An Introduction to Islamic Cosmological Doctrines

OTHER WORKS BY SEYYED HOSSEIN NASR IN ENGLISH

Three Muslim Sages

Ideals and Realities of Islam

Science and Civilization in Islam

An Annotated Bibliography of Islamic Science (3 vols.)

Man and Nature: The Spiritual Crisis of Modern Man

Islam and the Plight of Modern Man

Islamic Science: An Illustrated Study

The Transcendent Theosophy of Sadr al-Din Shirazi

Islamic Life and Thought

Knowledge and the Sacred

Islamic Art and Spirituality

Muhammad - Man of Allah

Traditional Islam in the Modern World

The Islamic Philosophy of Science

Sufi Essays

The Essential Writings of Frithjof Schuon (editor)

Shi'ism (editor)

Expectation of the Millennium (editor)

Islamic Spirituality—Foundations (editor)

Islamic Spirituality—Manifestations (editor)

The Need for a Sacred Science

An Introduction to Islamic Cosmological Doctrines

CONCEPTIONS OF NATURE AND METHODS
USED FOR ITS STUDY BY THE
IKHWĀN AL-ṢAFĀ', AL-BĪRŪNĪ, AND IBN SĪNĀ

Revised Edition

Seyyed Hossein Nasr

State University of New York Press

Published by
State University of New York Press, Albany

Printed in the United States of America

For information, address the State University of New York Press,
State University Plaza, Albany, NY 12246

Production by Christine M. Lynch
Marketing by Lynne Lekakis

Library of Congress Cataloging-in-Publication Data

Nasr, Seyyed Hossein.
An introduction to Islamic cosmological doctrine / Seyyed Hossein Nasr.
p. cm.
Includes bibliographical references (p.) and index.
ISBN 0-7914-1515-5 (alk. paper). — ISBN 0-7914-1516-3 (pbk. : alk. paper)
1. Islamic cosmology. 2. Bīrūnī, Muḥammad ibn Aḥmad, 973?–1048. 3. Avicenna, 980–1037. 4. Ikhwān al Ṣafā'. I. Title.
B745.C6N3 1993
113'.0917'671—dc20 92-25842
CIP

10 9 8 7 6 5 4 3 2 1

Dedicated in Humble Gratitude
to my Parents
Seyyed Valīallāh and Ashraf Nasr
to Emad Kia
and to
Sidi Ibrāhīm 'Izz al-Dīn
al-'Alawī

Contents

PART II. AL-BĪRŪNĪ

PART III. IBN SĪNĀ

Tables

Illustrations

Figures 5, 7, 11, 12, 13, and 15 are reproduced from al-Bīrūnī's Elements of Astrology, *translated by R. Ramsey Wright. Figure 16 is reproduced from an article by W. Hartner, "The pseudoplanetary nodes of the moon's orbit in Hindu and Islamic iconographies," in* Ars Islamica *5:118 (1938); also in W. Hartner,* Oriens-Occidens, *Hildesheim, 1968, pp. 349–404.*

Foreword

This study opens up a relatively unexplored, hence unfamiliar, aspect of Islam. The majority of modern Muslim rationalists will no doubt join in chorus with the formalist orthodox theologians to deny that its subject can be identified with Islam "in any true sense." But their perspective is false. The theme of Seyyed Hossein Nasr's study is one no less vital than the tracing out of one line in the complex process by which the Islamic Community gradually discovered its own nature and habitat.

To most Western readers also this study may appear no less paradoxical. It is commonly held that all scientific thought and writing in the medieval Islamic world was derived from the legacy of Greek thought, as modified by a number of orientalizing factors in the later Hellenistic age. So much has been written about the great Arabic scientists and philosophers and their influence upon the awakening mind of Europe that it comes as something of a shock to be confronted with the thickening web of "irrational" elements in the writings of such a personality as Avicenna.

It would be impossible within the compass of a preface to elucidate these paradoxes in detail. Its more limited aim must be to outline, for both Muslim and Western readers, a particular view of Islamic thought as it developed in the first seven centuries of Islamic history (the seventh to thirteenth centuries of our era), and to hope that, seen in the light of this development, the historical and religious significance of Seyyed Hossein Nasr's analysis will be more fully appreciated.

In the common exposition of both Eastern and Western scholars, the history of Islam is presented in a series of stages. After the first century or so of simple piety and political conflict, the energies of the Islamic Community were for a space of two or three centuries centered on the development of the schools of law and on theological dispute. Owing to the intellectual ferment resulting from the impact of Hellenism, the third and fourth centuries were the "Golden Age" of Islamic culture, when literature and science widened out in every direction, and economic prosperity also reached its climax. By the fifth century the legal and theological structures of both the Sunni and Shi'ite wings had been rigidly consolidated, and political issues had largely been removed from the sphere of controversy by the expanding hegemony of the Turks. The sixth century saw the beginnings of the process of decay, simultaneously with the infiltration of Ṣūfī mysticism into the general religious life of the Community; and with the Mongol invasions of the seventh century its course was irretrievably set toward a general intellectual and religious decadence.

The question raised by this presentation is whether these concepts of progress and decadence do not rest upon partial criteris which fail to take adequate account of the complexities and contradictions inherent in any society, and not least in Muslim society. From an ecumenical religious point of view, for example, one can scarcely doubt that the moral integration of the Christian West was far greater in the fourteen th century than in the twentieth; on this criterion, then, the Renaissance initiated a process of gradual decadence. So also in Islam, the course of moral and religious integration and the progress of the Community toward a deepening self-consciousness and universality call for entirely different standards of measurement than those by which the intellectual breadth or economic prosperity of the Islamic civilization in its "Golden Age" is judged.

From the beginning of its existence the Community was made aware (and daily reminded) by the Qur'ān of the purpose for which it was created and the destiny to which it was called. It was to represent on earth, before the eyes of all manking, the principle of Divine Justice, that is to say, of integral Reality, Harmony and Truth. Justice in this sense has little or nothing to do with the political or judicial application of man-made laws. It is a principle of order and wholeness: that all elements, endowments, and activities of life shall be in harmonious relation with one another, each fulfilling its proper purpose and ends in a divinely-appointed system of interlocking obligations and rights. If the Community were to fulfill its purpose, three needs must be continuously and adequately met. One was the continuing need of a spiritual intiution that should maintain its preceptions of the universals. The second was the *ḥikmah*, the "wisdom" to discern by the use of reason their proper application to particular cases. The thirs was the function of government to protect the integrity of the Community and the peaceful and harmonious coordination of other functions with it.

In the cold light of History, the Community was manifestly falling far short of this ideal. Spiritual intuition was too often dulled or replaced by theological disputes and formularies. The efforts of the jurists to define the applications of divine justice had produced, in the Sharī'a, magnificent (if rival) corpora of legal doctrine, but their legal logic was limited to prescription and contaminated by casuistry, while in other fields human reason was asserting itself as absolute and being exercised without restraint. The institution of government had been still more profoundly corrupted by the power of the sword and vitiated by theories and practices that disregarded even the Sharī'a, and the Community as a whole was unable to take effectual action to reform it because in all its social relationships also simple justice was sadly imperfect.

In spite of all this, however, the consciousness of its divine calling remained profoundly rooted within the Community. Although there is little evidence that in the early centuries it regarded itself as a sacral organization, there persisted an inner conviction that somehow and somewhere within it there was a continued effusion of divine Grace and divine Guidance. The idea was not yet conceived, much less defined, in metaphysical terms; its essence lay beyond human understanding, and it was perceived only in direct or indirect material indices, particularly in the form of *barakāt*. This was, again perhaps somewhat vaguely, connected with the idea of divine Justice. One might sat that the *barakāt* were manifested, in exemplary fashion, to correct specific instances of disregard of justice, of disharmony. There was thus an intimate link between it and the growht of Sufism, in both its spritual and its social aspects, and with the victory of Sufism it broke through on a new and grandiose scale. Alal of the vital religious forces and ideas were swept into the Ṣūfī movement and received in it their new and comprehensive formulation.

The pragmatic historian of Islam may again see in this the onset of a "decadence," a loss of freedom of thought and flexibility, a "stagnation" in the Islamic Community. What really happened was that from the sixth century the Community decisively turned away from the rationalizing and secular elements in the Hellenistic tradition to become more fully, what it had been in essence from the first, a Near Eastern religious community. Greek *falsafah* was replaced by Near Eastern *ḥikmah*, and the persistence of the basic constructions of Near Eastern religious thought is nowhere more strikingly evidenced than by the new Ṣūfī metaphysics. From the very dawn of articulated religious thought in ancient Sumer, the cosmos is regarded as one unified entity which embraces the whole of being, so that human societies but reflect the society of the Gods. But ancient Near Eastern though had been transformed by many influences before the rise of Islam. The later Islamic cosmology is thus a highly refined version of this basic concept. Its cosmos is now the Ptoplemaic structure of concentric spheres, its elements are the Aristotelian elements of fire, water, earth, and air, combined with the Plotinian emanations of pure intelligences and souls, transformed into or combined with the angels of the monotheistic religions, and controlled by the One Supreme Necessary Being, from whom all being is derived, being their origin and principle, and to which the whole creation yearns to return. The Muslim concept of Justice, Harmony, and controlled Order is extended to the whole cosmos, all of whose elements are maintained in the state of equilibrium whis is appropriate to their nature, and operate in an ordered hierarchy, from the ninth heaven to the lowliest minerals.

With the elaboration of this cosmoloty the Islamic Community acquires a new and central importance, not only in the terrestrial world but in the cosmos as a whole. For the ''Perfect Man,'' the cosmic individual in whom all its faculties are realized, is Muḥammad, and his Community inherits from him a kind of spiritual prerogative which invests it with special significance. The locus of the Divine Grace is the whole Community, to which the charisma of Muḥammad is transferred, giving it a supra-terrestrial extension. Material realizations cease to be of prime importance; the true realities are spiritual, apprehended through symbols, and not necessarily articulated in external structures. This transformation from the ''laic'' concentration of the early centuries upon the Community in this world into a mystical and charismatic Community was necessarily accompanied by a corresponding development of symbolism. Of course the daily business of life was still conducted in plain unmystical man-to-man relations, but the Muslims now lived in a world surrounded by symbols. The Sharī'a became a symbol of cosmic relations in the spiritual world, and the Qur'ān itself, like the snesual pleasures of love and wine at a lower level, acquired new ranges of symbolic meanings. The imperfections of the terrestrial community find their compensations in its spiritual counterpart in the ''World of Similiture'' (*'ālam al-mithāl*). More especially, for the great mass of Muslims, the scandal of its earthly governments is redeemed. The real government is not in the hands of temporal sultans but in the care of God's chosen ones, the unknown saints in their hierarchy, headed by the Pole, the *Quṭb*, who by Divine command and with the powers placed at their disposal supervise the affairs of the terrestrial world and protect the interests of the Community.

Such a mystical cosmology was not, however, the immediate creation of Sufism. Whence it came and how it entered Ṣūfī thought is here set out for the first time by Seyyed Hossein Nasr, in full and scholarly detail. It is almost a stratling revelation that its foundations were laid by the philosophical schools of the ''Golden Age,'' and that no other than

Avicenna himself, the "second master" of Aristotelian philosophy, furnished it with its cosmological symbolism. That it was the heirs of Hellenistic culture who generated the final flowering of Illuminationist Sufism seems the greatest paradox of all. It can only be explained by the working of an inner reason within all expressions of Islamic thought and culture, an inner reason which led each one of them unconsciously to make its contribution to the final elaboration of its central theme.

H. A. R. GIBB

Preface to the Second Edition

During the past three decades since this book first went to press, interest in cosmology as traditionally understood has increased greatly although the scientistic mentality which still dominates over many sectors of the contemporary land-scape continues to view pre-modern cosmologies as either puerile superstitions or rudimentary frameworks for the sciences of nature. To the extent that modern science is considered to be science as such and the only legitimate science of the natural order, this rejection of traditional cosmology based as it is upon the symbolic significance of cosmic phenomena and rapport between the physical and higher realms of existence cannot be helped. The very monolithic claims of modern science necessitate such a rejection. The scientific world view, however, is beginning to lose its totalitarian hold upon the minds of many contemporary men and women faced with the threat of the destruction of the environment resulting from the application of modern science and confronted with the new scientific cosmologies which, while changing from decade to decade, all share in excluding human beings qua human beings from the cosmos which they depict. To the extent that this rigid hold of modern science becomes losened and men begin to view modern science as a science of nature which is able to discover a great deal about the physical world but at the expense of overlooking certain essential dimensions of the cosmos, the significance of traditional cosmologies become more evident.

Moreover, the very poverty of the current Western philosophical scene has caused an ever greater number of seekers of *sophia* to turn to the traditional worlds of knowledge and to try to rediscover that supreme knowledge or *scientia sacra* which lies at the heart of all traditions. In this quest for re-discovery cosmology has come to occupy a place of great eminence and more and more the studies of non-Western traditions are beginning to pay attention to the domain of cosmology as can be seen in the numerous serious studies of the cosmologies of Hinduism, Buddhism, Jainisim, the American Indian tradition, and even the tradition of the Australian Aborigines, just to cite a few examples, which have appeared in print. Even in the field of Jewish and Christian studies, a number of notable works dealing with cosmology have seen the light of day, a few affected, at least at the stage of their inception, by our treatment of Islamic cosmology in the present work.

The thrust to turn to the study of traditional cosmologies has also been abetted by concern for the natural environment. The severe environmental crisis, which how threatens human existence itself along with the life of other species on earth, has turned the attention of those interested in the deeper causes of the crisis to the study of the relationship between man and nature in traditional societies, and hence, to those cosmologies which have governed these relationships over the centuries. The process of reformulating a veritable metaphysics or even theology of nature is inseparable from the comprehension and revival of traditional cosmology.

This revival of interest has also led to all kinds of subjective and non-traditional interpretations of traditional cosmologies ranging from the occultist interpretations of certain archaic Western cosmologies, to pseudo-Hindu representations to "the joyous cosmology" associated with hallucigenic experiences. The present day cultural landscape is cluttered by not only generalized physics baptized as cosmology with extravagant extrapolations concerning aeons of time and billions of light years of space, but also occultist cosmologies of a pseudo-traditional character which seem to stand at the opposite extreme of the mental spectrum, although in more than a few cases there are similarities with some of the tenets of what is called scientific cosmology in such a way that one can claim to be witness to yet another instance of the meeting of extremes. Despite this fact, however, for the first time in the history of modern West, serious cosmological studies of not only the non-Western but also traditional Western origin are beginning to appear, exercising a great deal of influence upon the whole field of religious studies, the philosophy of nature and also environmental studies.

It is strange, therefore, that although this book was the first to deal with traditional Islamic cosmology in the English language and appeared before the wave of interest in various traditional cosmologies began to appear, it has not been followed by studies of the same scope and nature as far as Islamic cosmology is concerned. One or two later works, such as A. Heinen's *Islamic Cosmology*, have dealt with the more popular religious cosmology of Islam, although there is as yet no thorough study in any European language of Quranic cosmology based on the inspired commentaries. Moreover, we ourselves have devoted a number of essays to intellectual and philosophical cosmology in some of our later studies. *An Introduction to Islamic Cosmological Doctrines* remains, however, still the only book of its kind in this field. Since its appearance, it has been rendered into several other languages and the English edition, first published by Harvard University Press in 1964, and later in a revised edition in 1978, has been out of print for some years. It is with this fact and the scholarly situation in this field in mind that this new edition is now seeing the light of day. A number of corrections have been made in the original text and the extensive original bibliography has been brought up to date.

The present book does not deal with the many schools of Islamic cosmology which developed during later periods of Islamic history, from the Ismā'īlī, to the *ishrāqī*, to the Ibn 'Arabian to the Ṣadrian associated with the school of "transcendent theosophy (*al-ḥikmat al-muta'āliyah*)" of Mullā Ṣadrā. But it does treat in detail the formative period of the development of major schools of Islamic cosmology which became a permanent strand in the tapestry of later Islamic intellectual life and helped to create, on the basis of the Quran, the *Ḥadīth* and their inspired commentaries, the vision of the cosmos within which Muslims have lived for the past millenium. The present work has already influenced a number of studies in specific fields and schools of Islamic thought. It is hoped that this new edition which makes possible the continued availability of this book, will help in a humble fashion to guide others toward not only a better understanding of the contents of Islamic cosmology as contained in the works of the Ikhwān al-Ṣafā', al-Bīrūnī and Ibn Sīnā, but also further research into that universe of meaning which is the Islamic cosmos. May this book open a door to that cosmos whose phenomena sing the praise of God's power and wisdom, whose heavens descend from the Divine Empyrean and whose earth, reflecting the heavens, contains in harmony the multiplicity of species and forms which have issued from the inexhaustible "treasury of the Invisible World."

wa'l-Llāh^{u} a'lam

Seyyed Hossein Nasr
Bethesda, Maryland
June 1992
Dhu'l-ḥijjah 1412

Introduction

Most of the studies made currently by Western orientalists as well as by contemporary modern Muslim scholars of the cosmological and natural sciences in the Islamic world have been carried out with the aim of establishing a relation between these sciences and those cultivated in the modern world. Only rarely has attention been turned to the general world view of the Muslims themselves, a view in whose matrix they studied the particular sciences of Nature. Our aim in this book, which is a revised and elaborated version of a thesis presented to the Department of the History of Science and Learning at Harvard University in 1958, is to clarify some of the cosmological principles and to bring into focus the contours of the cosmos in which the Muslims lived and thought, and which to a certain extent still provides the framework in which they envisage the world. Of course we do not in any way deny the validity and significance of the historical studies which on the one hand relate the Muslim sciences to their Babylonian, Egyptian, Greek, Indian, Chinese, and Persian origins, and on the other clarify the role which these sciences had to play in the formation of Latin scholasticism and the study of the natural sciences in the Western world from the thirteenth to the seventeenth centuries. But our aim in this book is primarily to study the Muslim cosmological sciences in themselves, and to try to envisage the world in its totality in the manner seen by those who cultivated these sciences, and not as viewed by one who stands on the outside and seeks to dissect the Muslim world view into its constituent elements according to the historical sources from which they were adopted.

The Muslim cosmological and natural sciences are as closely bound to the metaphysical, religious, and philosophical ideas governing Islamic civilization as the modern sciences are related to the religious and philosophical background which in the sixteenth and seventeenth centuries brought these new sciences into being and which has sustained and nourished them ever since. This close relation is best observed in the case of Muslim students who, upon the most cursory contact with the modern sciences, usually lose their spiritual footing and no longer feel in harmony with their tradition, whereas the same students might have studied traditional mathematics and the natural sciences for years without being in any way alienated from the Islamic revelation. The difference lies in the manner and perspective in which the materials and facts of the sciences are interpreted in each case, although sometimes the facts are the same in both instances. Consequently, the knowledge of the general Islamic vision of the cosmos provides not only a key for a true understanding of the Muslim sciences and a necessary background for any basic study of the history of medieval science, but also the principles which, being intrinsically bound with the immutable and nonhistorical essence and spirit of the Islamic Revelation, must guide the Muslims in judging all other sciences of Nature with which they come in contact. Only when the contour of the Islamic conception of the cosmos is clearly delineated will the Muslims be able to absorb and integrate those elements of foreign sciences which are in conformity with the spirit of their tradition into their own world view.

The Muslim world until now has had no need to be conscious of the cosmos in which it has lived. But now faced with the challenge of the modern sciences which are the fruit of a totally different conception of the world, the Muslims must bring into light the Islamic conception of the cosmos if they are to avoid the dangerous dichotomy which results from a superficial "harmony" between the Islamic perspective and the modern sciences to be seen so often in the writings of modern Muslim apologists. If the modern sciences are going to be anything more than an artificial "tail" grafted upon the body of Islam or even an alien element, the ingestion of which may endanger the very life of the Islamic world, the Muslims must find the universal Islamic criteria in the light of which the validity of all sciences must be judged.

As the title of this work implies, it is no more than a humble introduction to the study of the Islamic cosmological sciences. We have taken but a few steps, hoping that in the future further studies will correct and complete the elementary study undertaken here.

We are most grateful to Professors H. A. R. Gibb, H. A. Wolfson, and I. B. Cohen of Harvard University under whose direction this study was first undertaken. We are also thankful to Messrs. T. Burckhardt, L. Massignon, H. Corbin, and L. Gardet for their useful suggestions and for permission to quote from their works. We likewise humbly thank our masters in the traditional sciences in Persia, Sayyid Muḥammad Kāẓim 'Aṣṣār, Muḥammad Ḥusain Ṭabāṭabā'ī, Sayyid Abu'l-Ḥasan Qazwīnī Rafī'ī, Jawād Muṣliḥ, and Murtaḍā Muṭahharī who have taught us many things not contained in books.

The staff of Widener Library was most kind in its assistance as were the staffs of the libraries in Tehran, and especially Mr. M. T. Dānishpazhūh, the director of the central library in Tehran University. We are also deeply grateful to Professor Yusuf T. K. Ibish, Miss Maude Harrison, Mr. Mehran Nasr, and Dr. E. Daenecke for proofreading the text, and to M. Kathleen Ahern of the Harvard University Press for copy-editing the manuscript.

SEYYED HOSSEIN NASR

Faculty of Letters
Tehran University
Ṣafar 1380 A.H. (Lunar)
Shahrīwar 1339 A.H. (Solar)
August 1960 A.D.

List of Transliterations

Arabic characters

ء	ʾ
ب	b
ت	t
ث	*th*
ج	j
ح	ḥ
خ	*kh*
د	d
ذ	*dh*
ر	r
ز	z
س	s
ش	*sh*
ص	ṣ
ض	ḍ
ط	ṭ
ظ	ẓ
ع	ʿ
غ	*gh*
ف	f
ق	q
ك	k
ل	l
م	m
ن	n
ه	h
و	w
ي	y
ة	ah; at (construct state)
ال	(article) al- and 'l- (even before the anteropalatals)

long vowels

ا ى	ā
و	ū
ي	ī

short vowels

ـَـ	a
ـُـ	u
ـِـ	i

Diphthongs

ـَـو	aw
ـَـي	ai (ay)
ـيّ	īy (final form ī)
ـُوّ	uww (final form ū)

Persian letters added to the Arabic alphabet

پ	p
چ	*ch*
ژ	*zh*
گ	g

The world consists of the unity of the unified, whereas the Divine Independence resides in the Unity of the Unique.

Ibn ʻArabī—al-Futūḥāt al-makkīyah

In the Name of God Most Merciful and Compassionate

PROLOGUE

Islam and the Study of Nature

Cosmological Sciences and the Islamic Revelation

In a traditional civilization like that of Islam the cosmological sciences are closely related to the Revelation because in such civilizations the immutable revealed principle, or the "presiding Idea," manifests itself everywhere in social life as well as in the cosmos in which that civilization lives and breathes. In such civilizations the cosmological sciences integrate the diverse phenomena of Nature into conceptual schemes all of which reflect the revealed principles and the central Idea of which they are so many applications in the domain of contingency. In this manner cosmology repeats the process of traditional art which likewise selects from the multiplicity of forms those that are in conformity with the spirit of the tradition in whose bosom it has come into being.

The relation between Revelation and the people who are its receptor is much like that of form to matter in the Aristotelian theory of hylomorphism. Revelation, or the Idea in its manifested aspect, is the form while the mental and psychic structure of the people who receive it acts as the matter upon which this form is imposed. The civilization which comes into being in this manner, from the wedding of the above "form" and "matter," is dependent upon the psychic and racial qualities of the people who are its bearers in two ways. The first is that the Revelation is already spoken in the language of the people for whom it is meant, as the Quran insists so often; and the second, that the "matter" of this civilization plays a role in its crystallization and further growth.

The Truth in its unlimited and infinite essence is thus particularized by the specific form of the Revelation as well as by the characteristics of the people who are destined to receive it. This particularization of the Truth has a direct bearing upon the study of Nature and the whole cosmological perspective which is concerned for the most part with the world of forms.[1] Unlike pure metaphysics and mathematics

[1] Although Nature is often considered by the ancient and medieval cosmologists as the principle of change and is therefore related to the world of corporeal and subtle manifestation, sometimes it is universalized into a principle transcending the world of forms altogether as is seen in the writings of Ibn 'Arabī on Universal Nature (*ṭabī'at al-kull*) in the *Futūḥāt al-makkīyah* and other texts. See T. Burckhardt, "Nature can overcome nature" in Burckhardt, *Alchemy*, trans. W. Stoddart (Baltimore, 1971), pp. 123–138.

which are independent of relativity, cosmological sciences are closely related to the perspective of the "observer" so that they are completely dependent upon the Revelation or the qualitative essence of the civilization in whose matrix they are cultivated. And even within the same civilization several cosmological sciences may exist which study the same domain but according to different perspectives.

In traditional civilizations the study of Nature may be made for the sake of utility as is seen in ancient and medieval technology where aspects of Nature were studied with the aim of discovering the qualities which might make them useful to the daily needs of the society. Or such a study may be made with the aim of integrating cosmic existence into a pervasive rational system as with the Peripatetics, or into a mathematical system as with Archimedes. Or it may be with the aim of describing in detail the functioning of a particular domain of Nature, as in the biological works of Aristotle, and the medieval natural historians, or, again, in connection with the making of objects in which process art and industry before the machine age were always combined as in the medieval guilds and the branches of Hermeticism connected with them. Finally, Nature may be studied as a book of symbols or as an icon to be contemplated at a certain stage of the spiritual journey and a crypt from which the gnostic must escape in order to reach ultimate liberation and illumination, as is seen in the writings of Illuminationists and Ṣūfīs like Suhrawardī and Ibn 'Arabī.[2] Moreover, all of these different manners of studying Nature are sometimes superimposed upon each other in the writings

[2] In Islam where the Revelation has taken the form of a sacred book, the symbolism of the word is of special significance. The Quran often calls Nature a book which is the macrocosmic counterpart of the Quran itself and which must be read and understood before it can be put away.

The 8th/14th century Ṣūfī master 'Azīz al-Nasafī, in his *Kashf al-ḥaqā'iq*, compares Nature to the Quran in such a way that each genus in Nature corresponds to a *sūrah*, each species to a verse, and each particular being to a letter. Concerning this book of Nature he writes: "Each day destiny and the passage of time set this book before you, sura for sura, verse for verse, letter for letter, that you may learn the content of these lines and letters. . . . But he who finds for himself the eye of the eye and the ear of the ear, who transcends the world of the commandment (spiritual world), he obtains knowledge of the whole book in one moment, and he who has complete knowledge of the whole book, who frees his heart from this book, closes the book and sets it aside. He is like one who receives a book and reads it over and over until he finally knows its content; such a man will close the book and set it aside. This is the sense of the words 'On that day We will roll up the heavens as one rolleth up written scrolls' (Sura 21:104), and that other passage: 'And in his right hand shall the heavens be folded together' (Sura 39:67) whence it can be seen that the people of the left have no share in the folding together of the heavens." F. Meier, "Nature in the monism of Islam," *Spirit and Nature* (New York, 1954), pp. 202–203.

of a single author, especially in the Islamic civilization which forms the subject of our present study.

The symbols used to interpret and understand Nature depend upon the form of the Revelation, or Idea, dominant in a civilization which sanctifies and emphasizes a particular set of symbols as distinct from the general symbols inherent in the nature of things.[3] As for the symbols which are in the nature of things, like the colors of plants and flowers, or the light and heat of the Sun, they are independent of the subjectivism of the individual observer but are rather ontological aspects of things, enjoying a reality that is independent of our subjective whims.[4]

Therefore, any basic study of the cosmological sciences of a civilization must take into account not only the historical borrowing of ideas and facts from earlier cultures but also this intimate connection between Revelation and the symbols used to study Nature. Only in this way will one come to understand why each civilization chooses a particular set of phenomena out of the multiplicity of Nature as a subject for study, and why it develops a particular set of cosmological sciences to the exclusion of other possibilities.

Despite the difference in the forms of the ancient and medieval cosmological sciences, there is an element which they shared in common, this element being the unicity of Nature which all of these sciences sought to demonstrate and upon which they are all based. This unicity is the natural consequence of the Unity of the Divine Principle which formed the basis of all the ancient "Greater

[3] "Moreover, a distinction must be made between two kinds of symbols; those of nature and those of Revelation. The first have spiritual efficacy only by virtue of their 'consecration' or 'revalorisation' by the *Avatara*, or the revealed Word, or by virtue of a very exalted degree of knowledge which restores to them their fundamental reality. Before the Fall, every river was the Ganges, and every mountain was Kailasa, for the Creation was still 'interior,' 'the knowledge of good and evil' not having yet 'exteriorised' or 'materialised' it; likewise for the sage every river is still a river of Paradise. Natural symbolism, which assimilates, for example, the sun to the divine Principle, derives from a 'horizontal' correspondence; revealed symbolism, which makes this assimilation spiritually effective—in ancient solar cults and before their 'petrifaction'—derives from a 'vertical' correspondence; the same holds good for gnosis, which reduces phenomena to 'ideas' or archetypes." F. Schuon, *Stations of Wisdom*, trans. G. E. H. Palmer (London, 1961), pp. 96–97.

[4] "The science of symbols—not simply a knowledge of traditional symbols—proceeds from the qualitative significances of substances, forms, spatial directions, numbers, natural phenomena, relationships, movements, colours and other properties or states of things; we are not dealing here with subjective appreciations, for the cosmic qualities are ordered both in relation to Being and according to a hierarchy which is more real than the individual; they are then, independent of our tastes, or rather they determine them to the extent that we are ourselves conformable to Being; we assent to the qualities to the extent that we ourselves are 'qualitative.' " F. Schuon, *Gnosis, Divine Wisdom*, trans. G. E. H. Palmer (London: John Murray, 1959), p. 110.

Mysteries" and which, either veiled in a mythological dress or expressed directly as a metaphysical truth, is to be found as the central Idea in all traditional civilizations.[5] Ancient cosmologies are not childish attempts to explain the causality of natural phenomena as they may appear to the untrained eye; rather, they are sciences whose central object is to show the unicity of all that exists.[6]

The question of the Unity of the Divine Principle and the consequent unicity of Nature is particularly important in Islam where the idea of Unity (*al-tawḥīd*) overshadows all others and remains at every level of Islamic civilization the most basic principle upon which all else depends. But it must not be thought that this goal of finding and displaying the unicity of Nature is dependent upon a particular method to the exclusion of others. The Muslims used many "ways of knowing" to formulate sciences based on the idea of the unicity of Nature which is itself derived from the twin source of Revelation and intellectual intuition. In the case of the Islamic sciences, as in all other instances, the ends of a science lie outside of that science which may employ many means to reach those ends but cannot determine its goal itself. The Muslims employed many methods in the various sciences, from observation and ratiocination to contemplation and illumination, but the goal toward which these methods were aimed—that is, the demonstration of the interrelatedness of all things—came from the Revelation which, as we have already noted, determines from "above" the particular cosmological sciences cultivated in a tradition.

Returning to the basic principle of Unity in Islam, it can be said that this doctrine is expressed in the most universal manner possible

[5] The attitude toward Nature is always a reflection of the attitude toward metaphysics, the "earth" being a reflection of "heaven" in the religious and symbolic sense.

The cosmological sciences are the "Lesser Mysteries" and metaphysical knowledge the "Greater Mysteries" in whose light the "Lesser Mysteries" are usually absorbed as the Alexandrian cosmological sciences were integrated into the perspective of Islamic gnosis. See T. Burckhardt, "Nature de la perspective cosmologique," *Etudes Traditionnelles*, 49:218 (1948).

[6] This conception is also expressed in the *Golden Verses of Pythagoras*:

> If Heaven will it, thou shalt know that Nature,
> Alike in everything, is the same in every place.

"I have already said that the homogeneity of Nature was, with the unity of God, one of the greatest secrets of the mysteries. Pythagoras founded this homogeneity upon the unity of the spirit by which it is penetrated and from which, according to him, all our souls draw their origin. This dogma which he had received from the Chaldeans and from the priests of Egypt was admitted by all the sages of antiquity . . . These sages established a harmony, a perfect analogy between heaven and earth, the intelligible and the sentient, the indivisible substance and divisible substance, in such a manner that that which took place in one of the regions of the Universe or of the modification of the primordial ternary was the exact image of that which took place in the other." A. Fabre d'Olivet, *The Golden Verses of Pythagoras* (New York, 1917), p. 251.

in the first *Shahādah*, *Lā ilāha illa'Llāh*, usually translated as "there is no divinity but the Divine," but which in its most profound sense means there is no reality outside of the Absolute Reality, thereby negating all that is other than Allah.[7] This formula which is the Quranic basis of the Ṣūfī doctrine of the Unity of Being (*waḥdat al-wujūd*) does not imply that there is a substantial continuity between God and the world, or any form of pantheism or monism; rather, it means that there cannot be two orders of reality independent of each other.

The formula of Unity is the most universal criterion of orthodoxy in Islam; that doctrine may be said to be Islamic that affirms this unity in one way or other. The Prophet of Islam did not come to assert anything new but to reaffirm the truth which always was, to re-establish the Primordial Tradition (*al-dīn al-ḥanīf*), and to expound the doctrine of Divine Unity, a principle that is reflected in one way or another in all the traditions before Islam.

The ancient cosmological sciences were for the most part based upon the unicity of Nature and searched for the transcendent cause of things and were, therefore, far from un-Islamic even if they antedated the historical manifestation of Islam. It was this common factor of seeking to discover and demonstrate the unicity of Nature among such ancient cosmological sciences as those of the Pythogoreans and Hermeticists that made them conformable to the form of the Islamic Revelation and easily assimilable into its perspective. The form of the Islamic Revelation was in this way directly responsible for the integration of the ancient sciences into Islam as well as for the types of sciences cultivated in the Muslim world itself. The doctrine of the unicity of Nature which is based upon that of Unity and which thus relies on the essence and spirit of the form of Revelation in Islam, is, therefore, the ultimate aim of all the sciences of Nature, and the degree to which a science succeeds in expressing this unicity the criterion by which the success and validity of that science are judged.[8]

[7] "Islam, as a religion, is a way of unity and totality. Its fundamental dogma is called *Et-Tawḥīd*, that is to say unity or the action of uniting. As a universal religion, it admits of gradations, but each of these gradations is truly Islam in the sense that each and every aspect of Islam reveals the same principle. . . . The formula of '*Et-Tawḥīd*' or Monotheism is a Sharaite commonplace. The import that a man gives to this formula is his personal affair, since it depends upon his Sufism. Every deduction that one can make from this formula is more or less valid, provided always that it does not destroy the literal meaning; for in that case one destroys the unity of Islam, that is to say its universality, its faculty of adapting and fitting itself to all mentalities, circumstances and epochs." Abdul Hadi, "L'Universalité en l'Islam," *Le Voile d'Isis*, January 1934.

[8] Since we consider this principle as basic to the understanding of the Islamic sciences we shall seek to apply it throughout this work as our guiding principle.

In addition to the specific form of the Islamic Revelation, we must also consider the "matter" upon which this "form" was imposed, that is, the racial, psychological, and linguistic character of the people who were destined to form the substance of the Islamic civilization. For, as we already have mentioned, this "matter" also has a role to play in the general formation of the civilization and consequently in the cosmological sciences that are developed and the general view that is held with regard to Nature.

Islam was revealed in the Arabic language to a people who were of the stock of the Semitic nomads and later spread among the Persians, Turks, Mongolians, Negroes, and other racial and ethnic groups without losing its original character. This gives Islamic spirituality a nomadic trait even when it manifests itself in a sedentary environment. Moreover, the Revelation of Islam was given in the form of a sacred book, the Holy Quran, whose centrality and importance in all facets of Islamic culture and more specifically in the attitude toward Nature, can hardly be overemphasized. The Quran, this intertwining of the beauty of the geometry of the crystal and the profusion of the plant, refers constantly to the phenomena of Nature as signs of God to be contemplated by the believers.[9] And it is for this reason that throughout Islamic history "apart from a small number of investigators inspired by Greek philosophic ideals, the Muslims who engaged in the pursuit of science did so, like the Hebrews, in order to discover in the wonders of Nature the signs or tokens of the glory of God."[10]

The pre-Islamic Arabs to whom the Quran was first addressed had a great love for Nature and like all the nomads who wander endlessly in the great expanses of virgin Nature had a deep intuition of the

[9] It is quite significant that the phenomena of Nature, the events taking place within the soul of man, and the verses of the Quran are all called *āyāt*, the human soul and Nature being respectively the microcosmic and macrocosmic counterparts of the celestial archetypes contained in the Divine Word.

There are many verses of the Quran in which Nature and natural phenomena are mentioned, as for example the verse "We shall show them our portents upon the horizons and within themselves, until it be manifest unto them that it is the Truth." (Quran, XLI; 53. This and subsequent translations of the Quran in this book are from the edition of Muḥammad Pickthall.)

"سنريهم آياتنا في الآفاق وفي أنفسهم حتى يتبين لهم أنه الحق."

The Quran also contains explicitly a cosmology and angelology with its own specific terminology of the *kursī*, *'arsh* etc., which became the subject of exegesis and commentary by the later Muslim sages who developed Quranic cosmology to monumental proportions.

[10] R. Levy, *The Social Structure of Islam* (Cambridge, England, 1957), p. 460.

presence of the Invisible in the visible. Islam, which has always preserved the form of the spirituality of Semitic nomads, emphasized this particular trait of the nomadic spirit and made of Nature in Islam a vast garden in which the handiwork of the invisible gardener is ever present. Islam also emphasized the close relation between man and the rest of creation; the benediction upon the prophet (*al-ṣalāt 'ala'l-nabī*) in its most universal sense being the benediction upon the totality of manifestation.

Another point emphasized in the Quran is that human reason, which is a reflection of the Intellect, when healthy and balanced leads naturally to *tawḥīd* rather than to a denial of the Divine and can be misled only when the passions destroy its balance and obscure its vision.[11] Reason, therefore, when not impeded by external obstacles does not lead to rationalism in the modern sense of the word, that is, a negation of all principles transcending human reason, but becomes itself an instrument of Unity and a way of reaching the intelligible world.[12] Likewise, Islamic art, instead of being "rationalistic" as it might at first appear, leads the observer through the abstract symbols of geometry to the principle of Unity which can be represented only "negatively" and abstractly. This activity of reason within rather than outside of the basic tenets of the Revelation is ultimately the cause for Islam's ability to respond to the need for causality on the part of its adherents within the tradition rather than see this need seek the satisfaction of its thirst outside of the faith, as was to happen with Christianity at the end of the Middle Ages. It is also this conception of reason that made the study of the mathematical sciences so widespread in the Islamic world and enabled the Muslims to adopt the Pythagorean notion of mathematics so easily as a part of their world view.[13]

[11] The role assigned to the Intellect and its reflection on the human level—that is, reason—is one of the elements that distinguish Islam from Christianity. Christianity is essentially a way of love and its mysteries remain forever veiled from the believer, at least in the ordinary interpretation of the religion. Islam, on the contrary, is gnostic, and its final aim is to guide the believer to a "vision" of the spiritual realities. That is why there has always been in Christianity the question of preserving the domain of faith from intrusion by reason, whereas in Islam the problem has been to overcome the obstacles placed before the intelligence by the passions in order to enable the believer to reach the very heart of the faith which is the Unity of the Divine Essence.

[12] "En effet, selon la perspective islamique, la raison (*al-'aql*) est avant tout ce par quoi l'homme accepte les vérités révélées, qui, elles, ne sont ni irrationnelles, ni seulement rationnelles. C'est en cela que réside la noblesse de la raison et par suite celle de l'art; dire que l'art découle de la raison ou de la science comme l'attestent les maîtres de l'art musulman, ne signifie donc nullement qu'il soit rationaliste et qu'il faille le retrancher de l'intuition spirituelle, bien au contraire." T. Burckhardt, "Fondements de l'art musulman," *Etudes Traditionnelles*, 55:162–163 (1954).

[13] See introduction by S. H. Nasr to *Science and Civilization in Islam* (New York, 1970).

Aside from these general considerations regarding the Islamic attitude toward Nature and the sciences, a word must also be said about the character of the Arabic language as the vehicle of both the Revelation and most of the Muslim sciences. This language, which is without doubt the *lingua franca* of the Islamic world as well as the sacred language of Islam, has not only a precision which makes it an excellent instrument for scientific discourse but also an inner dimension which enables it to be the perfect vehicle for the expression of the most esoteric forms of knowledge. This flexibility made it easy for the early translators to translate Greek, Syriac, Sanskrit, and Pahlavi texts into Arabic, to coin new words with relative ease, and expand the meaning of already existing terms to include new concepts. The character of the Arabic language itself therefore was influential in the study of all the sciences in the Islamic world, including those concerning Nature.

In the sciences of Nature, the Muslims had a rich vocabulary of Arabic words to express all the diverse concepts and ideas connected with the cosmological sciences. For the word "Nature" itself, corresponding to the Latin *natura* and Greek *physis*, the Arabic word *ṭabī'ah* from the root (*ṭb'*) came to be used but with a somewhat different meaning from that in the classical languages.[14] The early Arabic translators also occasionally used the terms *kiyān* from the Syriac *kjōnō* as synonymous with *ṭabī'ah*.[15] In the Quran the word *ṭabī'ah* itself does not appear, but *ṭab'* is used several times[16] and is

[14] Muslim authors in the later centuries have usually distinguished between *ṭibā'* as the essential attributes of something, or, in other words, that which makes a thing behave and manifest itself as it does, and *ṭabī'ah* as that which gives movement or rest to a thing without possessing a will of its own.

"الطباع يقال للصورة الصفة الذاتية لكل شيء. الطبيعة قد تختص بما يصدر عنه الحركة
والسكون فيما هو فيه اولاً و بالذات من غير ارادة."

Khwājah Naṣir al-Dīn al-Ṭūsī, *Sharḥ al-ishārāt wa'l-tanbīhāt* (Tehran, 1378 [1958]) II, 56.

[15] L. Massignon, "La Nature dans la pensée islamique," *Eranos Jahrbuch*, 14:144–148 (1946).

[16] For example, "Our hearts are hardened—Nay, but Allah hath set a seal upon them for their disbelief" (Quran, LV, 155).

"قلوبنا غلف بل طبع الله عليها بكفرهم."

Also, "Allah hath sealed their hearts so that they know not" (Quran, IX, 92).

"وطبع الله على قلوبهم فهم لا يعلمون."

Fakhr al-Dīn al-Rāzī in his *al-Tafsīr al-kabīr* (Cairo, 1357 [1938], IX, 98) interprets *ṭab'* in these verses to mean the veil which hides God from man.

interpreted by both Sunni and Shī'ah commentators to mean the veil which separates man from God. Certain Ṣūfīs like Ḥallāj also contrast *ṭabī'ah* with Divine grace. The term *ṭab'* has also been used by certain authors in opposition to *maṭbū'*. These two terms may have been the origin of the Latin *natura naturans* and *natura naturata*[17] and bear nearly the same meaning as their Latin counterparts.

To express the relation and contrast between the Creator and the world the Muslim authors have usually used the pair of terms *ḥaqq* and *khalq*. In the dominant Sunni school of Ash'arite theology the absolute transcendence of God with respect to the world (*tanzīh*) and the "infinite" gulf separating *khalq* from *ḥaqq* is emphasized to such a degree that the individual nature of things, as well as Nature as a distinct domain of reality, melts away in the absolute power of the Creator. "Horizontal" causality is denied; of the ten categories of Aristotle pertaining to creatures, only substance, place, and quality are considered to have an objective reality; and time and space as well as "matter" are divided into "atoms."[18] All partial and immediate causes are absorbed into the Ultimate Cause, and God is considered as the direct cause of all things. For example, fire does not burn because it is its nature to do so, but because God so willed it. Moreover, what appear to us as "laws of nature" are due to habit and have no more than a juridical status,[19] the only real laws being those revealed by God through his prophets. The Ash'arite theologians emphasize above all else the discontinuity between the finite

[17] There is, in fact, a book by Jābir ibn Ḥayyān by the name of *al-Ṭab' wa'l-maṭbū'*. "Les termes scholastiques *natura naturans* et *natura naturata* paraissent être calqués sur l'arabe." O. Kraus, *Jābir ibn Ḥayyān* (Cairo, 1943), II, p. 137, n. 2.

[18] "Pour le théologien musulman, le temps n'est donc pas une 'durée' continue, mais une constellation, une 'voie lactée' d'instants (de même l'espace n'existe pas, il n'y a que des points)." L. Massignon, "Le Temps dans la pensée islamique," *Eranos Jahrbuch*, 20:141 (1952).

For the various forms of atomism in Islam, see S. Pines, *Beiträge zur islamischen Atomenlehre* (Berlin, 1936), and M. Fakhry, *Islamic Occasionalism and its Critique by Averroes and Aquinas* (London, 1958).

This trait of seeing the aspect of discontinuity of the cosmos and of its various conditions, such as time and space, is a trait of the spirit of the Semitic nomad, who feels the fragility of this world above all else, and manifests itself in many facets of Islamic intellectual life.

[19] "La distinction entre 'raison' et 'loi' ne touche en somme que le mode de la connaissance. Car toute chose, pour le kalām ash'arite, n'a d'existence que par le statut juridique que Dieu lui octroie. Il n'est de loi que positive revélée et les 'lois de la nature' sont de simples 'coutumes de Dieu', que l'expérience et la répétition des actes nous font connaître, à titre, en quelque sorte, de constatation provisoire. Le miracle en conséquence se définira comme une 'rupture d'habitude' (*khāriq al-'āda*)." L. Gardet and M. M. Anawati, *Introduction à la théologie musulmane* (Paris, 1948), pp. 430–431.

and the Infinite,[20] all the stages of the cosmic hierarchy above the "physical world," being absorbed, in their view, in the Divine Principle.

In the perspective of the Ṣūfīs, especially those belonging to the school of Ibn 'Arabī, and the theosophers (*ḥakīms*)—that is, the followers of that combination of Peripatetic philosophy, *Ishrāqī* theosophy[21] and gnosis which was perfected by Mullā Ṣadrā—as well as in the view of the early Muslim Peripatetics themselves, the other aspect of the relation between the Divine Principle and its manifestation came to be emphasized. The continuity between the two was stressed inasmuch as this relation is as real as the discontinuity considered by the theologians. One can say on the one hand that the infinite is absolutely separate from the finite, or the Creator from creation; and on the other, that since there cannot be two absolutely distinct orders of reality—this view being considered as polytheism (*shirk*)—the finite must somehow be none other than the Infinite.[22] The *Ishrāqī* sages and Ṣūfīs, without denying the absolute transcendence of God, have emphasized this second relationship and through the use of symbolism (*tashbīh*)[23] have sought to show that the manifested world is nothing but the shadow and symbol of the spiritual world and that the whole of cosmic manifestation is connected to its Divine Principle through its very existence.

Islam as the religion of the middle way stands between *tashbīh* and *tanzīh*, or immanence and transcendence, each of which taken alone can lead to serious error but which taken together express the just relationship between God and the Universe. In treating of the

[20] Usually an "atomistic" view of Nature, whether it be Greek, Ash'arite, or *Nyāya-Vaisésika*, is based on the aspect of the discontinuity between the cosmos and the Metacosmic reality, while the modes of thought which deny the existence of atoms, such as the Aristotelian, Hermetic, or Illuminationist (*Ishrāqī*), emphasize the aspect of continuity between the finite and the Infinite.

[21] We are using "theosophy" here in its original meaning, as it was used until quite recently by men like Jacob Böhme, and not in any way resembling that given it by the pseudo-spiritualist movement which came into being at the beginning of this century under this name.

[22] It is essential here to give this relationship in negative rather than affirmative terms so as not to confine it within a limited formulation.

[23] The symbolic interpretation of Nature is given scriptural authority by such Quranic passages as: "Seest thou not how Allah coineth a similitude: A goodly saying, as a goodly tree, its root set firm, its fruit at every season by permission of its Lord? Allah coineth a similitude for mankind in order that they may reflect" (Quran, XIV, 24–25).

« أَلَمْ تَرَ كَيْفَ ضَرَبَ اللَّهُ مَثَلًا كَلِمَةً طَيِّبَةً كَشَجَرَةٍ طَيِّبَةٍ أَصْلُهَا ثَابِتٌ وَفَرْعُهَا فِي السَّمَاءِ

تُؤْتِي أُكُلَهَا كُلَّ حِينٍ بِإِذْنِ رَبِّهَا وَيَضْرِبُ اللَّهُ الْأَمْثَالَ لِلنَّاسِ لَعَلَّهُمْ يَتَذَكَّرُونَ ».

Islamic cosmological sciences and the conceptions of Nature underlying them we shall deal only with those schools in whose teachings the light of the Divine does not totally absorb finite creation and shall therefore leave aside the various theological schools, like the Ash'arites. But it must not be forgotten that the view that the world is totally other than God and the belief that the finite cannot be absolutely other than the Infinite express different aspects of the same truth. Inasmuch as we are not dealing with matters of a purely rational order there is no question here of choosing between alternatives. Rather, the question involves the ability to discern in each instance the particular point of view from which this basic problem of the relation between the cosmos and its Source is being approached, the point of view which has a direct bearing upon the study of the cosmological sciences.

The Study of the Cosmological Sciences in Islamic History

In addition to being the last Revelation in time and therefore symbolically the synthesis of all the traditions before it, Islam spread geographically over the middle belt of the world and consequently became historically the heir of many of the earlier civilizations of Western Asia and the Mediterranean world. Alexandria, Antioch, Edessa, Nisibis, Ḥarrān, Jundishāpūr, and all the other centers of learning in Western Asia and North Africa became a part of the Muslim world and thereby provided the necessary material and substance for the later flowering of the Islamic arts and sciences.[24]

In the first century of Islam, when the religious and the spiritual forces were most intense, the different schools and perspectives which were to mark the later periods of Islamic history had not as yet manifested themselves; the tradition was still too close to its origin to become crystallized into its constituent elements. There was much interest in religious and literary sciences such as grammar, *ḥadīth*, or sacred history, and in some instances even in the pre-Islamic (*awā'il*) sciences as in the case of Khālid ibn Yazīd. But for the most part the spiritual seed which had been sown by the message of the Prophet

[24] For an account of the centers of learning in the ancient Near East and the means of transmission of the ancient sciences to the Muslims, see D. DeLacy O'Leary, *How Greek Science Passed to the Arabs* (London, 1929); M. Meyerhof, "On the transmission of Greek and Indian science to the Arabs," *Islamic Culture*, 2:17–29 (1937), and *Von Alexandrien nach Bagdad. Ein Beitrag zur Geschichte des philosophischen und medizinischen Unterrichts bei den Arabern.* Sitz-Ber. Berlin Akad. (Berlin, 1930); and F. Rosenthal, *The Classical Heritage in Islam*, trans. E. and J. Marmorstein (London, 1975).

did not bear fruit and did not manifest itself externally as far as the arts and sciences were concerned until the fourth and fifth Islamic centuries when the intensity of the religious fervor and the political power of the central government had already passed their culmination.[25]

With the establishment of the Abbasid caliphate, translations of Greek, Syriac, Pahlavi, and Sanskrit sources on the various sciences became available in Arabic, with the result that in addition to the earlier schools of grammarians and poets, traditionalists, commentators, historians, and Ṣūfī ascetics, all of whom relied almost entirely upon the Islamic revelation for their knowledge, there now began to appear new schools which also drew from non-Islamic sources. These new schools ranged from the logicians and rationalists, like the Mu'tazilites, to the astronomers and mathematicians, and finally to the followers of the more esoteric forms of the Greek, Alexandrian, and Chaldaean sciences connected with the Ṣabaean community in Ḥarrān.[26] During the third century, when the Islamic spirit began to become crystallized into its permanent forms, as reflected in the formation of the schools of law and the Ṣūfī brotherhoods, the various arts and sciences as well as philosophy also began to flourish, reaching their climax in the fourth and fifth Islamic centuries, which for this very reason we have chosen as the historic background for the subject of our discussion in this book.

The beginning of the fourth century witnessed the rise of Abū Naṣr al-Fārābī, Abu'l-Ḥasan al-Mas'ūdī, Yaḥyā ibn 'Adī, Ibrāhīm ibn Sīnān, Abu'l-Faraj al-Iṣfahānī, Abu'l-Ḥasan al-'Āmirī and many other figures who played an important role in the creation of the Islamic arts and sciences and, of more particular interest in our present study, in the cosmological sciences. The fourth century itself was not only a time of great activity in particular sciences but also in "the philosophy of Nature" and cosmology which had a permanent influence upon the sciences in the later centuries. It was the period in which the Ikhwān al-Ṣafā', al-Bīrūnī, Abu'l-Barakāt al-Baghdādī,

[25] With reference to the fourth century, Ṭaha Ḥusain writes: "During the course of their history, the Muslims have not known another century as rich in striking contradictions. Great material wealth and intellectual prosperity of the first order coexist with political decadence." Introduction to the *Rasā'il* of the Ikhwān al-Ṣafā' (Cairo, 1928), p. 3.

[26] For the general historical background of the Islamic sciences see George Sarton, *Introduction to the History of Science*, 2 vols. (Baltimore, 1927–1931), and A. Mieli, *La Science arabe et son rôle dans l'évolution scientifique mondiale* (Leiden, 1938 and 1966). See also S. H. Nasr, *Science and Civilization in Islam* (New York, 1970) and *Islamic Science – An Illustrated Study* (London, 1976); and M. Ullman, *Die Natur-und Geheimwissenschaften im Islam* (Leiden, 1972).

Ibn Sīnā, Abū Sulaimān al-Manṭiqī, and Abū Ḥayyān al-Tawḥīdī lived and wrote. It was also a time when such important encyclopedias as the *Mafātīḥ al-'ulūm* of Muḥammad ibn Aḥmad ibn al-Khwārazmī, compiled in 366/976,[27] and the *Fihrist* of Ibn Nadīm al-Warrāq of 378/988, made their appearance in Islamic intellectual life. During this century there were also several noteworthy Hermeticists like Abū Sa'īd ibn 'Abd al-Jalīl al-Sijzī, Abu'l-Qāsim al-Majrīṭī, and Shamalghānī al-Kūfī[28] and many Ṣūfī authors some of whom, like Ḥakīm al-Tirmidhī in his *Nawādir al-uṣūl*, dealt with the cosmological sciences.[29] Likewise, in the mathematical sciences, such famous names as Abū Zaid al-Balkhī, Abu'l-Wafā', Abū Sahl al-Kūhī, 'Abd al-Raḥmān al-Ṣūfī, and Ibn Yūnus attest to the great activity in these sciences during the fourth Islamic century.

Similarly, in the fifth century, although perhaps to a somewhat lesser extent, the Muslim arts and sciences continued to flourish. Such figures as Ibn al-Haitham, 'Alī ibn 'Īsā, 'Umar Khayyām, al-Ghazzālī, Abū Isḥāq al-Zarqālī, Nāṣir-i Khusraw, and Abu'l-Ḥasan ibn Marzbān Bahmanyār extended the tradition of the previous century down to the Seljuq period and elucidated the teachings of the earlier masters.

It is due to the great activity in these two centuries that all of the authors whose doctrines we wish to study in this book have been chosen from this period. In studying the conceptions of Nature in the writings of the Ikhwān al-Ṣafā', al-Bīrūnī, and Ibn Sīnā, who can be considered as the dominant figures in the various sciences in this most

[27] Two dates are given: the lunar Islamic year, left, and the solar Christian year, right.

[28] Although many Ṣūfīs have made use of Hermetic symbols, and Alexandrian Hermeticism became integrated into Islamic gnosis, one must distinguish clearly between *taṣawwuf* and Hermeticism and philosophy, which in the eyes of the Muslims is also connected with the name of Hermes or the prophet Idrīs and is considered, like all Revelation, to be of divine origin. As Ibn 'Arabī writes: "The knowledge of the philosophers is of another kind than that of positive religion [and, therefore, Sufism]; whereas the latter is based on the law of Muḥammad—upon whom be peace—the former is founded upon the law of Idrīs." 'Abd al-Wahhāb al-Sha'rānī, *Kitāb al-yawāqīt* (Cairo, 1305 [1887]), I, 133; also H. Corbin, *Avicenne et le récit visionnaire* (Tehran, 1952) II, 16.

[29] The Ṣūfī conception of Nature did not become explicitly enunciated until the 6th/12th and 7th/13th centuries, when the gnostic doctrines of Islam were formulated in the writings of Ibn 'Arabī, Ṣadr al-Dīn al-Qunawī, 'Abd al-Karīm al-Jīlī, and other masters of that school. But it must not be thought that there is a discontinuity between these masters and the earlier Ṣūfīs who remained content with the exposition of the practical rather than the theoretical aspect of the spiritual life. The later Ṣūfī conception of Nature as the Breath of the Compassionate (*nafas al-raḥmān*) is closely connected with the symbolism of invocation (*dhikr*) which has always formed the basic technique of Sufism.

On the question of *dhikr*, see L. Gardet, "La Mention du nom divin en mystique musulmane," *La Revue Thomiste*, 52:642–679 (1952); 53:197–216 (1953); G. C. Anawati and L. Gardet, *La Mystique musulmane* (Paris, 1961), Pt. 4.

active of all periods of Islamic history, we are in reality studying the basic elements of Islamic cosmological doctrines which are to be found in one form or another in the writings of most of the later Muslim authors. Our choice of these particular authors is therefore not accidental; rather, through them we hope to gain a glimpse of general doctrines not limited to the particular period in which these authors lived.

It may of course be asked why the fourth and fifth centuries were a period of great activity in the sciences. The reason is to be sought partially in the historical circumstances of the time.[30] If we divide the Islamic community into the two categories of the Sunni and the Shī'ah, we find that during the period of strength of the Sunni caliphate, both Umayyad and Abbasid, there was a different social and political background for the growth of the arts and sciences from that which characterized the period when the central authority had weakened and Shī'ah elements had become powerful.

In order to understand the reason for this distinction we must return to the first two centuries of Islamic history. From certain sayings of 'Alī ibn Abī Ṭālib and especially the writings of Imām Ja'far al-Ṣādiq, the first and sixth Shī'ah *imāms*, it is quite evident that the Hermetic sciences were early integrated into the Shī'ite perspective. One need only remember that Jābir ibn Ḥayyān, the most celebrated of all Muslim alchemists, was the disciple of Imām Ja'far and considered all of his works to be no more than an account of the teachings of his master.[31] Moreover, the discussions of Imām Riḍā, the eighth Shī'ah *imām*, with Ma'mūn and 'Imrān al-Ṣābī, made the intellectual sciences (*al-'ulūm al-'aqlīyah*) once and for all legitimate in the world of Shī'ism.[32]

[30] We are indebted to Professor H. A. R. Gibb for much of what follows regarding the history of this period. It is unfortunate that his analysis, made in his courses on Islamic history, has never appeared in printed form so that reference to it might be made here.

[31] Certain Western scholars like Julius Ruska have doubted the very existence of Jābir because some of the writings attributed to him have been shown to have been written during later centuries. While it must be admitted that much of the Jābirian corpus was not written by Jābir himself, due to the tendency in traditional sciences to identify the various manifestations of a school with its founder, one cannot simply deny the existence of Jābir with such arguments. Moreover, from a certain point of view the figure of a Jābir or a Pythagoras as conceived by their followers is more important for the understanding of the spiritual and intellectual forces dominant in a particular epoch than a picture which is the result of historical analysis based on only the written evidence which has survived the decaying influence of time.

[32] 'Abd al-Ḥujjat Balāghī, *Kitāb maqālāt al-ḥunafā' fī maqāmāt Shams al-'Urafā'* (Tehran, 1948), p. 11.

The early acceptance of Hermeticism[33] by the Shī'ites made them the proponents of a synthetic physics,[34] a "periodic" conception of time[35] as consisting of different cycles, or *adwār* and *akwār*, and the tradition of Hippocratic medicine tied to alchemy. Likewise, it made them opposed to the rationalistic elements of Aristotle's philosophy and many aspects of his physics. Consequently, when philosophy did finally become integrated into the Shī'ite perspective, it was not in the form of pure Aristotelianism but as that form of wisdom called *ḥikmah* in which Illuminationist and gnostic doctrines play a central role and in which reason becomes only the first stage and discursive knowledge the most elementary form of knowledge to be followed by the direct contemplation of the intelligible realities.

In the Sunni world, "official" learning did not concern itself so much with either Hermeticism or Peripatetic philosophy, except to the degree that philosophical methods were adopted to theological ends by the great Sunni theologians like Imām al-Ghazzālī and Fakhr al-Dīn al-Rāzī.[36] In fact, from the beginning the Sunnis displayed a greater hostility toward the philosophers than the Shī'ah, as demonstrated by the historical evidence of the survival of philosophy, in its new wedding with illumination and gnosis in the form of *ḥikmah*, among the Shī'ites long after it had ceased to exist as a living tradition in the Sunni world.

[33] By Hermeticists, or *harāmisah*, the Muslim authors meant the followers of the ante-Diluvian prophet, Idrīs, or Ukhnūkh (Quran, XIX, 57; XXI, 85), whom they regarded as the founder of the arts and sciences as well as of *ḥikmah* and philosophy. See "Hermes . . .," in S. H. Nasr, *Islamic Studies* (Beirut, 1967), ch. 6.

[34] "Une *physique synthétique*, qui, bien loin d'opposer le monde sublunaire au ciel empyrée (et les quatre éléments corruptibles à la quintessence), affirme l'unité de l'univers; théoriquement par une science des *correspondances* entre les divers 'horizons' de l'univers . . . pratiquement par l'exploitation expérimentale systématique de ces correspondances, en 'provoquant des résultats' en astrologie horoscopique, en typologie (toxiques en médecine, caractères individuels et collectifs dans la combinaison des métiers et la science des cités), en alchimie (sublimation)." L. Massignon, "Inventaire de la littérature hermétique arabe," in A. J. Festugière, *La Révélation d'Hermès Trismégiste* (Paris, 1950), I, 389.

[35] The periodic notion of time forms a part of the Islamic perspective and is affirmed implicitly in the prophetic eras mentioned in the Quran.

For the "cyclic" notion of time in Islam, see Abū Bakr Sirāj ad-Dīn, "The Islamic and Christian conceptions of the march of time," *Islamic Quarterly*, 1:230ff (1954). This notion does not imply a return to the same point after the passage of a certain period of time, but the presence of a number of periods from the beginning of creation to the last day which have points of correspondence with each other, and at the beginning of each of which God sends a prophet into the world to reaffirm the truth of the previous revelations which have been forgotten.

[36] As for Hermeticism, many of its symbols were adopted by such Ṣūfīs as Ibn 'Arabī and Ṣadr al-Dīn al-Qunawī (sometimes pronounced Qunyawī) so that they became a permanent heritage of esoteric schools in the Sunni as well as the Shī'ite world.

The opposition of the Sunni doctors of the law to philosophy and most of the pre-Islamic (*awā'il*) sciences became more intense after the destruction of the Mu'tazilites and the triumph of Ash'arite theology during the 4th/10th and 5th/11th centuries. Likewise, the Sunni caliphate usually was more favorable to the purely religious disciplines such as the science of commentary, *ḥadīth*, and jurisprudence, and supported the other sciences like medicine and astronomy only to the extent that they corresponded to the needs of the community.[37]

When we take into account this difference in attitude of the Sunni and the Shī'ah toward the arts and sciences, it becomes somewhat easier to discover the causes underlying the great activity in the various sciences during the 4th/10th and 5th/11th centuries, the period which we have chosen to study in this book. For it is during these centuries that Shī'ism becomes important politically and socially. Already, during the reign of Ma'mūn, a century before the period in question, the appointment of Ṭāhir Dhu'l-Yamīnain to the governorship of Khurāsān in 205/821 marked the beginning of the semi-independent Ṭāhirid dynasty which after a half-century of rule was destroyed by Ya'qūb ibn Laith, the Saffārid.[38] The Ṣaffārids in turn ruled over the eastern provinces of Persia from 253/867 to 298/910 with the support of the caliphate, although internally they were nearly independent. In Transoxiana, also, the four sons of Asad ibn 'Abdallāh, who before his conversion to Islam had been called Sāmān, served Ma'mūn with great distinction and were rewarded with the governorships of Samarqand, Farghana, Shash, and Herat. The control of this family over these cities marked the beginning of the Sāmānid dynasty, which, like the Ṣaffārids, enjoyed internal independence and ruled over much of Transoxiana until 389/999, and whose members became the patrons of many of the most famous Persian scientists and poets. These Persian rulers, who had diminished the central authority of the caliphate, were not overthrown until the rise to power of the newly emigrated Turkish tribes in the area cul-

[37] By this statement we mean only a general tendency that seems to be present in Islamic history rather than a hard and fast rule. Many Sunni caliphs and princes, from the legendary Khālid ibn Yazīd to Hārūn al-Rashīd, and from Ma'mūn in the East to 'Abd al-Raḥmān III in Andalusia, and wazirs like Rashīd al-Dīn Faḍlallāh were ardent supporters of the arts and sciences and played an essential role in the propagation and cultivation of the sciences in the Islamic world. The early Abbasid caliphs also interested themselves in Greek learning in order to protect the faith of the community from the acquired instrument of Greek logic by the use of that instrument itself.

[38] For the history of the eastern territories of Islam, and especially Persia, during this period see S. Lane-Poole, *The Mohammadan Dynasties* (Paris, 1925), pp. 128ff, and W. Barthold, *Turkestan down to the Mongol Invasion*, rev. ed. (London, 1928), pp. 208ff.

minated in the conquest of eastern Persia by Maḥmūd of Ghazna, ending permanently the rule of the Persians in Central Asia.

If the rise of these independent dynasties meant a weakening of the authority of the caliphate, these dynasties nevertheless, accepted at least theoretically, the Sunni caliph and ruled in his name. Such, however, was not true of the Shī'ite Būyids or Buwaihids[39] who ruled Persia from 320/932 to 447/1055. The star of this family began to rise when 'Alī, the son of Buwaih, who was reputed to have descended from ancient Persian kings, was given the governorship of Karaj in 318/930. Soon, with the help of his brothers, Ḥasan and Aḥmad, he was able to expand the domain of his power and within a few years became the ruler of most of central Persia. From this base the Buwaihids expanded their political and military power until 334/945, when Aḥmad conquered Baghdad itself.

The caliph, al-Muktafī bi'Llāh, was forced to accept the power of the new conquerors. He gave to the three brothers the title of 'Imād al-Dawlah, Rukn al-Dawlah, and Mu'izz-al-Dawlah and the rank of *amīr al-umarā'*. The Buwaihids in turn treated the caliph with great respect; but, being Shī'ite, they no longer accepted his absolute religious and political authority. They thus succeeded in establishing Shī'ite rule over the lands of the Eastern caliphate for the first time in Islamic history, a rule which they were able to maintain in their family until the Turkish Ghaznawids and Seljuqs once again brought the eastern provinces under Sunni rule.

While the Eastern provinces of the Islamic world were being dominated by Shī'ite rulers, Egypt and much of North Africa had also fallen under the sway of Shī'ism, this time in the form of Ismā'īlism. The Fāṭimid dynasty had established itself in Egypt and competed with the caliphs in Baghdad for supremacy in the Muslim world. This new Shī'ite caliphate in turn played an important role in the fostering of the arts and sciences and the establishment of schools in which the scientific disciplines were taught.[40]

As a result of this brief survey of the history of the Muslim lands during the 4th/10th and 5th/11th centuries we have discovered that

[39] The name of this family in Persian is Būyih, "oe" being a middle Persian sound which appears in many Persian names such as Bābūyih, Muskūyih, and so on. Since this sound does not exist in Arabic, it has been transformed into "awaih" or "uwaih" by Arabic writers, hence Ibn Miskawaih, Buwaihids, and so on. Since the Arabic form of these words is more familiar to Western readers, we have transliterated the well-known ones in this form rather than in the original Persian.

[40] For the relation of Fāṭimid rule to a certain "realism" in Islamic art and its possible relation to the sciences, see R. Ettinghausen, "Realism in Islamic Art," in *Studi orientalistici in onore di Giorgio Levi della Vida* (Rome), 1:253ff (1958).

this was a period during which the authority of the central Sunni government had weakened and Shīʿite princes were ruling over a large segment of the Islamic world. Considering the more sympathetic attitude of Shīʿism toward the pre-Islamic sciences and philosophy which we have already mentioned, it is not surprising to discover that this period of Shīʿite domination coincides with a time of great activity in the various intellectual sciences. In fact it may be safely asserted that the rise of the Shīʿah in this period was the chief reason for the greater attention paid to the arts and sciences. The Shīʿah, both in Persia and in Egypt, founded schools in which the sciences were taught and established educational and scientific procedures that were later adopted by the Sunnis themselves, as exemplified by the adoption of al-Azhar—originally founded by the Fāṭimids—for Sunni learning and the building of the Niẓāmīyah school in Baghdad upon earlier Shīʿite models.

The 4th/10th and 5th/11th centuries constitute, therefore, the period of the formation of the Islamic arts, sciences, and philosophy and the period in which the basis of the Islamic sciences was laid, in such a way as to determine the general contour of these sciences as they have been cultivated in the Muslim world ever since. It may be said, then, that to study the sciences in this period is to study the root and formation of the various Islamic sciences and not just a passing moment in the long centuries of Islamic history.

The Intellectual Dimensions in Islam and the Class of Seekers of Knowledge

To understand the relation of the subject matter of this book to the totality of the intellectual life of Islam it is necessary not only to place the period under discussion within Islamic history but also to relate the perspectives of the authors under study to the general intellectual dimensions in Islam. The most essential division within Islam is the "vertical" hierarchy of the Sacred Law (*Sharīʿah*), the Way (*Ṭarīqah*) and the Truth (*Ḥaqīqah*), the first being the exoteric aspect of the Islamic revelation, divided into the Sunni and the Shīʿite interpretations of the tradition, and the latter two the esoteric aspects which are usually known under the denomination of Sufism. Or, one might say that the Truth is the center, the Way or "ways" the radii, and the Sacred Law the circumference of a circle the totality of which is Islam.[41]

[41] See F. Schuon, *L'Œil du cœur* (Paris, 1974), pp. 91ff. It is necessary to add that Islamic esotericism can also be found in various forms of Shīʿism in addition to Sufism.

Another division of the intellectual perspectives within Islam which is more immediately related to our present study is the classification of the various intellectual dimensions according to the modes of knowledge sought by each school.[42] From this point of view we may enumerate the seekers of knowledge in the earlier centuries of Islam as being the Quranic scholars and traditionalists, grammarians, historians and geographers, natural scientists and mathematicians, the Mu'tazilites and other theologians, the Peripatetic philosophers, the Neo-Pythagoreans and Hermeticists, the Ismā'īlī philosophers, and finally the Ṣūfīs.

In the later centuries, when the various schools became more crystallized, the major schools in the Sunni world became more or less confined to those of the jurists, the theologians, and the Ṣūfīs, the last-named having absorbed the gnostic elements of such pre-Islamic traditions as Hermeticism. Philosophy and the natural and mathematical sciences also continued to be cultivated but to a much lesser degree; philosophy, especially, in its rationalistic mode ceased to exist after the 6th/12th century in the Sunni world.

In the Shī'ite world, likewise, the school of the theologians and jurists as well as those of the Ṣūfīs, who, as we noted, stand in a sense above the Sunni-Shī'ah division, remained dominant. But, in addition, with the weakening of rationalism under the attack of theology and Sufism in the 5th/11th and 6th/12th centuries, the new school of Illuminationist, or *Ishrāqī*, theosophy came to be established by Suhrawardī and his followers, one that has exercised a great influence upon the intellectual life of Persia ever since. *Ishrāqī* theosophy was in turn re-interpreted and combined with the tenets of Shī'ism by Ṣadr al-Dīn al-Shīrāzī, commonly known as Mullā Ṣadrā, who during the Safavid period opened the last new intellectual perspective in Islam[43] and who, has continued to dominate the intellectual life of Shī'ism to the present day. During the Safavid period, also, the study of the mathematical sciences was revived in Persia by Bahā' al-Dīn al-'Āmilī and others, but in this case it was mostly a question of

[42] There is also the general division of the sciences in Islam into the transmitted (*naqlī*) and intellectual (*'aqlī*), which we have not considered here. For this traditional division of the Muslim sciences, see Ibn Khaldūn, *The Muqaddimah*, trans. F. Rosenthal (New York, 1958), II, 436ff.

[43] For an account of the teachings of Suhrawardī and the significance of his school, see the two prolegomena of H. Corbin to Suhrawardī, *Opera Metaphysica et Mystica*, vol. I (Tehran, 1977) and vol. II (Tehran, 1977). Regarding the *Ishrāqī* school and the school of Mullā Ṣadrā see also S. H. Nasr, "Suhrawardī," "The School of Ispahan," and "Ṣadr al-Dīn Shīrāzī," in *A History of Muslim Philosophy*, ed. M. M. Sharif (Wiesbaden, 1963–66); and "Ṣadr al-Dīn Shīrāzī, his life, doctrines and significance," *Indo-Iranica*, 14:6–16 (December 1961). See also the monumental work of Corbin, *En Islam iranien*, 4 vols. (Paris, 1971–1972).

reviving the teachings of Khwājah Naṣīr al-Dīn al-Ṭūsī and the other earlier Muslim mathematicians rather than founding a new school.

We can say, therefore, that the dominant perspectives in Islamic history touching upon the study of Nature are those of the mathematicians, Hermeticists, Peripatetics, Ismā'īlīs, Illuminationists, gnostics, or Ṣūfīs, and finally the theologians, the majority of whom have followed a "philosophy of Nature" in which Nature and natural cause are absorbed into the Divine omnipotence.

To discover more specifically how these perspectives appear in the 4th/10th and 5th/11th centuries, we turn to the evidence of some of the Muslim authors themselves. In his *Treatise on Being* (*Risālat al-wujūd*) 'Umar Khayyām, one of the most significant figures of the 5th/11th century, writes concerning those who seek ultimate knowledge, as follows:

Seekers after knowledge of God, Glorious and Most High, are divided into four groups:

(1) The theologians (*Mutakallimūn*) who became content with disputation and satisfying proofs and considered this much knowledge of the Creator, excellent is His Name, as sufficient.

(2) The philosophers and metaphysicians [of Greek inspiration (*ḥukamā'*)] who used rational arguments and sought to know the laws of logic and were never content with satisfying arguments, but they too could not remain faithful to the conditions of logic and with it became helpless.

(3) The Ismā'īlīs and *Ta'līmīyūn* who said that the way of knowledge is none other than receiving information from a trustworthy (*ṣādiq*) informer, for in reasoning about the knowledge of the Creator, His Essence and Attributes, there is much difficulty, and the reasoning of the opponents and the intelligent is stupefied and helpless before it. Therefore, it is better to seek knowledge from the words of a trustworthy person.

(4) The people of *taṣawwuf* who did not seek knowledge by speculation or thinking but by purgation of their inner being and purifying of their disposition. They cleansed the rational soul from the impurities of Nature and bodily forms until it became a pure substance. It came face to face with the spiritual world (*malakūt*) so that the forms of that world became reflected in it in reality without doubt or ambiguity. This is the best of all paths because none of the perfections of God are kept away from it, and there are no obstacles or veils put before it.[44]

[44] Tehran National Library, MS. Bayāḍī (dated 659). Also Afḍal al-Dīn al-Kāshānī, *Muṣannafāt*, ed. Mujtabā Mīnovī and Yaḥyā Mahdavī (Tehran, 1952), vol. I, Introduction; and 'Umar Khayyām. "Az nathr-i fārsī-yi Khayyām," *Sharq*, 1:167–168 (1309 [1930]). (Throughout the book we have made use of suitable translations if they have existed in English, French, or German. Where such translations have not been available we have translated the Arabic and Persian texts.)

Several centuries later, when the various perspectives had become more crystallized, Sayyid Sharīf al-Jurjānī, the 9th/15th century Persian *ḥakīm*, in his glosses upon the *Maṭāli' al-anwār*, writes:

> To gain a knowledge of the beginning and the end of things, there are two ways possible: one the way of argument and examination (or observation), and the other the way of asceticism and self-purification (*mujāhadah*). Among the followers of argument and examination, those who attach themselves to one of the religions are called the theologians and those who do not follow the religion of any prophet are called the Peripatetics. Among the followers of the way of asceticism and self-purification, those who bind themselves to the *Sharī'ah* are called Ṣūfīs and those who do not have such a bond are called the Illuminationists.[45]

When we consider the intellectual position of the authors we have considered in this book in the general background of the various Islamic intellectual perspectives, it becomes possible for us to understand from what point of view the cosmological sciences are being considered in each case and what relation that point of view has with respect to the totality of Islamic intellectual life. In the writings of the Ikhwān al-Ṣafā' we encounter a wealth of Neo-Pythagorean and Hermetic symbols, a source upon which the Ismā'īlīs relied greatly during the later centuries. With al-Bīrūnī we meet one of the most eminent of Muslim mathematicians and astronomers and at the same time the independent scholar and historian in search of the knowledge of other lands and epochs. As for Ibn Sīnā, he was undoubtedly the greatest of the Muslim Peripatetics and in his writings one can discover the Peripatetic philosophy of Nature in its most lucid and thorough form. Moreover, the later works of Ibn Sīnā, especially the visionary narratives, present us with a vision of the cosmos which was adopted later by the *Ishrāqīs* and which presents many elements in common with the views of the Ṣūfīs on Nature and on the role of cosmology in the journey of the gnostic toward illumination.

In considering the writings of the Ikhwān al-Ṣafā', al-Bīrūnī, and Ibn Sīnā, therefore, we are dealing not only with three of the most important authors of the most active period of the Islamic arts and sciences, but also with the general views of the school of Hermeticists and Neo-Pythagoreans, mathematicians, historians, and scholars, and finally with the Peripatetic and indirectly the *Ishrāqī* and Ṣūfī

Likewise, al-Ghazzālī, in his *al-Munqidh min al-ḍalāl*, divides the seekers of knowledge into the *mutakallimūn*, *bāṭinīyah* (Ismā'īlīs), *falāsifah* and *ṣūfīyah*; see W. Montgomery Watt, *The Faith and Practice of al-Ghazali* (London, 1953), pp. 26ff.

[45] Sayyid Sharīf al-Jurjānī, *Sharḥ maṭāli' al-anwār* (Tehran, 1315 [1897]), p. 4.

conception of Nature.[46] It would then perhaps not be too audacious if we consider the present book as a general introduction to the Islamic cosmological sciences without our having taken into account all of the important authors who have contributed to this subject over the centuries. In choosing the specific writers of the 4th/10th and 5th/11th centuries we hope to demonstrate not only what this or that particular author has thought during a specific period, but, more importantly, what views each particular perspective in Islamic civilization has held concerning the sciences of Nature.

[46] The identification of an individual school with a particular author is legitimate in Islamic history because there, as in other traditions, the intellectual perspective dominates over individualistic modes of thought; and, as it is said in Arabic, the *mā qīla*, what is said, is more important than the *man qāla*, he who has said it. These authors therefore, present us with the views of nearly all the major Islamic intellectual perspectives excluding that of the theologians whom, as we mentioned, do not consider Nature to have a separate reality. As for the basic gnostic doctrines of Ibn 'Arabī and his followers, as far as the cosmological sciences are concerned, many of their principles are found, though perhaps in a less transparent form, in the writings of the Ikhwān al-Ṣafā' and Ibn Sīnā; for as we remarked earlier, the Alexandrian and Hermetic cosmological sciences, or "Lesser Mysteries," were absorbed in the light of the "Greater Mysteries" of Islamic gnosis.

That is what shows thee His Omnipotence, Exalted be He; that He hides Himself from thee by that which has no existence outside of Him.

Ibn ʻAṭā'allāh al-Iskandarī-*Ḥikam*

PART I

Ikhwān al-Ṣafā' wa Khullān al-Wafā'

(The Brethren of Purity)

CHAPTER 1

The Rasā'il *of the Ikhwān al-Ṣafā'* —*Their Identity and Content*

Having been hidden within the cloak of secrecy from its very inception, the *Rasā'il* have provided many points of contention and have been a constant source of dispute among both Muslim and Western scholars.[1] The identification of the authors, or possibly one author, the place and time of the writing and propagation of their works, the nature of the secret brotherhood the outer manifestation of which comprises the *Rasā'il*—these and many secondary questions have remained without any definitive historical answers.

Many early Muslim sources have given the name of a group of scholars from Baṣra as the authors of the *Rasā'il*. Ibn al-Qifṭī, in his *Akhbār al-ḥukamā'*,[2] mentions that according to Abū Ḥayyān al-Tawḥīdī the authors of the *Rasā'il* were Abū Sulaimān Muḥammad ibn Ma'shar al-Bastī, Abu'l-Ḥasan 'Alī ibn Hārūn al-Zanjānī, Abū Aḥmad al-Mihrjānī, 'Awfī and Zaid ibn al-Rifā'ī. Shahrazūrī, on the other hand, in his *Nuzhat al-arwāḥ*, gives a somewhat different list of authors,[3] consisting of Abū Sulaimān Muḥammad ibn Mas'ūd al-Bastī, known as al-Muqaddasī, Abu'l-Ḥasan 'Alī ibn Wahrūn al-Ṣābī, Abū Aḥmad al-Nahrjūrī, 'Awfī al-Baṣrī and Zaid ibn al-Rifā'ī. Abū Ḥayyān al-Tawḥīdī himself claims that the wazīr, Abū 'Abdallāh al-Sa'dān, who was killed in 375/985, had in his service a

[1] The name of the Ikhwān al-Ṣafā', the authors of the *Rasā'il*, is itself of interest. The word *ṣafā'* appears in the Quran (II, 153) and is used widely among the Ṣūfīs to denote the interior purity which makes gnosis (*ma'rifah*) possible and which is the ultimate aim of *taṣawwuf*. Certain Ṣūfī masters have derived the word *ṣūfī* itself from *ṣafā'*. For example, Abū Ḥasan al-Qannād says:

„ اَلصُّوفِي مَأْخُوذٌ من الصفاءِ وهو القيام لله عزّوجلّ في كلّ وقت بشرط الوفاءِ. "

Abū Naṣr al-Sarrāj al-Ṭūsī, *Kitāb al-luma'* (London, 1914), p. 26.

[2] Ibn al-Qifṭī, *Akhbār al-ḥukamā'* (Cairo, 1326 [1908]), pp. 58–63. See also Ẓahīr al-Dīn al-Baihaqī, *Tatimmah ṣiwān al-ḥikmah* (Lahore, 1351 [1932]), p. 21.

[3] From the manuscript of *Ta'rīkh al-ḥukamā'* of Shahrazūrī, quoted by Jalāl Homā'ī, *Ghazzālī-nāmah* (Tehran, 1936), p. 35.

group of scholars, including Ibn Zar'ah (331/942–398/1007), Miskawaih al-Rāzī (died 421/1029), Abu'l-Wafā' al-Buzjānī, Abu'l-Qāsim al-Ahwāzī, Abū Sa'īd Bahrām, Ibn Shāhūyah, Ibn Bakr, Ibn Ḥajjāj al-Shā'ir, Shūkh Shī'ī (died 391/1000), and Ibn 'Abīd al-Kātib whose sayings were compiled and collected to form the *Rasā'il.*[4] Regarding one of the alleged authors, Zaid ibn Rifā'ī, Abū Ḥayyān writes:

> He stands in no definite relation with any one system. He knows how to form his school from all sides . . . If one could but unite Greek philosophy and the religious law of Islam, the perfection of the faith, they the Ikhwān thought, would be reached. With this design, they wrote fifty tracts on all branches of philosophy.[5]

Not only is there a difference of view as to the authors of the *Rasā'il*, but also regarding the part of the Islamic community from which they originated. The modern discussions find their echo among the medieval Muslim authors themselves. Ibn al-Qifṭī, giving his own view, considers the Ikhwān as followers of the school of the Mu'tazilah, which was rationalistic in its approach.[6] Ibn Taimīyah, the Ḥanbalī jurist, on the other hand, tends toward the other extreme in relating the Ikhwān to the Nuṣairīs, who are as far removed from the rationalists as almost any group to be found in Islam.[7] Between these two extremes there have been the views expressed over the centuries that the *Rasā'il* were written by 'Alī ibn Abī Ṭālib, al-Ghazzālī, Ḥallāj, Imām Ja'far al-Ṣādiq, or various Ismā'īlī *dā'īs*, or "missionaries."[8]

Considering the great respect paid to the *Rasā'il* by the Ismā'īlīs,[9] the extensive use of them, particularly in the Yemen, and the fact that

[4] Al-Tawḥīdī, *Risālah fi'l-ṣidāqah wa'l-ṣadīq* (Constantinople, 1301 [1883], pp. 31–33). Dates have been given in the case of those authors for whom they have been established with certainty.

[5] S. Lane-Poole, *Studies in a Mosque*, 2nd ed. (London: Sydney, Eden, Remington, 1893), pp. 193–194.

[6] 'A. 'Awā, *L'Esprit critique des 'Frères de la Pureté': Encyclopédistes arabes du IVe/Xe siècle* (Beirut, 1948), p. 48.

[7] *Ibid.*

[8] For a general discussion of these opinions as well as those of the moderns, see A. L. Ṭībāwī, "Ikhwān aṣ-Ṣafā and their Rasā'il," *Islamic Quarterly*, 2:28–46 (1955).

[9] Some Ismā'īlī scholars have even called it "a Quran after the Quran."

„ إنّ رسائل الاخوان هى القرآن بعد قرآن او هى قرآن العلم كما ان القرآن هو
قرآن الوحى وهى قرآن الامامة وذلك قرآن النبوة.»

A. Tāmir, *La Réalité des Iḫwān aṣ-Ṣafā' wa Ḫullān al-Wafā'* (Beirut, 1957), p. 17.

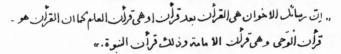

"the work is accepted by the Ismā'īlīs as belonging to their religion, and is still regarded as esoteric . . .,"[10] it is not surprising to find most modern scholars, Muslims and non-Muslims alike, claiming Ismā'īlī authorship for the work. A. Tāmir, for example, has given a very detailed and convincing account of the Ismā'īlī nature of the *Rasā'il*, whose contents he calls "the Ismā'īlī philosophy."[11] It is interesting to note, however, that the well-known modern Ismā'īlī scholar, H. F. al-Hamdānī, although emphasizing the importance of the *Rasā'il* in the Ismā'īlī mission in the Yemen, disclaims Ismā'īlī authorship for the work and instead attributes the treatises to the 'Alīds.[12] And A. L. Ṭībāwī, basing his conclusion on the fact that the Ikhwān opposed the hereditary and concealed *imām*, claims that the connection between the *Rasā'il* and the Ismā'īlīs is of later origin.[13] He makes a more general association, stating that the "Ikhwān aṣ-Ṣafā'

[10] V. A. Ivanov, *The Alleged Founder of Ismailism* (Bombay, 1946), p. 146.

[11] «وهذه الفلسفة هي بالحقيقة الفلسفة الاسماعيلية التي بذر بذورها اخوان الصفاء»

Tāmir, *La Réalité des Iḫwān aṣ-Ṣafā'* . . ., p. 8, and also in his Introduction to the edition of *Risālat jāmi'ah al-jāmi'ah* (Beirut, 1959), pp. 1–58, where he gives as the final reason for the Ismā'īlī origin of the *Rasā'il* the fact that their number is equivalent to the numerical value of the name of the man 'Abdallāh ibn Muḥammad, who according to Ismā'īlī authorities composed the work:

«ومما يمكن من امر فلدينا دليل آخر يلقي نوراً ساطعاً على الموضوع: وهو ان الامام عبدالله
بن محمد عندما وضع رسائل اخوان الصفاء جعل عددها (٥٢) رسالة لحكمة فلسفية
وتأويلية كان يقول بها وتقضي بان رسائل اخوان الصفاء دائرة علمية ناموسية حقيقية
ويجب ان يكون في الدائرة الناموسية الدينية، صورة لما في الدائرة العلمية،
وكما وان في الدائرة العلمية معرفته في الدائرة الدينية الناموسية ولهذا جعل
عدد الرسائل ٥٢ مطابقاً لعدد ركعات الصلوات الخمس وهذا العدد نفسه جاء
مطابقاً لعدد حروف اسمه بحساب الجمل على هذه الصورة:

ع ب د ا ل ل ه ب ن م ح م د = عبدالله بن محمد

٧ ٢ ٤ ١ ٣ ٣ ٥ ٢ ٥ ٤ ٨ ٤ ٤ = ٥٢

(pp. 17–18).

Zākī Pāshā, in his introduction to the 1928 Cairo edition of the *Rasā'il*, also argues for the Ismā'īlī origin of the work.

[12] H. F. al-Hamdānī, "*Rasā'il* Ikhwān aṣ-Ṣafā' in the literature of the Ismā'īlī Ṭaiyibī Da'wā," *Der Islam* (Berlin), 20:291ff (1932).

[13] "Ikhwān aṣ-Ṣafā and their *Rasā'il*," *Islamic Quarterly*, 2:33 (1955).

may be taken as symbolizing the Shī'a attempt, while al-Ghazālī represents the Sunni attempt at a synthesis."[14]

A somewhat different approach is considered by 'A. 'Awā in his analytical study of the *Rasā'il.* Rather than identifying the Ikhwān too closely with any group, 'Awā calls them by the vague name of post-Mu'tazilites.[15] In this opinion he is in agreement, although in a somewhat vague fashion, with some of the early Western students of the Ikhwān.

Serious interest in the *Rasā'il* on the part of Western scholars was manifested in the nineteenth century with the translation made by Fr. Dieterici in a somewhat free and disorderly fashion over a period of thirty years, of most of the *Rasā'il.*[16] He realized early in his studies on the Ikhwān their importance in bringing together in an encyclopedic manner a great deal of Islamic learning and in uniting the various sciences in a unified world view.[17]

Another early German study which was to have a considerable influence during the succeeding decades was G. Flügel's article on the Ikhwān.[18] He emphasized there the rationalistic and Mu'tazilite nature of the *Rasā'il.* Considering the interests and particularly the rationalistic tendencies of the Mu'tazilites on the one hand and the cosmological and metaphysical views of the Ikhwān on the other, the assertion of Flügel is hardest of all to understand. Yet this view is supported again in the twentieth century by such scholars as E. G. Browne and R. A. Nicholson, while Miguel Asín Palacios considers the work to be a combination of Mu'tazilite and Shī'ite inspiration.[19] In a somewhat similar fashion, S. Pines, referring to the role of the Prophet, claims that "the *Rasā'il Ikhwān aṣ-Ṣafā'* are, in this point

[14] "The idea of guidance in Islam," *Islamic Quarterly*, 3:148 (1956).

[15] *L'Esprit critique . . .*, p. 49. Later in the work 'Awā states more specifically that "c'est avec les Frères de la Pureté que la scolastique dogmatique (*kalām*) nous paraît répondre véritablement à ses motifs les meilleurs, au monisme universel faisant de la vérité du savoir et de l'idéal de l'action un ensemble unique, un tout homogène et réconcilié" (p. 305). 'Awā follows Dieterici in considering Abū Ḥayyān al-Tawḥīdī as being "incontestablement aussi un des propagateurs de l'association" (*Ibid.*, p. 309). Although al-Tawḥīdī's encounter with al-Muqaddasī is known, there is no proof that al-Tawḥīdī participated in the writing of the *Rasā'il.*

[16] Fr. Dieterici, *Die Philosophie der Araber im X. Jahrhundert*, vol. II: *Die Naturschauung und Naturphilosophie der Araber im zehnten Jahrhundert aus den Schriften der lautern Brüder, Der Darwinismus im X. und XI. Jahrhundert* (Leipzig-Berlin, 1858–1891).

[17] Dieterici, *Die Philosophie der Araber*, vol. III: *Makrokosmos* (1876). He considers the Ikhwān as an association of scholars which included al-Tawḥīdī (*ibid.*, pt. 1, pp. 145ff).

[18] "Über Inhalt und Verfasser der arabischen Encyclopädie," *Zeitschrift der Deutschen morgenländischen Gesellschaft*, 13:1–43 (1859).

[19] E. G. Browne, *Literary History of Persia*, I (London, 1909), p. 292; R. A. Nicholson, *Literary History of the Arabs* (London, 1956), p. 370; M. Asín Palacios, *El original árabe de la disputa del asno contra Fr. Anselmo Turmeda* (Madrid, 1914), p. 11.

as in many others, an attempt to bridge the gap between the two currents of thought. They are, on one hand, imbued with Shī'ite—more especially Ismā'īlite—doctrines; on the other hand, they closely follow and indeed plagiarize the political theory of al-Fārābī."[20]

The history of the rise of early Ismā'īlism, the Fāṭimid movement, the doctrinal and political relations between Ismā'īlīs and Bāṭinīs and Qarāmiṭah, are among the most obscure and difficult problems of Islamic history. But for our purpose here it is more suitable, if not exactly correct, to combine the foregoing movements and parties under one heading which we shall call Ismā'īlī.[21] With this generalization then, we can safely assert that the great majority of Western scholars consider the Ikhwān and their *Rasā'il* to be connected with the Ismā'īlī movement. Casanova, in 1915, had already defended this position,[22] to be followed in his stand by Goldziher,[23] MacDonald,[24] Lane-Poole,[25] Massignon,[26] and Ivanov,[27] just to mention some of the better-known authors in this field.

A few Western scholars—as, for example, Stern and Sarton—have accepted the opinions of early Muslim writers on the authorship of the *Rasā'il* and have attributed the work to a group of scholars probably from Baṣra. After abandoning this view, Stern once more returned to it after publication of the *Kitāb al-imtā'* of Abū Ḥayyān al-Tawḥīdī in which the group of scholars are mentioned.[28] Recently, in a profound study on the relation between the Ṣabaeans and the

[20] S. Pines, "Some Problems of Islamic Philosophy," *Islamic Culture*, 11:71 (1937).

[21] Massignon defines the *Qarāmiṭah* as (1) the general movement of reform during the third century which ended with the establishment of the Fāṭimids in 297/910; and (2) groups of Arabs and Nabaṭaeans of southern Mesopotamia who assembled there after the war of Zanj. L. Massignon, "Esquisse d'une bibliographie ḳarmate," in *Essays Presented to E. G. Browne* (Cambridge, England, 1922), pp. 329ff.

[22] P. Casanova, "Notice sur un manuscrit de la secte des Assassins," *Journal Asiatique* (1898), pp. 151–159.

[23] I. Goldziher, *Le Dogme et la loi de l'Islam* (Paris, 1920), p. 202. Goldziher believed that the *Rasā'il* were an important source for the Ismā'īlīs from which they drew a great deal.

[24] D. MacDonald, *The Development of Muslim Theology, Jurisprudence and Constitutional Theory* (New York, 1903), p. 188. MacDonald compares the Ikhwān to the lodges of the Masons and relates them to the *Qarāmiṭah*.

[25] Lane-Poole, *Studies in a Mosque*, p. 186.

[26] Massignon also relates the Ikhwān to the *Qarāmiṭah*. See his "Esquisse d'une bibliographie ḳarmate," p. 329.

[27] Ivanov rejects completely the existence of a Baṣra group of scholars. He writes, "I would be inclined to think that this was a kind of camouflage story circulated by the Ismailis to avoid the book being used as a proof of their orthodoxy." V. A. Ivanov, *The Alleged Founders of Ismailism*, pp. 146–147. He considers the *Rasā'il*, in fact, to have been written under Fāṭimid patronage "in connection with general work on the philosophy of Ismailism." *A Guide to Ismaili Literature* (London, 1933), p. 31.

[28] M. Stern, "The authorship of the Epistles of the Ikhwān aṣ-Ṣafā'," *Islamic Culture*, 20:367–372 (1946).

Ismā'īlīs, Corbin has identified the Ikhwān as a group or association of learned men who were at the same time the voice of the Ismā'īlī movement.[29]

Before forming a judgment on this difficult problem of the authorship of the *Rasā'il*, it is best to turn to the work itself for help. Since everyone agrees that the *Rasā'il* were written by the Ikhwān aṣ-Ṣafā', then whatever the Ikhwān tell us about themselves, their purpose, and the organization of their brotherhood, is at the same time information about the authors of the *Rasā'il*. They write, "The reason why the Brethren of Purity assemble is that each of them sees and knows that he cannot attain what he wishes concerning his well-being in this world and the attainment of success and salvation in the next world except through the cooperation of each one of them with his companion."[30] The aim of the Ikhwān is, therefore, neither the mere collection of facts nor a simple desire to create some sort of eclecticism as they have been accused by certain authors anxious to find in their writings originality and novelty above everything else.[31]

Rather, the purpose of the Ikhwān, according to their own definition, seems to be educational in the fullest sense of the word—that is, to bring to fruition and perfection the latent faculties of man so that he may gain salvation and spiritual freedom. Practically every chapter of their long work reminds the reader that in this world he is a prisoner who through knowledge must free himself from his earthly prison. All the sciences they consider—whether astronomy, angelology, or embryology—are discussed, not with the aim of a purely theoretical or intellectual interpretation or for their practical application, but to help untie the knots in the soul of the reader by making him aware, on the one hand, of the great harmony and beauty of the Universe and, on the other, of the necessity for man to go beyond material existence. And in order to reach this end they combine in their ideal education the virtues of many nations.

[29] "Au Xme siècle, une société de pensée qui s'est donnée le nom de 'Frères de la Pureté et Amis de la Fidélité,' a laissé en une vaste encyclopédie de 52 traités un mouvement de pensée ismaélienne." H. Corbin, "Rituel sabéen et exégèse ismaélienne du rituel," *Eranos Jahrbuch*, 19:187 (1950).

[30]

« وينبغي ان تعلم ان العلة التي تجمع بين اخوان الصفاء وهي ان يرى ويعلم
كل واحد منهم انه لا يتم له ما يريد من صلاح معيشته الدنيا ونيل الفوز والنجاة
في الآخرة الا بمعاونة كل واحد منهم لصاحبه. »

Rasā'il (henceforth referred to in the notes as *R*), Cairo, 1928, IV, 218.

[31] Or, as M. von Horten has put it, "einen unschöpferischen Eklektizismus"; see his *Die Philosophie des Islam* (Munich, 1923), p. 261.

They define the ideal and morally perfect man as of

East Persian derivation, Arabic in faith, of 'Irāqī, that is, Babylonian, education, a Hebrew in astuteness, a disciple of Christ in conduct, as pious as a Syrian monk, a Greek in the individual sciences, an Indian in the interpretation of all mysteries, but lastly and especially, a Ṣūfī in his whole spiritual life.[32]

If we consider the purpose rather than the sources of the *Rasā'il*, it is hard to explain the work away as being eclectic, because what may historically be drawn from diverse sources is brought together and unified with a single end in view. And since that end conforms almost completely to the spirit of the *ḥadīth* of the Prophet, "the world is the prison of the faithful and the paradise of the unbelievers,"[33] it is more difficult to call it in any way un-Islamic if we accept the definition of "Islamic" given in the Prologue.

Not only do the Ikhwān identify themselves spiritually with *taṣawwuf*, whose ultimate end is to awaken the initiate from the "dream of negligence" through spiritual education and spiritual training, but their account of their own organization corresponds—although on a plane that is more exterior and social—to that of the Ṣūfī brotherhoods. The Ikhwān divide themselves into four categories:

1. Those possessing purity of physical substance, excellence of conception and assimilation. Members must be at least fifteen years old. These brothers are called the pious and the compassionate (*al-abrār al-ruḥamā'*) and belong to the class of the masters of crafts.

2. Those possessing tenderness and compassion toward other men. Members must be at least thirty years of age. This grade corresponds to the philosophical faculty, and the members in it are called the brothers of religious and learned men (*akhyār* and *fuḍalā'*), the class of political chiefs.

3. Those possessing the ability to fight wars and insurrections in the spirit of calm and mildness which leads to salvation. They represent the power of Divine law which men receive at the age of forty. They are called the noble men of learning and virtue (*al-fuḍalā' al-kirām*) and are the kings and sultans.

[32] Tj. de Boer, *The History of Philosophy in Islam*, trans. E. R. Jones (London: Luzac & Co., 1933), p. 95. For us there can be nothing more convincing than this statement of the spiritual inclination and affiliation of the Ikhwān with *taṣawwuf*. See also A. L. Ṭībāwī, "Jamā'ah Ikhwān as-Ṣafā'," *Journal of the American University of Beirut* (1930–1931), p. 14; and Dhabīḥallāh Ṣafā, *Ikhwān al-ṣafā'* (Tehran, 1330 [1951]), p. 13.

[33] «الدّنيا سجن المؤمن وجنّة الكافر.»

4. The highest degree, which is that of surrender, receiving of Divine help and direct vision of the Truth. This is the angelic period which one only reaches at the age of fifty,[34] and is the preparation for heavenly ascension. The prophets like Abraham, Joseph, Jesus, Muḥammad, and sages like Socrates and Pythagoras belong to this stage.[35]

One can see in this classification the well-known division between craft, royal, and sacerdotal initiations which existed also in medieval Europe. The unity of the final goal through the hierarchy of the various grades is also evident. What has driven many people to accuse the Ikhwān of eclecticism, however, is not this unity but their mention of ancient sages along with the prophets. We have already explained in the Prologue, however, the validity of this procedure of integrating into Islam that which accepts the Unity of the Divine Principle. In fact, among many Muslims, especially the Ṣūfīs, the idea that God has revealed the Truth in some form to all peoples is an obvious consequence of the Quranic Revelation itself. Likewise, as Ṭībāwī says:

> The Brethren of Purity believe that the Truth is one without it being the private work of anyone. God has sent His Spirit to all men, to Christians as to Muslims, to blacks as to whites.[36]

In the opinion of the authors of the *Rasā'il*, individualism is the source of bewilderment and error. Seeing Greek or other ancient sages mentioned by the Ikhwān, then, in no way destroys their purpose of education through integration and toward that final aim, which is to free their disciples from the prison of this world; nor does it make them eclectic in other than a historical sense.

In a curious and significant passage, the Ikhwān identify themselves with the Primordial Tradition and the *philosophia perennis* which they seek to expound in its full blossoming only after the last of the prophets has brought his religion to the world.

> Know oh my brother, that we are the society of the Brethren of Purity, pure and sincere beings with generous hearts. We have slept in the cavern of Adam, our father, during the lapse of time which has brought back to us the vicissitudes of time and the calamities of events until finally, after our dispersion across various nations, there comes the moment of our encounter in the realm of the Master of the Eternal Religion, the moment when we see our Spiritual City elevated in the air . . . [37]

[34] These ages are not to be taken literally as corresponding to chronological years, for obviously according to the Ikhwān themselves some sages reached the highest stage before they were "biologically" fifty years old.

[35] *R.*, IV, 119ff; also, 'Awā, *L'Esprit critique* . . ., pp. 261–263.

[36] "Jamā'ah Ikhwān aṣ-Ṣafā'," p. 60.

[37] *R.*, IV, 85.

According to their own conception, then, the Ikhwān are expounding eternal wisdom, or what Suhrawardī later calls the *ḥikmah ladunīyah*, which man has always possessed in some form but which now is expounded fully by the Ikhwān after having been hidden (in the cave) throughout the previous periods of the history of humanity. After their temporal appearance, if the Ikhwān claim to draw their doctrines from ancient sources it is not to collect a "museum" but to build a unified citadel and to guide their disciples to the single Truth which they believe underlies the many sources from which they draw their material and inspiration. The ultimate "grace," or *barakah*, for them, however, comes from Islam which is the final Revelation of the Truth in the present cycle of humanity.

The Ikhwān and Philosophy

While certain scholars have thought the purpose of the Ikhwān to have been the reversal of the contemporary political situation by the restoration of a philosophical system capable of serving as a basis for life,[38] the majority of those who have studied their doctrines believe that their aim was to combine religion and philosophy.[39] The Ikhwān themselves, in fact, often speak of the virtues of philosophy as a way of finding the Truth and their desire to combine it with the Divine law, or *nāmūs*, of the prophets.[40] Their aim, however, is not that of an Ibn Rushd or even a Thomas Aquinas, because here again the Ikhwān give a connotation to the word "philosophy" which differs greatly from the rationalistic, syllogistic meaning given to it by the Aristotelians. Instead, they identify philosophy with *ḥikmah*,[41] in opposition to the great number of early Muslim writers who use philosophy as being almost synonymous with purely human wisdom and *ḥikmah* as a wisdom which has its ultimate source in the Revelations given to the ancient prophets. Philosophy for the Ikhwān is "the similitude as much as possible of man with God." It is "the means which again draws the elite of men or the angels on earth near to the Creator Most High."[42] Its use is the "acquisition of the specific

[38] Ṭaha Ḥusain, Introduction to the *Rasā'il*, p. viii.

[39] Jalāl Homā'ī considers their purpose to be twofold: (1) to cleanse the *Sharī'ah* of all impurities by combining it with philosophy; and (2) to give the essential truths of philosophy by going to its very sources. *Ghazzālī-nāmah*, p. 82.

[40] This word, which comes from the Greek word *nomos*, meaning law or harmony governing some domain, and also possibly from the Arabic root *nms* meaning concealed, is used by the Ikhwān to specify the universal laws revealed through the prophets. See the article on *nāmūs* in *The Encyclopaedia of Islam* (first edition).

[41] *R.*, III, 324. [42] *R.*, I, 221.

virtue of the human race, that of bringing to actualization all the sciences which man possesses potentially . . . By philosophy man realizes the virtual characteristics of his race. He attains the form of humanity and progresses in the hierarchy of beings until in crossing the straight way (bridge) and the correct path he becomes an angel . . . "[43] One may easily see that there is a more intimate connection between this conception of philosophy and the Pythagorean-Socratic aim of the purification of the soul of man than there is with Peripatetic logic.[44]

The Ikhwān are quite aware also of the characteristics of the type of philosophy which is not *ḥikmah*, and regard it in a manner similar to the religious authorities in Islam. In the discussion between man and the animals at the end of the section on zoology, the parrot in addressing man is made to say:

> And as for your boast that you have philosophers and logicians among you, why, they are not the source of benefit to you, but lead you into error and unbelief . . . because they turn men aside from the path ordained by God, and, by their disagreements, make the ordinances of religion of no effect. The opinions and beliefs of all are at variance one with another. Some pronounce the Universe to be the most ancient; some believe matter to be so; some endeavour to establish the antiquity of forms . . .[45]

The particularly noticeable feature of the treatment of philosophy, in its relation to Islam by the Ikhwān is their identification of *īmān*, the interior aspect of *islām*, with the "divine service of the philosophers."[46] This differentiation is similar to the distinction made by the Ṣūfīs between *islām*, *īmān*, and *iḥsān* as three degrees of the Tradition, the latter two being not only simple faith but also wisdom and gnosis (*ma'rifah*).[47] There is this difference, however: whereas the Ṣūfī practices connected with *īmān* and *iḥsān* derive completely from the Revelation of the Prophet Muḥammad—upon whom be peace—the liturgy described by the Ikhwān seems to be more closely related to the religion of the heirs of the prophet Idrīs, that is, the Ḥarrānians who were the principal inheritors in the Middle East of what

[43] *Risālat al-jāmi'ah*, ed. Dj. Saliba (Damascus, 1949), I, 101. (Henceforth this work will be referred to in the notes as *Jāmi'ah*.)

[44] This conception of philosophy is echoed several centuries later in the writings of the Persian sages following Suhrawardī, among them Mīr Dāmād and Mullā Ṣadrā, who call philosophy a doctrine whose totality comprises not only Aristotelian philosophy, but Illuminationist theosophy and gnosis as well.

[45] Ikhwān al-Ṣafā', *Dispute between Man and the Animals*, trans. J. Platts (London: Allen, 1869), p. 202.

[46] *R.*, IV, 301–302. Corbin, "Rituel sabéen . . .," *Eranos Jahrbuch*, 19:208 (1950).

[47] For an explanation of the Ṣūfī distinction between *islām*, *īmān*, and *iḥsān*, see F. Schuon, *L'Œil du cœur*, pp. 91ff.

has been called "Oriental Pythagoreanism" and who were the guardians and propagators of Hermeticism in the Islamic world. The philosophic liturgy of the Ikhwān took place three evenings each month, at the beginning, middle, and some time between the 25th and the end of the month. The liturgy of the first night consisted of personal oratory; that of the second of a *cosmic text* read under the starry heavens facing the polar star; and that of the third night of a philosophical hymn (implying a metaphysical or metacosmic theme) which was a "prayer of Plato," "supplication of Idrīs," or "the secret psalm of Aristotle." There were also three great philosophical feasts during the year, at the time of entry of the sun into the signs of the Ram, Cancer, and Balance. The Ikhwān correlated these feasts with the Islamic feasts of *'īd al-fiṭr* at the end of Ramaḍān, *'īd al-aḍḥā*, the 10th of *Dhu'l-ḥijjah*, and the *'īd al-ghadīr* on the 18th of the same month, the date of the investiture of 'Alī ibn Abī Ṭālib by the Prophet as his successor at Ghadīr Khumm, a major Shī'ite day of celebration which they made correspond to the fall feast. For the winter season, however, there was a long day of fasting instead, for the time when "the seven sleepers are sleeping in the cave."[48]

The connection between philosophy and liturgy and *ḥikmah* leads us to place the Ikhwān more in the line of the heirs of Hermeticism and what has been called "Neo-Pythagoreanism," which through the Ḥarrānians and Nuṣairis entered into Shī'ah Islam early in its history. However partial or ill-defined such a relationship may seem historically, it is, from the nature of the doctrines, more plausible than the theory that the Ikhwān adopted simply "theoretical" and "academic" philosophy and added it to the *Sharī'ah* without the ability to remain faithful to one or the other.

Identity and Significance of the Ikhwān

After this long search into the identity and significance of the Ikhwān we find ourselves confronted with many contradictory opinions among students of the subject. It can safely be asserted, however, that given the cosmological and symbolic rather than rationalistic tendency of the Ikhwān we must exclude them from the school of the Mu'tazilites as well as from the followers of Aristotle, namely the *Mashshā'īyūn* (or *Mashshā'ūn*). For the same reasons, and for additional ones to be discussed later in conjunction with the sources of the *Rasā'il*, the Ikhwān may be connected with Pythagorean-Hermetic doctrines, much of which was best known in Islam under the name of

[48] Corbin, "*Rituel sabéen . . .*," pp. 210–211.

the corpus of Jābir ibn Ḥayyān. Moreover, considering the extensive use made of the *Rasā'il* by the Ismā'īlīs during later centuries and the presence of certain basic ideas such as *ta'wīl* in both groups, we may loosely connect the Ikhwān with Ismā'īlism, especially with what has been called "Ismā'īlī gnosis." But it is perhaps more significant, especially with respect to their cosmological doctrines, to describe them as a Shī'ah group with Ṣūfī tendencies whose exposition of the cosmological sciences was to influence the whole Muslim community during the later centuries. The conception of Nature held by the Ikhwān was to have almost as great an influence among the Twelve-Imām Shī'ites as upon the Ismā'īlīs. The similarity also between much of the *Rasā'il* and *taṣawwuf* must be especially emphasized with reference to cosmology, from which al-Ghazzālī and Ibn 'Arabī were to draw many formulations.

As an attempt at a synthesis[49] on the part of the Shī'ah during the fourth century[50] the *Rasā'il* soon gained wide popularity and great importance.

> In effect, it is, by its own showing, a hand-encyclopaedia of Arabian philosophy in the tenth century . . . Its value lies in its completeness, in its systematizing of the results of Arabian study.[51]

The *Rasā'il* were widely read by most learned men of later periods, including Ibn Sīnā and al-Ghazzālī,[52] have continued to be read up to our own times, and have been translated into Persian, Turkish, and Hindustani. From the number of manuscripts present in various libraries in the Muslim world, it must be considered among the most popular of Islamic works on learning.[53] But the work is not just

[49] Ṭībāwī, "The Idea of guidance . . .," *Islamic Quarterly*, 3:148 (1956).

[50] Although it is hard to state the exact date of the composition of the *Rasā'il*, it is fairly safe to place them within the fourth century and even more precisely the latter half of that fruitful century. P. Casanova, in "Une date astronomique dans les Epîtres des Ikhwān aṣ-Ṣafā," in *Journal Asiatique*, 5:5–17 (1915), interpreted an astronomical passage from the fourth epistle to determine the date of the writing of the *Rasā'il* as lying between 418 and 427. Abū Ḥayyān, however, claims to have read them in 373/983.

[51] Lane-Poole, *Studies in a Mosque*, p. 191.

[52] Muḥammad Taqī Dānishpazhūh, "Ikhwān-i ṣafā," *Mihr*, 8:610 (1331 [1952]). For a detailed discussion of the influence of the Ikhwān see also Ṭībāwī, *Jamā'ah Ikhwān aṣ-Ṣafā'*, chap. VI.

[53] The organization of the Ikhwān had already expanded considerably in the fourth century, as shown, for example, by the fact that Abu'l-'Alā' al-Ma'arrī met a branch of them in Baghdad between 393 and 400. Their *Rasā'il* were read and made use of by al-Ghazzālī and Ibn al-Haitham, and its orthodoxy debated by Ibn Taimīyah. The Druzes and Assassins certainly read the *Rasā'il* extensively, and, as we have already seen, the Yemeni Ismā'īlīs held it in great veneration. Introduced into Spain by al-Majrīṭī and al-Kirmānī, they were also to influence two of the most celebrated authors from the Maghrib, Muḥyī al-Dīn ibn 'Arabī and Ibn Khaldūn. See Lane-Poole, *Studies in a Mosque*, p. 192, and 'Awā, *L'Esprit critique* . . ., pp. 314ff.

"popular" in the sense of being for everybody, as has often been said. The *Rasā'il* contain many profound metaphysical and cosmological ideas, mostly stated in a symbolic and, in a way, simple language which, from the point of view of a mind accustomed to long-drawn-out discussions, seems "popular" and "naïve." Besides, in the *Risālat al-jāmi'ah* and the very rare *Jāmi'at al-jāmi'ah*,[54] the Ikhwān present their doctrines in a more compact, hidden, and esoteric manner, although usually not departing from the general subject matter of the *Rasā'il.*

Taken as a whole, the writings of the Ikhwān present us with the conception of the Universe under which a large segment of the Shī'ah as well as the Sunni world has lived for a thousand years. Although they do not contain explicitly the esoteric science of a Muḥyī al-Dīn ibn 'Arabī or Muḥyī al-Dīn al-Būnī, they do explain in simple language, and often with great beauty, the main outlines of the conception of Nature which is to be found in many later Muslim works throughout the centuries.

The Sources of the Rasā'il

The lack of historical evidence for the lives and doctrines of what Proclus calls the "Golden Chain of the Pythagorean philosophers"[55] and what in the Islamic world is called the Jābirian corpus, makes the tracing of the sources of the *Rasā'il* a very difficult task. There can be little doubt, however, that the *Rasā'il*, in their cosmological aspects, draw most of all upon Pythagorean and Jābirian sources. The Ikhwān claim again and again that they are the followers of the tradition of Pythagoras and Nicomachus,[56] especially in their treatment of numbers as the key to the understanding of Nature and the symbolic and metaphysical interpretation of arithmetic and geometry. Moreover, they identify Pythagoras with the Ḥarrānians with

[54] See V. A. Ivanov, *A Guide to Ismaili literature*, p. 31. The *Risālat al-jāmi'ah* has also been attributed to al-Majrīṭī although this attribution is completely rejected by Tāmir and other Ismā'īlī authorities. As for the *Jāmi'at al-jāmi'ah*, whose text has recently been edited and made known for the first time by Tāmir, it is concerned to a great extent with the question of death, the afterlife, and resurrection while following the general metaphysical and cosmological pattern of the *Rasā'il.*

[55] For a general description of the Pythagorean doctrines of number and harmony, see K. S. Guthrie, *Pythagoras Sourcebook and Library. The Four Biographies and all the Surviving Fragments of the Pythagorean School* (Yonkers, New York, 1920).

[56] *R.*, I, 24. «والارثماطيقى هو معرفة خواص العدد وما يطابقها من معانى الموجودات التى ذكرها

فيثاغورس ونيقوماخس.»

whom, as has already been pointed out, the Ikhwān have many affinities.[57]

As for the relation of the Ikhwān to Jābir, it has been said that the *Rasā’il* are an "encyclopédie scientifique dont le caractère pythagorisant et la tendance ismaélito-bāṭinite présentent plus d'une analogie avec les écrits jābiriens."[58] Jābir himself claimed not only to have possessed the knowledge of the Greek sages, especially Pythagoras and Apollonius of Tyana (Bālīnās),[59] but also to have known the wisdom of the ancient Yemenites, which Jābir is said to have learned from Ḥarbī the Ḥimyarite,[60] and to have been acquainted with the sciences of the Hindus. Whatever the significance of these references may be, there can be no doubt that the Jābirian corpus contains many elements from Pythagorean and Hermetic sources, as well as certain ideas from Persia, India, and even China.

The intimate relation existing between the *Rasā’il* and the Jābirian corpus[61] naturally makes the sources of Jābir those of the Ikhwān as well.[62] In fact the *Rasā’il* in their content affirm the same general

[57] *R.*, III, 201. «وانّ فيثاغورس كان رجلاً حكيماً موحّداً من اهل حرّان.»

[58] P. Kraus, *Jābir ibn Ḥayyān*, Introduction to vol. I, p. lxiv.

[59] See the translation by de Sacy of "Le Livre du secret de la créature par le sage Bélinous," *Notices et extraits des manuscrits*, 4:107–168 (1798). This book, called in Arabic *Kitāb sirr al-khalīqah lī Bālīnūs*, contains many of the fundamental cosmological doctrines of Jābir. The doctrines of Apollonius are presented in a more complete manner in *The Book of Treasures* of Job of Edessa (Cambridge, England, 1936). An important difference between the Ikhwān on the one hand and Jābir and Job of Edessa on the other is that for the Ikhwān, fire, air, and so forth, are simple elements, whereas for the latter two, heat, cold, wetness and dryness are simple substances from which the elements have come into being.

[60] Kraus, *Jābir ibn Ḥayyān*, Introduction to vol. I, p. xxxvii. It is significant to see the reference to Yemen which is to be found again in later centuries in the writings of the *Ishrāqī* school.

[61] This close relation is partially indicated by the numbers used by Jābir and the Ikhwān. Jābir makes the number 17 in the sequence of 1:3:5:8 the key to the understanding of all of Nature. This number, which was also central to the Pythagoreans because of its equivalence to the number of consonants of the Greek alphabet and also related to the harmonic ratio 9:8, is found in Nuṣairī and Ḥarrānian as well as the common Islamic sources, where 17 is the number of daily units (*rak‘ah*) of prayer. Among the Shī‘ah, $51 = 3 \times 17$ is particularly important since it is considered as the number of the *rak‘ah* of prayer performed daily by ‘Alī ibn Abī Ṭālib. Now, aside from the last treatise on talismans and magic which was added later, the *Rasā’il* consists of 51 treatises, which of course again is a product of 3 and 17. Particularly, the section dealing with the sciences of Nature or physical treatises consists of 17 *Rasā’il*, 17 being the key to the interpretation of the physical world according to Jābir. See Kraus, *Jābir ibn Ḥayyān*, II, 199ff.

[62] The Ikhwān were quite conscious of the long tradition of science and wisdom which had existed before them. In the dialogue between the animals and man, the enterpriser (the interlocutor) addresses a Greek who had been boasting of the scientific achievement of his people, saying: "You boast most unreasonably of these sciences; for you did not

sources. One sees in these treatises the Pythagorean-Hermetic influence closely tied to the doctrines and practices of the Ḥarrānians, and, in certain subjects, the influence of Peripatetic philosophy as well, but usually not considered solely from a syllogistic point of view. There is, moreover, much Persian and Indian influence in the sections dealing with geography, ecology, music, and linguistics—following the tradition of Ibn Muqaffa' and al-Jāḥiẓ. Finally, there is the influence of the Quran which pervades the whole perspective of the Ikhwān. They interpret certain parts of ancient cosmology in terms of the Quranic terminology of the pedestal (*kursī*) and throne (*'arsh*),[63] and make constant reference to Islamic angelology based on the Quran.

The sources of the Ikhwān should not, however, be considered solely as historical texts. In a long passage they themselves inform the reader of the universality of their sources, which include Revelation and Nature in addition to written texts. They write:

> We have drawn our knowledge from four books. The first is composed of the mathematical and natural sciences established by the sages and philosophers. The second consists of the revealed books of the Torah, the Gospels and the Quran and the other Tablets brought by the prophets through angelic Revelation. The third is the books of Nature which are the ideas (*ṣuwar*) in the Platonic sense of the forms (*ashkāl*) of creatures actually existing, from the composition of the celestial spheres, the division of the Zodiac, the movement of the stars, and so on . . . to the transformation of the elements, the production of the members of the mineral, plant and animal kingdoms and the rich variety of human industry . . . The fourth consists of the Divine books which touch only the purified men and which are the angels who are in intimacy with the chosen beings, the noble and the purified souls . . .[64]

There are, then, four "books" from which their knowledge derives: the mathematical and scientific works written before them; the

---

discover them by your own penetration, but obtained them from the scientific men among the Jews of Ptolemy's times [reference must be to the Hermetic and sacred sciences traditionally associated with the Hebrew prophets]; and some sciences you took from the Egyptians in the days of Psammetichus, and then introduced them into your own land, and now you claim to have discovered them." The king asked the Greek philosopher: "Can it be as this (jinn) says?" He replied, saying, "It is true: we obtained most of the sciences from the preceding philosophers, as others now receive them from us. Such is the way of the world—for one people to derive benefit from another. Thus it is that Persian sages obtained their astrology and the sciences of observation (of the heavenly bodies) from the sages of India. Similarly, the Israelites got their knowledge of magic and talisman from Solomon, the son of David." Ikhwān, *Dispute between Man and the Animals*, pp. 133–134.

[63] 'Awā, *L'Esprit critique* . . ., pp. 306ff. From another point of view the terms *kursī* and *'arsh* can also be translated as throne and firmament respectively.

[64] *R.*, IV, 106.

Scriptures; the archetypes, or Platonic "ideas," of the forms of Nature; and the angelic, or what in contemporary terms may be called intellectual intuition. This intertwining of domains, now considered as quite separate and distinct, is itself the key to the understanding of the *Rasā'il*, as it is one more consequence of the existence of the one Truth which according to the Ikhwān underlies all things. And if Scripture or angelic vision can be here a source of the knowledge of the cosmos, it is because as yet the distinction between Nature and Supernature has not been made absolute. One may say that for the Ikhwān the supernatural has a "natural" aspect, just as the natural has a "supernatural" aspect. Moreover, the use of Revelation and intellectual intuition, in addition to the observation of Nature and the reading of more ancient books about Nature, stems from the ultimate purpose of the Ikhwān, which is to "see" and realize the unicity of Nature.[65] To demonstrate this unicity they have to appeal constantly to those powers and faculties in man which themselves possess the power of synthesis and unification so that they can integrate the peripheral and multiple activity of the observational faculties into the central and unifying vision of the Intellect.[66]

The Organization of the Rasā'il

Despite the repetitious character of certain of the ideas of the *Rasā'il*, the order of presentation of the subject matter follows the Ikhwān's philosophy and reflects the importance which they attach to the study of Nature in comparison with theology on the one hand and mathematics and logic on the other. In their classification of the sciences they divide them into three categories:

I. The primary [propaedeutic] sciences (*riyāḍīyah*)
II. Religious sciences (*al-sharī'at al-waḍ'īyah*)
III. Philosophical sciences (*al-falsafīyat al-ḥaqīqīyah*)

[65] The spirit of the Ikhwān in studying natural sciences in a religious manner and treating Nature as a domain inseparable from Revelation was followed universally during the Middle Ages and Antiquity. "On oublie trop que dans l'antiquité et au moyen âge l'expérience religieuse est constamment liée à l'expérience scientifique et, faute de se souvenir de ce fait, on se heurte, dans l'examen des textes, à d'incessantes contradictions. Qu'il s'agisse de la physique grecque, de la kabale hébraïque, de l'astrologie chaldéenne, de la science extrême-orientale des mutations ou de l'alchimie occidentale, toutes ces techniques, tous ces systèmes reposent sur un fait universel et commun: l'initiation à des mystères." R. Alleau, *Aspects de l'alchimie traditionnelle* (Paris, 1955), p. 29.

[66] Throughout this treatise the word Intellect will be used not as the equivalent of reason, as is done currently, but as the universal and supra-individual faculty which as Aristotle said "is the object of its own knowledge."

These in turn are divided in the following manner:

I. Primary sciences:
  1. Reading and writing
  2. Lexicography and grammar
  3. Accounting and business transactions
  4. Prosody and metrics
  5. Doctrines of good and evil omens
  6. Doctrines of magic, amulets, alchemy, stratagems, and so on
  7. Business and handicraft
  8. Commerce, agriculture, and so on
  9. Stories and biographies

II. Religious sciences:
  1. Science of Revelation
  2. Exegesis
  3. Tradition (*ḥadīth*)
  4. Jurisprudence and law
  5. Asceticism and *taṣawwuf*
  6. Interpretation of dreams

III. Philosophical sciences:
  1. Mathematics (*riyāḍīyāt*) consisting of the *Quadrivium*
  2. Logic
  3. Natural sciences, which in turn are divided into seven parts:
    (a) Principles governing bodies, consisting of knowledge of *hylé*, form, time, space, and motion (*'ilm al-mabādī al-jismānīyah*)
    (b) The heavens, consisting of the sciences of the stars, the motion of the planets, reasons for the stationary character of the earth, and so on (*'ilm al-samā'*)
    (c) Generation and corruption, consisting of knowledge of the four elements, their change into each other, and the minerals, plants, and animals coming into being from them (*'ilm al-kawn wa'l-fasād*)
    (d) Meteorology, consisting of the knowledge of the change of weather due to the effect of the stars, winds, thunder, lightning, and so on (*'ilm al-ḥawādith al-jawwīyah*)
    (e) Mineralogy (*'ilm al-ma'ādin*)
    (f) Botany (*'ilm al-nabāt*)
    (g) Zoology (*'ilm al-ḥayawān*)

4. Theology (*al-'ulūm al-ilāhīyah*)
   (a) Knowledge of God and His Attributes
   (b) Knowledge of the spiritual world (*'ilm al-rūḥānīyāt*)
   (c) Knowledge of souls (*'ilm al-nafsānīyāt*)
   (d) Politics (*'ilm al-siyāsah*), consisting of the knowledge of prophethood, kingship, the common people, the elite, and man considered in himself[67]

Using this division of the sciences as their base, the Ikhwān have organized their *Rasā'il* so as to include all fields of knowledge from the mathematical and logical sciences to the natural and corporeal, and from there to the psychological, and finally the theological. With this purpose in mind, the fifty-two *Rasā'il*, not including the *Risālat al-jāmi'ah* which comes at the end as a summary, are divided into four books in the following manner:

I. Mathematical and educational treatises:
   1. Properties of numbers
   2. Geometry
   3. Astronomy
   4. Geography
   5. Music
   6. Educational values of these subjects
   7–8. Various scientific disciplines
   9. Actions and sayings of the prophets and sages
   10–14. Logic (including the Isagoge, the Ten Categories, Perihermenias, Prior and Posterior Analytics)

II. Sciences of natural bodies:
   1. Explanation of the notions of matter, form, movement, time, space, and so forth
   2. The sky and the Universe
   3. Generation and corruption
   4. Meteorology
   5. Formation of minerals
   6. Essence of Nature
   7. Species of plants
   8. Explanation of the generation of animals and their species
   9. Composition of the human body
   10. Perception of the senses and their object
   11. Embryology

[67] *R.*, I, 202–208. The comprehensive nature of this classification is due to the connection of the Ikhwān with the craft guilds in addition to "academic" education.

12. Man as a microcosm
13. Development of particular souls in the human body
14. Limits of human knowledge and science
15. Maxims of life and death
16. Characters pertaining to pleasure
17. Cause of the diversity of languages, their system of transcription and calligraphy

III. Psychological and rational sciences:
1. Intellectual principles according to Pythagoras
2. Intellectual principles according to the Ikhwān
3. That the Universe is a macrocosm
4. Intelligence and the intelligible
5. Periods and epochs
6. Essence of passion
7. Resurrection
8. Species of movement
9. Cause and effect
10. Definitions and descriptions

IV. Theological sciences—on the *nāmūs* and the *sharī'ah*
1. Doctrines and religions
2. The character of the path leading to God
3. Explanation of the doctrine of the Ikhwān
4. Ways of life of the Ikhwān
5. Essence of faith and the virtues of the believing initiates
6. Essence of the Divine *nāmūs*, conditions and virtues of the prophets
7. The manner of appealing to God
8. State of spiritual beings
9. Politics
10. Hierarchy inherent in the Universe
11. Magic and talisman

Following the Ikhwān as closely as possible in their study of the cosmos, and considering for the most part the second book, we shall begin our research into the cosmological views of the Ikhwān with the principles governing Nature, then the hierarchy in the Universe, to be followed by a study of various parts of the Universe beginning with the heavens and then descending to the sublunary world. Then making a study of meteorology, geography, mineralogy, botany and zoology, we shall terminate our exposition with the study of man as the terminal link in the chain of terrestrial beings as well as the microcosm in whom multiplicity returns once again to Unity.

CHAPTER 2

The Principles of the Study of the Cosmos and the Hierarchy of the Universe

The universe described in the *Rasā'il* is a unified whole whose various parts are held together by the analogy which exists between them. As the Ikhwān write, "The whole world is one as a city is one, or as an animal is one, or as man is one."[1] Its parts are held together like the organs of a living body which derives its being and sustenance from the Divine Word.[2] The language with which this interrelation is expounded is that of symbolism, particularly numerical symbolism. Everywhere within the Universe the key to the understanding of things is numbers, which, like the morning sun, disperse the fog of the unintelligibility of things considered only in their terrestrial opaqueness.

The Ikhwān emphasize the symbolic character of this world in many passages, as, for example, when they write:

> He made these His works manifest, to the end that the intelligent might contemplate them; and He brought into view all that was in His invisible world, that the observant might behold it and acknowledge His Skill and Peerlessness, and Omnipotence, and Soleness, and not stand in need of proof and demonstration. Further, these forms, which are perceived in the material world, are the similitudes of those which exist in the world of spirits save that the latter are composed of light and are subtle; whereas the former are dark and dense. And, as a picture corresponds in every limb

[1] «وانها كلها عالم واحد، كمدينة واحدة، او كحيوان واحد، او كانسان واحد.»
Jāmi'ah, I, 386.

[2] «ان العالم كله بافلاكه العالية وسماواته السامية وما فيه من الانوار الروحانية والانفس المتحركة والقوى السارية في اركان الجسمانية، والاجسام الطبيعية وجميع الموجودات و سائر المخلوقات، مما حوته السماوات والارض، من اعلى عليين الى اسفل سافلين كله جسم واحد، منتهى بقبول الفيض الكلي من باريه سبحانه وان كلمة الله تعالى متصلة به تمده بالافاضة والجود، ليتم ويبقى في الوجود.»
Jāmi'ah, I, 635–636.

with the animal it represents, so these forms, too, correspond with those which are found in the spiritual world. But these are the movers, and those the moved . . . The forms which exist in the other world endure; whereas these perish and pass away.[3]

In this world of symbols the Ikhwān study Nature with the purpose of discerning the wisdom of the Maker. "Know," they write, "that the perfect manufacturing of an object indicates the existence of a wise and perfect artisan even when he is veiled and inaccessible to sense perception. He who meditates upon botanical objects will of necessity know that the beings of this reign issue from a perfect artisan . . ."[4]

Of the many types of symbolism which the Ikhwān use, numbers are the most important because through numbers they are able to relate multiplicity to Unity and bring to light the harmony which pervades the Universe.[5] Regarding their treatise on music, the Ikhwān write:

One of the aims of our treatise on music consists of demonstrating clearly that the whole world is composed in conformity with arithmetical, geometrical and musical relations. There, we have explained in detail the reality of universal harmony. We understand, therefore, that thus considered, the body of the world resembles an animal or the unique system of a single man or the totality of a city which shows also the Unity of its Maker (*mukhtari'*), the Creator of forms (*muṣawwir*), or of its Composer *mu'allif*), that is God.[6]

[3] Ikhwān al-Ṣafā', *Dispute between Man and the Animals*, trans. J. Platts, pp. 122–123.

«ثمّ اعلم ايها الملك العادل انّ هذه الصّور والاشكال والهياكل والصفات التّي
تراها في عالم الاجسام وجواهر الاجرام هي مثالات واشباه اصباغ تلك الصوّر التّي في
عالم الارواح غير ان تلك نورانيّة شفافة وهذه ظلمانيّة كاسفة ومناسبة هذه الى تلك
كنسبة التّصاوير والنقوش التّي على وجوه الارواح وسطوح الحيطان الى هذه الصّور و-
الاشكال التّي عليها هذه الحيوانات من اللحم والدّم والعظام والجلود لان تلك الصور التّي في عالم
الارواح محرّكات وهذه متحرّكات والتّي دون هذه ساكنات صامتات ومحسوسات فانيات
فاسدات وتلك ناطقات معقولات روحانيّات غير مرئيّات باقيات.»

R., II, 232.

[4] *R.*, II, 130.

[5] For an exposition of the basic relation between mathematics and music among the Pythagoreans, see H. Kayser, *Akroasis, die Lehre von der Harmonik der Welt* (Stuttgart, 1947); English trans. R. Lilienfeld as *Akróasis, The Theory of World Harmonics* (Boston, 1970).

The Ikhwān once again demonstrate their strong Pythagorean tendencies when they in their treatise on music state that "the science of proportions—itself known under the name of music—is indispensable to all kinds of professions."

[6] *R.*, I, 160.

The science of number (*'ilm al-'adad*) is considered by the Ikhwān as the way leading to the grasp of Unity,[7] as a science which stands above Nature and is the principle of beings[8] and the root of the other sciences, the first elixir and the most exalted alchemy.[9] It is, moreover, the first effusion (*faiḍ*) of the Intellect imprinted upon the Soul[10] and the "tongue which speaks of Unity and transcendence."[11] No wonder, then, that the *Rasā'il* always compare the relation of God to the world—or, metaphysically speaking, of Being to existence—as that of One to the other numbers.[12] In the more esoteric *Risālat al-jāmi'ah*, it is implied in one place that Being (*al-wujūd*) corresponds to one, and the Infinite, or the Divine Essence, to zero. Zero, therefore, symbolizes the Divine Ipseity, which is above all determinations including Being.[13] As 'Awā writes:

[7] *Jāmi'ah*, I, 173. „فانه الطريق الى التوحيد."

[8] *R.*, III, 201. „ان الموجودات بحسب طبيعة العدد."

[9] „ان صور العدد فى النفوس مطابقة لصور الموجودات فى الهيولى وهى انموذج من
العالم الاعلى وبمعرفته يتدرج المرتاض الى سائر الرياضيات والطبيعيات وما فوق
الطبيعيات وان علم العدد هو "جذر العلوم" وعنصر الحكمة ومبداء المعارف
واسطقس المعانى، الاكسير الاول والكيمياء الاكبر..."

Jāmi'ah, I, 9. Later they identify the first elixir with God. *Ibid.*, p. 16.

[10] „فكان علم العدد تأييدا من العقل للنفس، وكان اول جود فاض من العقل على النفس."
Jāmi'ah, I, 28.

[11] *Jāmi'ah*, I, 30. „وان علم العدد هو لسان ينطق بالتوحيد والتنزيه."

[12] *R.*, I, 28. This statement is made over and over throughout the *Rasā'il*. Referring to the creatures, the Ikhwān state that they proceed from God and return to Him, just like the generating and reduction of numbers with respect to unity. "Know, brother, that the Creator, Most Exalted, created as the first thing from his light of Unity the simple substance (*al-jawhar al-basīṭ*) called the Active Intellect (*'aql*)—as 2 is generated from one by repetition. Then the Universal Soul was generated from the light of the Intellect as 3 is generated by adding unity to 2. Then the *hylé* was generated by the motion of the Soul as 4 is generated by adding unity to 3. Then the other creatures were generated from the *hylé* and their being brought to order by the Intellect and the Soul as other numbers are generated from 4 added to what went before it . . ." *R.*, I, 28–29. The complete text of the treatise on arithmetic has been translated by B. R. Goldstein as "A Treatise on Number Theory from a Tenth Century Arabic Source," *Centaurus*, 10:129–160 (1964).

[13] *Jāmi'ah*, II, 295. Iamblichus likewise wrote that the series of numbers should be carried below one to zero (*to ouden*), which is their source. P. Tannery, *Mémoires scientifiques* (Toulouse, 1912) II, 196.

En un mot, "la théorie du nombre" est, aux yeux des Frères de la Pureté, la sagesse divine et est au-dessus des choses. Les choses ne sont formées qu'après le modèle des nombres.[14]

As we have already noted, the Ikhwān believed themselves to be the disciples of Pythagoras and of such followers as Nicomachus, especially in considering numbers as the cause of all things and the key to the understanding of the harmony pervading the Universe.[15] The basic question to be asked, therefore, is the exact meaning of the Pythagorean numbers which the Ikhwān employ constantly. A full study of this subject would require—to say the least—a treatise of its own and lies outside of our range of discussion. Considering the affinity of the Ikhwān with the Pythagoreans, however, particularly in mathematics, it is essential to define briefly the meaning of number and geometry according to this ancient Greek school, which was to have disciples until the very end of the Graeco-Roman period, and which was so influential in the formation of Muslim intellectual sciences.

The Pythagorean Notion of Arithmetic and Geometry

As Schuon has stated so accurately concerning the traditional notion of numbers:

This is numbers in the Pythagorean sense, of which the universal rather than the quantitative import is already to be divined in geometrical figure; the triangle and the square are "personalities" and not quantities, they are essentials and not accidentals. Whilst one obtains ordinary numbers by addition, qualitative number results, on the contrary, from an internal or intrinsic differentiation of principial unity; it is not added to anything and does not depart from unity. Geometrical figures are so many images

[14] *L'Esprit critique des Frères de la Pureté* . . ., p. 62.

[15] « وهى مطابقة لقول الحكماء والفيثاغوريين فى الاخبار عن كون الموجودات عن البارى،
سبحانه كَكون الاعداد عن الواحد. واسباب الكائنات الكليات والجزئيات عن
البارى عزّ وجلّ وترتيبها فى الوجود كترتيب العدد الصحيح عن الواحد الذى قبل
الاثنين وهذا القول اصوب الاقوال واصح المقالات وابين الدلالات. ولذلك
وافق مذهب اهل هذا الرأى، مذهب اخواننا الكرام ... »

Jāmi'ah, II, 23.

"Pythagoras was the first who spoke of the nature of numbers. He taught that the nature of numbers is in relation with that of Nature. Whoever knows the nature of numbers, their species and genus and their properties, can know the quantity of species

of unity; they exclude one another or rather, they denote different principial quantities; the triangle is harmony, the square stability; these are "concentric," not "serial," numbers.[16]

The Pythagorean numbers, being a qualitative rather than just a quantitative entity, cannot be identified simply with division and multiplicity as can modern numbers. They are not identical with quantity, that is, their nature is not exhausted by their quantitative aspect alone. On the contrary, because they are a "projection of unity" which is never totally separated from its source, the Pythagorean numbers, when identified with a certain existing entity in the world of multiplicity, integrate that entity into Unity, or Pure Being, which is the source of all existence. To identify a being with a certain number is to relate it to its Source by means of the inner bond which relates all numbers to Unity.

The misunderstanding of this conception of numbers has made many ancient works, including the *Rasā'il*, appear ridiculous in the eyes of many modern readers.[17] Yet ancient sources as well as the Ikhwān have repeated many times exactly what they mean by numbers and how they make use of them. Just to cite an example, the famous first-century (A.D.) Pythagorean, Nicomachus, whose *Introduction to Arithmetic* and *Theologoumena Arithmetica* are among the most important and influential expositions of this school's theory of numbers, asks regarding the primacy of arithmetic over the rest of the *Quadrivium*:

Which then of these four methods must we first learn? Evidently, the one which naturally exists before them all, is superior and takes the place of origin or root, and, as it were, of mother to the others. And this is arithmetic, not solely because we said that it existed before all others in the mind of the creating God like some universal and exemplary plan, relying upon which as a design and archetype example the Creator of the Universe sets in order his material creations and makes them attain to their proper ends; but also because it is naturally prior in birth, inasmuch

---

of beings and their genus." Dieterici, *Die Philosophie der Araber*, vol. II: *Lehre von der Weltseele*, p. 441.

[16] F. Schuon, *Gnosis, Divine Wisdom*, trans. G. E. H. Palmer, p. 113, n. 1.

[17] "It would be ridiculous if one wished before having acquired any notion concerning the value and use of the algebraic signs, to explain a problem contained in these signs. This is, however, what has often been done relative to the language of Numbers. One has pretended, not only to explain it before having learned it, but even to write of it, and has by so doing rendered it the most lamentable thing in the world. The savants seeing it thus travestied have justly made it reflect, by the same language upon the ancients who have employed it." Fabre d'Olivet, *The Golden Verses of Pythagoras*, p. 228.

as it abolishes other sciences with itself, but is not abolished together with them.[18]

As for the meaning of numbers and their relation to Nature, he says:

> All that has by nature and with systematic method been arranged in the Universe seems both in part and as a whole to have been determined and ordered in accordance with number, by the forethought and mind of Him that created all things; for the pattern was fixed, like a preliminary sketch, by the domination of number pre-existing in the mind of the world-creating God, number conceptual only and immaterial in every way, so that with reference to it, as to an artistic plan, should be created all these things, times, motions, the heavens, the stars, all sorts of revolutions.[19]

Similar definitions may be found in the writings of many other members of this school. In the Islamic world, Jābir, who employs numbers exclusively as the basis of the balance, also uses the qualitative number of the Pythagoreans, since the Jābirian balance is essentially an instrument for measuring the tendency of the World Soul toward each substance.[20] As for the Ikhwān, number for them is "*the spiritual image resulting in the human soul from the repetition of Unity.*"[21] It is, therefore, the "projection of unity," a projection which is never divorced from its source. And since numbers are the projection of the number one, the *Rasā'il* do not consider one itself to be the beginning of numbers. They believe two to be the first number and unity itself the origin and principle of all numbers.

In geometry, also, they follow the Pythagoreans by describing the "virtues" and "personalities" of various geometrical figures.[22] The final aim of geometry is to permit the faculties of the soul to reflect and meditate independently of the external world so that finally "it wishes to separate itself from this world in order to join, thanks to its celestial ascension, the world of the spirits and eternal life."[23]

The double aspect of mathematics, as a quantitative and qualitative science, makes this form of knowledge in a way "the ladder of Jacob." The use of mathematics in the study of the world of quantity

[18] Nicomachus, *Introduction to Arithmetic*, trans. M. L. D'Ooge (Chicago; Ency. Brit. 1953), p. 813. This work, which was translated into Arabic by Thābit ibn Qurrah, became one of the main sources of information in the Muslim world about the Pythagorean notion of numbers.

[19] Nicomachus, pp. 813–814.

[20] Or, as Corbin has said: "Puisque la Balance a pour principe et raison d'être de mesurer le Désir de l'âme du monde incorporé à chaque substance" ("Le Livre du Glorieux de Jābir ibn Ḥayyān," *Eranos Jahrbuch*, 18:84 [1950]).

[21] *R.*, I, 25 (italics ours).

[22] *R.*, I, 58–59.

[23] *R.*, I, 65.

becomes, therefore, a bridge by means of which one can journey from that world to the world of the archetypes. Number, because of its symbolic aspect, becomes not only the instrument of division but also that of unification and integration. The Pythagorean numbers as used by the Ikhwān, by virtue of their inner identification with the "Platonic ideas," or archetypes, of creation, have the power of synthesis in addition to that of analysis which they possess as a result of having a quantitative aspect.

In a further study of numbers which involves their odd-even, rational-irrational, and similar properties, the Ikhwān divide numbers into four groups: unities, dozens, hundreds, and thousands (much like the Chinese) and relate this fourfold division to the fourfold division which they see everywhere in Nature. They write:

> God himself has made it such that the majority of the things of Nature are grouped in four such as the four physical natures which are hot, cold, dry and moist; the four elements which are fire, air, water and earth; the four humours which are blood, phlegm, yellow bile and black bile; the four seasons . . . the four cardinal directions . . . the four winds . . . the four directions envisaged by their relation to the constellations (*awtād*); the four products which are the metals, plants, animals and men.[24]

If numbers are so closely bound to the "book of Nature," they are also intimately connected with the "book of Revelation"—that is, the letters of the Arabic alphabet, Arabic being the language of the Islamic Revelation. The Ikhwān use Table I for the numerical values of the letters:[25]

TABLE I. THE NUMERICAL VALUE OF LETTERS ACCORDING TO THE IKHWĀN AL-ṢAFĀ'

a	b	j	d	h	w	z	ḥ	ṭ	i,y	k	l	m
1	2	3	4	5	6	7	8	9	10	20	30	40
n	s	ʿ	f	ṣ	q	r	sh	t	th			
50	60	70	80	90	100	200	300	400	500			
kh	dh	ḍ	ẓ	gh	bgh	jgh						
600	700	800	900	1000	2000	3000						

[24] *R.*, I, 27.

[25] *R.*, I, 26. For a discussion of the value of the letters of the Arabic alphabet and their symbolic meaning drawn from the *Jafr jāmiʿ* of Nasībī and *Shaṭḥīyāt* of Baqlī, see L. Massignon, *Essai sur les origines du lexique technique de la mystique musulmane* (Paris, 1954), pp. 90–101. There are actually thirteen different systems of numeral symbolism of which six, called *al-dawā'ir al-sittah*, are most frequently used. See Ibn Sīnā, *Kunūz al-muʿazzimīn* (Tehran, 1331 [1952]), Introduction by J. Homā'ī, p. 40.

The science of the numerical symbolism of letters, *'ilm al-jafr*, which is comparable to sciences of a similar nature that existed among the ancient Pythagoreans, the Hindus, and the medieval Kabbalists, is said by masters of this science in Islam to have come down from 'Alī ibn Abī Ṭālib. It plays a very important role in *taṣawwuf* and among many Shī'ite schools and is basic for the symbolic interpretation (*ta'wīl*) of certain Quranic texts.[26] The Ikhwān also make some use of it so that in a way they place numbers as the link and deciphering code between the book of Revelation and that of Nature.[27] The constant reference to numbers which we shall see in the following chapters, and the language of analogy which the Ikhwān employ so often, are so many ways of seeing Unity within multiplicity and multiplicity as the projected image of Unity.

The Hierarchy of Being

The creation of the world by God, or the manifestation of existence by Being, is compared by the Ikhwān to the generation of numbers from One. Having divided all beings into the particular and general, they further divide the latter category itself into nine "states of being," since 9, by virtue of coming at the end of the decimal cycle, closes that cycle, and symbolically brings to an end the series of numbers. The creation of the Universe, beginning with the Creator, descending through the multiple states of Being, and ending with the terrestrial creatures whose final link is man, is outlined in the following manner:

1. Creator—who is one, simple, eternal, permanent.
2. Intellect (*'aql*)—which is of two kinds: innate and acquired.
3. Soul (*nafs*)—which has three species: vegetative, animal, and rational

[26] Of the 28 letters of the Arabic alphabet, 14, or half of them, appear at the beginning of the various *sūrahs*. The Ikhwān, like Jābir and al-Majrīṭī, divide the alphabet into 14 letters corresponding to the septentrional signs of the Zodiac and 14 to the meridional; this division is also one of luminous and tenebrous qualities of soul and body. The 14 letters at the head of the *sūrah* correspond to the dark signs since due to inverse analogy the 14 visible signs are dark for the soul, and vice versa (*R.*, III, 152). This correlation between Nature and the Quran points to the correspondence which exists between the cosmic milieu and Revelation in the mind of Muslim authors. See L. Massignon, "La Philosophie orientale d'Ibn Sīnā . . .," *Mémorial Avicenne*, 4:9 (Cairo, 1954).

[27] "De même que le *ta'wīl* amène à éclore le sens ésotérique, alchimie et théurgie, médecine et astrologie, sont pour leur part autant d'exégèse du texte cosmique." Corbin, "Le Livre du Glorieux . . .," p. 77.

4. Matter (*hayūlā'*)—which is of four kinds: matter of artefacts, physical matter, universal matter, and original matter.
5. Nature (*ṭabī'ah*)—which is of five kinds: celestial nature and the four elemental natures.
6. Body (*jism*)—which has six directions: above, below, front, back, left, and right.
7. The sphere—which has its seven planets.
8. The elements—which have eight qualities, these being in reality the four qualities combined two by two:

   Earth—cold and dry
   Water—cold and wet
   Air—warm and wet
   Fire—warm and dry

9. Beings of this world—which are the mineral, plant, and animal kingdoms, each having three parts.[28]

There is an important distinction to be made in this table of generation. The first four numbers are simple, universal beings—the numbers 1 to 4 already containing in themselves all numbers, since $1 + 2 + 3 + 4 = 10$—while the other beings are compound.[29]

The Ikhwān describe the production of the "great chain of Being" in the following manner:

> The first thing which the Creator produced and called into existence is a simple, spiritual, extremely perfect and excellent substance in which the form of all things is contained. This substance is called the Intellect. From this substance there proceeds a second one which in hierarchy is below the first and which is called the Universal Soul (*al-nafs al-kullīyah*). From the Universal Soul proceeds another substance which is below the Soul and which is called Original Matter.[30] The latter is transformed into the Absolute Body, that is, into Secondary Matter which has length, width and depth.[31]

[28] *R.*, III, 185, 203–208. B. Carra de Vaux, *Les Penseurs de l'Islam*, IV (Paris: Geuthner, 1923), 109–110. In the text, numbers 2 to 9 in the outline are given as 1 to 8 so that with the Creator the total becomes 9. It should be noted that each general being is itself divided into a number of species equal to the number of that being. This ontological hierarchy is the basis of the Ikhwān's study of Nature and cosmology.

[29] It is from this point of view that the Ikhwān, in other places in their *Rasā'il*, divide the hierarchy of Being into the fourfold division of God, Universal Intellect, Universal Soul, and *hylé*. (*R.*, I, 28.)

[30] The hierarchy outlined here follows in many ways that of Jābir except that Jābir in his *Kitāb al-khamsīn* places Nature after the soul. See Kraus, *Jābir ibn Ḥayyān*, II, 150.

[31] Dieterici, *Die Lehre von der Weltseele*, p. 15. *R.*, II, 4f.

The Relation between God and the Universe

The bringing into being of various creatures by God does not in any way nullify in the mind of the Ikhwān the fundamental distinction between God and the Universe. The Universe is "all the spiritual and material beings who populate the immensity of the skies, who constitute the reign of multiplicity which extends to the spheres, the stars, the elements, their products and to man."[32] This Universe, which they sometimes call a city or an animal, but always something distinct from the Divine Unity, is related to God by its existence (*wujūd*), its persistence in being (*baqā'*), its completeness (*tamām*), and its perfection (*kamāl*). The Universal Intellect, which is at the same time a great veil hiding God as well as the great gate to His Unity,[33] inherits the four above-mentioned virtues from God and transmits them to the Universal Soul, which remains passive and feminine with respect to the Intellect.[34]

The Ikhwān also make use of the symbolism of love (*'ishq*) in terms similar to those used by the Ṣūfīs in order to show the attraction between God and the Universe. According to them, the whole world seeks the Creator and loves Him. In fact, the Creator is really the only Beloved (*ma'shūq*) and the only object of desire (*murād*).[35] They make the power of yearning (*shawq*) the very cause of the coming into being

[32] *R.*, I, 99. The Ikhwān write at times that God is above Being, while in other instances they imply that Being is divided into God and Universe. See R. L. Fackenheim, "The conception of substance in the philosophy of the Ikhwān aṣ-Ṣefā' (Brethren of Purity)," *Medieval Studies*, 5:117 (1945).

[33] «انّ العالم كلّه بما فيه، داخل في امر الله عزّ وجلّ، غير خارج عنه ولا هارب منه، وانّه في قبضته وتحت ارادته، فاوله، واعلاه، واقربه من باريه هو العقل وهو مثل الحجاب الاعظم، والباب الاكبر، الّذى منه الوصول الى توحيد الله عزّ وجلّ.»

Jāmi'ah, II, 33. The twofold aspect of the Intellect as created and uncreated seems to be implied here.

[34] *R.*, III, 188.

[35] «المعشوق، المطاع المحبوب، المراد المطلوب، على الحقيقة هو البارى سبحانه وان الخلائق كلّها وجملة العالم باسرها مشتاقة اليه.»

Jāmi'ah, II, 159. Interpreting the Quranic verse «وَإِنْ مِنْ شَيْءٍ إِلَّا يُسَبِّحُ بِحَمْدِهِ.» they say,

«التسبيح بحمده هو المسارعة الى امتثال امره ونهيه اليه والدّنوّ منه.»

of things and the law governing the Universe.[36] It was through *shawq* for Allah that the Universal Soul brought the outermost sphere of the Universe, the *Muḥīṭ*, into existence. The *Muḥīṭ* in turn rotated to form the sphere below it, this process continuing all the way down to the sphere of the moon.[37]

Contrary to many followers of Hellenistic philosophy and cosmology, and particularly the Peripatetics, the Ikhwān believe in instantaneous creation rather than in the eternity of the world, and they severely criticize the *dahrīyūn*, or those who believe in the eternity of the world.[38] According to them, God has created the first four universal beings in the series of effusions (*faiḍ*) instantaneously. The other beings in the Universe, on the other hand, have been brought into existence directly by the Universal Soul "acting with the permission of Allah Most High."[39] The *Rasā'il* emphasize that the relation of God to the world is not just that of a mason to a house or of an author to a book:

> The world in relation to Allah is like the word in relation to him who speaks it, like light, or heat or numbers to the lantern, Sun, hearth or the number One. The word, light, heat and number exist by their respective

[36] "God is the first Beloved of the Universe." Everything which is not God proceeds from Him and aspires to return to Him. This aspiration is the law of the Universe—the *nāmūs*, and the prophet is in fact called *ṣāḥib al-nāmūs*, the possessor of the Law.

„اعلم ان وقوف الافلاك عن الدوران هو موت العالم وبطلان حياة الكل ومفارقة النفس الكلية الفلكية من الاجسام كلها دفعة واحدة وتلك هي القيامة الكبرى والبوار الكلي وبطلان الجملة .."

R., III, 275.

[37] *Jāmi'ah*, I, 276–278. Jābir also considers the *shawq* of the soul for Allah as the cause of the coming into being of the world. Kraus, *Jābir ibn Ḥayyān*, II, 156.

[38] According to the Ikhwān the Universe is not *qadīm*, or eternal, but *muḥdath*, or created. One day it will die when the Universal Soul leaves it, as a man dies when the soul leaves his body.

„العالم محدث مبدع مخترع كائن بعد ان لم يكن وان مبدعه ومخترعه ومحدثه وخالقه ومصوره هو الباري جل جلاله ابدعه كما شاء وكيف شاء .."

R., II, 76. They write regarding the death of the Universe:

„ان الله هو المعشوق الاول وان كل الموجودات اليه تشتاق ونحوه تقصد واليه يرجع الامر كله لان به وجودها وقوامها وبقاءها وثباتها وكمالها لانه هو الوجود المحض وله البقاء والدوام ..."

R., II, 77.

[39] *R.*, III, 330–332.

sources, but without the sources could neither exist nor persist in being. The existence of the world is thus determined by that of Allah . . .[40]

The use of numerical or light symbolism does not prevent the Ikhwān from emphasizing the absolute transcendence (*tanzīh*) of God with respect to the world.[41] Yet, they know also that His Qualities are "lines drawn by the fiat of effusion in the Book of the Universe like verses engraved in souls and in matter."[42]

The notion of the transitory and imperfect nature of this world and its corollary, the absolute perfection of God, which are so characteristic of the Islamic perspective, are expounded again and again throughout the *Rasā'il.* "There is no one in the world," they write, "who possesses every noble quality and every blessing . . . Perfection is for the Most High God alone, and for none besides."[43]

Also contrary to the Peripatetics and certain other Greek schools and their followers in the Muslim world, the influence of God in the Universe is not limited to the heavens nor bound by the "position" of God as the "Prime Mover." The Ikhwān envisage a Universe whose anatomy is based upon an ontological and not just a logical hierarchy. One of the Ikhwān tells us:

> I have heard that some foolish men suppose that the favours of God, Most High, do not pass the lunar sphere. Were they to attentively regard and reflect upon the circumstances of all existing things, they would learn that His goodness and loving kindness comprehends all—small and great.[44]

In this Universe of purpose where "God, Most High, has created nothing in vain,"[45] there are correspondences and analogies, descents and ascents of souls, differentiation and integration, all knit into a harmonious pattern which is very far from a "rationalistic castle." It is rather the "cosmic cathedral" in which the unicity of Nature, the interrelatedness of all things with each other and the ontological dependence of the whole of creation upon the Creator, is brought into focus.

The Universal Intellect and Soul

As numbers 2 and 3 in the hierarchy of beings, standing just below the Creator, the Intellect and Soul assume the role of the principles

[40] *R.*, III, 319. [41] *R.*, IV, 252–256. [42] *R.*, IV, 225.
[43] Ikhwān, *Dispute between Man and the Animals*, trans. J. Platts, p. 34.
[44] *Dispute* . . ., p. 120. [45] *Ibid.*

of the whole Universe; the duality upon which things are based returns to them in one way or another.

Various people have said that the world is made of form and matter, others light and darkness, substance and accident, spirit and body, Guarded Tablet and Pen, expansion and contraction, love and hate, this world and the next, cause and effect, beginning and end, exterior and interior, high and low, heavy and light.[46]

But, according to the Ikhwān, "in principle all these views are the same; they disagree only in secondary aspects and in expression." In all these cases the duality refers to the Intellect and Soul which contain in themselves the active and passive principles through which the life and activity of the Universe can be understood. Creation is the "dynamic" and "feminine" aspect of the Divine. It itself possesses an "active" and "masculine" aspect which is called Nature and which is the source of all activity in the Universe; and a "passive" and "feminine" aspect which to us appears as the "matter" or "inert" base of this activity.[48]

In the chain of causation, the Intellect can be said to have only an efficient Cause which is God.[49] With respect to God, the Intellect is purely passive, in obedience, tranquillity, and permanent desire for union with the Divine Principle. Since the Intellect is the highest being in the Universe, its passivity with respect to God may be said to symbolize the passivity of the whole of creation with respect to the Creator. The Universe can only receive while the Creator can only give.[50]

The Universal Soul in turn acts passively, and like "matter," with respect to the Intellect, which is active with respect to it. It has only two causes, the efficient one being God and the formal one the Intellect.[51] The Universal Soul receives from the Intellect all the virtues, forms, and positive qualities, and transmits them in turn to the whole of the Universe.[52]

The Universal Soul is to the Universe what the human soul is to the human body, and it has, therefore, for its field of action—in the geocentric cosmos where the earth lies stationary at the center with nine concentric spheres around it—the whole of the Universe from

[46] *Jāmi'ah*, II, 7–8. [47] *Jāmi'ah*, II, 8.

[48] For a full explanation of the active-passive polarization in the Universe, see T. Burckhardt, "Nature sait surmonter nature," *Etudes Traditionnelles*, 51:10ff (1950).

[49] The Ikhwān interpret by symbolic interpretation (*ta'wīl*) the Quranic verse (XVII, 89): "And verily we have displayed for mankind in this Qur'ān all kinds of similitudes . . ." to justify this assertion scripturally.

[50] *R.*, III, 187ff. [51] *R.*, III, 233. [52] *R.*, III, 235.

the outermost sphere which is the *Muḥīṭ* to the center of the earth.[53] It is also the prime-mover which makes the sphere of the fixed stars perform its diurnal motion.[54] All bodies in the Universe are like tools in the hand of the Universal Soul which performs all actions through them in the same way as a carpenter uses his tools for various ends.[55] All change in the Universe, therefore, is directed by the Soul.

The Ikhwān emphasize the dominance of the Universal Soul over the whole Universe:

> This Universal Soul is the spirit of the world as we have exposed it in the treatise where we said that the world is a great man. *Nature is the act of this Universal Soul.* The four elements are the matter which serve as its support. The spheres and the stars are like its organs, and the minerals, plants and animals are the objects which it makes to move.[56]

The Universal Soul can be divided in several ways according to what aspect of its multiple activities is envisaged. The Ikhwān sometimes divide its forces into fifteen parts: seven superhuman, one human, and seven subhuman. The two divisions immediately above are the angelic and prophetic, while the two immediately below are the animal and vegetative.[57] In this vast cosmos, from the outermost heaven which symbolizes the spiritual and intellectual world to the earth which being farthest away from heaven symbolizes material existence, the parts of the Soul move according to three motions:

(1) Away from the outer sphere (*Muḥīṭ*) toward the world of generation and corruption and ultimately hell.
(2) Upwards toward heaven.
(3) Horizontal oscillation without knowledge of where to go, as in the souls of animals.[58]

[53] *R.*, II, 224.
[54] Carra de Vaux, *Les Penseurs de l'Islam*, IV, 107. Placing *al-nafs al-kullīyah*, or the Universal Soul, at the heaven of the fixed stars was already accomplished by Jābir. Kraus, *Jābir ibn Ḥayyān*, II, 137–138, n. 5.
[55] «وانّه لا فعل الاّ للنفس وانّها تفعل افعالها بقوّتها فى الاجسام وانّ الاجسام كلّها آلات وادوات و مفعولات بها.» *R.*, II, 56.
[56] Dieterici, *Lehre von der Weltseele*, 43ff. Also Carra de Vaux, *Les Penseurs de l'Islam*, IV, 107 (italics ours).
[57] *R.*, I, 240. Also 'Awā, *L'Esprit critique* . . ., p. 167.
[58] 'Awā, *ibid.*, p. 168. There is a striking resemblance between the three cosmic tendencies of ascent, descent, and horizontal expansion described by the Ikhwān and the

The cosmic tendencies and qualities which are to be found everywhere owe their existence to these fundamental tendencies of the Universal Soul which is the cause of all activity in the world.

Matter

The notion of matter is elaborately developed by the Ikhwān and along lines which separate their views from those of the Aristotelian school. According to the Ikhwān, Prime Matter is already far removed from Pure Being and possesses in itself only existence and persistence. It is, however, a positive spiritual principle rather than just potentiality. It is the first being in the descending scale of beings here considered that does not desire virtue and goodness by itself. However, it is still a "spiritual form emanating from the Universal Soul";[59] it is still simple, intelligible, and imperceptible to the senses. Coming after the numbers 1, 2, and 3, it has three causes, the efficient being God, the formal the Intellect, and the final the Soul.[60]

Primary Matter is to be distinguished from Secondary Matter, the latter being the first metaphysical step toward the concrete. Primary Matter first receives the three spatial dimensions to become the Absolute Body (*al-jism al-muṭlaq*), or "the matter of the all." Then Secondary Matter comes into being with God as its efficient cause, the Intellect as its formal cause, and the Soul as the final cause. As for the material cause, it belongs to Secondary Matter itself and resides in the simple substance which admits of three dimensions. Hence four causes come to act upon all bodies which are composed of Secondary Matter.[61]

As mentioned already, the Ikhwān use "matter" in four distinct ways:

(1) Matter of artificial works.
(2) Matter of natural objects.
(3) Universal Matter (or Secondary Matter).
(4) Original Matter.

These four types are described in the following manner:

The natural matter consists of fire, air, water and earth. All that is found in the sublunary sphere—the animals, plants, and minerals—come from

three Hindu *gunas*: *sattwa*, *tamas*, and *rajas*. See R. Guénon, *Man and his Becoming According to the Vedanta*, trans. R. C. Nicholson (London, 1945), pp. 51–52.

[59] *R.*, III, 230.

[60] *R.*, III, 233. Also 'Awā, *L'Esprit critique . . .*, pp. 168–169.

[61] *L'Esprit critique*, pp. 170–171.

these constituents and by corruption return to them. *Their creator is Nature* which is one of the forces of the celestial Universal Soul.

Universal Matter is the Absolute Body. From this Body is drawn the entire corporeal Universe, that is, the celestial spheres, stars, the elements and all other beings whatever they may be. They are all bodies and their diversity comes only from their diverse forms.

Original matter is a simple and ideal substance which cannot be sensed because it is none other than the form of unique existence; it is the primitive foundation. If this foundation receives quantity it becomes by virtue of that reception the Absolute Body about which one affirms that it has three dimensions—length, breadth and thickness. If this foundation receives quality, as, for example, the form of a circle, triangle or rectangle, it becomes a special body which is determined as being such and such. Thus quality is equal to 3, quantity to 2, and the primitive foundation to 1. Just as 3 comes after 2, so does quality come after quantity, and just as 2 comes after 1, quantity comes after the primitive foundation. In its existence the primitive foundation precedes quantity and quality as 1 precedes 2 and 3.

The primitive foundation, quantity, and quality are simple, ideal forms which cannot be sensed. When one of them is united to another, the first is matter at the same time that the second is form. Quality is form with regard to quantity, and quantity is matter for quality. Quantity in its turn is form for the primitive foundation, and the primitive foundation is matter for quantity.[62]

In summary, we can present the Ikhwān's notion of matter in the following hierarchy:

Original Matter—possessing no determination other than existence.

↓

Universal Matter—possessing quantity and the three dimensions (Absolute Body).

↓

Determined Body—formed of the union of Absolute Body playing the role of matter and a particular form.

Matter then possesses several levels of existence, each more "condensed" and "coagulated" than the next, beginning with the primary or original matter which does not even possess quantity and is a spiritual form, and ending with the matter of particular objects which are perceptible by the senses and are the terminal stage of manifestation, being as far away from the Divine Principle as the conditions of cosmic manifestation permit.

[62] *R.*, II, 4ff. Dieterici, *Die Naturschauung und Naturphilosophie der Araber . . .* (Berlin, 1861), pp. 2–3, and E. Duhem, *Le Système du monde* (Paris, 1913–1919), IV. 466–467.

Nature

The Ikhwān emphasize in their description of the Universal Soul that it is the cause of all actions in the Universe. Now, as the matter which was described above is acted upon in one way or another and is the receiver of action, so is one of the faculties of the Universal Soul the cause of all change and activity in the sublunary region; this faculty is called Nature.

> Nature is none other than one of the faculties of the Universal Soul of the spheres which is propagated in all the bodies existing in the sublunary region beginning from the sphere of the ether until the center of the world. Bodies below the sphere of the moon are of two kinds: simple and complex. There are four simple bodies: fire, air, water and earth; and three types of composed bodies: minerals, plants and animals. This faculty which I like to call Nature is spread within all things as clarity is spread in the air. Its Nature makes them move or rest, it governs them, it perfects them and makes each come to the place where it tends according to how it becomes them.[63]

All events occurring on earth and below the sphere of the moon are then due to this spiritual agent called Nature which orders all change and is the cause of all "physical" events we see here around us.[64] It is in the affirmation of this view that the Ikhwān write in another passage that:

> Nature is only one of the faculties of the Universal Soul which has expanded in all the sublunary bodies. In the language of religion (*shar'ī*) it is called the Soul in charge of maintenance and organization or order in the world by permission of Allah. In philosophic terminology, it is a natural force acting by the permission of the Creator on the bodies in question. Those who deny the action of Nature have not understood the true sense of these denominations . . .
>
> Know, Oh Brother, that those who deny the action of Nature say that there is no proper action except by the Alive, the Powerful [this is in reference to the Ash'arite theologians]. This saying is correct; however,

[63] Dieterici, *Lehre von der Weltseele*, p. 43; *Jāmi'ah*, I, 311; Carra de Vaux, *Les penseurs de l'Islam*, IV, 106–107.

[64] «اعلم انه لما كان الذين يتكلمون في الحوادث والكائنات التي هي دون فلك القمر من الحكماء والفلاسفة العلماء ينسبون هذه الآثار والافعال كلها الى الطبيعة.» *Jāmi'ah*, I, 309.

«الطبيعة... قوة من قوى النفس الكلية وهي سارية في جميع الاجسام التي دون فلك القمر من لدن كرة الاثير الى منتهى مركز الارض.» *Jāmi'ah*, I, 311.

they think that the Alive, the Powerful, does not bring into existence except by means of a body . . . They do not know that there is along with the body a substance which is ultimately spiritual and invisible. This is the Soul, which they describe as being an accident, by means of which change occurs in the body. It is this, that is, the Soul, by means of which actions appear in bodies.[65]

The concern of the Ikhwān in describing nature is more with what the Latins, with a somewhat different connotation, called *natura naturans* and not so much with *natura naturata*, which forms the subject matter of the modern natural sciences.

The *Rasā'il* emphasize the importance of understanding and accepting the presence of this spiritual force called Nature which is the performer of all actions. In fact, they often identify materialists with those who deny Nature, for they know that the cosmological and metaphysical aspects of the traditional sciences such as astrology, and not the predictive aspect, which is completely secondary, derive directly from this conception of an organic Universe where the sub-lunary parts have no autonomy of their own independent of the Universal Soul[66] and its faculty Nature, any more than human limbs have any autonomy of motion independent of the human will which moves them. The consideration of "inert matter" to which motion and life are incidental is diametrically opposed to the Ikhwān's conception of the activity of the physical domain as being due to the force of Nature which pervades it throughout. The Universe for the Ikhwān acts more like a live organism whose motions come from a force within rather than a cadaver to which external motion has been added.

The Spheres and the Elements

The astronomy of the Ikhwān—which will be discussed in greater detail below—conforming to the general view of medieval cosmologists, places the earth at the center of the Universe with the Moon, Sun, and the planets rotating about it. Beyond the sphere of Saturn there is the Sphere of Fixed Stars and finally the outermost sphere, or *Muḥīṭ*. In the heavens, which possess circular motion, perfect circular

[65] *R.*, II, 55. See also *R.*, II, 112–113.

[66] According to the Ikhwān, the Universal Soul acts through three agents: the 12 signs of the Zodiac, the heavens (*aflāk*) and the planets. *Jāmi'ah*, I, 313. The action of these agents upon the sublunary region which underlies the whole of astrology is a necessary consequence of the function of the Universal Soul as the cause of all action in the world. Moreover, the agents of the Universal Soul act upon this world as a soul upon a body, not as almost "material rays" or any gross ideas of the kind entertained by so many modern astrologers.

form and movement are joined to matter to bring into being the quintessence, or the substance, of which the heavens are made. By the quintessence the Ikhwān mean a substance having such properties that "on the one hand the celestial bodies accept neither generation nor corruption nor change nor transformation nor augmentation nor diminution, and that on the other hand their movements are all perfect, thus circular."[67] The "quintessence" or "fifth element," of the Ikhwān, however, differs from the ether of Aristotle or Ibn Sīnā. Whereas the latter school considers the cosmos as being completely divided into two regions, the sublunary made of the four elements and the celestial made of ether which does not possess any of the four essential qualities of hot, cold, wet, and dry, the Ikhwān conceive of a unified cosmos in which the quintessence also possesses the four qualities.[68] Otherwise it would not be possible to assign to the planets and the signs of the Zodiac the qualities which are the basis of astrology. This distinction between a divided and unified cosmos is to be found throughout the Middle Ages among the Aristotelian and Hermetic schools.

By the elements, the Ikhwān—like nearly all other Muslim authors—mean the four elements mentioned by Empedocles and Aristotle, that is, fire, air, water, and earth, which, as described above, possess in pairs the combination of the four qualities of heat, cold, dryness and moistness. They refer to the sphere of the elements as *usṭuqus*, from the Greek term *stoichos*, meaning support or base, since the elements are the ground from which the creatures of the earth come into being. The elements are the constituent parts of all the members of the three kingdoms of minerals, plants, and animals. Nature acts upon these elements in various ways, and the soul appropriate to each kingdom and each species is added to this mixture by the Universal Soul in order to bring particular members of each species into being. The elements cannot act by themselves but are always subservient and passive to the force of Nature which acts upon them from above and within.

Time, Space, and Motion

The physics of the Ikhwān, unlike that of Aristotle, does not have the problem of motion as its central subject. In fact, in order to under-

[67] *R.*, II, 39.

[68] The Ikhwān do, however, agree with the Peripatetics that the ether is beyond corruption and heaviness and lightness. Sometimes they even imply that it is beyond the four qualities, but most often assign qualities to the planets and signs of the Zodiac. See *R.*, II, 26ff, 39–42.

stand fully the physics of the Ikhwān, it is necessary to go beyond not only the Cartesian conception of matter but also the *materia* of the Stagirite. One can say about the Ikhwān with respect to the problem of motion what has been said about the early pre-Socratic Greek philosophers:

> If we would understand the sixth-century philosopher, we must disabuse our minds of the atomistic conception of dead matter in mechanical motion and of the Cartesian dualism of matter and mind. We must go back to the time when motion was an unquestionable symptom of life, and there was no need to look for a "moving cause." Matter or body requires a distinct moving cause only when it has been deprived of its own inherent life . . . Motion was inherent in the divine stuff because it was alive . . .[69]

The Universe which the *Rasā'il* describe is, like the cosmos of the ancient Greeks, one which is alive, being composed of a body and the Universal Soul which animates the whole of it. Consequently, the question of motion does not have the same status with the Ikhwān as it does with either Aristotle or the Cartesians.

Inasmuch as things do move, however, and events do take place in time and space, the conception of these primary matrices of physical events and necessary conditions of terrestrial existence must be described. Time and space, which are intimately connected with motion, are considered in the *Rasā'il* more from their cosmological aspect than from the kinematic point of view.

The Ikhwān reject the Aristotelian notion of time as being nothing but the measure of movement, although they still relate it to the motion of the heavens, which are the generators of space as well as of time.[70] But they consider also the psychological aspect of time, about which they write:

> Time is a pure form, an abstract notion, simple and intelligible, elaborated in the soul by the faculties of the spirit. It is born there through meditation upon the regular repetition of nights and days around the earth and resembles the generation of numbers by the repetition of One.[71]

[69] F. M. Cornford, *Principium Sapientiae* (Cambridge University Press, 1952), pp. 179–181.

[70] *Jāmi'ah*, I, 177. «ولمّا كان الفلك هو سبب وجود المكان، وعدد حركاته هو الزمان.»

«لما كان الزمان مقدار حركة الفلك.»

Jāmi'ah, I, 48. Inasmuch as the Universal Soul is the cause of motion of the heavens, it is also the cause of space and time.

[71] *R.*, II, 15.

Time is also intimately connected with creation and in fact is created with the world. Likewise, the last Day (*yawm al-qiyāmah*) is not just another day in time but the termination of time itself.[72]

As for space, it has no reality independent of this world, but is, on the contrary, one of the conditions of physical existence. It is therefore useless to ask whether there is vacuum or plenum outside of the Universe. There is neither one nor the other because there is no space outside the cosmos and the Universe cannot be said to be in space.[73] Rather, all that is in space is by nature dependent upon the Universe. From a physical point of view space, or place, is the boundary of bodies as defined by Aristotle and the Muslim Peripatetics.[74] From a more inward point of view it is an abstract, simple, intelligible idea, "a form abstracted from matter and existing only in the consciousness,"[75] rather than either the surface of a substance or the void. The Ikhwān, as a matter of fact, reject the possibility of a void; since, according to them, and following the argument of the Aristotelians, a void must be in a place, or what is currently called space; but place is a quality of bodies and cannot be found except where there are bodies, so that where there are no bodies there is no place or space and, therefore, no void. On the contrary, space for the Ikhwān is something always filled, even when it seems empty to the senses. "Not a span of space is there," they write, "but what is occupied by spirits who dwell therein."[76] They never say, however, that all of space is filled only by "material" or "physical" beings; for them space dwelt in by spirits is as "full" as one filled by water.

The question of motion is inseparable from the Universal Soul and its faculties inasmuch as all motion is due to this soul. As the Ikhwān state: "We call 'souls' certain real substances, living and moving by their essences, and we designate under the name 'move-

[72] *Jāmi'ah*, II, 48–49.
[73] «وليس خارج العالم شيئ آخر، لا خلاء ولا ملاء، وليس في مكان، وكلّ ما فيه مكان موكّل به،
وكلّ واحد من العالم بمكان هو اليق به من امكنة العالم...»
Jāmi'ah, II, 24.
[74] *R*., III, 361. «وكل موضع تمكن فيه المتمكن، وهي نهايات الاجسام..»

For the definition of place given by Aristotle, see his *Physics*, bk. IV, chap, iv; also H. Wolfson, *Crescas' Critique of Aristotle* (Cambridge, Mass., 1929) chap. II.
[75] *R*., II, 9–10.
[76] Ikhwān, *Dispute between Man and the Animals*, trans. J. Platts, p. 229.

ment' the actions of a soul on a body."[77] And again: "By its active life the soul models the matter of the body as well as that of the exterior world."[78]

Universal Soul, then, is the cause of motion, while "movement is a form imposed on a body by the Universal Soul after it has been shaped, and rest is the absence of this form."[79] Comparing movement to light, the Ikhwān consider motion not as a material activity but a spiritual form. "Movement is a spiritual and complimentary form (*al-ṣūrat al-rūḥānīyah*) which traverses all parts of moving bodies and expands within them instantaneously like light in order to terminate abruptly their rest."[80]

They give several different classifications of motion, one being according to the objects moved, that is, the movement of the seven heavens, the fixed stars, planets, comets, meteors, air, wind, and other meteorological phenomena; seas, streams, rain, motion of the interior of the earth such as earthquakes, or of beings like the minerals inside the earth, the plants and trees on the surface of the earth, and finally the animals in various directions of space.[81] To realize that all of these movements, which are so diverse in appearance, are due ultimately to a single agent who is the Universal Soul is to see in a striking way the unicity of Nature. To show further the interrelatedness of all things, the Ikhwān also classify the motions of the Spirit (*rūḥ*), in a manner similar to that of bodies, and relate the two to each other. For example, they compare the motion of the interior of the earth with the abrogation (*naskh*) of previous *sharī'ahs* by the Prophet Muḥammad—upon whom be peace—and the motion of the planets to the *sharī'ah* of the various prophets.[82]

Another method of classification closer to the Aristotelian, and in a way reducible to it, is outlined on the following page.

The Ikhwān, however, do not proceed much further in discussing the intricacies of motion in a manner that one finds in the writings of Ibn Sīnā or Abu'l-Barakāt al-Baghdādī. The main interest of the authors of the *Rasā'il* remains the unified and organic Universe whose unicity they seek to bring to light through analogy and symbolism.

[77] *R.*, III, 306. „قد بيّنا انّ المحرّك والمسكّن للاجسام هي النفس“

R., III, 305. It should be emphasized that the souls in various species in the world such as the animal and vegetative do not actually signify a plurality of souls but various functions of the single Universal Soul.

[78] *R.*, I, 225. [79] *R.*, II, 12. [80] *R.*, II, 12.

[81] *Jāmi'ah*, II, 238. [82] *Jāmi'ah*, II, 253ff.

- Motion
  - Physical (*jismānī*)
    1. Generation (*kawn*)—passage of something from potentiality to act by which things come into existence.
    2. Corruption (*fasād*)—the reverse of generation.
    3. Augmentation (*ziyādah*)—stretching of the extremities of a body with respect to its center.
    4. Diminution (*nuqṣān*)—opposite of augmentation.
    5. Alteration (*taghyīr*)—change of quality of an object, such as its color.
    6. Translation, or local movement (*naqlah*)—passage in space and time from one point to another.
       - Straight (*mustaqīmah*)
       - Circular (*mustadīrah*)
       - Combination of the two (*murakkabatun minhumā*)[83]
  - Spiritual (*rūḥānī*)

The Analogy of Microcosm and Macrocosm and the Great Chain of Being

All the principles and concepts which have been explained thus far are integrated by the Ikhwān into the closely related ideas of the analogy of the microcosm and macrocosm and the chain, or hierarchy, of being. Both of these ideas are universal and far from being limited to Greek, Islamic, or Christian cosmologies, have their exact counterparts in China, India, and elsewhere. They are moreover, "conceptual dimensions" which through their beauty and profundity can lead the soul far beyond the domains of the physical aspects of Nature. Both ideas, in fact, belong to the domain of theology and metaphysics as well as to cosmology. The Ṣūfī doctrine concerning the Universal Man (*al-insān al-kāmil*), the Hindu conception of *Purusa*, and the Chinese *Chen-jen* all attest to the universality of the macrocosm-microcosm analogy and its importance in domains beyond that of the sciences of Nature. In the study of the Universe, also, these ideas hold a vital position, because they serve as the central link in showing the unicity of Nature and in demonstrating the inward relation between man and Nature; consequently, the study of Nature in medieval science acts as a support for spiritual realization, as con-

[83] *Jāmi'ah*, II, 237. *R.*, II, 10–13.

versely, the study by man of himself leads to his understanding of the inner aspects of Nature.[84]

The essential techniques of numerical symbolism and analogy, which, as we mentioned above, form the basic language of the Ikhwān, are used throughout the *Rasā'il* in the context and the service of illuminating the reality and beauty of the relation between the microcosm and macrocosm and the hierarchy of Being. To a reader unsympathetic to this perspective, such efforts may seem artificial and unreal. If, however, one possesses the "conceptual perspective" necessary for an understanding of these symbols, the beauty and grandeur of these analogies become evident. A physical "application" of this doctrine, which is easier to visualize than its literary description, is found in the medieval cathedral and the Hindu temple. Both of these buildings are the "body of the Universal Man" as well as a miniature cosmos, and reflect in their beauty the grandeur of the conceptions which underlie their construction. In Islam, also, *taṣawwuf* itself and much that is the fruit of the Ṣūfī spirit, whether it be in poetry or in architecture, express in the last analysis the doctrine of the Universal Man[85] which along with Unity (*al-tawḥīd*) comprises the essence of Islamic spiritual doctrines.

Nearly every chapter of the *Rasā'il* and every domain of Nature that is studied is elucidated and elaborated with reference to the analogy between man and the Universe. The Ikhwān write:

> Know, oh Brother, that by the Universe (*'ālam*) the sages (*ḥukamā'*) mean the seven heavens and the earths and what is between them of all creatures. They also call it the great man (*al-insān al-kabīr*) because it is seen that the world has one body in all its spheres, gradation of heavens, its generating elements (*arkān*) and their productions. It is seen also that it has one Soul (*nafs*) whose powers run into all the organs of its body, just like the man who has one soul which runs into all of his organs. We desire to mention in this treatise the form of the world and describe the composition of its body as the body of man is described in a book of anatomy. Then in another treatise we shall describe the quality of the Soul of the world and how its powers run into the bodies in this world from the most

[84] These remarks, which have been drawn from a general study of medieval cosmological texts, are emphasized over and over by the Ikhwān throughout the *Rasā'il*.

[85] For an exposition of the doctrine of the Universal Man and its function in cosmology, see R. A. Nicholson, *Studies in Islamic Mysticism* (Cambridge, England, 1921), chapter on "The Perfect Man"; also *De l'homme universel* (Paris, 1975) by 'Abd al-Karīm al-Jīlī, trans. T. Burckhardt.

high sphere of *Muḥīṭ* to the lowest point which is the center of the earth.[86]

Our study of the heavens and earth, the three kingdoms, and finally man as the microcosm will fully demonstrate how this analogy exists. Often in their study of the Universe, the Ikhwān give analogies from the microcosm to illustrate an otherwise difficult concept concerning cosmology. For example, the relation of the Universal Soul to the Universe, described above, becomes concrete and vivid when compared to the human soul and body. Or the comparison of the death of the Universe to human death makes what appears as a far-away event a very "real" one. But the Ikhwān also apply analogies in the reverse sense, explaining the constitution of the human being by correspondences drawn from the heavens and earth, again in order to make vivid and "real" some aspect of man, and, what is more important perhaps, to demonstrate his cosmic qualities and significance. We shall explore this aspect fully in the chapter on man as the microcosm, which begins with the statement: "Our end consists of showing here how man can be considered as a small world".[87] This implies that the knowledge of man's soul is essential to a knowledge of the external world.

In making analogies between various parts of the cosmos and man, the part of the cosmos above the Moon, which is the most beautiful and perfect part of the Universe, is compared to the Universal Man (*al-insān al-kullī*),[88] while the sublunary region, where change occurs and where good and evil souls are mixed together, is compared to the particular man (*al-insān al-juz'ī*). The human being is created between the Universal and particular man and takes part in the nature of each.[89] Also, particular man is created from the Universal Man just as in the creation of the world the sublunary region is generated from the heavens and is always passive and obedient with respect to them.[90]

The cosmological chain, starting from Unity, which symbolizes

[86] «اعلم ايها الاخ ان معنى قول الحكماء العالم انه يعنون به السماوات السبع والارضين وما بينهما من الخلائق اجمعين. وسموه ايضا انسانا كبيرا لانهم يرون انه جسم واحد بجميع افلاكه واطباق سماواته واركان امهاته ومولداتها ...»
R., II, 20.

[87] *R.*, II, 318.

[88] The Ikhwān use a different term for Universal Man from that of the Ṣūfīs, the latter usually using *kāmil* rather than *kullī*, although the term *kāmīl* is also known to the Ikhwān.

[89] *Jāmi'ah*, I, 612–615.

[90] «في معرفة الانسان الكلي الكامل، الذي من أجله خلق الانسان الجزئي ...»
Jāmi'ah, I, 610.

the Creator, up to the number 9, which is the domain of the three kingdoms, already contains the basis of the chain of being. The chain of being essentially means that all beings in the Universe exist according to a continuous hierarchy which is ontological as well as cosmological. A particular entity has a position in the great chain of being depending upon the degree to which it participates in Being and Intelligence; or, one might say, upon the degree to which it possesses the perfections and virtues which in the absolute sense belong only to Pure Being, or God, who is transcendent with respect to the chain. The Ikhwān, like the Ṣūfīs, make the hierarchy of being dependent upon the degree to which anything possesses beauty or, in other words, participates in the Absolute Beauty which is an inner attribute of God.

Starting from the highest heaven, which is nearest to the Divine, the hierarchy of being descends through the heavenly spheres—symbolizing the angels—and down to the world of the four elements, of which the heaviest, the earth, is the one farthest away from the pure light of heaven. The elements then are mixed to various degrees by the Soul which from them forms the three kingdoms. The process terminates with man, who is the final term of the effusion: "The unity and complexity of his soul and body respectively make him 'the antipode of God.' "[91] By virtue of this position, man is the central link in the great chain; below him stands the animal kingdom, and above, the world of the angels, and he is connected to one domain as well as to the other.[92]

According to the Ikhwān, the qualities and perfections belonging to the various levels of the hierarchy of being are not in any way "subjective" or "anthropomorphic," but, being a part of their ontological status, are completely independent of the whims and fancies of the "thoughts" of men. In the three kingdoms of mineral, plant, and animal, good and evil (*maḥmūd* and *madhmūm*) souls are mixed independently of human will. The beautiful and good qualities of these kingdoms are manifestations of the good souls, while what is ugly is due to the evil souls, which the Ikhwān call "satanic forces" (*shayāṭīn*).[93] These qualities, being an inherent part of each object,

[91] *R.*, III, 3–5. 'Awā, *L'Esprit critique* . . ., p. 172.

[92] «ولمّا كان آخر مرتبة الانسان متّصلا بأول مرتبة الملائكة ، وآخر مرتبة الحيوان متّصلا بأوّل مرتبة الانسان ، وجب ان يكون الانسان مجموعًا من العالمين متوسطًا بينهما .» *Jāmi'ah*, I, 342.

[93] *Jāmi'ah*, I, 367ff.

are transmitted along with that object. For example, if a plant possesses certain good qualities, it transmits them to the animal that eats it. Or if the flesh of a particular animal has evil qualities, these qualities affect the man who eats that flesh. This effect, however, is not just physical; rather, the soul of man is also affected by it.[94] One can derive from this view of the Ikhwān the reason for the dietary prohibitions existing in various religions like Islam and Judaism, each of which is established in conformity with the spiritual and psychological "economy" of a segment of humanity.

In the three kingdoms, each end member is connected to the first member of the next domain.[95] Minerals are connected below to water and earth, and their lowest types are alum, hyacinth, and vitriol, which are very close to earth. Red gold, on the other hand, stands highest among the minerals and approaches the world of the plants. Among plants, moss is the lowest order approaching the mineral kingdom, while the palm tree, which already has a differentiation of sexes, stands between the plant and animal worlds. Among animals, the snail is mentioned as being closest to the plant world and the elephant—being highest in intelligence among the animals—nearest to man. Inasmuch as this hierarchy is based on the degree of intelligence and the development of interior faculties rather than on external similarities, we find that the Ikhwān name the elephant rather than the monkey as the animal closest to man. This is a good example of the difference between the traditional idea of gradation which is based on interior qualities and ontological status and the modern theories of evolution which are based on the physical behavior and the external similarities of creatures.

The whole chain of being, the cosmos and man, the qualities of the Universe and its parts, as well as of man, the prophets and kings, the three kingdoms and the angels—all this is summarized by the Ikhwān in a diagram which conceptualizes their relation with each other. In the diagram of Figure 1 the viewer is faced once more with the unicity of Nature and the interrelatedness of all things from the "highest of

[94] *Jāmi'ah*, I, 379–382.

[95] «واعلم يا اخي بان اول مرتبة الحيوان متصل بآخر مرتبة النبات وآخر مرتبة الحيوان متصل باول مرتبة الانسان كما ان اول المرتبة النباتية متصل بآخر المرتبة المعدنية واول المرتبة المعدنية متصل بالتراب والماء ...»

R., II, 143.

the high" to the "lowest of the low," which is a constant theme of the medieval cosmological sciences.[96]

The chain of being described by the Ikhwān possesses a temporal aspect which has led certain scholars to the view that the authors of the *Rasā'il* believed in the modern theory of evolution.[97] From what we have discussed thus far, however, the divergence of the Ikhwān from modern theories of evolution should be clear. First of all, according to the *Rasā'il* all changes on earth occur as acts of the

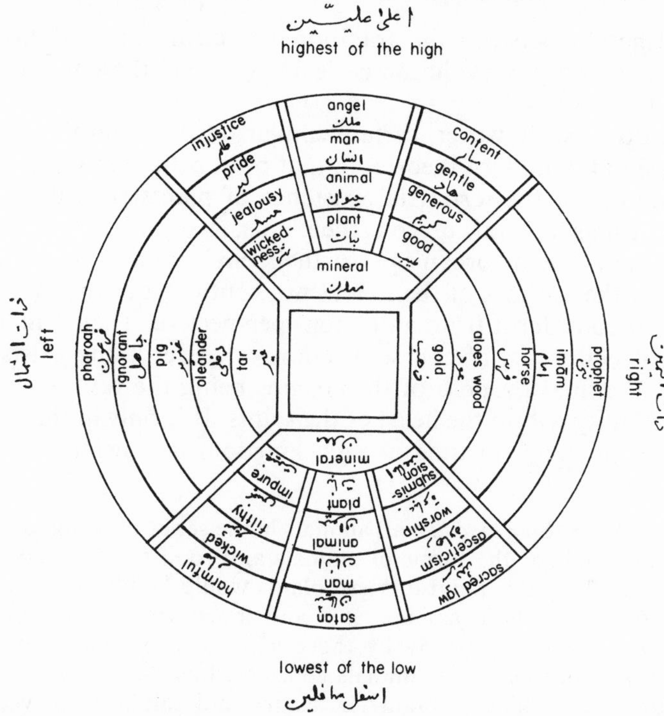

Figure 1. The cosmic hierarchy according to the Ikhwān al-Ṣafā'.

Universal Soul and not by an independent agent acting within bodies here on earth. Secondly, according to the Ikhwān this world is a shadow of another world more real than it, and the "idea" of everything in this world actually exists in the other, so that there is no

[96] *Jāmi'ah*, I, 488.

[97] Dieterici, *Der Darwinismus im X. und XI. Jahrhundert* (Leipzig, 1878). De Boer correctly refutes Dieterici's thesis and asserts that the Ikhwān imply a gradation and not evolution in its modern sense. Tj. de Boer, *History of Philosophy in Islam* (London, 1933), p. 91.

question of a species changing into another, because the "idea" of each species is a form which is beyond change and decay. In the words of the Ikhwān:

> The species and genus are definite and preserved. Their forms are in matter. But the individuals are in perpetual flow; they are neither definite nor preserved. *The reason for the conservation of forms, genus and species, in matter is the fixity of their celestial cause* because their efficient cause is the Universal Soul of the spheres instead of the change and continuous flux of individuals which is due to the variability of their cause.[98]

The distinction between the traditional doctrine of gradation and the modern theory of evolution is clearly stated in these words of the Ikhwān themselves.

There do exist, however, certain similarities between the views of the Ikhwān and modern theories in that both believe that the date of the beginning of the terrestrial existence of plants precedes that of animals, just as minerals precede the plants. Also, the Ikhwān believe in the adaptation of organisms to their environment, much in the manner of the authors of the nineteenth century, but the authors of the *Rasā'il* consider it from a different perspective. Their whole conception of Nature is, of course, teleological. Everything exists for a purpose, the final purpose of the cosmos being the return of multiplicity to Unity within the heart of the saints. It is only in this context that the appearance in time of each kingdom is considered. As the Ikhwān write:

> Plants come before (*taqaddama*) animals in the series of beings and serve them as material for the forms of animals and food for the nutrition of their bodies. From this point of view, plants would be like a mother who eats raw food, digests it, assimilates it and transforms it into pure milk which is absorbed very gently by those who drink it. The plants subsequently present this to the animals considered as their sons . . . Plants occupy an intermediate position—necessary and salutary—between the four elements and the animals. All the parts of the vegetables which the animals consume such as seeds, leaves, fruit, and so on, come from the four elements digested and transformed by the plants . . .[99]

As minerals serve plants and plants animals, so do animals in turn serve man, who therefore comes to this world later than all of them, since each has come after the kingdom upon which it depends.[100]

[98] Quoted in Carra de Vaux, *Les Penseurs de l'Islam* IV, 107 (italics ours).
[99] *R.*, II, 154.
[100] «اعلم يا اخي بأنّ الحيوانات كلّها متقدمة الوجود على الانسان بالزمان.»
R., II, 55. The Ikhwān also subdivide the kingdoms according to the order of creation.

The Ikhwān imply in their writings, without always stating it clearly, that the coming into being of the sublunary region after the heavens, the mineral after the elements, the plants after the minerals, the animals after the plants, and finally, man after the animals, is temporal as well as *in principio*. But since the gradation from the elements to minerals and higher realms is a return toward the heavenly perfections, there is no question of an indefinite gradation of physical forms. Once the origin has been reached again, there is no further step to be taken. In the perfect man, who has realized his Divine Origin, the process has come to an end. Man's "evolution" is therefore inward; God does not create something after man as he created man after the animals, because man, by virtue of being able to return to his origin, fulfills the purpose of the whole of creation. All other orders of beings were created in order that this final stage of reunion might take place. Once the reunion has occurred, there is no metaphysical necessity for another form to be created.

Man is the link between the three kingdoms and the heavens and therefore the channel of grace for the terrestrial environment; the three kingdoms depend upon him, and man in turn has the right to make use of them.[101] In the section of the *Rasā'il* called "Dispute between Man and the Animals" at the end of the treatise on zoology, the members of the animal kingdom complain to the king of the *jinn* for man's cruelty against them. In the trial, none of man's boastings about his own beauty, wit, learning, reason, science, or art can overcome the virtues of the animals. At the end, the only point which justifies the domination of man over the animal kingdom is that among men there are a few who become angels on earth, that "among men there are a few saints and sages who have the natures of cherubim."[102]

In the Universe, where the wisdom of the Creator is to be seen everywhere, every occurrence has its reason and shows the wisdom

---

For example, marine animals are said to precede land animals, while among land animals those with more perfect sexual organisms come after those that lay eggs, which in turn come later than those generated in putrescences. *R.*, II, 155ff.

[101] «فصار الانسان واسطة بين الحيوان وبين عالم الافلاك يفيض عليه مما يفاض عليه، وصار الحيوان خادماً للانسان بحسب حاجته اليه، وصار النبات بين الاركان والحيوان.»

Jāmi'ah, I, 419–420.

[102] Ikhwān, *Dispute between Man and the Animals*, trans. J. Platts, pp. 226–227.

of God, so that each creature possesses those faculties which conform to its needs. With respect to the animals, the Ikhwān write:

> Providential wisdom stipulates that an animal be given no other organs than these. If it were otherwise the animal would be hindered and its safety and continued existence endangered.[103]

"Adaptation to the environment" is not the result of struggles for life or "survival of the fittest," but comes from the wisdom of the Creator, Who has given to each creature what corresponds to its need. In the deepest sense, what separates all these ideas of the Ikhwān from their modern counterparts is that for the Ikhwān the hands of God were not cut off from creation after the beginning of the world—as is the case with the deists. On the contrary, every event here "below" is performed from "above" by the Universal Soul, which is God's agent. Consequently, the purpose of the study of Nature is to see these "vestiges of God"—the *vestigia Dei* as the medieval Latins used to express it—so that, thanks to the analogy existing between the Universe and man, the soul through this knowledge of cosmic realities can come to know itself better and ultimately be able to escape from the earthly prison into which it has fallen. "Thy soul, oh Brother, is one of the pure forms. Use your efforts then to know it. Thou willst succeed probably in saving it from the ocean of matter to raise it from the abyss of the body and deliver it from the prison of Nature."[104]

[103] *R.*, II, 144.

[104] *R.*, II, 17.

CHAPTER 3

The Individual Cosmological Sciences

Astronomy and Astrology

In the Islamic sciences, as in Greek and Latin astronomy where *astrologia* and *astronomia* are often used interchangeably, there is no clear distinction between the words signifying astronomy and astrology; the term *nujūm* can mean one as well as the other. For the Ikhwān, also, the two studies are closely bound together, because not only are the heavenly bodies moving objects whose motions and periods can be studied and measured, but they are also the seats of the various faculties of the Universal Soul, which is the cause of all change in the world of generation and corruption. Astrology, then, must be considered always in the light of the metaphysical principles which underlie the cosmology of the Ikhwān. However, since astronomy and astrology are studied separately today, we shall try as much as possible to separate the science of the constitution and movement of the heavens from the study of both their symbolic and spiritual qualities and their influence on earthly phenomena. The Ikhwān themselves divide the science of *nujūm* into three parts: (1) the science of spheres, stars, their dimensions, movements, and so on (*'ilm al-hai'ah*), (2) the science of astronomical tables (*zīj*), and (3) judicial astrology (*'ilm al-aḥkām*). Our separation of astronomy and astrology, therefore, can perhaps be partially justified by their own views, although general astrology, which includes more than just judicial astrology, also enters into the first category.

In the *Rasā'il* great importance is attached to the study of the heavens, a subject which enters every branch of natural science because of the influence of the heavens upon all sublunar events. Also, the ancient character of the history of astronomy is fully realized and, in fact, this science is considered to have been originally not a purely human form of knowledge, but a science revealed to the prophet Idrīs or Hermes Trismegistus who "journeyed to Saturn" in order to bring to earth the science of the heavens.[1] The study of the heavens has, therefore, an aspect of revealed truth and is of a sacred nature.

It has already been mentioned that the Ikhwān follow the general scheme of the ancient astronomers in placing the earth at the center, followed by the seven planets, Moon, Mercury, Venus, Sun, Mars, Jupiter, and Saturn, then the heaven of the fixed stars and finally the outermost sphere, or the *Muḥīṭ*, which was added by Muslim astronomers to the spheres of Ptolemy to account for the precession of the equinox. They also follow the Ptolemaic system of epicycles in order to explain the retrograde motion and changes in the periods of the planets. In explaining this retrograde motion they write that the body of each planet dominates over a small sphere which is called the "sphere of rotation,"[2] (*falak al-tadwīr*), implying, contrary to the majority of Greek astronomers, that the epicycle is a solid sphere. Such a view of the nature of the heavenly sphere was already held by al-Farghānī, from whom the Ikhwān probably learned it. The cosmos of the Ikhwān is the traditional, finite cosmos beyond which there is "neither void nor plenum."[3] Moreover, they equate the heavens of the fixed stars with the *kursī*, or Pedestal, (Quran II, 255) and the ninth heaven with the *'arsh*, or Throne (Quran IX, 129; LXIX, 17) in order to conform to Quranic cosmology.

According to the Ikhwān, the stars are luminous, spherical bodies —altogether 1029 in number, of which seven are wandering and the rest stationary.[4] The spheres are hollow, transparent, and concentric like the skins of an onion. More precisely, each "sphere" consists of two concentric, hollow spheres with a certain depth, the inner one moving within the outer in such a way that the movements become slower as one approaches the earth.[5] As for the signs of the Zodiac, they are located in the *Muḥīṭ* and are divided into six northern and six southern signs. The Ikhwān follow the regular astrological practice of dividing the signs also into four parts in the following manner:

(1) Aries, Leo, Sagittarius—fire, hot, dry, east.
(2) Taurus, Virgo, Capricornus—earth, cold, dry, south.

[1] «يحكى عن هرمس المثلث بالحكمة وهو ادريس النبي عليه السّلام انه صعد الى فلك زحل و دار معه ثلاثين سنة حتى شاهد جميع احوال الفلك ثم نزل الى الارض فخبر الناس بعلم النجوم. قال الله تعالى: ورفعناه مكاناً علياً.» R., I, 92.

[2] For the general description of the heavens, see *R.*, I, 73ff.

[3] *R.*, III, 24. «لا خلاء ولا ملاء.»

[4] *R.*, I, 73, and *R.*, II, 27.

[5] *R.*, II, 26ff.

(3) Gemini, Libra, Aquarius—air, hot, wet, west.
(4) Cancer, Scorpio, Pisces—water, cold, wet, north.[6]

In the cosmos described by the Ikhwān, the Sun plays a central role. "God has placed the Sun at the center of the Universe just as the capital of a country is placed in its middle and the ruler's palace at the center of the city."[7] Below it stand Venus, Mercury, Moon, the sphere of air, and the earth, and above it there are another five spheres, those of Mars, Jupiter, Saturn, the fixed stars, and the *Muḥīṭ*. The Sun is thus "the heart of the Universe"[8] and "the sign of God in the heavens and earth."[9] It is also the source of light for the whole Universe, light which in the most direct way symbolizes the effusion of Being. Just as the spirit (*rūḥ*) gives life to the heart (*qalb*) of man, so does the Intellect "with the permission of Allah" give life to the Sun and Moon and through them to the whole of the Universe of which they are the first and second, or symbolically the masculine and feminine, principles which, by their wedding, generate all things.[10]

Certain numbers connected with the motion of the heavens played a fundamental role in ancient Babylonian, Hindu, and Egyptian cosmology and religion, as well as among the Pythagoreans. The Ikhwān, for whom numbers are so important, are fully aware of the symbolic significance of many of these numbers, particularly 9, 12, 7,

[6] *R.*, I, 77. The principles of astrology which the Ikhwān describe are the same as those followed by other Muslin astrologers and will be discussed more fully in the chapters on al-Bīrūnī.

[7] *R.*, II, 25.

[8] *Jāmi'ah*, II, 112. "فكان القلب من الانسان بمنزلة الشمس في عالم الافلاك"

In medieval cosmology Mercury is usually placed above the Moon, although it is closer to the Sun than Venus. The reason is that from the outer limit of space to the terrestrial milieu there is a continual "temporal contraction" so that the greater speed of Mercury over Venus justifies the place of Mercury above the sphere of the Moon. For a masterly discussion of this subject, see T. Burckhardt, *Clé spirituelle de l'astrologie musulmane d'après Ibn Arabi* (Paris, Editions Traditionnelles, 1950), p. 12.

[9] *Jāmi'ah*, II, 111.

[10] *Jāmi'ah*, I, 538ff. The motion of the Sun in the middle of the heavens gives the spirit of life (*rūḥ al-ḥayāt*) to the heavens above and below it (*Jāmi'ah*, II, 255). The Ikhwān compare the relation of the world to God with the emanation of light from the Sun (*ibid.*, p. 256). In all this they make use of a universal symbolism which can be found among nearly all people. In expounding further the symbolism of light, they give a commentary of the *āyat al-nūr* (Quran, XXIV, 35) interpreting light (*al-nūr*) as the Universal Intellect, niche (*mishkāt*) as the Universal Soul, glass (*zujājah*) as the prime form (*al-ṣūrat al-ūlā*), a shining star (*kawkabun durrīyun*) as individual form (*al-ṣūrat al-mujarradah*), the blessed olive tree (*shajarah mubārakah zaitūnah*) again as the Universal Soul, and light upon light (*nūrun 'alā nūr*) as the light of the Intellect over the light of the Soul. (*Jāmi'ah*, II, 293–294.)

and 28, which correspond to the number of the spheres, constellations (or divisions of the Zodiac), the planets, and lunar mansions.

The Pythagoreans who think that beings correspond to the nature and properties of numbers know also the perfection of Divine Wisdom which is its origin. In fact, the numbers 7, 9, 12, 28 are the first numbers which are called complete (*kāmil*), odd square, exceeding and perfect respectively. Also the cause of the exclusivity of those numbers comes on the one hand from the fact that $7 = 3+4$; $12 = 3 \times 4$; $28 = 7 \times 4$ and on the other hand $7 + 12 + 9 = 28$. Thus noble beings correspond to noble numbers.[11]

As with other sciences, so in astronomy the purpose of study is "to prepare pure souls and make them desirous of celestial ascent."[12]

Besides the above numbers, whose symbolism is easy to grasp, the Ikhwān give numbers for the thickness (or height) and diameter of the various spheres and the relative sizes of the planets, without specifying clearly either the sources of their knowledge or any possible significance these numbers may have outside of their literal values.

In Table II we give the distances to the various spheres in earth radii instead of in actual miles. Duhem has interpreted the data in such a way that "diameter" actually signifies a "semidiameter," thus making the values given by the Ikhwān closer to those of al-Battānī and al-Farghānī. This table, given by Duhem, is based on the distances mentioned in the *Rasā'il.*[13]

TABLE II. THE PLANETARY DISTANCES ACCORDING TO THE IKHWĀN AL-ṢAFĀ'

Distance	*Corrected (in terms of Earth Radii)*	*Uncorrected*
Sphere of air	16½	16½
To perigee of Moon	34	34
To apogee of Moon and perigee of Mercury	67	67
To apogee of Mercury and perigee of Venus	172	172
To apogee of Venus and perigee of Sun	1 087	2 107
To apogee of Sun and perigee of Mars	1 187	2 307
To apogee of Mars and perigee of Jupiter	8 843	17 619
To apogee of Jupiter and perigee of Saturn	14 370	28 673
To apogee of Saturn	21 975	43 883
External surface of the sphere of fixed stars	33 975	67 883

[11] *R.*, I, 94–95. Like the Pythagoreans, the Ikhwān also relate the motion of the heavens to music. As they say: "If sidereal time were evaluated by the movement of celestial individuals—movement which is proportional and harmonious—the notes which would result from it would resemble those of music." *R.*, I, 151.

[12] *R.*, I, 91ff.

[13] *R.*, II, 44; P. Duhem. *Le Système du monde* (Paris: Hermann, 1906–13), II, 52. The Ikhwān are evidently using the principle also used by the Greeks that there is no wasted space in the cosmos. The size of the cosmos given in the text, however, is larger than most of the other values given during the Middle Ages. Medieval planetary distances were

As for the relative size of the planets, they are given in Table III.[14]

TABLE III. THE RELATIVE SIZE OF PLANETS IN THE *Rasā'il*

Moon	$\frac{1}{28}$ (size of earth)
Mercury	$\frac{1}{28}$
Venus	$\frac{5}{12}$
Sun	$5\frac{2}{5}$
Mars	$1\frac{1}{6}$
Jupiter	$4\frac{5}{6}$
Saturn	$4\frac{1}{2}$

(Fixed stars are all greater than the earth, fifteen having a diameter $4\frac{3}{4}$ as great as that of the earth.)

According to the *Rasā'il*, the movements of the heavens are divided into five categories:

(1) Rotation imposed upon each planet by its sphere of rotation.
(2) Rotation imposed at the center of each sphere of rotation by the sphere carrying it.
(3) Rotation imposed upon the sphere carrying the planet (the deferent) by the principal sphere (the epicycle) of the planet.
(4) Rotation imposed upon fixed stars by their principal sphere.
(5) Rotation around the elements by the enveloping sphere and the whole sky. This last sphere moves from east to west daily with respect to the Northern Hemisphere.[15]

Following al-Farghānī among Muslim astronomers, and especially Ptolemy among the Greeks, whom they always consider their master and whose system of astronomy they follow in detail, the Ikhwān consider the motion of the heavens as being from Orient to Occident, this movement becoming slower and slower as one moves farther from the supreme heaven, which is the unerring sphere of diurnal movement, toward the earth. To this motion is added the precession of the equinox which is the rotation of the fixed stars about the signs of the Zodiac in the period which the Ikhwān consider to be 36,000 years. In fact, they equate the "Great Year" of the Chaldaeans (36,000 years, the time for all the planets to be in conjunction at the spring equinox) with the time of revolution of the orb of the fixed stars found by Hipparchus to be also 36,000 years. The Ikhwān call the end of this cycle,

based in the case of the Sun and the Moon on the determination of Aristarchus and Hipparchus and of the other planets on the principles established by Ptolemy, especially in his *Hypotheses*, and perfected by later Hellenistic astronomers and mathematicians —in particular Proclus in his *Hypotyposis*.

[14] Duhem, *Le Système du monde*, II, 53.

[15] *R.*, I, 73ff; Duhem, II, 125.

that is, the time of the conjunction of the planets at the spring equinox, the "Last Day," or *qiyāmat al-qiyāmah*.[16]

Since all cycles of time—whether they be days, months, or years—are dependent upon the motion of the heavens, the Ikhwān consider the various periods of heavenly movement, especially the 36,000-year period, as being fundamental in determining the cycles of events on earth, whether these be natural or historical. They inform us:

There are some revolutions and conjunctions which are accomplished only once in a long time and others once in a very short time. A very long period is that of the revolution which occurs only once in 36,000 years. The conjunction of the stars at the end of the 36,000 years marks a cycle from the time when the planets have reunited together at the first degree of the sign of the Ram to the time when they come back to this point after the lapse of this time. The tables of Sindhind, [that is, those of the Indians], call this lapse of time a year of the disposition of the world.[17]

After re-emphasizing the dependence of all sublunary events upon the heavens, they continue:

Everything which in this world is produced quickly, lasts a short time, disappearing rapidly [to be reborn new]; and that depends upon a motion of the universal sky which is rapid, of short duration, and returns quickly to its beginning . . .

A movement which is slow, of long duration, which comes back to its principle after a long time, is the movement of the fixed stars around the sphere of the signs, a movement which occurs once in 36,000 years. The apogee and perigee of the planets take part in this movement.

During the lapse of time of this movement, civilization in this world of generation and corruption is transported from one quarter of the earth to another. Continents replace the seas, and seas come to replace solid earth. The mountains change into seas and seas into mountains.

Every 3,000 years the fixed stars, apogees, and nodes of the planets pass from one sign to another after having traversed all the degrees of these signs. Every 9,000 years they pass from one quadrant to another . . . By the effect of their intermediate cause the zeniths of the stars and the incidence of their rays at diverse points of the earth are modified and with them the climate of diverse countries . . .

It is by these primary and intermediate causes that the domination of the world passes from one people to another, that cultures as well as desolation may be transported from one quarter of the earth to another. All these events happen by virtue of the power determining the conjunctions which occur in regulated times and circumstances.[18]

[16] *Jāmi'ah*, I, 321.
[17] *R.*, III, 244; Duhem, II, 216.
[18] *R.*, III, 246–259.

Likewise, with respect to the atmosphere and geological changes, they write:

This is why the diverse regions of the earth are modified. The layers of air are changed above diverse places and countries by which the properties of these layers of air pass from one state to another . . . It is for this reason that cultivated earth becomes desert, and deserts become cultivated earth; steppes become the sea and the sea becomes steppes or mountains.[19]

Since the heavens are the abode of the angels, some of whom are actually aspects or various faculties of the Universal Soul, it is natural that heavenly bodies should be moved by the Soul. According to the Ikhwān, the Universal Soul exercises a special force on all celestial phenomena. This force, which is called the particular soul of each celestial body, becomes the guide for that body and the agent in whose activity it participates. Of the cognitive and active forces of the Soul, it is naturally the active which makes bodies pass from potentiality to actuality and which, for the heavenly bodies, becomes the cause of movement. As to why the heavens move, the Ikhwān explain that the motion occurs so that

the Universal Soul may receive plenitude and prime matter attain perfection; that is the final term of the union of the soul with this substance. It is for this end that rotation of the heavens and the creation of things are produced, in order that the Soul may manifest its plenitude in matter and that matter receiving these forms, this emanation and all this superiority, come to its perfection.[20]

The perfection of movement and beauty characteristic of the heavens exists since "they [the heavens] have obtained this as a gift from the angels, who constitute the armies of the Most High God, and serve Him with faithful service."[21]

As the metaphysical foundations of astrology gradually disappeared, astrology became restricted to the prediction of individual events, and it is in this aspect that it is presently known in the West. In medieval times, especially in the Islamic world, astrology had a greater significance, as we have seen to some extent in our study of astronomy above, and the prediction of mundane events was considered always a secondary and inferior aspect of it. The important part was the cosmological role of astrology, which tried to show the dominance of "heaven" over "earth," the unfolding of all creation

[19] *R.*, II, 80; Duhem, II, 219.

[20] *R.*, I, 73ff; Duhem, II, 169.

[21] Ikhwān, *Dispute between Man and the Animals*, trans. J. Platts, p. 155. According to the *Rasā'il*, angels obey God as the five senses obey man's reason.

from a Unique Principle, and the helplessness and passivity of earthly creatures before the angels, or divine agents, who are symbolized by the planets. The Ikhwān, who use astrology in this second sense in practically every chapter of the *Rasā'il*, are not even sympathetic to the prediction of events. They write quite plainly:

> Astrology does not pretend and has not the right to pretend to an anticipated knowledge of events. Many people believe that astrology proposes to study the science of the unseen (*ghaib*), but they are definitely wrong. What they call the science of the unseen is really the science of indetermination, the gratuitous pretention of anticipating the future without recourse to any symptom or reasoning, be it causal or deductive. *In this sense the unknown is accessible neither to the astrologers, nor diviners, nor prophets, nor sages. It is the work of God only.*[22]

Sometimes they even belittle and admonish those astrologers whose function for the most part is to predict daily events. In the dispute between man and the animals, the parrot accuses the astrologers in strong terms, saying: "Again, as to your mentioning astrologers [you should know that] their doings only pass with the ignorant. Women and children put faith in them. They have no position in the estimation of the Wise."[23] Later, even when they do admit that astrologers can foresee the possibility of the occurrence of certain events, the Ikhwān emphasize that they cannot prevent them since "only prayer can forestall disasters."[24]

The planets in their motion do have a marked influence upon events in the world of generation and corruption, particularly upon the generation of plants, animals, and the human foetus;[25] this influence exists because the planets are agents of God and not because they are separate powers in the Universe. As agents of God they are given the power—thanks to the analogy that exists between the various parts of the cosmos—to cause the generation of a particular set of things as they pass through each part of the Zodiac. Each planet has a spiritual force which emanates throughout the Universe and, as we shall see, plays a major role in the life of the members of the three kingdoms on earth.[26]

[22] *R.*, I, 105–106 (italics ours).
[23] Ikhwān, *Dispute* . . ., p. 195.
[24] *Dispute* . . ., pp. 198–199.
[25] «ونريد ان نذكر تأثيرات الكواكب السبعة فى النطفة وفى الجنين واحدا واحدا وشهرا شهرا الى الكون قياسا على سائر المواليد من الحيوانات والحوادث والكائنات.»
R., II, 353.
[26] *R.*, II, 124–126.

Particularly important is the influence of the Sun, which is to the Universe as the heart is to the body, while the other planets are like the other organs. The Ikhwān describe in detail the effects of the Sun in each sign of the Zodiac. Its effect is related to the health and sickness of animals, conditions of mountains and valleys on the earth, well-being and misfortune of people, and political conditions of kingdoms.

The Moon, as the second principle of the Universe, has the greatest influence after the Sun but mostly confined to feminine cycles occurring on earth. It also influences the ripening of fruits, the growth and decay of plants which give fruit, the generation of mushrooms, the production of certain minerals such as rock salt, and the generation of certain animals like the birds. The Ikhwān also believe that the extent of animal life on earth depends upon the stations of the Moon.[27]

The influence of the seven planets is greatly elaborated and repeated often throughout the *Rasā'il* and even extended to sacred history as well as to the realm of Nature. For example, the Ikhwān, like later Ṣūfīs such as 'Abd al-Karīm al-Jīlī in his *al-Insān al-kāmil*, make each planet correspond to one prophet and to each period of history, which is divided into epochs according to the revelation of the prophetic messages of Adam, Noah, Abraham, Moses, Jesus, and Muḥammad—upon all of whom be peace—the last period lasting until the Day of Judgment when all the planets will come together again, and God will create a new day.[28] This doctrine was to be used later by the Ismā'īlīs, but as it is with most of the cosmological views of the Ikhwān, so in the case of astrology—one cannot identify it exclusively with the theological views of one particular group. Cosmology differs from theology and cannot be integrated into its view. It belongs essentially to the metaphysical, and therefore the most universal, aspect of the tradition, and, like metaphysics, cuts across the theological and "legal" (*shar'ī*) divisions within Islam. It is not surprising, then, to find among later Shī'ite and Sunni authors many of the astrological and astronomical doctrines of the Ikhwān. This is true also of many of the other sciences. If an orthodox author like al-Ghazzālī wrote a treatise against the Bāṭinīs, he was attacking their theological and propaedeutic doctrines but not all of their sciences, so that we find in his cosmology, as in that of Ibn Masarrah and Ibn

[27] *Jāmi'ah*, II, 103. The influences of the Moon as well as the other planets are given in much greater detail. However, since our aim here is to present the principles of the sciences and not the details of the sciences themselves, the discussion is limited to these few examples.

[28] *Jāmi'ah*, II, 145ff.

'Arabī, many points which are to be found either as a seed or as a full-grown idea in the writings of the Ikhwān.

The World of Generation and Corruption

The world of generation and corruption comprises the same domain as the sublunary region; it is always subject to change, to coming into being and passing away. In a very Pythagorean fashion the Ikhwān consider the transition from the heavens to the world of generation and corruption as the change from the odd to the even number, the odd number being the masculine, active, and intellectual principle, and even the feminine, passive, and material one. They also compare heaven to the land of pure forms and hell to the sublunary region which is in a continuous state of generation and corruption.[29] In this region new forms are continually imposed upon matter. "When the new form is more noble it is said that there is generation. Corruption is the name of the operation in the reverse direction."[30]

Forms in the sublunary region are divided into groups of noble and evil qualities as well as into general categories, one being the four elements, which are the universal generating or "material" powers (*ummahāt*), and the other, the three kingdoms—mineral, plant, and animal—which are the generated (*muwalladāt*) powers. Transition between the two occurs by means of two types of exhalation: (1) humid and gaseous (*bukhārāt*), and (2) humid and aqueous (*'uṣārāt*).[31]

The exhalations make transition possible only under the direct influence of the planets which, as agents of the Universal Soul, govern all acts below the heavens, so that one is reminded once again of the unicity of Nature and the dependence of terrestrial changes upon celestial forces.

Meteorology

In ancient and medieval sciences, and going back to Aristotle himself, meteorological phenomena comprise all the natural events which occur between the surface of the earth and the sphere of the Moon. These phenomena include not only weather changes—winds, storms, rain, snow, thunder, lightning, rainbow, and so on, but also shooting stars, meteors, comets, and other events which are now a part of

[29] *R.*, II, 52 [30] *R.*, II, 51.

[31] *R.*, II, 50. In this instance, as well as in the field of meteorology, the Ikhwān follow Aristotle completely, whereas in many other branches of physics and metaphysics they differ from his views, as we have already seen.

astronomy. In this domain Aristotle had a very great influence, not only upon the Peripatetics who followed him closely, but also upon those like the Ikhwān whose conception of Nature differed greatly from that of the Stagirite.

The Ikhwān divide the air in the sublunary region into three divisions:

(1) Higher layer, or ether (*athīr*), which is heated by contact with the lunar circle.
(2) Middle layer (*zamharīr*), which is extremely cold.
(3) Lower layer (*nasīm*), which has moderate temperature.

They describe in detail the influence of seas and other bodies of water upon the humidity of the air and conversely the influence of the atmosphere upon conditions on earth. They also discuss the dependence of the heat in the atmosphere and on earth upon the intensity and angle of incidence of the rays of the Sun. They demonstrate by the extreme differences of temperature between the North Pole and Equator the validity of their assertions.[32] Here, as in many other instances, the Ikhwān appeal to observation of events in Nature and are always certain that the organic and unified conception of the Universe which they present is not just a creation of man's imagination imposed upon the Universe, but that all manifestations of Nature, if studied deeply, display this unicity.

The authors of the *Rasā'il* follow the Arab rather than Greek tradition of the twenty-four winds existing in the atmosphere, of which only four (*al-Ṣabā*, *al-Dabūr*, *al-Janūb*, and *al-Shimāl*) are known to man. These winds, however, perform the same function as in the meteorology of Aristotle. Likewise, the phenomena of rain, snow, and so forth, follow the Peripatetic explanation of the contact of water vapor with cold air under specified conditions.

Thunder, according to the Ikhwān, is caused by hot vapor which instead of falling has risen higher and reached the *zamharīr* region, where it is compressed within the moist vapors of the atmosphere. The dry vapors, however, try to escape, because having been heated they naturally expand. The attempt to escape bursts the moist envelope, setting up a rumbling sound in the air.[3] Lightning, the sister phenomenon of thunder, is caused when the water vapor comes into contact with the uppermost heated region, which is fiery. The Ikhwān interpret the fact that although lightning and thunder occur together we see the lightning first and hear the thunder only later as being

[32] *R.*, II, 57–59. [33] *R.*, II, 66.

due to the fact that light is a spiritual entity while sound is only physical.

The rainbow, which because of its beauty and color symbolism was the focus of so much attention in the works of Muslim and also Christian authors during the Middle Ages and the Renaissance, is explained in the *Rasā'il* as a phenomenon which occurs in the *nasīm* portion of the atmosphere opposite the setting or rising Sun. It is caused by the reflection of sunlight by particles of water present in the air. The top of its curve approaches the *zamharīr* region. It has four colors which from the top downward are red, yellow, green, and blue, corresponding to the four elements. The Ikhwān reject strongly the popular practice of predicting future events by the intensity of the colors of the rainbow.[34]

Somewhat above the region of rainbows, there are found meteors and shooting stars which move in the *zamharīr* region. If the subtle, dry water vapor arising from mountains and dry places reaches the boundary of the *zamharīr* and *athīr*, by contact with the latter it will catch fire and become a glowing body in the shape of a vertical cone. Meteors are not fallen stars from heaven, since only a heavy body falls to earth.[35] As for falling stars, the ones in *zamharīr* do not actually fall; only those in *nasīm* do. Being liquid in nature they move in circular motion, since fluid bodies naturally take the circular shape which offers the least resistance to motion.

Finally there are the comets, which are made of subtle dry and moist exhalations condensed by the influence of Saturn and Mercury until they are transparent like crystal. They originate near the sphere of the Moon and move like planets until they are gradually dissipated.[36] Believing that comets are evil omens, the Ikhwān, by fasting and prayer, ask God for protection from their evil.[37] In their explanation of comets, as well as other meteorological phenomena—which seem naïve to the modern reader—the Ikhwān, like many other medieval scientists, are trying to show how, out of the womb of the four elements and the patriarchal influence of the heavens, the very

[34] *R.*, II, 67–69.

[35] *R.*, II, 70–73. The verse of the Quran, "And verily we have beautified the world's heaven with lamps, and we have made them missiles for the devils" (Quran, LXVII, 5) «لقد زيّنا السماء بمصابيح وجعلناها رجوما للشياطين.» they believe refers to something other than meteors.

[36] *R.*, II, 70–74.

[37] «ويرتدعون عن معصية الله وينقادون الى طاعة الله ويظهرون الدعاء والتضرّع والتوبة والندم والتطوّع بالصوم والصلاة والصدقة.» *R.*, II, 75.

diverse and ever-changing phenomena of the atmosphere can come into being, manifesting multiple appearances while preserving an inner reality which is one and the same for all of them.

Geology and Geography

The spherical earth with a circumference of 2267 *farsakhs* (equivalent to 6,800 miles),[38] upon which the three kingdoms live and die, is, according to the Ikhwān, in its form and movement like an animal,[39] and from the point of view of man's entelechy a prison. Its surface consists of three-quarters sea and one-quarter land upon which there are mountains and deserts. Mountains in time become seas, and seas mountains—as shown by remains of animals in rocks; forests become deserts and deserts lakes.[40] Geological changes occur under the influence of the movements of the heavens, which not only influence the earth directly but also indirectly through the change of weather conditions, which in turn affect the surface conditions of the earth.

The Ikhwān are fully aware of such effects of the atmosphere as the weathering of mountains and rocks which causes the formation of sands. These sands are carried by rivers into oceans where they form deposits on its floor.[41] The Ikhwān also describe the resistance of various types of mountains to weathering processes. Some are granite and hard like those of Tihāmah near Mecca; others are soft like those of Ṭabaristān and Palestine and permit more vegetation and have many caves. In these caves, water in the course of time may purify into quicksilver which is the base of metals. Mountains also have different heights, structures, and so on, which the Ikhwān discuss as part of the physical geology of those regions of Western Asia with which they were familiar.

There are the seven traditional seas[42] and the seven climates (*aqālīm*) which, having a Quranic as well as a pre-Islamic source, are

[38] The *farsakh* in Arabic, or *pārsang* in Persian, is a unit of length equal to three miles.

[39] »وانها أعني الارض حية. متحركة بما عليها. تشبه بجملتها صورة حيوان واحد تام الخلقة عجيب البنية...«

Jāmi'ah, I, 195–196.

[40] The Ikhwān like a number of other medieval Muslim authors such as al-Bīrūnī, easily identified stones bearing animal imprints with fossils and therefore believed in the inundation of present land masses.

[41] *R.*, II, 81–86.

[42] The Ikhwān enumerate them as the Roman Sea (*baḥr al-rūm*), Red Sea (*baḥr al-qalzam*), Indian Sea (*baḥr al-hind*), Sea of Gog and Magog (*baḥr ya'jūj wa ma'jūj*), and Caspian Sea (*baḥr al-jurjān*). *R.*, II, 50.

accepted by nearly all Muslim authors on geography. The quarter of the earth which is land is divided according to Figure 2.[43]

The first zone is 3,000 by 150 *farsakhs*, being the longest and widest, and the seventh is 1,500 by 70 *farsakhs*, the shortest and narrowest. Each climate has its particular conditions, not only physical ones like the amount of heat, light, moisture, and so forth, which are connected to the "body of the Universe," but also "psychic" conditions related to the Universal Soul animating the whole Universe and

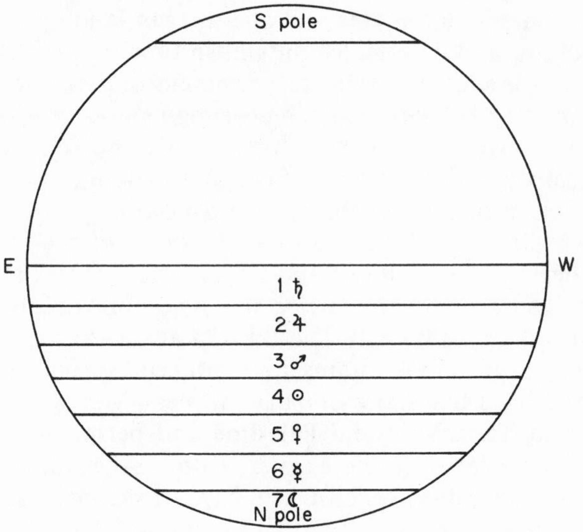

Figure 2. The seven climates and the planets.

symbolized by the planets, each of which—as an agent of God and a faculty of the Universal Soul—governs a climate. Therefore, not only is there a profound ecological relation between the flora, fauna, men, and climatic conditions of a region but also between the aspects of Nature as a combination of subtle and physical parts and the civilizations and religions which rise in those climates. Just as the amount of sunshine influences the color of the skin of the people living in a certain zone, so do these subtle or psychic aspects of Nature influence the soul of the people living in a particular climate. The Ikhwān discuss in great detail the totality of conditions due to physical and subtle influences which modify the bodies and souls of the peoples in

[43] *R.*, I, 116ff.

each region. For example, the fourth climate dominated by the Sun is the one in which most of the great prophets of humanity have arisen.[44] Or the first climate, near the equator, is considered to be the one in which the four elements are best mixed and moisture is so abundant that God chose the clay from this zone out of which to create animals and man.[45]

In their geography, the Ikhwān do not discuss at any length the symbolism of directions which play so great a role among so many Muslim authors, especially the followers of the *Ishrāqī* school. Like the *Ishrāqīs*, however, the Ikhwān do identify Heaven with the East or the place of the rising of the Sun.[46] In their consideration of geography, they combine the physical elements with what one may call "sacred geography," the science which had a major role to play in the construction of sacred cities like Jerusalem and Mecca and in the orientation of the rites of various religions. In their journey toward Unity, they make no effort to separate with any finality the "sacred" and the "profane" or to distinguish between the outer manifestations of Nature and what they consider to be its inner qualities.

The Three Kingdoms

Like all terrestrial beings, the minerals—of which over 900 kinds may be found on earth—come into being as the result of a series of causes both celestial and terrestrial.

> The efficient cause of mineral substances is Nature, which acts with the permission of Allah. Sulphur and Mercury constitute the material cause of these same substances . . . The third, or formal, cause is the revolution of the spheres and the movement of the stars about the four elements. The last cause, the final cause, consists in the utility which these substances offer to man and all the animals.[47]

Nature, therefore, which as a faculty of the Universal Soul is the cause of all activity here on earth, acts directly to bring about the generation of minerals, which are the first constructs that Nature brings forth on earth.[48]

[44] *R.*, I, 112ff. As a matter of fact, most of the prophets and sages of the religions of the world as they exist today do seem to have come from the region considered by the Ikhwān and other medieval geographers as the fourth climate.

[45] In the Islamic Tradition it is generally believed that the clay from which Adam was created came from between Mecca and Ṭā'if.

[46] "This Paradise which God gave Adam to dwell in, is a garden in the East, on the top of a ruby mountain." Ikhwān, *Dispute* . . ., pp. 46–47.

[47] *R.*, II, 78.

[48] *Jāmiʿah*, I, 328. «ان المعادن هى اوّل مفعولات الطبيعة ، التى هى دون فلك القمر.»

The sulphur-mercury theory of the constitution of metals, which lies at the core of Jābirian alchemy, is fully accepted by the Ikhwān. The sulphur, which *is not* "physical sulphur" but a principle, symbolizes the masculine and active principle and mercury the feminine and passive. The relation of these principles to the four elements and four basic tendencies can be summarized as shown in Figure 3.[49]

When these principles are combined in a perfect manner gold is formed, which is the perfect metal because "its spirit, soul, and body

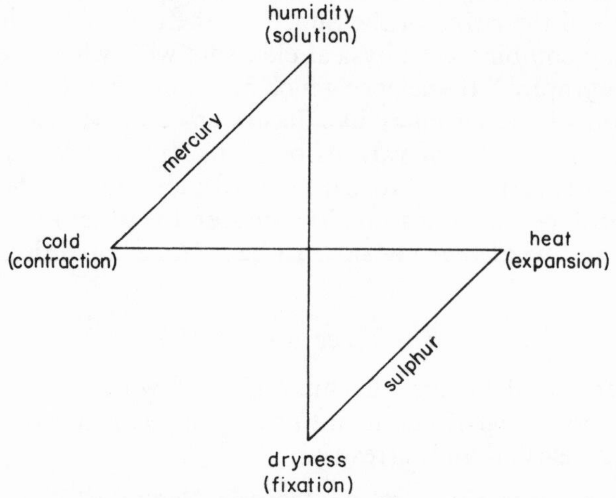

Figure 3. The four natures and the mercury-sulphur theory.

[airy, watery, and earthly elements] are all one.[50] As with man so with minerals, perfection implies the integration of a being into a unified whole. After gold comes silver, which for the Ikhwān, as for the alchemists, is the second most perfect metal. Although the Ikhwān do not speak a great deal about alchemy as such, they not only accept the Jābirian theory of metals and minerals but also the belief in the possibility of the transformation of one metal into another.[51]

As the formal cause of minerals, the heavens are specifically respon-

[49] For a full explanation of this scheme, see T. Burckhardt, "Considérations sur l'alchimie," *Etudes Traditionnelles*, 49:293 (1948).

[50] *R.*, II, 99.

[51] *Jāmi'ah*, I, 326–327. All of the Hermetic sciences, even when not discussed by the Ikhwān, can be considered as a natural consequence of their conception of Nature. A Universe which has a Universal Soul permeating every part of its "body" can easily accept those disciplines which seek either to control or to be aided by the psychic forces present in Nature. The Ikhwān treat magic, talismans, and similar studies in a separate chapter at the end of the treatise where they state that they are all due to the

sible for the many forms of minerals found on earth. There is a specific influence connected with each heavenly body and a general change of influence of the heavens, due to the precession of the equinox. As the Ikhwān have mentioned before, it is the angels (whose symbols are the planets) who keep order in the motion of the heavens and who generate the minerals as well as plants and animals.[52] These heavenly souls, or angels, act upon the elements to generate the beings below the sphere of the Moon, in a manner similar to that in which music acts upon the human soul.[53]

The Ikhwān also explain the intricate concordance which exists between the heavens as the active principle and the qualities and colors which they generate here below:

> There are certain substances which fire cannot melt—like crystal, hyacinth, chrysolite . . . The color, purity, density, of each of these substances are in rapport with the light of the star which lights it constantly, which casts its ray on the region of the earth particularly assigned to this stone, as we have shown in the treatise on plants. In effect, the color of yellow hyacinth, or pure gold, or saffron and other analogous vegetable colors are related to the rays of the Sun cast upon them. Such is the case for all the colors. Each color is related to a moving or fixed star . . . Black corresponds to Saturn, red to Mars, green to Jupiter, blue to Venus, yellow to Sun, white to Moon. That which is variegated with many colors belongs to Mercury.[54]

Minerals, according to the Ikhwān, are not dead objects but have a life of their own. They grow like fruits of trees and have love, desire, hatred, and repulsion just as animals do. They have a hidden perception (*shu'ūr khafiy*) and delicate sense like plants and animals.[55] Minerals exist potentially in the earth and become actualized at the

---

actions of spiritual (here meaning psychic) beings (*af'āl al-rūḥānīyīn*) in various domains of the cosmos (*Jāmi'ah*, II, 389–391). For our purpose it is important only to note that since there is, one might say, "open traffic" between heaven and earth, all questions like miracles, magic, and the like, which in either Aristotelian or modern rationalistic schools are considered as either too absurd to discuss or too difficult to fit into "the system", can be easily placed within the possibilities inherent in the cosmos.

[52] «افعال ملائكة الله الموكلين بحفظ عالمه وادارة افلاكه وتسيير كواكبه وتوليد حيواناته وتربية نبات ارضه وتكوين معادنها.»
R., II, 109.

[53] *R.*, II, 109.

[54] *R.*, II, 92; Duhem, *Le Système du monde*, p. 358. In the qualitative sciences, such as those presented by the Ikhwān, colors have an objective reality which is not secondary or accidental as Galileo and other seventeenth-century physicists understood it.

[55] The *Rasā'il* remind us, however, that the love and hate of the minerals is not known to man but only to God. *R.*, II, 94.

surface. They are grown as are the animals by the inception of the male sperm in the female womb of the earth[56] and participate in the life of Nature which permeates all things.

The final cause of the minerals, in a Universe where everything has a purpose and everything points to a finality, is to be utilized by the superior kingdoms. The minerals, like all beings, are created for the purpose of knowing God. Inasmuch as in the heart of the contemplative saint creation returns once again to its source and fulfills its purpose, all creatures fulfill their entelechy in contributing to this end. The Ikhwān emphasize that the minerals find their finality not so much in serving man considered only as an animal but in helping to keep in this world the few men "who have become angels" and so are a channel of the grace and light of heaven for all terrestrial creatures.

After the discussion on minerals, the authors of the *Rasā'il* turn to the study of plants.

> All bodies which push out of the earth, which need nourishment and which grow, are called plants. There are first the trees whose branches or roots are planted; secondly, plants with seeds whose seed, kernel or stem is planted; and finally herbs of all sorts.[57]

The vast kingdom thus defined forms the subject of the science of botany which is studied because "things which are well made indicate *ipso facto* the existence of the author [God] even if He be hidden and invisible."[58]

Plants, like other beings of this world, have their four causes which bring them into existence. Also, like minerals and animals, their form is visible but their cause of existence hidden.

> Although plants are obvious and visible creations, the cause of their existence is hidden and veiled from the perception of man. It is what the philosophers call "natural forces," what the *Sharī'ah* calls the "angels and troops of Allah appointed for the nurturing of plants, the generation of animals and the composition of minerals," and what we call "partial spirits."[59]

As for the four causes, they are very similar to the case of minerals; here the material cause is the four elements, the efficient cause Nature (or the Universal Soul), the formal cause the set of planetary influ-

[56] *Jāmi'ah*, I, 225. The Ikhwān here continue the tradition of regarding metallurgy as a type of obstetrics, a view which goes back practically to the dawn of man. See M. Eliade, *Forgerons et alchimistes* (Paris, 1956).

[57] *R.*, II, 135.

[58] *R.*, II, 130.

[59] *R.*, II, 130. See R. Levy, *The Social Structure of Islam* (Cambridge University Press, 1957), p. 490, n. 1.

ences, and the final cause the use of plants by animals as food. Considerations here are very similar to those described already with regard to the minerals. The only major difference is that the vegetative soul, which is one of the faculties of Nature, has been added in this kingdom and is the basic reason for the distinction between the two realms. This new faculty of Nature that has come into play in this kingdom has the seven biological functions of attraction, fixation, digestion, repulsion, nutrition, formation and growth.[60] Besides having these functions which distinguish plants from minerals, plants also have the sense of touch which they share in common with the animals. Also unlike minerals, plants cannot be transformed into one another. Each plant has a chyme (*kaimūs*) formed from a particular combination of the elements which always produces a specific type of plant.[61]

With plants as with minerals, there are numerous forms, each with characteristic colors, perfume, flower, and medical properties which are described in great detail. To describe the plants, the Ikhwān divide them into nine basic parts: root, vessel, branch, bough, leaves, color, fruit, shell, and germ. Complete plants, which are the most perfect, possess all of these parts, while the incomplete plants have only a certain number of them. All of the activities of plants are due to the vegetative soul, as has already been mentioned, so that in studying plants man is led once again to see the one force which manifests itself in so many ways. Beyond this lower unity, there is yet another which the Ikhwān describe as the agent behind the scene or as Nature, which, having at one level manifested itself in the mineral world, now under a new guise re-enters the world, this time in the realm of plant life.

Just as the plant kingdom possesses all the properties of the minerals, to which the vegetative soul is added, so animals possess all the faculties of plants to which movement and sensation are added. These additions form the parts of the animal soul which, as another faculty of Nature, comes into play at this level of creation. Animals, standing higher in the chain of being, have a diversity and complexity above that of plants and as a matter of fact become more and more complex as they are generated during later stages of the history of the world. They are classified in several ways, depending on what features are considered. According to the development of animal faculties, they are classified into five categories:

(1) Those having only the sense of touch, like clams.

[60] *R.*, II, 134. [61] *R.*, II, 132.

(2) Grubs which crawl on leaves and have the senses of taste and touch.
(3) Marine animals and those occupying dark places which have the senses of touch, taste, and smell.
(4) Insects and creeping things which have all senses except sight.
(5) Perfect animals having all the five senses.[62]

The Ikhwān also divide the animals according to their process of generation, following Aristotle but with less elaboration:

(1) Animals most complete and perfected which foster their young, conceive them, suckle and educate their children.
(2) Those which do not perform the foregoing functions but which leap the female, lay eggs, and hatch them.
(3) Those which do none of the above but come into being in putrefaction. They do not live a full year but are destroyed easily by changes of heat, cold, and so on.[63]

Finally there is the classification according to habitat:

(1) Animals which occupy the air, consisting of most of the birds and all the insects.
(2) Those of the sea, which includes all animals that swim in water like fishes, crabs, frogs, snails, and the like.
(3) Those that live on land, consisting of quadrupeds, cattle and wild beasts.
(4) Those which dwell on the earth, consisting of worms, and so forth.[64]

In all these discussions the Ikhwān give many details of the organs of various animals, always with the view of showing their purpose in the scheme of the Universe and the wisdom of the Creator. In fact, they state that only God, and not human reason, knows the profound reason for the function and organs of animals which He created as He wished.[65] But there is little doubt in the mind of the Ikhwān that all things, even the strangest of creatures, have been created for a purpose and according to Divine wisdom.

[62] *R.*, II, 157–158.

[63] *R.*, II, 164. In this world, the first category was generated later than the second, and the second later than the third.

[64] *R.*, II, 168–169.

[65] «كلّ ذلك لاسباب وعلل واغراض لا يعلم كنه معرفتها الا الله الذي خلقها وصوّرها كما شاء وكيف شاء.»

R., II, 162.

The four causes of the animals are similar to those of plants and minerals. However, because the animals are higher in the scale of Being, they reflect in a passive sense many qualities and virtues which make the right of men to dominate over them far from obvious. In the section, "Dispute between Man and the Animals," where the Ikhwān describe the animal kingdom always in terms of the spiritual virtues and beauty of design which its members possess, the obvious advantages of man—whether they be physical or mental—are offset one by one by the animals. Even man's assertion that he is superior to animals by virtue of his vertical, erect position is denied by animals who claim that the reason for man's erect position is that God created him weak and without means of acquiring food; therefore, He made him erect in order to enable him to pick fruit off the trees. The superiority of man over the animals is admitted only when the animals realize that among men there are a few who, having become saints and sages, fulfill the purpose of all of existence, including that of the animal kingdom.

CHAPTER 4

The Microcosm and Its Relation to the Universe

The Universe, whose anatomy we have just described, is found once again, in a complete but miniature model, in man considered as the microcosm, in accordance with the Arabic saying: "Man is the symbol of Universal Existence (*al-insān ramz al-wujūd*)." To present this analogy completely would require going into man's social, linguistic, cultural, and—above all—religious organizations, all of which find their counterparts in the Universe. Since, however, our purpose is to delineate the conception of Nature, we limit our consideration of the microcosm first of all to that aspect which relates man to other kingdoms on earth and to the heavens, and secondly to man's role as the termination of the cosmic process and as the point of return of multiplicity to Unity so that he is, in a way, the purpose of the whole Universe.

The body of man belongs to the animal kingdom and possesses much of the beauty and wisdom which the Creator has also placed within the physical frame of other animals. Making use of numerical symbolism, which means, as always, relating multiplicity to principial Unity, the Ikhwān describe the wisdom which God has used in the creation of the frame of man and certain of the animals in the following manner:

2—He has divided the body into two parts, left and right, to correspond to the first number, which is 2.

3—He has divided the constitution of animals into two extremities and a middle, corresponding to the first odd number, 3.

4—Four humours—the first square number.

5—Five senses—the first circular number; also the number of the elements plus the ether.

6—Six powers of motion in the six directions—the first complete number (*tāmm*)[1] and the number of the surfaces of the cube.

[1] They use the word "complete" to describe what is now called "perfect number," that is, a number equal to the sum of its parts.

7—Seven active powers—the first perfect number (*kāmil*) and the number of planets.
8—Eight natures (four simple and four mixed)—the first cubic number and the number of musical notes.
9—Nine levels (*ṭabaqāt*) of the body—the first odd square and the number of heavens.
12—Twelve openings for the senses and limbs—the first "excessive" number (*zā'id*) and the number of signs of the Zodiac.
28—Twenty-eight vertebrae of the backbone—the second complete number, and the number of stations of the Moon.
360—Three hundred and sixty veins—the number of degrees of the circle of signs and the number of days of the year.[2]

If man shares much with the animals in the design of his body, he differs in the important fact that among the creatures only he stands erect. This vertical position symbolizes an ontological and metaphysical ascent and the yearning of man to reach toward the spiritual world. As for man's head being separate from his body, the Ikhwān tell us that it is also due to his striving toward the heavens. Man stands with his head up and feet down, while the plants are just the reverse with their heads dug in the ground and "feet" toward heaven. The animals, which stand between the plants and man, have the neutral position, which is in the horizontal direction.[3] The fundamental difference between man and the animals is not, however, so much in physical characteristics; rather, it resides in the presence of the human soul, which, although a part of the Universal Soul,[4] differs profoundly from that of the animal. Man can be said to stand in the same relation to the animals as the heavens to the sublunary region.[5]

The body of man, from its very inception until its complete formation, is filled with lessons for the keen observer—not only from the point of view of medicine but also from that of acquiring wisdom. Al-Ghazzālī describes perfectly the spirit with which the body of man was studied by the Muslim sages. He tells us:

The science of the structure of the body is called anatomy: it is a great science, but most men are heedless of it. If any study it, it is only for the

[2] *R.*, II, 168–169. The Ikhwān again state the Pythagorean principle that the creatures are made according to the nature of numbers.

„ معنى قول الحكماء الفيثاغوريين انّ الموجودات بحسب طبيعة العدد ... "

In this correlation they use the term "perfect" in a symbolic sense not easily reducible to a mathematical definition. The number 7 plays a central role in Ismā'īlī cosmology (there being seven "original" *imāms* and seven cycles of history). The term excessive (*zā'id*) means that the sum of the divisors of the number is larger than the number itself.

[3] *R.*, II, 155–156.
[4] *R.*, III, 236.
[5] *Jāmi'ah*, I, 419: „ ولمّا كان الانسان هو للحيوان بمنزلة العالم العلوى للعالم السفلى . "

purpose of acquiring skill in medicine, and not for the sake of becoming acquainted with the perfection of the power of God. The knowledge of anatomy is the means by which we become acquainted with the animal life: by means of knowledge of animal life, we may acquire a knowledge of the heart, and the knowledge of the heart is a key to the knowledge of God.[6]

It is in the same spirit that the Ikhwān tell us that God has placed everything that is in the Universe in the microcosm. Man cannot know all that is in the Universe by going around and studying it because life is too short and the world too large; only by studying himself can he come to the knowledge of all things which already exist within him.[7]

The human body, in its embryonic growth, traverses the other kingdoms of Nature. During the 240 days, which is the "natural duration" of the inception of human beings from the time of the union of the parents until the moment of birth, the first period of four months is under the influence of the vegetative soul. During the fifth month the organs of the foetus begin to form although the foetus still remains in the middle of the embryo sac. At this time the animal soul becomes powerful and dominates the child until the date of birth. During each period the foetus is under the influence of a particular planet which, as the agent of the Universal Soul, gives form to the foetus and directs its growth just as the generation and growth of all other things in this world depend upon the Universal Soul. The case of the animals, in fact, does not differ greatly from that of the generation of the members of the other kingdoms.[8]

Once the body is born and begins to grow, it functions like a kingdom or a city, where the brain acts as the king to whom all other

[6] Al-Ghazzālī, *Alchemy of Happiness* (Albany, N.Y., 1873), pp. 38–39. Like the Ikhwān, al-Ghazzālī, compares the body to the Universe. "Our intention," he writes, "has been to show you that man is a great world, and that you might know what a multitude of services his body has to minister to him so that you might realize while in your enjoyment, in walking, in sleeping or at rest in your world, that by God's appointment, these numerous servants in your employ never suffer their functions to cease for a minute" (*ibid.*, p. 37). One sees how close is the spirit of the Ikhwān in studying Nature to that of al-Ghazzālī, who is among the greatest Sunni theologians as well as one of the most famous Ṣūfī masters.

[7] «ان العالم واسع كبير وليس في طاقة الانسان ان يدور في العالم حتى يشاهده كله لقصر عمره وطول عمران العالم فرأى من الحكمة ان يخلق لها عالماً صغيراً مختصراً من العالم الكبير وصوّر في العالم الصغير جميع ما في العالم الكبير.»

R., III, 9.

[8] *R.*, II, 353ff.

organs are subservient.[9] But it is the heart that is the center of the body as it is symbolically the center of man's being, and his most noble organ.[10] Not only in the process of spiritual realization is the heart central, but in the physiological process of breathing it also plays a major role. The air enters through the throat into the lungs where it is purified; then it enters the heart to carry away its heat. From the heart it penetrates into the pulsative arteries and reaches all parts of the body. The air on its return journey comes once again to the heart, from which it goes into the lungs and from there to the throat, carrying with it the heat of the body. Among most Muslim authors the heart is considered not only to be the central organ in the basic life-giving activity of breathing but also the seat of intelligence because, like intelligence, it is immediate and central and is therefore closer to sense experience and the rhythms of life (which the heart governs) than the rational faculty associated with the brain which acts in an indirect manner.

As for the body being like a city, the Ikhwān go to great lengths to develop the analogy in conjunction with, and as an aid to, the understanding of its analogy with the Universe. They tell us:

> Know then and may God give thee aid, that the body of man was constructed by the Creator like a city. Its anatomical elements resemble stones, bricks, trunks of trees, and metals which enter in the construction of the city. The body is composed of different parts and consists of several biological systems like the quarters of a city and its buildings. The members and organs are connected by diverse joints like the boulevards with respect to the quarters.[11]

Returning to numerical symbolism, they explain further:

> The body is composed of nine anatomical elements: the bone, brain, nerves, veins, blood, flesh, skin, nails, and hair . . .; of ten stages: the head, neck, chest, belly, abdomen, thoracic cavity, the pelvic girdle, the two

[9] *R.*, II, 162.

[10] «ان القلب في الجسد مصوّر على صورة الانسان ولذلك صار افضل الاعضاء التي في اجسام الحيوان.»

R., III, 118.

[11] *R.*, II, 320. To show how close they are in these considerations to what is considered by many as an authoritative Islamic viewpoint, we may once again quote al-Ghazzālī, who in practically the same words writes: "Know, Oh Student of Wisdom; that the body, which is the kingdom of the heart, resembles a great city" (*Alchemy of Happiness*, p. 19). The study of the conception of Nature of the Ikhwān is not the study of a peripheral "eclecticism" but of something that played an influential role in the formulation of the dominant cosmologies of later centuries.

thighs, the two legs, and the two feet; of 249 bones connected by 750 tendons distorted like cords.[12]

There are, moreover, eleven treasures in the body: these are the brain, spinal cord, lungs, heart, liver, spleen, gall-bladder, stomach, intestines, kidneys, and sexual organs—each filled with different substances. The inhabitants of this city—that is, the soul and its faculties—can circulate in 360 passages and have 390 rivulets to water their city. The city is bordered by walls having twelve sewers (the openings of the body) in order to evacuate the waste.

As for the inhabitants of this city, the Ikhwān tells us that the perfect construction of this city is performed by the collaboration of seven artisans which are the seven forces of the vegetative soul, that is, attraction, sustenance, digestion, repulsion, nutrition, growth, and formation. The policing in the city is assured, thanks to five agents: hearing, vision, smell, taste, and touch. Three tribes occupy it in an invisible manner and resemble in their activities the angels, men, and jinns. Their actions comprise the rational (*nāṭiqah*), animal, and vegetative souls. The tribes in question obey a unique Chief, that is, the intellect within man, a sole King capable of knowing, holding, and deciding the details of their problems. God ordained them to prostrate before the King in saying in the Quran (XXXVIII, 74–75): "The angels fell down prostrate, everyone saving Iblīs; he was scornful . . ."[13] Man himself is not to be identified with the city but rather with one of the inhabitants for he is the dweller in the house of the body.

Having expanded the horizon of the reader to the vision of a city, the Ikhwān now enlarge the scope of their analogy to include the whole of the Universe, painting a picture of great beauty in which the cosmic aspect of man and his correspondence with the Universe is delineated. The human soul, they inform us, runs through the whole body as the jinn, men, daemons, and angels run throughout the Universe. To the nine heavens there correspond the nine substances of the body: bone, brain, flesh, veins, blood, nerve, skin, hair, and nails, lying one above the other like the heavens; and to the twelve signs of the Zodiac the twelve openings of the body: the two eyes, nostrils, ears, nipples of the breast, mouth, navel, and channels of excretion. The seven planets, whose influence governs the sublunary region, correspond to the seven powers of the body: attraction, sensation, digestion, repulsion, nutrition, sleep and imagination, and the seven spiritual powers: the five senses, the power of speech, and

[12] *R.*, II, 320–321.

[13] *R.*, II, 321–322.

the intellectual faculty. The five senses correspond to the five moving planets, the power of speech to the Moon, and the intellectual faculty to the Sun, which illuminates all things. Also as the Moon receives its light from the Sun and casts it over the twenty-eight mansions, so does the power of speech receive its power from the intellectual faculty and transmit it through the twenty-eight letters of the (Arabic) alphabet.

Even the ailments of the body have their cosmic correspondence. A physical ailment, which is the weakening or the lack of functioning of some organ or parts that are channels of disposal of the wastes of the human body, is like the eclipse of a heavenly body. The following correspondence is established between the ailment of various parts of the body, and the planets:

Eyes—Jupiter
Ears—Mercury
Nostrils and nipples of breast—Venus
Channels of excretion—Saturn
Mouth—Sun
Navel—Moon[14]

Unlike rationalistic explanations, the symbolic and analogical language used to expound the inner relationships of Nature is not limited within the boundary of "either-or" propositions. The Ikhwān, having compared the body to the heavens, proceed to compare it to the sublunary region without contradicting their previous analogy; they present, rather, another aspect of the interrelation of all things with one another. Compared in this way, the four parts comprising the body (head, chest, belly, belly to foot) correspond to the four elements. As exhalations leave the earth so do various liquids, such as phlegm and saliva, leave the various openings of the body.

The body itself is like the earth, the bones like mountains, the brain like mines, the belly like the sea, the intestine like rivers, the nerves like brooks, the flesh like dust and mud. The hair on the body is like plants, the places where hair grows like fertile land and where there is no growth like saline soil. From its face to its feet, the body is like a populated state, its back like desolate regions, its front like the east, back the west, right the south, left the north. Its breath is like the wind, words like thunder, sounds like thunderbolts. Its laughter is like the light of noon, its tears like rain, its sadness like the darkness of night, and its sleep is like death as its awakening is like life. The days of its childhood are like spring, youth like summer, maturity like autumn, and old age like winter. Its motions and acts are like

[14] *R.*, III, 9–12.

motions of stars and their rotation. Its birth and presence are like the rising of the stars and its death and absence like their setting . . .[15]

Not only the individual microcosm but man's society, too, bears analogy to the cosmos where the Sun reigns as king.

The only relation of Mars to the Sun is like that of the head of the army to the king; that of Mercury to the Sun like that of the secretaries and ministers to the king; that of Jupiter like that of judges and learned men; that of Saturn like that of treasures and lawyers; that of Venus like that of members of the harem and singers; that of the Moon like that of rebels to the king who first obey him only to repudiate him and set up their own claim later, as the Moon gets its light from the Sun at the beginning of the month when opposite it and then imitates its light and becomes like it in appearance. Also the condition of the Moon resembles that of the planets and animals in this world in that the Moon begins to increase in light from the beginning of the month and reaches its perfection in the middle, then begins to decrease, dwindle away and disappear toward the end of the month. So it is with the people of this world who begin at first to increase and continue to increase until perfection and completion. They then begin to sink and diminish until they dwindle away and are annihilated.[16]

Through his five exterior senses man receives impressions which first reach the *sensus communis* and from there reach the five interior faculties, which are: imagination (*mutakhayyilah*), thought (*mufakkirah*), memory (*ḥāfiẓah*), speech (*nāṭiqah*), and production (*ṣāni'ah*).[17] The faculty of imagination, which is in front of the brain, receives the effects from the *sensus communis* which reach the brain through the "cobweb" of the nervous system. From there the sense impressions (*maḥsūsāt*) are transmitted to the faculty of thought at the center of the brain where the information is measured and evaluated and then stored in the memory for the time that it is needed.

The soul of man, however, does not gain certainty and knowledge of things through these sense impressions, but only from the Intellect.[18] In fact, the soul—as Plato asserts in the *Meno*—already possesses all knowledge in itself potentially.[19] It only needs to

[15] *R.*, III, 12–13. The "poetic" quality of this and many similar passages, reminds the reader that just as art in medieval times was a science (*ars sine scientia nihil*) so was science an art, and, like art, overlooked certain exterior appearances of things in order to bring out their inner reality.

[16] *R.*, III, 13–14.

[17] *R.*, II, 342ff.

[18] «النفس لا تنظر ذاتها الّا بنور العقل ولا تعرف حقائق الموجودات الّا بالنظر الى العقل.»
R., II, 351.

[19] «ان العلوم كلها فى النفس بالقوّة فاذا فكّرت فى ذاتها وعرفتها صارت العلوم كلها فيها بالفعل.»
R., II, 352.

recollect this knowledge, and the impression from the senses can do no more than to help in this recollection. Man's purpose on earth, in fact, is to recollect first of all where he came from, and so on this earthly journey prepare by the purification of his being for "the return to Allah."[20] The Ikhwān take the disciple from the heavens to earth to remind him that he should prepare to return once again to his original abode in Heaven. They describe the unicity of the vast domain of Nature so that by its study and contemplation the disciple can come to integrate and unify himself, and thereby to serve his final purpose on earth, which is the preparation for the journey to Heaven and even beyond all formal worlds to the Divine Presence. In a passage which is quite vivid in its symbolism and effective in its language, the Ikhwān compare the movement of the heavens with one of the central Muslim rites, the pilgrimage to the *Ka'bah* and its circumambulation, which symbolizes the reintegration of man in his Divine Prototype. The cosmos thus participates in the sacred rites of Islam, illustrating on the one hand that everything in the Universe is Muslim, that is, surrendered to the Divine Will, and on the other that the whole Universe participates with man in his process of spiritual realization.

They write:

> The earth which is found at the center of the world resembles the *Ka'bah* which is located at the center of the sacred sanctuary. The revolution of the outermost sphere (*Muḥīṭ*) and the other Celestial Spheres around the four elements resembles the rotation of the pilgrims around the *Ka'bah*.
>
> The double movement of apogee and perigee of the stars resembles the double journey of the pilgrims who approach and recede from Mecca in their going and returning. Each pilgrim carries with him his business, money, masterpieces, gifts, and rings before encountering on the sacred ground pilgrims coming from all the nations and belonging to all sects and all doctrines. The pilgrims make intimate contact among themselves and exchange during their stay merchandise and ideas. Once the rite of pilgrimage is accomplished, each returns to his country provided with the pardon and the satisfaction of Allah.
>
> Likewise, oh Brother, is the propagation by effusion of the forces of the superior beings from the outermost sphere to the center of the earth. Their union and provisional stay in matter of particular bodies gives rise to exchange among individuals belonging to the realm of generation and corruption—that is, minerals, plants and animals. Their enthusiastic return, once the end of their journey is reached, toward their point of departure resembles term by term the stages of human pilgrimage to

[20] *R.*, II, 352ff.

Mecca. The particular souls who regain—in passing beyond the outermost sphere—their original source, return happily to the world of Eternity.

Man should thus meditate on his original home and awaken from his ignorant sleep, and desire fervently to return to his celestial abode announcing finally *Labbaika Labbaika*, at Thy orders, to the call of God, "But oh! thou soul at peace! Return unto thy Lord content in His good pleasure!"[21]

And so multiplicity returns again to Unity, integrating in this process the whole of Nature and bringing everything to the Source from which nothing really ever departs.

21 « يَا أَيَّتُهَا النَّفْسُ الْمُطْمَئِنَّةُ ، اِرْجِعِي إِلَى رَبِّكِ رَاضِيَةً مَرْضِيَّةً ».

Quran, LXXXIX, 26–27; *R.*, II, 118–119.

The heavens revolve day and night
Like a potter's wheel.
And every moment the Master's wisdom,
Creates a new vessel. For all that exists
Comes from one hand, one workshop.

Maḥmūd Shabistarī—*Gulshan-i rāz*

PART II

Al-Bīrūnī

CHAPTER 5

The Life, Works, and Significance of al-Bīrūnī

A comprehensive study of the cosmological doctrines of Abū Raiḥān Muḥammad ibn Aḥmad al-Bīrūnī,[1] undoubtedly one of the most learned of Muslim scholars and scientists, is a doubly difficult task because, on the one hand, in those of his works which are still in existence no attempt is made to deal with this subject thoroughly and systematically, and on the other, the philosophical works which he has written, in which he probably treated this subject more fully, are no longer extant.[2] In order to discover the conception which underlies his many studies of the manifestations of Nature it is necessary to assemble small bits from his works where he almost "accidentally" gives the reader a glimpse of some of the aspects of his conception of Nature. Yet, until some of his philosophical writings, like the *Kitāb al-shāmil*, or *The Book of General Knowledge*, are found—an event which, at the present at least, seems unfortunately quite unlikely—there is little choice except to collect in a mosaic the picture of the Universe in which al-Bīrūnī lived and thought.

Abū Raiḥān al-Bīrūnī[3] was born outside (*bīrūn*) of the city of

[1] Much has been written on the pronunciation of al-Bīrūnī's name, whether it is Bairūnī, Berūnī, or Bīrūnī. The choice of Bīrūnī seems most plausible, however, as shown by the arguments presented in the *Al-Biruni Commemoration Volume* (Calcutta, 1951) and 'Alī Akbar Dehkhodā, *Sharḥ-i ḥāl-i nābighih-i shahīr-i Īrān . . . Bīrūnī* (Tehran, 1324 [1945]). Also, we have used the Arabic article "al" because although he was a Persian he wrote almost always in Arabic and referred to himself and was known as al-Bīrūnī throughout most centuries of Islamic history. In Persia he is referred to simply as Bīrūnī.

[2] For a discussion of the lost philosophical works of al-Bīrūnī, see Dhabīḥallāh Ṣafā, "Barkhī az naẓarhā-yi falsafī-yi Abū Raiḥān," *Indo-Iranica*, 5:6 (1952).

[3] For the biography of al-Bīrūnī, see Dehkhodā, *Sharḥ-i ḥāl-i nābighih-i shahīr-ī Īrān . . .*, pp. 1–21, and E. C. Sachau's Preface to his translation of al-Bīrūnī's *Fī taḥqīq mā li'l-hind*, hereafter cited as *Alberuni's India* (London: Kegan Paul, 1910), vol. 1. Accounts of al-Bīrūnī appear also in most of the traditional sources such as the *Tatimmah ṣiwān al-ḥikmah*, pp. 62–64; *'Uyūn al-anbā'* of Ibn Abī Uṣaibi'ah (Cairo, 1299 [1881]), II, 20–21; *Chahār maqālah* of Niẓāmī 'Arūḍī (Tehran, 1334 [1955]), pp. 46–120; and the *Kashf al-ẓunūn* of Ḥājjī Khalīfah. As a result of the celebration of the thousandth anniversary of the birth of al-Bīrūnī in 1973, numerous works concerning him and his ideas appeared throughout the world. The most important are mentioned in the supplementary bibliography. See also S. H. Nasr, *al-Bīrūnī, An Annotated Bibliography* (Tehran, 1973).

Khwārazm—the modern Khiva and ancient Chorasmia—in the year 362/973, in the region which was to produce some of the greatest scholars and sages of Islam. He showed an aptitude for the sciences early in life and is said to have studied under Abū Naṣr al-Manṣūr, the astronomer and mathematician who wrote a commentary on the *Spherics* of Menelaus and who himself had been a student of Abu'l-Wafā'.[4] The early part of his life was spent under the reign of the Ma'mūnīds of Khwārazm, called also the Khwārazmīyah, who were originally subordinate to the Sāmānīds but later became almost independent. Al-Bīrūnī traveled through other regions of Persia, spending from 388/998 to 403/1012 in Jurjān at the court of Shams al-Ma'ālī Qābūs ibn Wushmgīr. It was during this period in the year 390/1000 that he wrote the famous *al-Āthār al-bāqiyah.*

The rising power of the Turks in Central Asia culminated during the reign of Maḥmūd of Ghazna in the destruction of most of the small Persian kingdoms of the region. In 408/1017 Maḥmūd captured Khwārazm and the next year took Abū Raiḥān, who had been his political enemy, to Ghazna. As court astronomer and astrologer, al-Bīrūnī accompanied Maḥmūd on his many campaigns, including the celebrated invasion of India which provided al-Bīrūnī with the opportunity to study the diverse manifestations of Hinduism. In 422/1031, back in Ghazna, he composed what is perhaps his most famous work, *India,* as well as the *Kitāb al-tafhīm.*

Maḥmūd died in Ghazna in 421/1030. A feud followed among his sons, resulting in the victory of Mas'ūd, who was to become a great patron of al-Bīrūnī and to whom the major astronomical opus, *al-Qānūn al-mas'ūdī,* was dedicated in the same year that Mas'ūd came to power. Al-Bīrūnī lived the rest of his days in Ghazna, continuing to write and study until the very end of his life around 442/1051.[5]

The long life of al-Bīrūnī, which saw so much political turmoil and change in the outward conditions of life in Central Asia and Persia, also witnessed considerable change in his interests. Attracted early to mathematics and astronomy, in which he became one of the greatest authorities in the annals of the Muslim sciences, his attention turned later toward chronology and history and finally, during the latter part of his life, to optics,[6] medicine, mineralogy, and pharmacology as

[4] S. H. Barani, "al-Bīrūnī's scientific achievements," *Indo-Iranica,* 5:39 (1952).

[5] There is still some uncertainty as to the date of al-Bīrūnī's death. The recent research of Barani and Dehkhodā has shown that the date of his death is most likely 442/1051 or 443/1052; while Dh. Ṣafā believes it to be 440/1048.

[6] He wrote a work on optics called *Lama'āt* which was later used in the *Jāma-yi Bahādur Khānī.* Barani, "al-Bīrūnī's scientific achievements," p. 39.

shown in his *Kitāb al-ṣaidanah* (or *ṣaidalah*).[7] Throughout these changes, his interest in religion and cult remained strong; his quotations from the *Bhagavad-Gītā*, no less than his description of the religious feasts of the religions of Western Asia, give evidence of his intense interest and understanding of religion. His work on comparative religion remains among his most important contributions.[8]

Although practically nothing has remained of his philosophical works, it is known that al-Bīrūnī had studied philosophy deeply and was well versed in it, and was especially interested in the anti-Aristotelian philosophy of such philosophers as Muḥammad ibn Zakariyyā' al-Rāzī. Al-Bīrūnī spent many years in search of Rāzī's *Fī 'ilm al-ilāhī*, and other philosophical works, and yet wrote a treatise condemning Rāzī's errors.[9] He also studied, as much as it was possible at that time, the Vedanta and other texts of Hinduism which, if not philosophy in a modern or even Aristotelian sense, are certainly among the purest forms of wisdom. The attitude of Abū Raiḥān toward Greek philosophy in its Aristotelian vein is far from friendly, however.

Besides his major works that have remained extant—such as *al-Āthār al-bāqiyah*, *India*, *Kitāb al-tafhīm*, *Kitāb al-jamāhir fī ma'rifat al-jawāhir*, *al-Qānūn al-mas'ūdī*, the recently published *Kitāb al-ṣaidanah* and *Kitāb taḥdīd nihāyāt al-amākin*, al-Bīrūnī wrote a large number of smaller treatises dealing mostly with astronomy and geography but also with most other subjects of learning including philosophy. His works on philosophy, such as *Kitāb al-shāmil fi'l-mawjūdāt al-maḥsūsah wa'l-ma'qūlah*, *Kitāb fi'l-tawassuṭ bain Arisṭūṭālīs wa Jālīnūs fi'l-muḥarrik al-awwal*, *Riyāḍat al-fikr wa'l-'aql*, *Maqālah fi'l-baḥth 'an al-āthār al-'ulwīyah* and *Maqālah fī ṣifāt asbāb al-sukhūnat al-mawjūdah fi'l-'ālam wa ikhtilāf fuṣūl al-sanah*,[10] seem to be lost along with his many translations of such works as Euclid's

[7] "Al-Bīrūnī hat, wie so viele grosse muslimische Gelehrte, sehr mannigfaltige Studien betrieben, unter anderen auch Medizin und Philosophie in denen beiden er sich späterhin literarisch nicht betätigt hat." Al-Bīrūnī, *Das Vorwort zur Drogenkunde der Beruni*, ed. and trans. M. Meyerhof (Berlin, 1932), p. 4.

[8] See A. Jeffrey, "Al-Biruni's contribution to comparative religion," *Al-Biruni Commemoration Volume*, pp. 126–160.

[9] In his treatise, *Fī fihrist kutub Muḥammad ibn Zakariyyā' al-Rāzī* (ed. P. Kraus under the title *Epître de Beruni contenant le répertoire des ouvrages de Muhammad ibn Zakariya al-Razi*, Paris, 1936), al Bīrūnī praises al-Rāzī greatly and shows much respect for him (p. 1) but considers as "nonsense" his ideas drawn from Mani's *Sifr al-asrār* and his mixing Manichaeism and Islam (p. 4). See also Dh. Ṣafā, "Barkhī az naẓarhā-yi falsafī-yi Abū Raiḥān . . .," *Indo-Iranica* 5:6 (1952); and S. H. Nasr, "Al-Bīrūnī as philosopher," *Hamdard Institute* (Karachi, 1973).

[10] See Ṣafā, *ibid*., pp. 6–7.

Elements and Ptolemy's *Almagest* into Sanskrit.[11] His translation of the *Yoga sūtras of Patañjali* from Sanskrit, also assumed lost, was found sometime ago in Istanbul.[12] He also wrote a few literary works such as the story *Qāsim al-surūr wa 'ayn al-ḥayāt*, and *Urmuzdyār wa mihryār*.[13] Al-Bīrūnī, in his *Fī fihrist kutub Muḥammad ibn Zakariyyā' al-Rāzī*, gives a list of 113 of his own works plus 25 others written by Abū Naṣr al-Mansūr ibn 'Alī ibn al-'Irāq, Abū Sahl 'Īsā ibn Yaḥyā al-Masīḥī, and Abū 'Alī al-Ḥasan ibn 'Alī al-Jīlī under his own direction. Ḥājjī Khalīfah, in his *Kashf al-ẓunūn*, mentions fifteen other works not mentioned in the *Fihrist* which al-Bīrūnī had written fourteen years before his death. Furthermore, seven other manuscripts have been found which are not mentioned in either work. If one includes Yāqūt's listing, which mentions translations from the Sanskrit and works written by others and attributed to al-Bīrūnī, the total comes to 180.[14]

The great bulk of the writings of al-Bīrūnī are in Arabic and a few in Persian, although his mother tongue was neither one nor the other, but Khwārazmī. He had a particular love for Arabic, whose value as a universal language he fully realized. He tells us:

> Les sciences de toutes les régions du monde ont été traduites dans la langue des arabes, se sont embellies, ont pénétré les coeurs, et la beauté de la langue a circulé dans les veines et les artères . . . Jugeant par moi-même: je fus éduqué dans une langue dont on peut dire que, si l'on voulait s'en servir pour exprimer les sciences, ce serait aussi étrange qu'un chameau sur le toit ou une girafe dans le harnais . . .[15]

[11] Ziauddin Ahmad, "Al-Biruni, his life and his works," *Islamic Culture*, 5:348 (1931).

[12] The title of the translation is *Kitāb batanjal al-hindī fi'l-khilāṣ min al-amthāl*, MS. Köpr. 1589. See also L. Massignon, "Al-Beruni et la valeur internationale de la science arabe," in *Al-Biruni Commemoration Volume*, p. 218. This manuscript, which was found by Massignon, was studied by J. W. Hauer; see his "Das neugefundene arabische Manuskript von al-Bīrūnis übersetzung des Pātañjala: Ein vorläufiger Bericht," *Orientalistische Literaturzeitung* (1930), pp. 33, 273–282. Its text after being studied twice by H. Ritter in *Le Livre du millénaire d'Avicenne* (Tehran, 1953, II, 134–148), and *al-Muntaqā min dirāsāt al-mustashriqīn* (Cairo, 1955, I, 59–72), was finally published by him in "Al-Bīrūnī's Übersetzung des Yoga-Sūtra des Patañjali," *Oriens*, 9:165–200 (1956).

[13] S. H. Barani, "Avicenna and al-Biruni," in *Avicenna Commemoration Volume* (Calcutta, 1956), p. 12.

[14] For a detailed bibliographical study of al-Bīrūnī, see D. J. Boilot, "L'œuvre d'al-Beruni. Essai bibliographique," *Institut Dominicain d'Etudes Orientales du Caire, Mélanges*, 2:161–256 (1955). See also Nasr, *op. cit.* The importance of al-Bīrūnī's treatise *Maqālīd 'ilm al-hay'ah*, which is the first work in the history of mathematics on spherical trigonometry and which was discovered only recently, should also be pointed out. See A. Qorbānī, *Bīrūnī-nāmah* (Tehran, 1353 [1974]).

[15] M. Meyerhof. "Etudes de pharmacologie arabe tirées de manuscrits inédits," *Bulletin de l'Institut d'Egypte*, 22:144–145 (1939–40).

Al-Bīrūnī wrote one of the masterpieces of medieval science, *Kitāb al-tafhīm*, apparently in both Arabic and Persian, demonstrating how conversant he was with both tongues. The *Kitāb al-tafhīm* is without doubt the most important of the early works on science in Persian and serves as a rich source for Persian prose and lexicography as well as for the knowledge of the *Quadrivium* whose subjects it covers in a masterly fashion.[16]

In addition to personal encounters with numerous Muslim, Christian, and Hindu scholars and sages of his time, al-Bīrūnī also had access to many ancient texts of the Greek, Babylonian, Manichaean, and Zoroastrian sciences. In fact, a work like *al-Qānūn al-mas'ūdī* is not only a compendium of Muslim astronomy but a source for much of ancient science, Chaldaean as well as Greek, whose original texts have been lost.[17] Besides having had a thorough knowledge of such astronomical-mathematical texts as the *Almagest*, *Elements*, various *Sinddhānta* and other Hindu works, al-Bīrūnī was also well acquainted with a remarkable number of writings dealing with "natural philosophy" and history. The sources referred to in the *Kitāb al-jamāhir fī ma'rifat al-jawāhir*, the most complete Islamic text on mineralogy, include Muslim scientists like al-Kindī, al-Jāḥiẓ, Muḥammad ibn Zakariyyā' al-Rāzī, Jābir ibn Ḥayyān, literary figures and historians and geographers like Naṣr ibn Ya'qūb al-Dīnawarī, Aḥmad ibn 'Alī, Abu'l-'Abbās al-'Ummānī, and Greek authors such as Aristotle, Archimedes, Apollonius of Tyana, Dioscorides, Plutarch, Ptolemy, Galen, Bolos Democritus, Plato, Heraclides, and Diogenes. He also quotes Arabic poetry—both Islamic and pre-Islamic—as well as Persian, Indian, Syriac, and Alexandrian works. Moreover, he

[16] «درمیان کتب نثر فارسی که باهمیت معروفند و براستی هم درخور اهمیت اند هیچ کتابی را جامع
همهٔ خصوصیات و مزایائی که در کتاب «تفهیم» فارسی موجود است سراغ نداریم. این کتاب
معتبرترین سند قدیمی علمی و ادبی فارسی بعد از اسلام و صحیح‌ترین مأخذ چند شعبه از فنون ریاضی
از بزرگترین استادان فن، و گرانبهاترین گنجینهٔ سرشار لغات و اصطلاحات و تعبیرات کهن و
اصیل فارسی است.»

J. Homā'ī, Introduction, p. (nūn-vāv) to *Kitāb al-tafhīm lī awā'il ṣinā'at al-tanjīm* (Tehran, 1316–18 [1937–39]).

[17] The text of *al-Qānūn al-mas'ūdī* has been published only recently and not yet completely studied. Professor E. S. Kennedy of the American University of Beirut, however, has already found several Babylonian astronomical ideas which were not known, or at least not used, by the Greeks but were present in al-Bīrūnī's work.

For an account of the contents of this work and the significance of al-Bīrūnī's astronomical doctrines, see the Introduction to the published edition of *al-Qānūn al-mas'ūdī* by Barani.

mentions often in the *Kitāb al-jamāhir . . .*, as well as in other works, passages from the Sacred Scriptures of many religions, including the Old and New Testaments, the Avesta and, of course, the Quran with which Abū Raiḥān was very well acquainted. And in his treatise *Ifrād al-maqāl fī amr al-ḍalāl*,[18] in discussing the times of prayer, he cites prophetic *ḥadīth*, 'Umar ibn al-Khaṭṭāb, al-Ash'arī, al-Shāfi'ī, and many other Muslim religious authorities, demonstrating further his profound knowledge of many of the sources of Muslim law and theology. Altogether, there are few fields that he left untouched in the sciences of his day.

Owing to the accidents of translation, al-Bīrūnī was not as well known or as influential in the Latin West as his contemporary, Ibn Sīnā. If his *al-Qānūn al-mas'ūdī* had been translated into Latin, it would probably have become as famous as the *Qānūn* of Ibn Sīnā. In the Muslim world, however, al-Bīrūnī has always remained an undisputed master of astronomy, astrology, geography, and mathematics. His *India* is unique in Muslim annals, and his *al-Āthār al-bāqiyah* is the best source of the chronology and religious events of Western Asia in ancient times. The *Kitāb al-tafhīm* served as inspiration in a direct manner for several important scientific treatises of later centuries, including *Kitāb rawḍat al-munajjimīn* by Shahrdān ibn Abi'l-Khair al-Rāzī and *Kaihān shinākht* by Ḥasan Kattān al-Marwazī, both written during the fifth century, *Jahān-i dānish* by Sharaf al-Dīn Muḥammad ibn Mas'ūd ibn Muḥammad al-Mas'ūdī and *Kifāyat al-ta'līm fī ṣinā'at al-tanjīm* by Sayyid al-'Ulamā' Abu'l-Maḥāmid ibn Mas'ūd ibn al-Zakī al-Ghaznawī, composed during the sixth century. The famous *Mu'jam al-buldān* of Yāqūt ibn 'Abdallāh al-Ḥamawī, written during the seventh century, as well as *Kitāb al-tafhīm fī ma'rifat istikhrāj al-taqwīm* of Maẓhar al-Dīn Muḥammad al-Lārī, belonging to the tenth century, is also based on al-Bīrūnī's work.[19] His writings came at the height of the intellectual activity of the fourth century and were themselves the finest attempt made at that time to unify many branches of Muslim learning as well as the sciences of those people from whom the Muslims inherited the ancient sciences. As such, his works served throughout the succeeding centuries as sources for the natural and historical sciences and acquired authority as the writings of an undisputed master. As an

[18] Al-Bīrūnī, *Rasā'ilul-Bīrūnī, Containing Four Tracts* (Hyderabad, 1948), pp. 160–180.

[19] For a discussion of al-Bīrūnī's influence, see the Introduction by Homā'ī to the Persian edition of *Kitāb al-tafhīm*.

astronomer and astrologer, especially, he became almost the prototype and ideal to be followed.[20]

A cursory reading of the works of al-Bīrūnī is sufficient to discover the deep faith which he had in Islam. He recognized the universality of Truth in his study of other religions and connected this universality itself with the Quranic texts which testify to the universality of prophecy.[21] His study of comparative religion did not make him in any way "eclectic" but on the contrary affirmed his Muslim religious beliefs. Referring to al-Bīrūnī's introduction to *Kitāb al-ṣaidanah*, Meyerhof justly remarks:

> Schon aus diesem kurzen Abschnitt kann mann deutlich seine naturwissenschaftlichen, philosophischen und historischen Neigungen klar erkennen; eine tief religiös-islamische Einstellung und grosse Bewunderung für den wissenschaftlichen Wert der arabische Sprache kommen hier klar zutage, als in Berunis bisher bekannten Schriften.[22]

Al-Bīrūnī was fully aware of the universal character of Islam and its unifying role in bringing various nations together. He tells us in the *Kitāb taḥdīd nihāyāt al-amākin*:

> And now Islam has appeared in the Eastern and Western parts of the world and has spread between Andalus in the West and parts of China and Central India in the East, and between Abyssinia and Nubia in the South and the Turks and the Slavs in the North. It has, as never before, united all the different nations in one bond of love . . .[23]

The study of geography, astronomy, and so on, is in fact appropriate because of its importance to the religious life of the Islamic community and should be studied with that end in view.[24] There is no question of "science for science's sake" in the mind of al-Bīrūnī, any more than there is "art for art's sake." The arts and sciences should both serve the ideal of Islamic life which for the Muslim community is the "good life" and the final goal to be sought. The validity of the study of the sciences is not to be determined, however, by practical utility, for utility does not determine the innate value of things.[25] On

[20] For the image of al-Bīrūnī in the mind of later generations, see Niẓāmī 'Arūḍī, *Chahār maqālah* (Tehran, 1955), pp. 110ff.

[21] ". . . it follows from his statement that all the inhabitants of the earth and the Hindus are subject to reward and punishment; that they are one great religious community" (Al-Bīrūnī in *Alberuni's India*, I, 295).

[22] Al-Bīrūnī, *Das Vorwort zur Drogenkunde des Beruni*, trans. M. Meyerhof, p. 14.

[23] S. H. Barani, "Kitābut-taḥdīd," *Islamic Culture*, 31:177 (1957).

[24] *Ibid.*, pp. 169–170.

[25] «الفضيلة الذاتية للشيء غير المنفعة العارضة لاجله.»

From p. 10 of manuscript of *Kitāb al-taḥdīd* quoted by Barani in "Kitābut-taḥdīd," p. 169.

the contrary, the validity of the study of the sciences is to be found in the Quranic injunction whereby man is commanded to contemplate heaven and earth which God has created by Truth (*bi'l-ḥaqq*).[26]

Although the devotion and sincerity of al-Bīrūnī as a Muslim is certain, his affiliation with the particular divisions within Islam is difficult to determine. As is the case with the works of so many authors of the fourth century, the writings of Abū Raiḥān do not specify in a clear manner whether he was a Sunni or a Shī'ite. He writes of both parties with much knowledge and insight but rarely gives any indication of his own preference. One can see, however, some attraction toward Shī'ism during the early years of his life and toward Sunnism during old age,[27] but this preference is far from definitive. In fact, Abū Raiḥān tells us that he wore a ring with two different types of the same stone, one of which was venerated by the Sunnis and the other by the Shī'ites. In this way he hoped to show that he belonged to both of them.[28]

Al-Bīrūnī also displays some knowledge of *taṣawwuf* despite his erroneous derivation of Ṣūfī from *sophos*, and in his *India* he often compares Hindu doctrines with those of the Ṣūfīs. Yet, there is little doubt that he himself was not a Ṣūfī.[29] He was a great scholar and scientist and a devout Muslim who had learned much by reading, observation, and thought and had gained mastery over many branches of knowledge, but he did not follow the way of purification of the soul and direct intellectual intuition, which in Islam belongs to *taṣawwuf*. He had the same veneration for Ṣūfī spirituality as the great majority of devout Muslims, without, however, ever participating in it himself.

Al-Bīrūnī also shows considerable interest in philosophy in its Socratic sense. Referring to a passage in *India* about wisdom, he tells the reader that "this passage reminds one of the definition of philosophy as the striving to become as much as possible similar to

[26] Al-Bīrūnī quotes the verse: «وَيَتَفَكَّرُونَ فِي خَلْقِ السَّمَاوَاتِ وَالْأَرْضِ رَبَّنَا مَا خَلَقْتَ هَذَا بَاطِلًا ..» Quran (III, 188), Barani (n. 25), p. 169.

[27] Meyerhof, "Etudes de pharmacologie arabe . . .," p. 144.

[28] Al-Bīrūnī, *Kitāb al-jamāhir* . . ., p. 215.

[29] «وكلام الصوفية يكاد أن يكون غير مفهوم عندهم فضلاً على غيرهم وخاصة كلام الحسين بن حلاج ...» From al-Bīrūnī, *Ifrād al-maqāl*, quoted by S. H. Barani in "Ibn Sina and al-Biruni," *Avicenna Commemoration Volume*, p. 13. Al-Bīrūnī's acquaintance with Ṣūfī terminology can be seen in his comparison of Ṣūfī doctrines with those of *Patañjali Yoga* in his *India*. See L. Massignon, *Essai sur les origines du lexique technique de la mystique musulmane*, pp. 42ff.

God."[30] On the other hand, he is strongly opposed to the syllogistic and rationalistic philosophy of Aristotle, an opposition whose various modes we shall investigate in a later chapter. He respects the scientific achievements of the Stagirite but thinks quite differently from the Peripatetics regarding such major questions as the meaning of creation and the eternity or non-eternity of the world. Al-Bīrūnī had made an intensive study of al-Rāzī and perhaps of other writers who had been imbued with Hermetic ideas. Were we to discover some of al-Bīrūnī's lost philosophical works, we could perhaps gain a more coherent understanding of the doctrines which he held in opposition to the Aristotelians.

It would be difficult to categorize al-Bīrūnī exactly according to the divisions of the seekers of knowledge which we gave in the introduction. Certainly he can be excluded from Ismā'īlī affiliations and in a direct manner from any Ṣūfī lineage. Nor can he be classified in any way with the Peripatetics whom he opposed on so many questions. Affirmatively he must first of all be considered as a devout Muslim, and secondly in a very vague way he may be classified with the *ḥukamā'*, not here referring specifically to the *Ishrāqī* school of later centuries or the followers of the Greeks, but to that group which in its "natural philosophy" considered the manifestations of Nature as signs of Divine Wisdom and sought to study things as the handiworks of God. Perhaps it would be even more justifiable, however, to envisage al-Bīrūnī as a devout Muslim scientist, compiler, and historian, for whom the role of reason lay in leading naturally to the Transcendent Cause of all things. We see again and again in his study of mathematics, geography, or astronomy how the most technical mathematical discussion or rational discourse leads quite naturally to the affirmation of some attribute of the Creator. The emphasis on this noble aspect of reason as a natural bridge to the suprarational realities and to religious faith, rather than as an obstacle against them, is a profound aspect of the Islamic spirit. In this sense, al-Bīrūnī can be considered among the most Muslim of those in Islamic civilization who devoted themselves to the study of the intellectual sciences and who synthesized the achievements of pre-Islamic cultures and developed them in the spirit of Islam.

[30] *Alberuni's India*, I, 29–30.

CHAPTER 6

The Creation of the World and Its Subsequent History

Al-Bīrūnī accepts fully the scripturally supported belief that the world was created *ex nihilo* and rejects completely the arguments of the Greek philosophers for the eternity of the world. Like the theologians who fought against the Greek idea of the eternity of the world because it led to a kind of "naturalism," al-Bīrūnī also devotes much time to combating this idea. According to him, the creation of the world is a manifestation of the power of the Creator, not something to be rejected by any arguments contrived by human reason. God is the Creator who has mastery over the whole Universe and knowledge of all its particulars and inner mysteries.[1]

Al-Bīrūnī, in the *Kitāb taḥdīd nihāyāt al-amākin*, gives a full account of his conception of the creation of the world and its scriptural history. He writes:

> Now I say: If by adducing rational proofs and true logical syllogisms, we can conclude that the world was created, and that the parts of its finite period, since its creation and existence, have had a beginning, we cannot by such proofs deduce the magnitudes of those parts, which will enable us to determine the date of the creation of the world.
>
> Let us consider the syllogism with the following composition: the body cannot be divested of temporal accidents, and all that cannot be divested of accidents is temporal; therefore the body must be temporal and not pre-temporal (?), and an accident to a body has been proved by the first figure (proposition?). But a succession of accidents cannot be infinite, for this necessitates a pre-eternity of time, and that is impossible. For if we say that

[1] «ثم الاعمال بالنيات ولن يحبط عند الله عمل انتوى فيه الخير للغير وهو اعلم بالسرائر والمجازي بما في الضمائر.»

Al-Bīrūnī, *Das Vorwort zur Drogenkunde des Beruni*, trans. M. Meyerhof, Arabic text, p. 17.

the past parts of time, i.e. periods, exist and are denumerable and cumulative, and all that exists is denumerable, beginning with the number one and ending with a finite number, then time must have a beginning at an assigned moment and must be finite, and it has been shown by the first figure that time has a beginning and is finite.

However, a knowledge of the parts that constitute the whole, I mean: years, months, and days, and their magnitudes, cannot in any way be realized by minds reasoning by syllogisms. It is possible for the beginning of time and the creation of the world to precede any assigned moment that we may fix, by an instant, or by a thousand thousands of years which are denumerable and finite. It all depends on how much truth there is in what one hears about this matter, for the Book of God and the true monuments have said nothing about it at all.

Again, those with a book of divine revelation, like the Jews, the Christians, and others like the Sabians and the Magians, have all agreed about dating events by the Era of the Creation of Mankind, but they differ greatly in their estimation of the duration of that era. They have not referred to the Era of the Creation of the World, except in the opening two verses of the Torah, which have the following content but not the exact wording: "In the beginning God created the heaven and the earth. And the earth was without form and void, and the spirit of God was moving upon the surface of the waters" (Genesis I: 1, 2). They considered that to be the first day of the week in which the world was created, but that was a period of time which cannot be measured by a day and a night, for the cause of these periods is the sun with its rising and setting, and both the sun and the moon were created on the fourth day of that week. How is it possible to imagine that these days are like the days of our reckoning! The Qur'an says: "A day in the sight of thy Lord is like a thousand years of your reckoning" (Sura 22: 47). In another verse, God says: "In a day the measure whereof is as fifty thousand years" (Sura 70: 4). Thus it is obvious that we cannot estimate that period with our method of reckoning, and that it is unverifiable since the beginning of creation.[2]

Al-Bīrūnī is obviously accepting the Scriptures as a source of knowledge about the creation of the world and understands clearly the symbolic nature of the account of creation in the Book of Genesis. But apparently he does not go so far as to follow the symbolic interpretation (*ta'wīl*) of the Scriptures that is prevalent among the Shī'ah and the Ṣūfīs, and is content with reaching certainty of the origin of the world in time (or with time) without having gained scriptural knowledge of its subsequent history. He then turns to the physical remains of the previous periods as the only means of

[2] Al-Bīrūnī, *The Determination of the Coordinates of Cities*, trans. Jamil Ali (Beirut, 1966), pp. 14–16; see also A. Z. Validi Togan, *Biruni's Picture of the World* (Calcutta, 1937–1938), pp. 53, 54.

knowledge of the history of the world.[3] But the remains are not deciphered according to the belief in the uniformity of conditions, that is, the hypothesis of "uniformitarianism"; on the contrary, the whole interpretation of the past, according to Abū Raiḥān, depends upon the qualitative nature of time which is basic to the comprehension of his doctrine.

The modern assumption of the uniformity of events of Nature throughout time, which has even been made the basis of the study of the past, considers that the forces acting in Nature, observable by the human senses at the present moment in the particular conditions chosen for the study of these forces by modern scientists, have been acting in the same manner throughout the history of the world. Moreover, it is assumed that any forces which cannot be observed now could not have acted in the past. This belief in the uniformity of conditions, which generalizes for all times and all of space the findings of scientists during the past few centuries, has been extended beyond the physical domain to the social, psychological, and even spiritual worlds and forms a common background of much of the study made by modern scholars of other civilizations, whether these studies be archaeological or historical.

The traditional doctrine, developed at great length by the Hindus in such cosmological treatises as the *Purānas*, is based upon the opposite view. It envisages the unfolding of time according to a universal law in such a manner that at each "cosmic moment" that which belongs to that particular moment is manifested. Therefore, far from being under a uniform condition, the cosmic environment, as well as human society which is closely wed to it, possesses certain characteristics and modes of existence belonging to the particular period in which it has come into existence. The "laws of Nature" are therefore not valid throughout the history of the cosmos, like the law of the rotation of a wheel inside a watch, but themselves change during the life of the world as the form and function of an organism alter during various periods of its life.

Al-Bīrūnī—perhaps because of his familiarity with Hindu cosmological doctrines—discusses the qualitative nature of time in greater detail than most other Muslim authors, although similar ideas are discussed by al-Mas'ūdī and al-Ṭabarī among others. The belief in the existence of the hermaphrodite, for example, which was a favorite topic of discussion for Graeco-Roman historians as well as for Muslim authors, was based on the belief that what does not exist at one period, but has been recorded historically, may have existed

[3] Togan, p. 55.

in another and may have had great significance as a part of the cosmic environment of that period, in which all events unfold according to universal laws operating at each point of the cycle.[4]

Al-Bīrūnī, much like other medieval authors, considers the generation of time as being due to the revolution of the Sun through the signs of the Zodiac.[5] It is the motion of the Sun that brings order out of chaos and generates all the periods by which time is measured. The periods of time generated by the movement of the heavens consists not only of days and nights, months and years, which have their own features and periodic changes, but greater cycles which govern historical and geologic changes. The *Āthār al-bāqīyah* is to a great extent the study of many of these periods and their reckoning among various peoples. Al-Bīrūnī is even aware of the differences of view among various groups regarding the cyclic notion of time for he writes:

> And some people maintain that *time* consists of cycles, at the end of which all created beings perish, whilst they grow at their beginning; that each such cycle has a special Adam and Eve of its own, and that the chronology of this cycle depends upon them.
>
> Other people, again maintain that in each cycle a special Adam and Eve exist for each country in particular, and that hence the differences of human structures, nature, and language [are] to be derived.[6]

But Abū Raiḥān has no patience with those who believe the world to be eternal or time to be without an end. So he writes: "Other people, besides, hold this foolish persuasion, that *time* has no *terminus quo* at all."[7] On the contrary, according to him time has a beginning as

[4] We do not mean by "cyclic" that time returns exactly to the same point or that an event repeats itself exactly. To quote Burckhardt: "Ce qui s'exprime dans cette superposition de rythmes, c'est, d'une part, que tout cycle de manifestation comporte une relative répétition, puisqu'il est fait d'images d'un même archétype 'polaire,' images qui sont nécessairement analogues entre elles; mais d'autre part, il ne comporte aucune répétition effective, puisque l'essence créative de l'archétype ne saurait jamais être épuisée par ses images ou symboles. L'analogie est la trace de l'Unité, et le caractère inépuisable est le reflet de l'infinité du Principe." (*Clé spirituelle de l'astrologie musulmane*, p. 43.) The traditional idea of cycles implies a qualitative notion of time in such a way that an analogy exists between two points in the unfolding of time. This conception can be symbolized by a helix whose turns have analogies with each other without ever repeating one another.

[5] Al-Bīrūnī, *Tamhīd al-mustaqarr li taḥqīq ma'na'l-mamarr*, in *Rasā'ilul-Bīrūnī*, p. 38. This work, which contains a discussion of transits and other astrological and astronomical subjects, has been translated into English: as *Al-Bīrūnī on Transits*, trans. Mohammad Saffouri and Adnan Ifram (Beirut, 1959).

[6] *Chronology of Ancient Nations*, trans. E. C. Sachau (London: W. H. Allen, 1879), p. 115. All quotations from the *Chronology*. . . are taken from E. C. Sachau's translation.

[7] *Chronology* . . ., p. 116.

well as an end which is ordained by the Creator. As al-Bīrūnī says concerning the eclipse of the Sun and Moon in connection with the end of time: "Both do not happen together except at the time of the total collapse of the Universe as the Almighty has said: 'Then when the sight shall be dazzled and the Moon shall be eclipsed and the Sun and Moon shall be in conjunction.'"[8]

Al-Bīrūnī is quite clear about the change of conditions of the world through time. With regard to geologic observation he writes:

> And what is told by the Hindus and other people regarding mountains after investigation and study seems on the surface to be in vain because they have recorded their observations thinking that whatever they have seen has always been and will always be the same. This is done in consideration of the fact that by examination it has been discovered that in the course of evidence the mountains have not remained in the same state, and that all of a sudden, or in the course of time changes and variations have occurred. Therefore, we cannot consider the present state and conditions which we have discovered by observation to have been always the same. Likewise, the observations of the people of India and other peoples regarding mountains is precisely like the observations of previous ages regarding the heavens.[9]

In a similar manner, with respect to the legend of the great physical size of earlier generations, he writes:

> As regards the (superhuman) size of the bodies (of former generations), we say, if it be not necessary to believe it for this reason, that we cannot observe it in our time, and that there is an enormous interval between us and that time, of which such things are related, it is therefore by no means impossible.[10]

With regard to the belief in the life of early prophets and manifestations of Nature which did not exist in his own time, al-Bīrūnī expresses the same belief in the qualitative conception of time:

> Now, personal observations alone, and conclusions inferred therefrom, do not prove a long duration of the human life, and the huge size of human bodies, and what else has been related to be beyond the limits of possibility. For similar matters appear in the course of time in manifold shapes.

[8] *Kitāb al-jamāhir . . .*, "Chapter on Pearls . . .," trans. F. Krenkow, *Islamic Culture* 15:421 (1941).

[9] From the second question asked by al-Bīrūnī of Ibn Sīnā. See al-Bīrūnī and Ibn Sīnā, *al-As'ilah wa'l-ajwibah*, ed. S. H. Nasr and M. Mohaghegh (Tehran, 1973), p. 12. These questions and answers are also to be found in partial form in many earlier sources such as 'A. Dehkhodā, *Sharḥ-i ḥāl-i nābighih-i shahīr-i Īrān . . .*, pp. 29ff; and *Nāma-yi dānishwarān-i nāṣirī* (Tehran, 1296 [1878]), II, pp. 585–604.

[10] *Chronology of Ancient Nations*, p. 97.

There are certain things which are bound to certain times, within which they turn round in a certain order, and which undergo transformations as long as there is a possibility of their existing. If they, now, are not observed as long as they are in existence, people think them to be improbable, and hasten to reject them as altogether impossible.

This applies to all cyclical occurrences, such as the mutual impregnation of animals and trees and the forthcoming of the seeds and their fruits. For, if it were possible that men did not know these occurrences, and then they were led to a tree, stripped of its leaves, and were told what occurs to the tree of getting green, of producing blossoms and fruits etc., they would certainly think it improbable, till they saw it with their own eyes. It is for the same reason that people who come from northern countries are filled with admiration when they see palm trees, olive trees, and myrtle trees, and others standing in full blossom at winter time, since they never saw anything like it in their own country.

Further, there are other things occurring at times in which no cyclical order is apparent, and which seem to happen at random. If, then, the time in which the thing occurred has gone by, nothing remains of it except the report about it. And if you find in such a report all the conditions of authenticity, and if the thing might have already occurred before that time, you must accept it, though you have no idea of the nature or of the cause of the matter in question.[11]

Al-Bīrūnī also shares the belief of most ancient and medieval writers that somehow the peoples of earlier cycles of history were closer to man's celestial origin and lived a more integral life. He even implies that the ancients possessed more knowledge than the people of his own time. "What we have of sciences," he writes "is nothing but the scanty remains of bygone better times."[12] Therefore, not only is cyclic revolution a certainty, for ". . . the cyclical revolutions of times is nothing very special, but is simply in accordance with the results of scientific observation,"[13] but there is also a dissolution caused by the vicissitudes of time. The changes in man and his society, moreover, have their analogy with the cosmic environment, which also changes at its various levels of existence, including the physical domain, according to the universal laws of manifestation which govern the world of becoming at every "cosmic moment" of its history.

[11] *Chronology . . .*, pp. 91–92 (italics ours).
[12] *Alberuni's India*, p. 152.
[13] *Ibid.*, p. 152.

CHAPTER 7

The Role of Nature and the Methods of Its Study

On Nature and Its Function

Nowhere in his extant works does al-Bīrūnī give a complete exposition of the meaning of the term Nature either as a technical philosophic term, such as is given by the Peripatetics, or as a specific universal function, as the Ikhwān al-Ṣafā' understood it. There is, nevertheless, hidden in the writings of Abū Raiḥān the conception of Nature as the principle of activity, as that which brings about change in the cosmos. As he tells us:

> There is no doubt that the *Vis Naturalis* (the creative power of Nature), in all work it is inspired and commissioned to carry out, never drops any material unused, if it meets with such; and if there is abundance of material, the *Vis Naturalis* redoubles its creating work.[1]

There is, consequently, not only a creative power of Nature which brings form into being, but also an "economy" and plan. Nature is neither "dead matter" possessing motion, nor "primary matter," nor the *hylé*. On the contrary, the *hylé* is the intermediary through which the forces of Nature act on matter, or in al-Bīrūnī's words:

> Now, as regards the motion of that which is above matter, we say that the *hylé* is the middle term between matter and the spiritual divine ideas that are above matter, and that the *three primary forces* exist in the *hylé* dynamically *en dynamei*. So the *hylé* with all that is comprehended in it, is a bridge from above to below.[2]

[1] Al-Bīrūnī, *Chronology of Ancient Nations*, trans. E. C. Sachau, p. 93. In discussing the Hindu conception of Nature, he writes: "Next comes *Nature*, which they call *sharikāra*. The word is derived from the idea of *overpowering*, *developing*, and *self-assertion*, because matter when assuming shape causes things to develop into new forms, and this growing consists in the changing of a foreign element and assimilating it to the growing one. Hence it is as if *Nature* were trying to overpower those *other* or foreign elements in this process of changing them, and were subduing that which is changed (*Alberuni's India*, I, 41). Quotations from *Alberuni's India* in this and following chapters are from the translation of E. C. Sachau (see above, Chapter 5, n. 3).

[2] *Alberuni's India*, I, 41.

The idea of "economy" in Nature—considered not simply anthropomorphically but with regard to the Divine plan—is closely allied to teleology; for if there were no purpose in things it would be meaningless to speak of waste or utility. Al-Bīrūnī is well aware of this relation and presents the belief in the "economy" of Nature in conjunction with that of the purposefulness of all things in the Universe. The faculties of each creature are made for a particular purpose to fit within the harmony of the total scheme of Nature.[3] For example, he writes: "As to the question why the springs have the most copious water in winter, we must observe: the All-Wise and Almighty Creator, in creating the mountains, destined them for various purposes and uses."[4] And again: "Praise therefore be unto Him who has arranged creation and created everything for the best."[5]

The "economy of Nature" implies that, in al-Bīrūnī's words, "there is no waste or deficiency in His Work."[6] To cite an example, he writes:

> The bees kill those of their kind who only eat, but do not work in their beehives. Nature proceeds in a similar way; however, it does not distinguish, for its action is under all circumstances one and the same. It allows the leaves and fruit of the trees to perish, thus preventing them from realising that result [for] which they are intended in the economy of Nature. It removes them so as to make room for others.
>
> If thus the earth is ruined, or is near to being ruined, by having too many inhabitants, its ruler—for it has a ruler, and his all-embracing care is apparent in every single particle of it—sends it a messenger for the purpose of reducing the too great number and of cutting away all that is evil.[7]

If there is this design in Nature there must be some explanation for the strange phenomena that are occasionally observed. One type of such manifestation is strange because it differs radically from what man is accustomed to witnessing. Al-Bīrūnī writes:

> Of a similar character is a fountain called "the pure one" in Egypt, in the lowest part of a mountain which adjoins a church. Into this fountain sweet, smooth-running water is flowing out of a source in the bottom of the mountain. If, now, an individual who is impure through pollution or menstruation touches the water, it begins at once to stink, and does not

[3] *Kitāb al-jamāhir . . .*, p. 3.

[4] *Chronology of Ancient Nations*, p. 252.

[5] *Alberuni's India*, I, 170.

[6] *Kitāb al-jamāhir . . .*, p. 3. «لا إسراف فيه ولا تقتير.»

[7] *Alberuni's India*, I, 400–401.

cease until you pour out the water of the fountain and clean it; then it regains its nice smell.

Further, there is a mountain between Herat and Sijistan, in a sandy country, somewhat distant from the road, where you hear a clear murmur and a deep sound as soon as it is defiled by human excrement or urine.

These things are natural peculiarities of the created beings, the causes of which are to be traced back to the simple elements and to the beginning of all composition and creation. And there is no possibility that our knowledge should ever penetrate to subjects of this description.[8]

There are yet other strange phenomena which appear to man as "faults of Nature," as imperfections in the Divine plan.

To this category belong, for example, animals with supernumerary limbs, which occur sometimes, when Nature, *whose task it is to preserve the species as they are*, finds some superfluous substance, which she forms into some shape instead of throwing it away; likewise, animals with imperfect limbs, when Nature does not find the substance by which to complete the form of that animal in conformity with the structure of the species to which it belongs; in that case she forms the animal in such a shape, as that the defect is made to lose its obnoxious character, and she gives it vital power as much as possible.[9]

The "economy" and design of Nature is not based upon purely human judgment. The conception of al-Bīrūnī differs profoundly from the idea of "simplicity" and "economy" found in the philosophical systems of some seventeenth- and eighteenth-century European thinkers because he has no intention of substituting human reason for Divine Wisdom. Neither human needs nor purely human ideals of perfection determine the harmony, design, and purpose of the Universe. As al-Bīrūnī tells us in regard to "faults of Nature":

Frequently, however, you find in the functions (actions) of Nature which it is her office to fulfill some fault (some irregularity), but this only serves to show that the Creator who had designed something deviating from the general tenor of things is infinitely sublime, beyond everything which we poor sinners may conceive and predicate of Him.[10]

Nature, therefore, is a power which forms and orders things according to a Divine plan and without any waste. The perfection and "economy" of the cosmos, however, is not to be judged by human standards at all. It is the Divine Wisdom which rules and orders the Universe and gives form to creatures, often in a manner which

[8] *Chronology of Ancient Nations*, p. 235.

[9] *Ibid.*, pp. 92–93 (italics ours).

[10] *Ibid.*, pp. 294–295.

demonstrates the transcendence of Divine Wisdom and Beauty above any human criteria of purposefulness and harmony. Man discovers the harmony and beauty of Nature not by projecting his own limited perspective upon the cosmos but by realizing his weakness and submitting to the Wisdom of the Creator.

The Methods Used to Study Nature

The view of modern science which selects a particular manner of studying Nature and then considers this "method" as the only possible and legitimate way is a quite recent one. In Islamic sciences—as we see in the case of al-Bīrūnī—there is no single path toward the understanding of Nature; observation and experimentation, reason and reflection, as well as Sacred Scripture and ancient sources, lead to the knowledge of the Universe. The answers received from Nature depend always upon the questions put to her as well as the way the questions are asked. Moreover, the "facts" found by observation and experimentation possess meaning only within the total framework which for al-Bīrūnī is the Islamic world view.

Al-Bīrūnī was a master of observation not only in astronomy but also in geology, geography, and the study of organic phenomena. His numerous studies of descriptive geography, such as *Kitāb taḥdīd nihāyāt al-amākin*, his description of the flora, fauna, and minerals of various regions of the earth, as well as his remarkable description of the Indus Valley where al-Bīrūnī argues for its sedimentary origin,[11] show him as a master observer of the multiple forms of Nature.

When discussing a problem regarding the details of some particular aspect of Nature, he always appeals to Nature itself as it functions in its own way rather than as it behaves when directed and placed under artificial conditions. In a passage whose contents do not agree with modern biology but which shows al-Bīrūnī's appeal to observation, he writes:

> The formation of scorpions out of figs and mountain-balm, that of bees from the flesh of oxen, that of wasps from the flesh of horses, is well known to all naturalists. We ourselves have observed many animals, capable of propagating their species, that had originally grown out of plants and other materials by a clear process of formation, and who afterward continued their species by sexual intercourse.[12]

[11] *Alberuni's India*, I, 196ff. For a description of the plants, minerals, and so on, from China to Europe, see A. Z. Validi Togan, *Al-Bīrūnī's Picture of the World.*

[12] *Chronology of Ancient Nations*, p. 214.

He also appeals to observation in order to question certain Aristotelian doctrines: "If it be established by us that the existence of a vacuum inside and outside of this world is impossible, then why does a glass vessel, whose inside air has been sucked out, when inverted into water pull the water upward?"[13] He asks this question despite the fact that he himself does not believe in the possibility of the existence of a vacuum.[14] In another question he observes the peculiar property of water which expands upon solidification and points to its conflict with Aristotelian physics. "Why does ice remain near the surface of the water," he asks "rather than sink to the bottom although ice contains earthy parts and is heavier than water because of its solidity and coldness?"[15]

The appeal to experiment to verify or deny opinions is used as often by al-Bīrūnī as the appeal to observation. For example, to deny a commonly held opinion about the change of sweet into salt water he writes:

> People say that on the 6th [of January] there is an hour during which all salt water of the earth is getting sweet. All the qualities occurring in the water depend exclusively upon the nature of that soil by which the water is enclosed if it be standing, or over which the water flows if it be running. Those qualities are of a stable nature, not to be altered except by a process of transformation from degree to degree by means of certain *media*. Therefore this statement of the waters' getting sweet in this hour is entirely unfounded. *Continual and leisurely experimentation will show to anyone the futility of this assertion.*[16]

Besides using observation and experiment, al-Bīrūnī appeals often to measurement. He realizes fully the importance of numbers and geometry, for he writes:

> Counting is innate to man. The measure of a thing becomes known by its being compared with another thing which belongs to the same species and

[13] This is the sixth of eight questions asked by al-Bīrūnī of Ibn Sīnā on physical sciences. Dehkhodā, *Sharḥ-i ḥāl-i nābighih-i shahīr-i Īrān . . .*, p. 57; *al-As'ilah wa'l-ajwibah*, p. 47.

[14] *Chronology of Ancient Nations*, p. 254.

[15] The eighth question on physical sciences he asked of Ibn Sīnā. Dehkhodā, p. 58; *al-As'ilah wa'l-ajwibah*, p. 49.

[16] *Chronology of Ancient Nations*, p. 240. (Italics ours.) In another passage from the *Kitāb al-jamāhir* . . . on the favorable conditions for the formation of pearls al-Bīrūnī writes: "This is the desired condition, as has been reported to us, and is similar to what the adepts of alchemy want, and there is no proof for it except experiment and no guide to it except experience" (F. Krenkow, trans. "Chapter on pearls . . .," *Islamic Culture* [1941], p. 39).

is assumed as a unit by general consent. Thereby the difference between the object and this standard becomes known.[17]

For example, "by weighing, people determine the amount of gravity of heavy bodies."[18]

Al-Bīrūnī cannot be considered a follower of the Pythagoreans in the same way as the Ikhwān al-Ṣafā'. Nevertheless, he definitely has a feeling for harmony and for the role of geometry in Nature. Showing his appreciation of this aspect of mathematics, he writes:

So all numbers are found in physical appearances of the works of the soul and life, and especially in flowers and blossoms. For the leaves of each blossom, their bells and veins, show in their formation certain numbers (numerical relations) peculiar to each species of them. Now, if anybody wants to support his theory by referring to one of these species, he *can* do so (that is, there is material enough for doing so), but who will believe him?[19]

By this question, al-Bīrūnī does not imply that he himself is skeptical about the relation between numbers and species, for he continues:

. . . Among the peculiarities of the flowers there is one really astonishing fact, viz., the number of their leaves, the tops of which form a circle when they begin to open, is in most cases conformable to the laws of geometry. In most cases they agree with the chords that have been found by the laws of geometry, not with conic sections. You scarcely ever find a flower of 7 or 9 leaves, for you cannot construct them according to the laws of geometry in a circle as isosceles [triangles]. The number of their leaves is always 3 or 4 or 5 or 6 or 18. This is a matter of frequent occurrence. Possibly one may find among the species hitherto known such a number of leaves; but, on the whole, one must say Nature preserves its *genera* and *species* such as they are. For if you would, for example, count the number of seeds of one of the many pomegranates of a tree, you would find that all the other pomegranates contain the same number of seeds as that one the seeds of which you have counted first. So, too, Nature proceeds in all other matters.[20]

Al-Bīrūnī mentions also the relation between the regular geometric figures and the elements, in the manner of Plato's *Timaeus* and following its example. He asks:

How many figures can be inscribed within a sphere? When the faces of the polyhedra are equilateral and equiangular and all equal and of one kind, only five; and these five are related by resemblance to the four elements and the sphere. When, however, the faces are of various kinds, there is no limit to the number.

[17] *Alberuni's India*, I, 160. [18] *Alberuni's India*.
[19] *Chronology of Ancient Nations*, p. 294. [20] *Ibid.*, pp. 294–295.

With regard to the five referred to: there are, first, the cube, bounded by six squares, called earthy; second, the icosahedron, by twenty equilateral triangles; it is a watery one; third, the octahedron, by eight equilateral triangles, the airy body; fourth, the tetrahedron, by four equilateral triangles, the prickly body, *ḥassakī*, fiery; and fifth, the dodecahedron by twelve pentagons.[21]

But al-Bīrūnī does not develop these ideas to any great extent. For the most part he uses mathematics with the idea of harmony in mind but without developing explicitly the science of arithmetical and geometric symbolism.

Al-Bīrūnī applies measure to the study of Nature in many ways; in astronomy as exemplified in *al-Qānūn al-mas'ūdī*, as well as in geography and physics. In geography, particularly, he uses mathematics in many novel ways and may be considered the founder of the science of geodesy.[22] In *al-Kitāb fi'l-usṭurlāb*, for example, al-Bīrūnī describes his own method for determining the circumference of the earth. The circumference is measured by climbing a mountain close to the sea and observing the setting of the sun and the dip of the horizon. Then the value of the perpendicular from the mountain is found. From this value one can determine the ratio of the earth's circumference to the height of the mountain by multiplying this height by the sine of the complementary angle of the dip, to use al-Bīrūnī's own description, and dividing the resultant by the versed sine of this dip, and finally multiplying this quotient by 2π.[23] He then adds that "such matters, however, need actual experiments, and could be verified only by testing."[24]

Al-Bīrūnī was given the opportunity to try this method in Northern Dabistān in the province of Jurjān, but because of lack of assistants and other difficulties he did not get any satisfactory results. He did

[21] Al-Bīrūnī, *Elements of Astrology*, p. 20. Quotations from al-Bīrūnī's *Elements of Astrology* in this and following chapters are from the translation by R. Ramsay Wright (London: Luzac & Co., 1934).

[22] See S. H. Barani, "Muslim researches in geodesy," and J. H. Kramers, "Al-Bīrūnī's determination of geographical longitude by measuring the distances," in *Al-Biruni Commemoration Volume*, where the application of spherical trigonometry for the measurement of the distance between cities is discussed. In his *Ifrād al-maqāl fī amr al-ḍalāl*, chap. 28, published in *Rasā'ilul-Bīrūnī*, al-Bīrūnī gives a geometric technique for measuring shadows to find distances between two places and heights of mountains.

[23] This operation can be presented mathematically in the following manner: If α = angle of depression of the horizon and h = height of the mountain, then $(h \times \cos\alpha)/(1 - \cos\alpha) = R$, where R = radius of the earth. Carra de Vaux, *Les Penseurs de l'Islam*, II, 30. C. Nallino, *'Ilm al-falak ta'rīkhuhu 'ind al-'arab fi'l-qurūn al-wusṭā* (Rome, 1911), pp. 290–292.

[24] See Barani, "Muslim researches in geodesy," p. 33.

not despair, however, for in the *Kitāb taḥdīd nihāyāt al-amākin* he describes another attempt which he made in India to use this method and in which he was quite successful. Since this method is an excellent

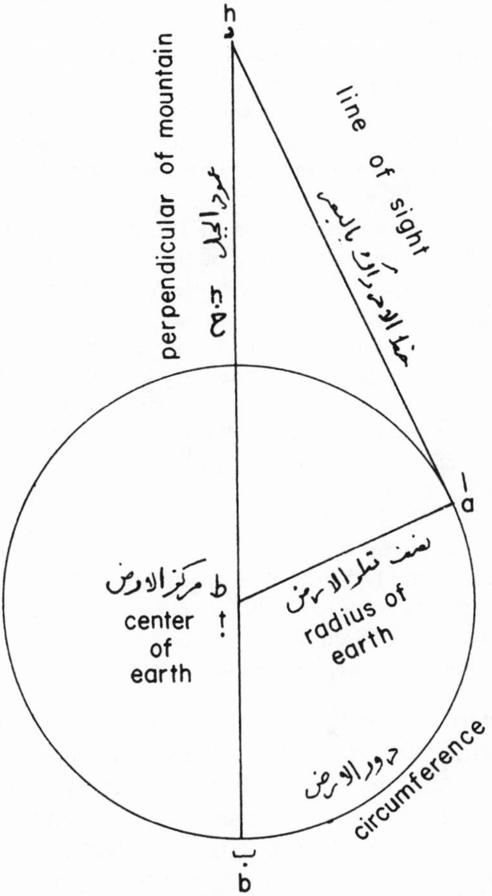

Figure 4. Al-Bīrūnī's measurement of the circumference of the earth.

example of the application of measurement to the physical domain, we produce here his own account of the second attempt to apply it:

When in the country of India, I found a mountain adjacent to a level-faced plain; I first ascertained its height at sea-level. I then imagined the sight line passing on its peak and connecting the earth with the sky, that is, the horizon (*dā'irat al-ufuq*). I found through my instrument that its horizon inclined from the Eastern and Western lines a little less than $\frac{1}{3}$ and $\frac{1}{4}$ degrees. So I took the dip of the horizon as 34 minutes. I then ascertained the altitude of the mountain by taking the heights of its peak in two different places, both of which were in a line with the bottom of the mountain's perpendicular. I found it $652\frac{1}{20}$ cubits. Now the mountain's perpendicular (*hḥ*) stands erect on (*abḥ*), the Earth's sphere; we carry it straight down to (*ḥṭb*), which would necessarily pass through the Earth's center (*ṭ*) on account of the attraction of the heavy weight on it. Now the tangent touching the Earth from the peak of the mountain (*h*) passing to the horizon is (*ha*). We join (*ṭ*) and (*a*), and thus is formed the right-angled triangle (*hṭa*), of which the angle at (*a*) is known to be the right angle and the values (of the other two angles) are also known; the angle (*ahṭ*) being equal to the complementary angle of the dip of the horizon having 89 degrees and 26 minutes, with a sine of $0^p, 59', 59'', 49''', 2''''$, and the angle (*hṭa*) being equal to the dip of the horizon itself, that is, 34′, with a sine of $0^p, 0', 35'', 36'''$. And thus this triangle will also be of known sides in the proportion in which (*ṭh*) will be sine 1 (that is, 90°) and (*ṭa*) (half-chord) will be sine for the complementary angle to the dip of the horizon. Therefore (*hḥ*) would be the excess in the sine 1 over the sine for the complementary angle to the dip of the horizon, and would come to $0^p, 0', 0'', 10''', 57'''', 32'''''$, and its ratio to (*ṭa*), the sine for the complementary angle to the dip, would be the same as the ratio of the cubits of (*hḥ*), the perpendicular of the mountain (that is, $652\frac{1}{20}$ cubits) to the cubits of (*ṭa*), the radius of the Earth.

In this manner the radius of the Earth would be 12,851,359 cubits 50′, 42″, and the circumference 80,780,039 cubits 1′, 38″, and a single one of the 360 degrees 224, 388 cubits 59′ 50″.

The mile for a single degree would amount to 56° 0′ 50″ 6‴.[25]

If we accept the value found by Nallino for the Arabic cubit (*dhirā'*) as being 4,933 millimeters, the above method gives the circumference of the earth as $25{,}000\frac{2}{7}$ English miles, not far different from the value found by the astronomers of al-Ma'mūn. If the earth were a perfect sphere instead of a geoid, the value found by al-Bīrūnī would be extremely close to modern measurements. As it stands, it is among the best geodetical measurements made during the medieval period.

Another instance of the use of measurement by al-Bīrūnī is his well-known determination of the specific density of minerals described in the *Kitāb al-jamāhir* . . . He uses the hydrostatic principle that "si l'on pèse un certain volume d'une substance dans l'air et dans l'eau, il se manifeste une différence, le poids dans l'eau étant

[25] This passage has been translated and fully explained by Barani in "Muslim researches in geodesy," pp. 35–41.

moindre, mais que le chiffre de cette différence est égal à celui du poids du volume de l'eau déplacée."[26]

Abū Raiḥān, without describing the instruments he uses, gives a table indicating: (1) the weight of water displaced, (2) the weight of the object in water, and (3) the weight of the object. He gives the weight to three figures for nine metals based on the weight of gold and for nine gems based on the weight of Oriental sapphire. These values differ only in the third place from modern measurements.[27]

The above examples demonstrate al-Bīrūnī's role as a careful observer and experimenter. He has often been admired by modern scholars for this aspect of his research because it is this particular approach to Nature which has been so actively pursued since the seventeenth century. With al-Bīrūnī, however, it is not the only approach, or the only legitimate way of acquiring knowledge. He applies measurements of this kind to that aspect of the physical domain where multiplicity is most evident, without seeking to apply such techniques everywhere. The type of knowledge arrived at by experiment and observation, which is completely legitimate on its own level, is integrated into the knowledge which transcends it and the universal perspective in which the study of the details of Nature find their meaning. Al-Bīrūnī, moreover, following to its conclusion the logic of things, never takes that which is improbable as being impossible or that which is probable as being certain. For him, observations and experiments in the physical domain and the use of logic are not only handmaids of rationalism or purely human modes of thought but are subservient to the intellectual principles of Islam whose essence, as well as form, lies above what is purely human.

[26] J. J. Clement-Mullet, "Pesanteur spécifique de diverses substances minérales, procédé pour l'obtenir d'après Abou'l-Raihan Albirouny," *Journal Asiatique*, 11:384 (1858).

[27] See *ibid.*, pp. 389–399. Also E. Wiedermann, *Beiträge zur Geschichte der Naturwissenschaften. Sitzungsberichten der physikalisch-medizinischen Sozietät in Erlangen*, VIII (1920–1921), 163–166; XXXI (1920–1921), 31–34.

CHAPTER 8

The Universe and Its Parts

The Heavens

In none of the sciences did al-Bīrūnī excel as much as in astronomy and astrology. Although many modern scholars try to discount his astrological studies, there is no doubt that soon after his death he became well known in the Muslim world as the perfect master of astrology as well as astronomy, which were almost always combined under one discipline in Islam. The astronomical and astrological works of al-Bīrūnī are so numerous that until today they have not yet been fully studied.[1] A detailed treatment of their content would require many volumes and lies outside the scope of the present treatise. We aim to treat here only that aspect of his work which has a cosmological significance.

Al-Bīrūnī is aware of the belief in the Divine source of astronomy, its origin being traditionally attributed to the prophet Idrīs or Hermes.[2] He follows the traditional Muslim, and to a great extent Greek, account not only of the origin of astronomy but of the order of the stars, planets, and elements. The cosmos has a spherical shape with the outermost heaven of fixed stars forming its boundary. Below it lie the heavens of Saturn, Jupiter, Mars, Sun, Venus, Mercury, and Moon and finally the sublunary region of the four elements with the Earth at the center. The heavens, which are made of ether (*athīr*), are called in their totality the higher world (*al-ʿālam al-aʿlā*), while the sublunary region of generation and corruption is called the lower

[1] Several well-known studies of al-Bīrūnī's astronomical doctrines were made by Nallino, Schoy, and Wiedemann at the beginning of this century (see George Sarton, *Introduction to the History of Science*, I, 108–109). More recently, several other studies have been added in European languages. See M. Lesley, "Biruni on rising times and daylight length," *Centaurus*, 5:121–141 (1959); E. S. Kennedy and A. Muruwwa, "Bīrūnī on the solar equation," *Journal of Near Eastern Studies*, 17:112–121 (1958); and S. H. Barani's introduction to the printed edition of *al-Qānūn al-masʿūdī*. Kennedy has also made several other major studies of al-Bīrūnī's astronomy. See Nasr, *Al-Bīrūnī: An Annotated Bibliography*, pp. 43ff.

[2] Al-Bīrūnī, *Chronology of Ancient Nations*, p. 188.

world (*al-ʿālam al-asfal*).[3] The heavens, however, are not absolutely different from the world of the elements, because they both possess the four fundamental qualities of heat, cold, moistness, and dryness; moreover, the heavens act upon the sublunary region in a cosmos whose parts are unified.

There are certain distinguishing features of al-Bīrūnī's astronomy, however, which set him apart from some Muslim and many Greek astronomers. In contrast to most Greek mathematical astronomers, he believes in the physical existence of the crystalline sphere; moreover, he does not simply try to explain the astronomical phenomena mathematically while ignoring the physical reality of the spheres which are used to explain celestial motion.[4]

> The celestial sphere is a body like a ball revolving in its own place; it contains within its interior objects whose movements are different from those of the sphere itself, and we are in the center of it. It is called *falak* on account of its circular movement, like that of a whirl of a spindle, and its name, *athīr* (ether) is current among philosphers.
>
> There are eight such spheres, each one enclosed within another, like the layers of an onion; the smallest sphere is that which is nearest to us, within which the Moon is always traveling above, rising and setting, within its limits. To each sphere there is a certain amount of space between the outer and inner boundaries so that the planet to which it belongs has two distances, the one further, the one nearer.[5]

Contrary to most Muslim astronomers, who added a ninth sphere to the eight of Ptolemy in order to explain the precession of the equinox, al-Bīrūnī remains content with the eight spheres of the Greeks. As he tells us: "Now we on our own part were already obliged to assume an eighth sphere, but there is no reason why we should suppose a ninth one."[6] He uses the Aristotelian argument

3 «العالم بكليته جرم مستدير الشكل متناه حواشيه بعضه ساكن في جوفه، واذا انتقل جزء
من نوع ساكن الى مكان نوع آخر منه تحرك على استقامة نحو حيّزه حركة عرضية، وما
حول هذه الساكنات في اطرافه فهو متحرك حركات مستديرة مكانية حول الوسط الذي
هو حقيقة السفل ومركز الارض - وجملة هذا الجرم الموجود يسمى عالماً بالاطلاق و
ربما فصل فسمى المتحرك منه على استدارة عالماً اعلى، والمتحرك على استقامة عالماً اسفل.»

Al-Bīrūnī, *al-Qānūn al-masʿūdī*, I, 21–22. "The sun is the middle of the planets, Saturn and Moon their two ends, and the fixed stars are above the planets." (*Alberuni's India*, II, 66.) See also *Elements of Astrology*, trans. R. Ramsay Wright, pp. 43ff. This work is hereafter cited as *EA*.

4 *Chronology of Ancient Nations*, p. 248.

5 *EA*, p. 43.

6 *Alberuni's India*, I, 225.

that a moved object must be moved by an outside mover and considers the special nature attributed to the ninth sphere in order to conclude that "the theory of the ninth sphere is proved to be an impossibility."[7]

In conformity with the nonmythological perspective of Islam, al-Bīrūnī rejects the mythological cosmology of the Hindus. While being acquainted with *brahmāṇḍa* or "egg of Brahman" of the Hindus and many aspects of its profound symbolism,[8] he remains more within the geometrical and abstract astronomical tradition inherited from the ancient civilizations of the Middle East and Greece which is focused upon geometric harmony and mathematical symbolism and is nonmythological.

In his determination of the size of the various planetary spheres and bodies, al-Bīrūnī follows the principles and even at times the values given by Ptolemy.[9] As he tells us:

> The distances of the Sun and Moon from the center of the earth in terms of the earth's radius is also made clear in the fifth book of *Majisti*; astronomers are agreed that the furthest distance of any planet is the nearest of that which is immediately above it and thus the ratio between the nearest and farthest distance is known in the case of each planet.[10]

Using this principle, he gives the following sizes of the planetary orbits and the planets:[11]

TABLE IV. SIZE OF THE PLANETARY ORBITS AND PLANETARY VOLUMES ACCORDING TO AL-BĪRŪNĪ[a]

Heavenly Body	*Volume in terms of the Earth's Volume = 1*	*Nearest Distance Compared with Radius of Earth (1081, 19′, 21″)*
Moon	1′, 33″	36 395
Mercury	14″	69 416, 4′, 23″
Venus	1′, 34″	183 656, 2′, 3″
Sun	167, 20′	1 254 638, 7′, 11″
Mars	1, 27′	1 363 361
Jupiter	95, 14′	9 919 443, 1′, 3″
Saturn	92, 08′	17 914 241, 2′, 33″

[a] Source: *Elements of Astrology*, trans. R. Ramsay Wright, p. 115.

The diameter of the girdle of the Zodiac, that is, the size of the cosmos, is given as $44{,}964{,}005\frac{13}{30}$ *pārsangs*, a large number but one that is still within the bounds of the imagination, and therefore preserves the sense of the "cosmos," or order, which underlies the hierarchical, finite Universe of medieval science. Al-Bīrūnī is not

[7] *Alberuni's India*, p. 226. See also *EA*, pp. 43ff.
[8] *EA*, pp. 43ff; *Alberuni's India*, I, 223.
[9] *EA*, p. 115. [10] *EA*, p. 116. [11] *EA*, p. 117.

dogmatic about the figures he gives, for he knows that in the case of physical sciences that must be based on experiment at a distance and on reports of observations, "it is inevitable that there should be controversies . . ."[12]

Without deviating from the geocentric system universally accepted during the Middle Ages, al-Bīrūnī is quite aware of the existence of the heliocentric system which was known not only among some Greek astronomers like Aristarchus of Samos, but was also taught by certain sages whom al-Bīrūnī met in India.[13] In fact, until the end of his life he remained neutral on this question and realized, correctly, that the choice between the two hypotheses was not one to be made by astronomy but something which depended on the one hand upon the cosmological and psychological questions which have a profound bearing upon human culture and on the other upon the science of physics. He writes:

I have seen the astrolabe called Zūraqī invented by Abū Sa'īd Sijzī. I liked it very much and praised him a great deal, as it is based on the idea entertained by some to the effect that the motion we see is due to the Earth's movement and not to that of the sky. By my life, it is a problem difficult of solution and refutation . . .

For it is the same whether you take it that the Earth is in motion or the sky. For, in both cases, it does not affect the Astronomical Science. It is just for the physicist to see if it is possible to refute it.[14]

He emphasizes the indifference of the helio or geocentric systems to astronomy again when he writes:

Besides, the rotation of the Earth does in no way impair the values of astronomy, as all appearances of an astronomic character can quite as well be explained according to this theory as to the other. There are, however, other reasons which make it impossible. This question is most difficult to solve. The most prominent of both modern and ancient astronomers have deeply studied the question of the moving earth, and tried to refute it. We, too, have composed a book on the subject called *Miftāḥ 'ilm al-hai'ah* (*Key of Astronomy*),[15] in which we think we have

[12] *EA*, p. 118.

[13] See *Alberuni's India*, I, 276ff, where he describes the views of Brahmagupta and others about the rotation of the Earth. In *al-Qānūn al-mas'ūdī*, I, 49, al-Bīrūnī states that the disciples of the famous Hindu astronomer Āryabhaṭa assigned the first movement from east to west to the Earth and a second movement from west to east to the fixed stars.

[14] Dehkhodā, *Sharḥ-i ḥāl-i nābighih-i shahīr-i Īrān . . .*, p. 12; Barani, "Al-Bīrūnī's scientific achievements," *Indo-Iranica* 5:47 (1952). See also A. Z. Validi Togan, "al-Biruni wa ḥarikati 'arz," *Islam Tetkikleri Enstitüsü Dergisi*, 1:90–94 (1953).

[15] This work seems unfortunately to have been lost; at least no trace of it has yet been found in any library.

surpassed our predecessors, if not in the words, at all events in the matter.[16]

Toward the end of his life al-Bīrūnī finally decided in favor of the geocentric system mainly for physical reasons. His calculation of the speed needed for the rotation of the Earth seemed to him unreasonable and too great to be conformable to terrestrial conditions.[17] There is no doubt that the change from geocentric to the heliocentric system involved changes in physics as well as in theology and the general religious perspective which were not to be brought about until several centuries later and then in Europe and not in the Muslim world.

To explain the motion of the planets, al-Bīrūnī adopts the Ptolemaic system of epicycles with the later accretions and refinements added by Muslim astronomers.

> Each planet has a small orbit known as an epicycle, *falak al-tadwīr*; the earth is not within it but the orbit is entirely above us. On the circumference of this epicycle the planet moves, when on the upper part towards the east in accordance with the succession of signs, and when on the lower towards the west; during such movement it completes its revolution and adheres closely to the circle.[18]

As for the apparent motion of the Sun:

> The *auj* of the Sun is the highest point which it attains in its orbit: the circumstance that there is a highest point is explained by the fact that it does not travel on the circumference of its own *mumaththal* orbit, but rather on the circumference of another orbit in the same plane but with a different center. This is its eccentric orbit *falak al-auj*. The earth is inside this orbit; consequently there is one point where it is nearest to the earth, and another opposite to that, furthest from the earth.[19]

Al-Bīrūnī discusses in great detail the motion of the planets and their irregularities, as, for example, retrograde motion. Here a brief quotation suffices:

> All the planets are constantly revolving on the circumference of their epicycles; beginning from their summits they travel towards the east in the direction of succession, and therefore in the opposite direction to the Moon, which travels westward and contrary to succession from its summit.[20]

[16] *Alberuni's India*, I, p. 277. See also C. A. Nallino, *'Ilm al-falak . . .* (Rome, 1911), p. 250.

[17] Al-Bīrūnī, *al-Qānūn al-mas'ūdī*, I, 59ff; also, S. Pines "La Théorie de la rotation de la terre," *Journal Asiatique*, 244:305 (1957).

[18] *EA*, p. 61. [19] *EA*, p. 88. [20] *EA*, p. 92.

The relation of the position and movement of a planet with respect to the center of the Universe, the Earth, and its boundary, the Zodiacal belt, is illustrated by al-Bīrūnī in the accompanying diagram:[21]

Al-Bīrūnī is also quite well aware of the long discussion over the centuries regarding the significance of the precession of the equinox and "trepidation." The former type of motion he discusses with some

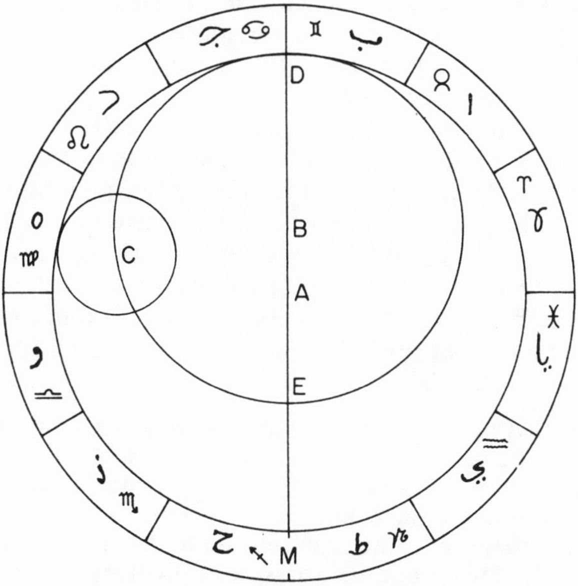

Figure 5. Planetary motion and the Zodiac. (A) center of the world; (B) center of deferent; (C) center of epicycle; (DE) apogee and perigee of deferent; (M) *mumaththal* orbit.

frequency, while he expresses general skepticism about trepidation and the possibility of its observation.[22] He describes the precession of the equinox and the "nodes of the Moon" in the following manner:

The nodes of the Moon make a complete revolution in eighteen years, seven months, and nine days, while each of the fixed stars and the apogees of the planets take according to the calculation of our ancestors thirty-six

[21] *EA*, p. 92. (See Appendix for the explanation of astrological symbols.)
[22] *EA*, p. 101.

thousand years, but to those of our own time twenty-three thousand seven hundred and sixty years.[23]

In his account of the chronologies of various nations, al-Bīrūnī mentions the eschatological significance of the period of the precession of the equinox. Yet nowhere does he give this astronomical phenomenon the same significance which we found in our study of the Ikhwān al-Ṣafā', or as is found in the Hindu cosmological treatises dealing with the *Yugas* and in Ṣūfī cosmological treatises such as certain chapters of the *Futūḥāt al-makkīyah* of Ibn 'Arabī. Al-Bīrūnī remains content with compiling the views of various religions on the significance of this astronomical motion without seeking to interpret them in detail.

As for the question of light and its connection with heavenly bodies, there is not as much emphasis placed upon solar symbolism by al-Bīrūnī as by the Ikhwān and other Muslim authors, some of whom have called the Sun "the heart of the Universe" (*qalb al-'ālam*). According to al-Bīrūnī, the Sun does remain the central body whose movement generates and brings order out of chaos but, curiously enough, in contradiction to the views of other Muslim writers, it is not the source of light for either the Universe or even for the planetary system. As he tells us:

Many assert that light is exclusively the property of the Sun, that all the stars are destitute of it, and that since the movements of the planets are obviously dependent on those of the Sun, it may be assumed by analogy that their light is in the same position.

But others believe that all the planets are luminous by nature with the exception of the Moon, and that its special peculiarities are its paleness and absence of brilliancy. This opinion is more in accord with the truth (as long as there is no evidence to the contrary) and [with the fact] that their concealment under the rays of the Sun is just like their non-visibility in diffused daylight, which by its intensity so affects our vision, that we are unable to perceive them. But anyone who looks out from the bottom of a deep pit by day may see a planet which happens to pass over the zenith, because his vision is relieved from the intensity of light by the surrounding darkness and strengthened by it, for black concentrates and strengthens vision, while white dissipates and weakens it.

Whether the higher planets are self-luminous or not, they are always to be seen in the same condition. For if the Moon were above the Sun, it

[23] *EA*, pp. 100–101. Al-Bīrūnī also realized that the change in the axis of the earth with respect to the heavens causes a slight change in geographic latitude, or "rotation of latitude," which, unlike the longitude, does not therefore remain fixed throughout time. From p. 33 of MS. *Kitāb taḥdīd nihāyāt al-amākin*, quoted by Barani in "Kitābut-taḥdīd," p. 171.

would cease to present the phenomena of waning, *inthilām*, and would always appear as full Moon.

The situation, however, with regard to Venus and Mercury is this, that if they are not luminous, there would be a difference in the amount of their light when at their greatest distance from the Sun, and when approaching their disappearance in its rays at conjunction, for indeed they are lower than the Sun, and no such difference is observable.

It is therefore preferable to regard the planets as self-luminous, while the special characteristics of the Moon and the variety of the phases of its light are due to three things, its captivity (by the Sun, conjunction), *bastagī, giriftagī*, its pale colour and absence of brilliance, and its position below the Sun.[24]

The Sublunary Region

As in Aristotle's cosmology, so in that of al-Bīrūnī, the Moon marks the boundary between the world of change and the incorruptible heavens. Above it lie the unchanging heavenly spheres and below it the world of generation and corruption. As for the Moon itself, it is a "non-luminous globular body and its brightness is due to the rays of the Sun which falls upon it as they do upon the earth, mountains, walls or the like, the other sides of which are not illuminated."[25]

Al-Bīrūnī describes in detail the contents of the sublunary world:

In the center of the sphere of the Moon is the earth, and this center is in reality the lowest part. The earth is, as a whole, globular, and in detail is rough-surfaced on account of the mountains projecting from it and the depressions on its surface, but when considered as a whole it does not depart from the spherical form, for the highest mountains are very small in comparison with the whole globe. Do you not see that a ball of a yard or two in diameter, covered with millet seeds and pitted with depressions of similar size, would still satisfy the definition of a sphere? If the surface of the earth was not as uneven, water coming from all sides would not be retained by it, and would certainly submerge it, so that it would no longer be visible. For water while it shares with earth in having a certain weight, and in falling as low as possible in air, is nevertheless lighter than earth, which therefore settles in water sinking in the form of sediment to the bottom. Moreover water, although it does not penetrate earth itself, sinks into the interstices thereof, and there becomes mixed with air, and as a result of the intimate contact becomes suspended in the air. When the air escapes to the outside, the water regains its natural state in the same way as rain falls from the clouds. On account of the various irregularities projecting from the surface, water tends to collect in the deepest places giving rise to streams.

[24] *EA*, pp. 67–68. [25] *EA*, p. 65.

The earth and the waters together form the one globe, surrounded on all sides by the air; as much of the latter as is in contact with the sphere of the Moon becomes heated in consequence of the movement and friction of the parts in contact. Thus is produced the fire which surrounds the air, less in amount in the proximity of the poles owing to the slackening of the movement there.[26]

Al-Bīrūnī's attempts to find the dimensions of the elements from the surface of the earth to the orbit of the Moon.

Is it possible to state the dimensions of the four elements in these terms? [he asks and goes on to answer the question affirmatively]. The earth with

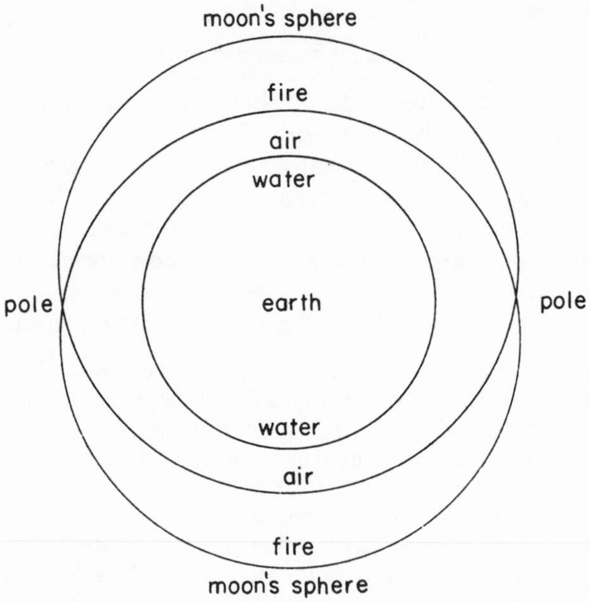

Figure 6. The elements in the sublunary world.

the mountains projecting from it like teeth is solid, and the water surrounds it occupying the hollows, but these two elements form the one globe, whose dimensions have been above stated. Now when the radius of the earth is deducted from the distance of the Moon at perigee, the remainder is the distance between the surface of the earth and the Moon's orbit occupied by the air, viz., 35 213 $\frac{1}{10}$ *parsangs*. When the measurement of the volume of the earth, viz., 5,305,498,589$\frac{4}{5}$ cubic *parsangs*, is deducted from that of the sphere whose radius is the nearest distance of the Moon from the center of the earth, viz., 200,356,658,322,333$\frac{1}{3}$ *parsangs*, there

[26] *EA*, pp. 45–46.

remain 200,351,352,823,$743\frac{8}{15}$ *parsangs*. This is the dimension of air and fire together, but it is impossible to determine the amount of these elements separately. Above the air in the moist vapours occur the various phenomena of wind, cloud, snow, and rain, also thunder, lightning, thunderbolts, rainbows, haloes, and like. Above it likewise in the dry smoky vapours are the stars with tails and locks, shooting stars, stars . . .[27]

We see from these passages that in the case of al-Bīrūnī, as in that of the Ikhwān al-Ṣafā' and of most other Muslim scientists, the four elements, which are the principles of this world of change, are responsible in their many activities for the diverse phenomena which comprise the manifestations of Nature in the physical domain.

A large number of these phenomena concern the changes occurring at the surface of the earth, especially geological ones. The concept of slow geologic change was widely held among Muslim scientists even before al-Bīrūnī. Aside from such specifically modern concepts as the Darwinian theory of evolution, there are many modern geological ideas, such as the change of land and sea, sedimentation, rise of mountains, and so on, which are to be found in various medieval Muslim treatises, particularly those of al-Bīrūnī. Undoubtedly this conception of great changes in the structure of the surface of the earth, and even the disappearance of such things as mountains which seem so solid and firm, is due not only to the ability of Muslim natural historians to travel over great distances and observe diverse geological conditions, but also to the emphasis of the Islamic perspective, supported by many Quranic verses, upon the transitory nature of all that is in this world. Much of the lesson that is drawn from natural history is, in conformity with the spirit of the Quran, pointed toward the basic Islamic doctrine that "all perishes save the face of Allah." The great changes in the surface of the earth quite naturally bring the devout Muslim face to face with the passing away in time not only of natural objects but of even the mightiest earthly powers and the greatest human achievements.

Al-Bīrūnī bases his study of the geological changes upon the records which the strata of rock have preserved. He writes often regarding the slow changes in conditions whose effects have been preserved in rocks:

We have to rely upon the records of the rocks and vestiges of the past to infer that all these changes should have taken place in very very long times and under unknown conditions of cold and heat: for even now it takes a long time for water and wind to do their work. And changes have been going on and observed and noticed within historical times.[28]

[27] *EA*, pp. 119–120.

[28] Validi Togan, *Biruni's Picture of the World*, pp. 57–58.

In his numerous travels al-Bīrūnī, as an acute observer, was able to see many regions of different geologic structures. He realized the great changes which had occurred in the past before the creation of man and afterwards during man's life on earth and up to the present time.[29] He even observed dislodging of strata in mountains which he attributed to recent internal upheavals. Several of his observations are particularly interesting. One deals with his discovery of fossils which, like the Ikhwān, he correctly identifies as the remains of sea animals which once lived in the locality that had now become land. As he tells us:

> Sea has turned into land and land into sea; which changes, if they happen [sic] before the existence of man, are not known, and if they took place later they are not remembered because with the length of time the record of events breaks, especially if this happens gradually. This only a few can realize.
>
> This steppe of Arabia was at one time sea, then was upturned so that the traces are still visible when wells or ponds are dug; for they begin with layers of dust, sand and pebbles, then there are found in the soil shells, glass and bones which cannot possibly be said to have been buried there on purpose. Nay, even stones are brought up in which are embedded shells, cowries and what is called "fish-ears," sometimes well-preserved, or the hollows are there of their shape while the animal has decayed.[30]

Another remarkable geological observation of al-Bīrūnī concerns his identification of the Ganges Plain as a sedimentary deposit. After his travels in India, where he studied the Ganges Plain carefully, he writes:

> One of these plains is India, limited in the south by the above-mentioned Indian Ocean, and on three sides by lofty mountains, the waters of which flow down to it. But if you see the soil of India with your own eyes and meditate on its nature, if you consider the rounded stones found in earth however deeply you dig, stones that are huge near the mountains and where the rivers have a violent current, stones that are of smaller size at a greater distance from the mountains and where the streams flow more slowly, stones that appear pulverized in the shape of sand where the streams begin to stagnate near their mouths and near the sea—if you consider all this,

29 «وعلى مثله ينتقل البحر الى البر والبر الى البحر في ازمنة ان كانت قبل كون الناس في العالم
فغير معلومة وان كانت بعده فغير محفوظة لان الاخبار تنقطع اذا طال عليها الامد -
وخاصة في الاشياء الكائنة جزوا بعد جزو.»

Togan, pp. 55–56.

30 *Kitāb taḥdīd nihāyāt al-amākin*, p. 24, trans. F. Krenkow: "Bēruni and the MS. Sultan Fātiḥ No. 3386," in *Al-Biruni Commemoration Volume*, p. 199.

you can scarcely help thinking that India was once a sea, which by degrees has been filled up by the alluvium of the streams.[31]

Despite this affirmation of the gradual and slow nature of natural processes acting at the surface of the earth, al-Bīrūnī, like almost all medieval scientists, believes also in cataclysms and disasters which from time to time devastate the earth. The emphasis is often placed upon this violent aspect of change rather than the gradual in order, on the one hand, to awaken man from his customary slumber, which is closely allied to his confidence in the permanence of his immediate physical environment, and, on the other, to remind him that the hand of God never stops intervening in this world, that periodically it sends not only prophets but also natural agents to purify the terrestrial domain.

Abū Raiḥān discusses also the relation of cataclysms to the rhythm of history and the rise and fall of different peoples. He writes:

The disasters which from time to time befall the earth, both from above and from below, differ in quality and quantity. Frequently it has experienced one so incommensurable in quality or in quantity, or in both together, that there was no remedy against it, and that no flight or caution was of any avail. The catastrophe comes on like a deluge or an earthquake, bringing destruction either by the breaking in of the surface, or by drowning with water which breaks forth, or by burning with hot stones and ashes that are thrown out, by thunderstorms, by landslips, and typhoons; further by contagious and other diseases, by pestilence, and more of the like. Thereby a large region is stripped of its inhabitants, but when after a while, after the disaster and its consequences have passed away, the country begins to recover and to show new signs of life, then different people flock there together like wild animals, who formerly were dwelling in hiding-holes and on the tops of the mountains. They become civilized by assisting each other against common foes, wild beasts or men, and furthering each other in the hope for a life in safety and joy. Thus they increase to great numbers; but then ambition, circling round them with the wings of wrath and envy, begins to disturb the serene bliss of their life.[32]

It can be concluded, therefore, that just as man and the Universe are interrelated, so is the rhythm of man's society intimately connected to the cosmic ambiance.

The discussion of geology leads naturally to the study of the geographic division of the earth. The seven-fold climatic division of the world, which is mentioned in the Quran and which was widely known and employed by the Greeks and in pre-Islamic Persia, is an image

[31] *Alberuni's India*, I, 198. [32] *Ibid.*, I, 378–379.

upon Earth of the seven spheres of heaven. It is not something completely arbitrary, but rather, like all aspects of "sacred geography," it expresses a certain cosmic reality. Like most of his contemporaries, al-Bīrūnī, who is among the greatest of Muslim geographers, adopts

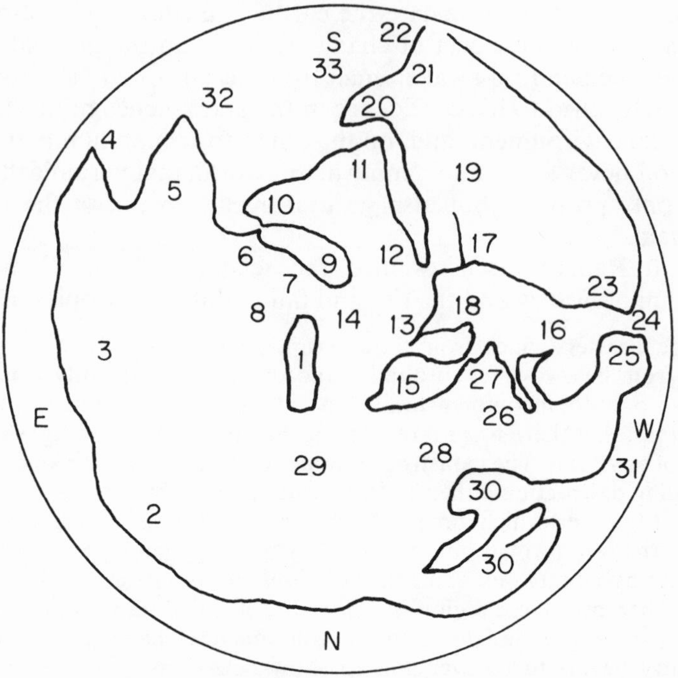

Figure 7. The geography of the Earth according to al-Bīrūnī. (1) Caspian. (2) Turks. (3) China. (4) Java. (5) India. (6) Makrān. (7) Persia. (8) Khurāsān. (9) Persian Gulf. (10) Oman. (11) Aden. (12) Qulzum. (13) Syria. (14) Irāq. (15) Pontus. (16) Mediterranean. (17) Alexandria. (18) Egypt. (19) Sudan. (20) Ras Berbera. (21) Mountains of the Moon. (22) Sofala al-zanj. (23) Morocco. (24) Zuqāq. (25) Andalusia. (26) Rūm. (27) Constantinople. (28) Slavs. (29) Khazars. (30) Baltic and Varangians. (31) Surrounding Ocean. (32) Dibācha Islands. (33) Islands of the Zanj Empire. [*Note*: Although in the R. Ramsay Wright edition of the Arabic text, region 22 is called "al-Zanj," or Zanzibar, more likely the correct reading, to which Professor M. Mīnovī has drawn attention, should be al-Zābij, meaning Java.]

the seven-fold division of climate, following in much of his terminology the old Persian division of the world into seven zones, *keshvars*. As he states:

> Members of this profession (geography) divided the habitable land into seven long strips from east to west parallel to the equator called "climates."

The principle of the division is that the middle points of contiguous strips differ from each other by half an hour in the length of the longest summer day.[33]

He is also aware, however, of other types of division—for example the threefold scheme of Firaidūn and Noah, the fourfold division of the Greeks (into Asia Major, Asia Minor, Libya, and Europe) and the ninefold classification of the Hindus.[34]

The world is described by al-Bīrūnī in the following manner:

> The reader is to imagine the inhabitable world, as lying in the northern half of the earth, and more accurately in one-half of this half—[that is], in one of the quarters of the earth.[35] It is surrounded by a sea, which both in the West and East is called the comprehending one; the Greeks call its western part near their country [*okeanos*]. This sea separates the inhabitable world from whatever continents or inhabitable islands there may be beyond it, both towards West and East; for it is not navigable on account of the darkness of the air and the thickness of the water, because there is no more any road to be traced, and because the risk is enormous, whilst the profit is nothing. Therefore people of olden times have fixed marks both on the sea and its shores which are intended to deter from entering it.[36]

In the fourth physical question which al-Bīrūnī asks Ibn Sīnā, he puts forward a question which has baffled modern geologists as it did many medieval natural historians. Al-Bīrūnī asks, "Why is it that a quarter of the earth is the site of agriculture and civilization while the other northern quarter as well as the two southern ones have remained uninhabited although the astrological laws of the two southern quarters are like the two northern?"[37] He does recognize a symmetry in the design of the world, however, for he says that "it is possible, nay, even likely, that each pair of quarters of the earth forms a coherent, uninterrupted unity, the one as a continent, the other as an ocean."[38]

The description of the seven climates, their ecological, cultural, religious, and astrological features, would lead this discussion too far

[33] *EA*, p. 138.

[34] *EA*, pp. 142–147. Al-Bīrūnī discusses in detail the cities located in each zone and the astrological influences acting upon them.

[35] Al-Bīrūnī calls this habitable quadrant *rub' ma'mūrah* (*EA*, p. 121).

[36] *Alberuni's India*, I, 196.

[37] Dehkhodā, *Sharḥ-i ḥāl-i nābighih-i shahīr-i Īrān* . . ., p. 54; *al As'ilah wa'l-ajwibah*, p. 41.

[38] *Alberuni's India*, I, 266. It is curious that on the question of symmetry he rejects the island in the South Pole which the Hindus called *Vaḍavāmukha*. In this and other passages in *India* and the *Chronology of Ancient Nations*, al-Bīrūnī hints at the existence of another continent opposite the Asiatic land mass, that is, America, to preserve the longitudinal symmetry of the earth.

afield. It suffices to state that the sevenfold division of the world is symbolically an affirmation of the passivity of the earth with respect to heaven and an acknowledgment that all things here below are

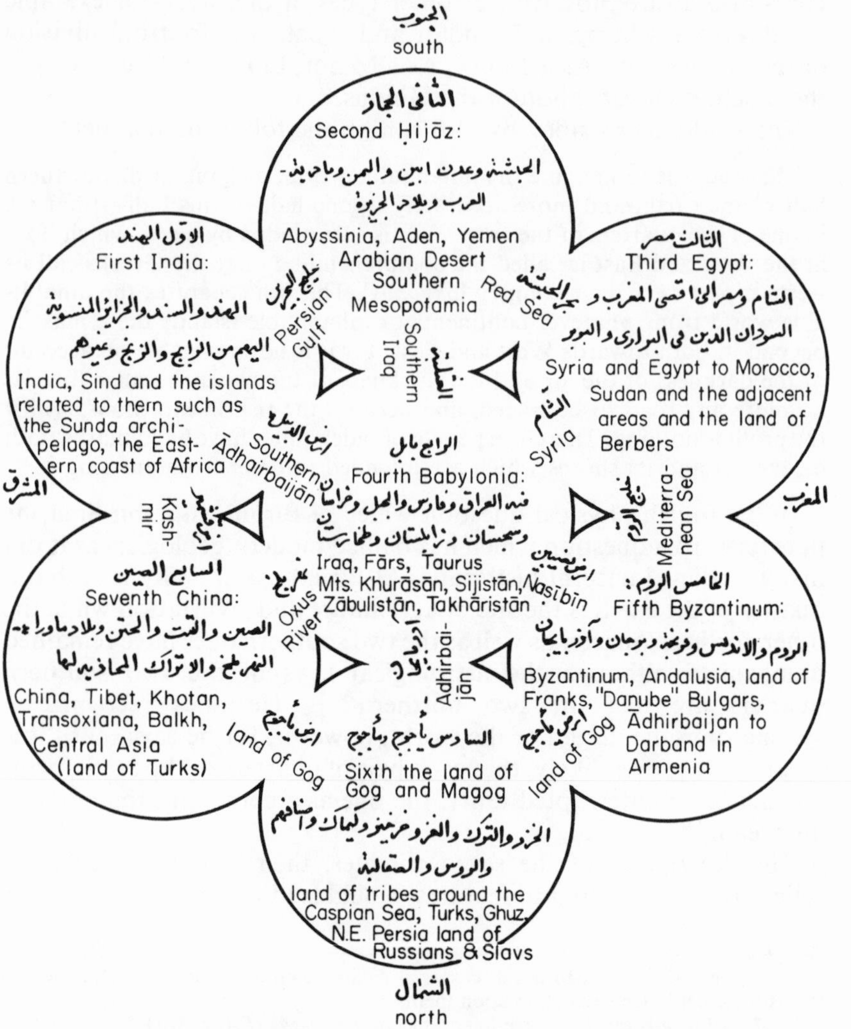

Figure 8. Al-Bīrūnī's representation of the seven climates.

made in the image of what exists above in the heavens. This sevenfold division was accepted not only in the Islamic world but also in Zoroastrian Persia and Greece and before that in Babylonia. Al-Bīrūnī makes the analogy even more clear by presenting the seven climates in a novel manner as seven circles, rather than strips, to make them conform in geometry as well as number to the seven spheres of heaven. In his *Kitāb taḥdīd nihāyāt al-amākin* he gives the diagram shown in Figure 8 which synthesizes into an intelligible whole the geography of the entire world known to the medieval Muslims.[39]

The world whose geography al-Bīrūnī describes in such great detail is occupied by the minerals, plants, and animals who comprise the totality of creatures possessing physical existence here on earth. Abū Raiḥān follows closely the usual scheme of medieval authors without, however, describing in any detail the plant and animal kingdoms. His study of them is pointed more toward their pharmacological and medical properties than anything else. Considering other kingdoms in their relation to man is legitimate for al-Bīrūnī, since—like the Ikhwān al-Ṣafā'—he believes that man, in the universal sense of this word, has "migrated" through the other realms in order to reach perfection and therefore contains within himself the nature of the creatures of the other realms.[40] This "migration" signifies the gradation of being in the Universe which according to al-Bīrūnī as well as most of his contemporaries is a hierarchy where each creature occupies a position in the ontological scale in conformity with its own nature.

The mineral kingdom which forms the base of support for the plants and animals is studied by Abū Raiḥān in greater detail than the others. The *Kitāb al-jamāhir* . . . which, as we have said, is the

[39] Validi Togan, *Biruni's Picture of the World*, p. 61. Al-Bīrūnī, *The Determination of the Coordinates of Cities*, p. 102. See also George Sarton's review of this book in *Isis*, 34:31 (1943–1944). For an explanation of the exact meaning of Muslim geographical terms, see *Ḥudūd al-'ālam, The Regions of the World*, trans. and explained by V. Minorsky (Oxford, 1931).

This division into six regions circumscribing a central climate bears a striking resemblance to the pre-Islamic Persian division of the world and must have been inspired by it; see E. Herzfeld, *Zoroaster and His World* (Princeton, 1947), II, 680; and F. Justi, *Handbuch der Zendsprach* (Leipzig, 1864), p. 81.

[40] «الّا ما يعنون في الانسان انّه بالغ اقصى مرتبة الكمال بالاضافة الى ما دونه من الحيوان
ويذهبون فيه الى سنخه وجوهره لا انّه صعد الى الانسانية من انواعها حتى ارتقى من
الكلبية الى الدبية ثم الى القردية الى ان يأنس ...»

Al-Bīrūnī, *Kitāb al-jamāhir* . . ., p. 80. It is interesting to note that al-Bīrūnī mentions specifically the monkey as the last animal through whom man has "migrated" to reach his present state. Some have argued that this passage announces the modern theory of evolution. For our part we still believe that it refers to the gradation in the chain of being, especially since al-Bīrūnī so often mentions the function of Nature as the preserver of the species. See in this connection J. Z. Wilczynski, "On the presumed Darwinism of Alberuni eight hundred years before Darwin," *Isis*, 50:459–466 (December 1959).

most complete medieval text on mineralogy, contains the description of minerals and metals from all over the Asiatic, European, and African continents. There, the author treats not only the colors, odors, hardness, and other qualitative physical properties but the weight and density of many of the minerals and of course their medical properties and "virtues." As for the formation of minerals and metals, al-Bīrūnī follows the exhalation theory and more specifically the sulphur-mercury theory of Jābir ibn Ḥayyān.

Au chapitre de la formation des métaux la combinaison du soufre et du mercure, et ces deux corps ont une si grande part dans leur production, que le soufre en est dit *le père* (*abū*), et le mercure *la mère* (*umm*). Il est dit encore en être *l'âme* (*rūḥ*), comme l'arsenic et le soufre en sont *l'ésprit* (*nafs*).[41]

Not only does al-Bīrūnī follow the alchemical theory of sulphur and mercury, which are the masculine and feminine principles, for the origin of metals, but he also believes in the growth of minerals and the perfection of metals into gold. Minerals have a "life" of their own; their extraction from the earth, which as M. Eliade has mentioned was considered by the ancients as a kind of obstetrics,[42] should therefore be for a noble purpose. In order for man to have the right to deprive the minerals and metals of the "life" they possess, he must spend the wealth accumulating from them in the way of God,[43] not to satisfy his own lust.

It is curious that after accepting the principles of the "natural philosophy" of alchemy, al-Bīrūnī rejects alchemy itself in a very categorical manner. Contemporary scholars have repeatedly discussed al-Bīrūnī's criticism and condemnation of this art. For example, Yūsuf 'Alī writes that "al-Bīrūnī considered alchemy to be a sort of witchcraft or magic, though he saw that the force behind its vogue was greed rather than want of intelligence."[44] Or, as Mohammad Haschmi states: "Beruni spricht über die Umwand-

---

[41] J. J. Clément-Mullet, "Pesanteur spécifique de diverses substances minérales, procédé pour l'obtenir d'après Abou'l-Raihan Albirouny," *Journal Asiatique*, 2:391–392 (1858).

[42] M. Eliade, *Forgerons et alchimistes*, Introduction and chap V.

[43] Al-Bīrūnī, *Kitāb al-jamāhir* . . ., p. 10. He quotes the verse:

« وَالَّذِينَ يَكْنِزُونَ الذَّهَبَ وَالفِضَّةَ وَلَا يُنْفِقُونَهَا فِى سَبِيلِ اللهِ فَبَشِّرْهُم بِعَذَابٍ اليمٍ . »

"They who hoard up gold and silver and spend it not in the way of Allah, unto them give tidings (O Muḥammad) of a painful doom" (Quran, IX, 34), in order to emphasize the fact that man does not have a right to exploit the other kingdoms for his own desires, which are insatiable, but may use them only in conformity with the law of God and in His way.

[44] A. Yusuf Ali, "Al-Bīrūnī's India," *Islamic Culture*, 1:481 (1927).

lung der Elemente. Er behauptet was die Natur hervorbringen kann, kann die Kunst nich nachmachen."[45] Aldo Mieli, in praising al-Bīrūnī, likewise points to his condemnation of alchemy and his opposition to its philosophy.[46]

All these judgments are quite understandable since al-Bīrūnī himself states:

> We understand by witchcraft, making by some kind of delusion a thing appear to the senses as something different from what it is in reality . . . One of the species of witchcraft is alchemy, though it is generally not called by this name.[47]

What has been partly overlooked, however, is the distinction between the belief in transformation and the cosmological principles of alchemy. It is true that al-Bīrūnī does not believe in the physical transformation of metals made possible by a human agent. It is also certain that he is not concerned with "spiritual alchemy" and therefore does not accept the science at its symbolic level of interpretation. Yet, what he does accept with all clarity is the cosmological doctrine of the male-female, or sulphur-mercury, theory of Jābirian alchemy and the belief in the growth and life of minerals. Abū Raiḥān, like many medieval Muslim scientists, rejected the idea of transmutation because of lack of evidence, while accepting the cosmological principles of alchemy in order to explain the origin and properties of the mineral kingdom.

Man and the World

In his study of the relation between man and the world, al-Bīrūnī accepts the analogy of microcosm and macrocosm which is so closely allied to the concept of the chain of being, without developing these topics in any detail. "And how should a man wonder at this," he asks, "it being undeniable that God has the power to combine the whole world in one individual (that is, to create a microcosm)!"[48] The body of man as the physical part of the microcosm is composed of diverse and contradictory elements of the cosmos held together in a unity.[49] He possesses five senses which bring

[45] M. J. Haschmi, *Die Quellen des Steinbuches des Bērūnī* (Bonn, 1935), p. 17.

[46] "Fra gli arabi più meritataménte celebri, ricordo anche Albiruni (973–1048) presso a poco contemporaneo ad Avicenna; esso, per quanto si occupasse meno di chimica, era assolutamente contrario alle falsificazioni alchimistiche, come si potrà facilmente vedere da un passo di una sua opera che riporteramo più oltre, trattando del discredito nel quale era caduta l'alchimia." A. Mieli, *Pagine di storia della chimica* (Rome, 1922), pp. 124–125. See also *ibid.*, pp. 231–233.

[47] *Alberuni's India*, I, 187.

[48] *Chronology of Ancient Nations*, p. 2.

[49] Al-Bīrūnī, *Kitāb al-jamāhir* . . ., pp. 6–7.

him knowledge of the physical world. But he exceeds other animals not by the acuteness of his senses but by the possession of Intellect by virtue of which he is God's vicegerent (*khalīfat Allāh*) on earth. It is because man is the vicegerent of the Creator that things in this world are ordered on his behalf, and he is given power over them.[50]

Of the five senses of man, the most important are hearing and sight, which lead him from the sensible to the intelligible world. As al-Bīrūnī writes: "Sight connects what we see to the signs of Divine Wisdom in creatures and demonstrates the being of the Creator from his creation."[51] Likewise, the ear is the channel through which man hears the word of God and His command. These two senses, according to Abū Raiḥān, are joined not in the brain but in the heart which is the seat of intelligence.

Man, the caliph of God on earth, who is given all these gifts and above all is endowed with intelligence, is put here on earth in order to administer to all creatures as a caliph rules over his realm. It is for man to use his sight to see "the signs of God in the horizon," and to use his reason in order to journey from the company of creatures to that of the Creator. Only in this way does he realize his noble nature and the purpose for which he was created.

[50] *Kitāb al-jamāhir* . . ., p. 4.
[51] *Ibid.*, p. 5. «أما البصر فللاعتبار بما يشاهد من آثار الحكمة في المخلوقات واستدلال على الصانع من المصنوعات.»

Al-Bīrūnī quotes the Quranic verse:

«سَنُرِيهِمْ آيَاتِنَا فِي الْآفَاقِ وَفِي أَنفُسِهِمْ حَتَّىٰ يَتَبَيَّنَ لَهُمْ أَنَّهُ الْحَقُّ.»

"We shall show them Our portents on the horizons and within themselves until it will be manifested unto them that it is the Truth" (Quran, XLI, 53) as proof of his statement.

CHAPTER 9

The Wedding of Heaven and Earth in Astrology

Principles of Astrology

The integration of astrology in its Alexandrian–Hermetic formulation into the monotheistic esotericism of Islam during the medieval period was due not so much to the conformity of judicial astrology with this perspective but to the fact that astrology contains a primordial symbolism of great contemplative value.[1] As traditionally considered, the metaphysical basis of astrology is the spontaneous identification of the rhythms of the heavens with the prototypes of the physical world, these prototypes existing in the heaven of the signs (*falak al-burūj*).[2] The signs of the Zodiac in their indefinite variety hide and reveal Pure Being at the same time. They are at once a veil which

[1] A distinction must be made between genethliac astrology, which is concerned with the casting of horoscopes for an individual, and the more general judicial astrology which deals with the whole of an institution, society, or ruler, and the relation of the cosmos to the human environment. See O. Neugebauer, "The history of ancient astronomy: problems and methods," *Astronomical Society of the Pacific*, 58:39 (1946). Al-Bīrūnī had knowledge of both types of astrology and practiced them throughout his life. In this study we seek to present only the principles of astrology without examining in any detail its many judicial or genethliac applications.

[2] "L'astrologie, telle qu'elle fut répandue au moyen âge dans les civilisations chrétienne et islamique et qu'elle subsiste encore en certains pays arabes, doit sa forme à l'hermétisme alexandrin; elle n'est donc ni islamique ni chrétienne dans son essence, et elle ne saurait d'ailleurs trouver une place dans la perspective religieuse des traditions monothéistes, étant donné que cette perspective insiste sur la responsabilité de l'individu devant son Créateur et qu'elle évite de ce fait tout ce qui pourrait voiler cette relation par la considération de causes intermédiaires. Si l'astrologie a néanmoins pu être intégrée dans les ésotérismes chrétien et musulman, c'est qu'elle perpétuait, véhiculée par l'hermétisme, certains aspects d'un symbolisme très primordial; la pénétration contemplative de l'ambiance cosmique, et l'identification spontanée des apparences—constantes et rythmiques—du monde sensible avec leurs prototypes éternels correspondent en effet à une mentalité encore primitive, au sens propre et positif de ce terme. Cette primordialité implicite du symbolisme astrologique se rallume au contact de la spiritualité, directe et universelle, d'un ésotérisme vivant, comme le scintillement d'une pierre précieuse s'allume lorsqu'elle est exposée aux rayons d'une lumière." T. Burckhardt, *Clé spirituelle de l'astrologie musulmane*, pp. 5–6.

covers the "face of the Beloved" and a prism which disperses the "light of Being" into its constituent colors which comprise the world of manifestation. The regular cycles of the heavens in their rhythms symbolize the "eternal essences" while their effects upon the Earth indicate the interrelatedness of the parts of the cosmos and the submission of the beings of this world to their heavenly prototypes. The basis of astrology is symbolically the indissoluble marriage between heaven and earth and the derivation of all things on earth from their celestial counterparts.

The Zodiac, which contains the archetypes of cosmic manifestation, is differentiated by the three basic conditions of cosmic existence, namely time, space, and number. The division of the Zodiac into twelve signs and into the qualitative directions of space depends upon

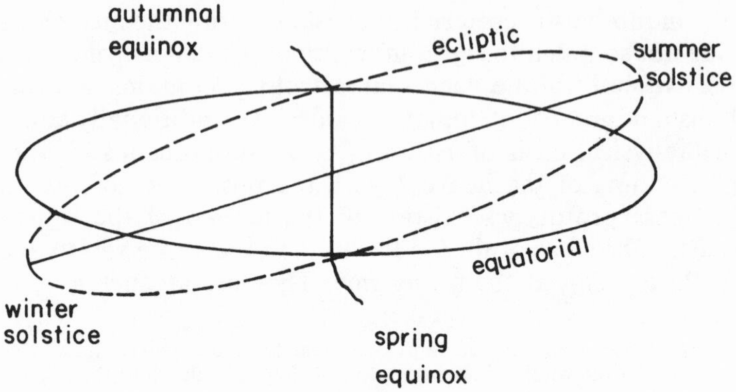

Figure 9. The ecliptic.

the motion of the Sun which, as the most direct symbol of the spiritual principle of the Universe, is responsible for the qualification of space and its determination out of the indefiniteness of circular motion as well as for the measurement of time. The annual path of the Sun differentiates space into four cardinal points corresponding to the two solstices and equinoxes (see Figure 9). Once these four points on the Zodiacal circle are specified, the other eight points become automatically determined because of the natural ternary and hexagonal division of the circle. To each corner of the square there correspond two opposite points so that altogether the circle is differentiated into twelve parts (see Figure 10).

The basic number of the Zodiac, 12, is a product of 4 and 3. As interpreted traditionally, these numbers symbolize the fourfold polarization of Universal Nature into the active qualities of heat and cold and the passive qualities of moistness and dryness which in their combination form the elements, and the three fundamental tendencies of the Universal Spirit (*al-Rūḥ*), which are (1) the descending movement away from the Principle, (2) horizontal expansion, and (3) ascent back to the Principle. The 12 signs, therefore, contain in their numerical symbolism the totality of the principles which govern the cosmos.[3]

Each sign of the Zodiac possesses several relations with the other signs, the most important perhaps being the trigonal and square (see Figure 11).[4]

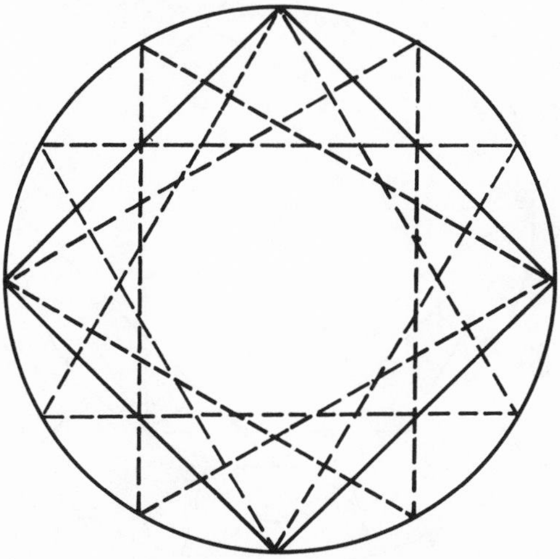

Figure 10. The twelve-fold differentiation of the circle.

Par suite cette réintégration ou multiplication, tous les points du zodiaque qui se trouvent en relation de trigone ont la même nature élémentaire mais se distinguent par les qualités relevant du ternaire de l'Esprit; et tous les points qui se trouvent en relation de carré ont la même qualité spirituelle mais se différencient par les contrastes élémentaires.[5]

The relation between the signs depends upon the angle they make with each other, so that the right angle implies contrast, an angle of 180 degrees opposition, of 120 degrees perfect synthesis, and of 60 degrees affinity. They are furthermore related in a symmetric fashion as

[3] *Clé spirituelle . . .*, pp. 14ff.
[4] Al-Bīrūnī, *Elements of Astrology* (*EA*), p. 225.
[5] Burckhardt, *Clé Spirituelle . . .*, p. 17.

shown in Figure 12.[6] The signs joined vertically, being equidistant from an equinoctial point, are equipollent, since the day hours of one are equal to the night hours of the other. Those joined horizontally correspond in their course since their day hours and night hours are equal and their ascensions at the equator identical.

The interrelation between the signs, which symbolizes the intertwining and weaving of cosmic tendencies into a pattern of indefinite

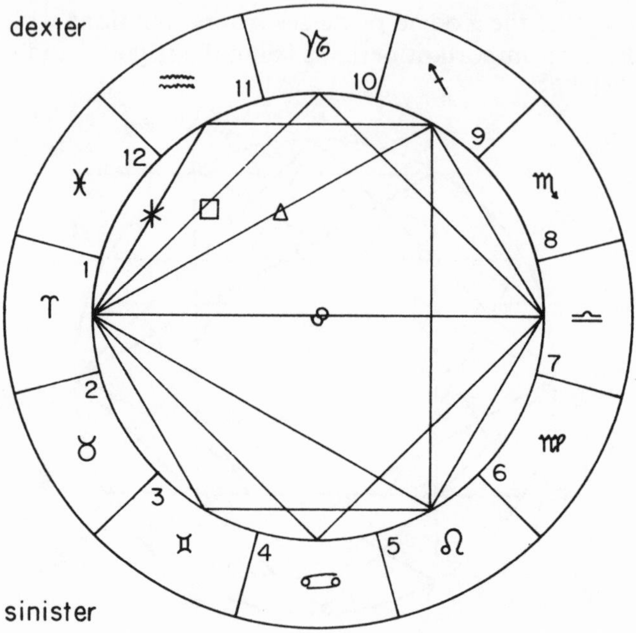

Figure 11. Relations between the Zodiacal signs. The signs used are ☌, conjunction; ☍, opposition; ✳, sextile; □, quartile; △, trine.

complexity yet principial simplicity, is complementary with the relation of the signs to sublunary qualities. First of all, the signs themselves possess certain qualities which in the unified cosmos of the astrological perspective are manifested throughout the Universe. As al-Bīrūnī states:

If they (the signs) are written down rows, upper and lower, the first sign above and the second below it, and so on to the last, all those of the upper row are hot and those of the lower cold, while the pairs so arranged are alternately dry and moist.[7]

[6] *EA*, p. 227. [7] *EA*, pp. 209–210.

To these fundamental qualities are added others which derive from them, such as the male and female, active and passive, fertile and barren, voiced and voiceless.

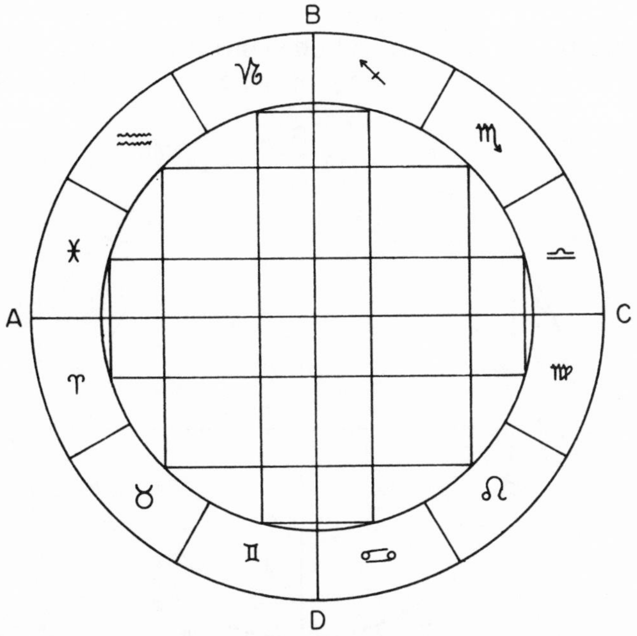

Figure 12. Equipollent signs and those with corresponding courses. The vertical lines join equipollent signs, the horizontal those corresponding in their course. ADC: northern half; CBA: southern half; DAB: ascending half; BCD: descending half.

TABLE V. THE FOUR NATURES AND THE ZODIACAL SIGNS

	Dry	*Moist*	*Dry*	*Moist*	*Dry*	*Moist*
Hot	Aries	Gemini	Leo	Libra	Sagittarius	Aquarius
Cold	Taurus	Cancer	Virgo	Scorpius	Capricornus	Pisces

Possessing this basic relation with the four fundamental cosmic qualities, the signs are naturally related to all cosmic manifestations which are themselves due to the various combinations of these qualities. Inasmuch as these combinations are limitless, the analogies to be drawn between them and the signs are also without end. For our purposes here, however, it is enough to mention only some of the more fundamental relations.

With respect to terrestrial existence, the relation of the signs to the cardinal points of the compass is of considerable significance because of the role of "sacred geography" and orientation in sacred rites and the architecture of temples and other structures which are based on the knowledge of the "anatomy of the cosmos." Al-Bīrūnī presents

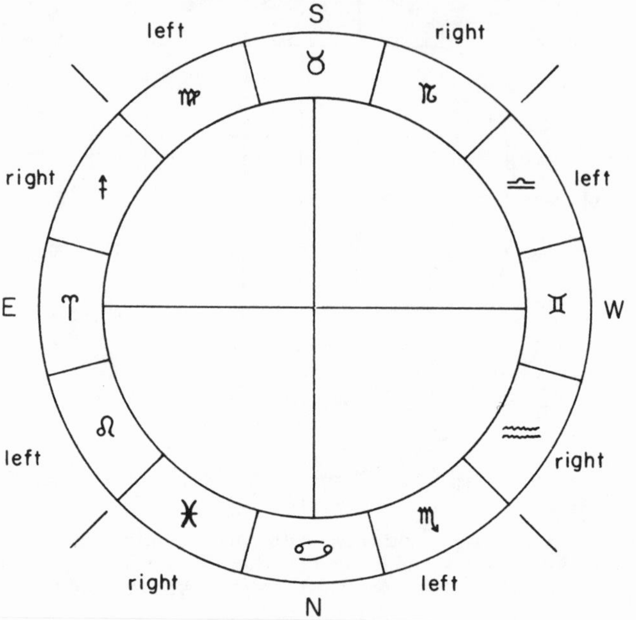

Figure 13. The signs and the directions.

this relation in Figure 13 where the directions as well as the dexter, sinister aspects of the signs are indicated.[8]

The relation of the signs to the winds follows that of the directions so that "a wind coming from a quarter associated with a particular sign is also associated with that sign; thus the East wind with Aries, the West with Gemini, the South with Taurus and the North with Cancer. Similarly with the intermediate quarters, a S.E. wind is related to Virgo or to Sagittarius according as it is nearer S. or E."[9]

The three kingdoms which are generated from the combination of the four elements, and therefore the four qualities, are also intimately

[8] *EA*, p. 215.
[9] *EA*, p. 215.

connected with the signs. Al-Bīrūnī describes this relation in the following manner:

The first triplicity is found of Aries, Leo and Sagittarius all of which are fiery in their nature withering and heavy, while the special domain of each is for Aries, fires in ordinary use, for Leo those present in minerals and plants, and for Sagittarius that which is distributed from the heart of animals throughout the body.

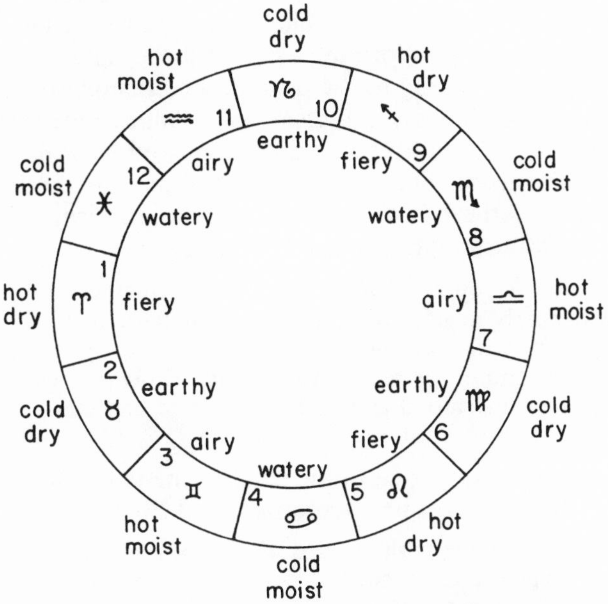

Figure 14. The signs and the elements and natures.

The second triplicity composed of Taurus, Virgo and Capricorn is earthy, generous with its wealth, and the interpretation of its effects is that Taurus is responsible for pastureland which is not sown, Virgo for plants which have neither berries nor seeds and small trees, Capricorn for sown crops and large and tall trees.

Gemini, Libra and Aquarius form the third triplicity which is airy in nature, sending winds abroad; and in detail Gemini is characterized by that quiet air which produces and sustains life, Libra, by that which causes trees to grow, fertilizes them and produces fruit, and Aquarius by destructive storms.

The fourth triplicity of Cancer, Scorpius and Pisces is watery in sympathy, Cancer denoting sweet pure water, Scorpius that which is turbid and Pisces that which is stinking, distasteful and alkaline.

[As for their relation to the seasons of year and periods of human life] Aries, Taurus and Gemini are vernal, changeable, govern childhood, the east and the east wind, the first watch of day and night. Cancer, Leo and Virgo are aestival, restful, govern youth, the south and the south wind and the second watch. Libra, Scorpius and Sagittarius are autumnal, changeable, govern adult life, the west and its wind, and the third watch, while Capricorn, Aquarius and Pisces are hibernal, peaceful, govern old age, the north and the north wind and the fourth watch.[10]

The human microcosm, which contains all of the Universe in itself, is likewise made up of the four qualities and possesses analogies with the signs, these analogies forming a part of the foundation of medieval Muslim medicine. Owing to the profound contemplative perspective which this relation implies, it is also used in many Ṣūfī treatises such as the *Gulshan-i rāz* of Maḥmūd Shabistarī and *al-Insān al-kāmil* of 'Abd al-Karīm al-Jīlī. The "elemental" relation is, of course, between the humours of the body which sustain the physical aspect of the microcosm and the signs. As al-Bīrūnī says:

> When therefore you know the active virtues, whether dryness or moisture, it will not be concealed from you what particular element of the world and what particular humour of the body each sign resembles. Each sign that is hot and dry is related to fire and yellow bile, each that is hot and moist to air and blood and each that is cold and moist to water and phlegm.[11]

The signs are also related to the parts of the body and may be said to form their macrocosmic counterparts. Al-Bīrūnī writes:

> The following are the various parts of the body which are related to the several signs. The head and face to Aries, the neck and windpipe to Taurus, the arms and hands to Gemini, the chest, breasts, sides, stomach and lungs to Cancer, the heart to Leo, the womb with its contents to Virgo, the back and buttocks to Libra, the genitals to Scorpius, the thighs to Sagittarius, the knees to Capricorn, the shanks to Aquarius and the feet and heels to Pisces.[12]

As the parts and humors of the body are dependent upon the signs, so are the diseases of the body, which according to traditional medicine are due to the disequilibrium of the qualities and humors in the body, dependent upon these celestial archetypes. Al-Bīrūnī gives exhaustive tables of the many correspondences existing between the two domains and assures the reader that "the signs are also indicative of the various diseases of man, of his complexion, figure, face, and the like . . ."[13]

[10] *EA*, pp. 230–231.
[11] *EA*, pp. 210–211.
[12] *EA*, p. 216.
[13] *Ibid.*

The illustrations of the analogies existing between the signs of the Zodiac and the cosmos could be carried out indefinitely. But enough has been said to demonstrate the contemplative and primordial symbolism of the Zodiac. "Standing" outside of the space of the cosmos the signs are the "heaven of the archetypes" of cosmic manifestation. Pure Being, which is metacosmic, is hidden by the signs while at the same time its polarization is manifested by them. They contain the four qualities of Universal Nature (*al-ṭabīʿat al-kullīyah*) and the three fundamental tendencies of the Spirit (*al-Rūḥ*) and therefore the archetypes or "ideas," of all the manifestations of Nature which we witness in the world.

Between the world of archetypes and the terrestrial environment lie the seven planets which from the contemplative point of view can be considered as modes of the Intellect in its macrocosmic aspect.[14] They are "the cosmic intermediaries between the immutable world of the archetypes and the terrestrial milieu,"[15] or, as al-Bīrūnī says, "[they] are spiritual forces which change the nature of bodies submitted to their influence . . ."[16] Likewise, the spheres of the planets form an intermediate domain belonging at the same time to the corporeal and subtle worlds.[17] As intermediaries, the planets "transmit" the fundamental qualities of the Universe from the archetypal world to the earth so that they themselves, like the signs, are identified with certain maleficent as well as beneficent qualities and other cosmic polarizations such as active-passive, male-female, and Oriental-Occidental differentiations. In al-Bīrūnī's words:

> All of the three superior planets and the Sun are male, Saturn among them, being like a eunuch. Venus and the moon are female, and Mercury hermaphrodite, being male when associated with the male planets, and female when with the female; when alone it is male in its nature. Some people say that Mars is female. But this opinion is not received.[18]

We have already mentioned the relation of the planets to the seven climates. Al-Bīrūnī also gives an exhaustive account of their relation to other aspects of the terrestrial environment, ranging from agricultural factors, minerals, spices, plants and animals to the human

[14] "Des modes de l'Intellect dans sa manifestation macrocosmique, modes qui réalisent ou mesurent les possibilités contenues dans la sphère indéfinie." Burckhardt, *Clé spirituelle* . . ., p. 25.

[15] *Ibid.*, p. 23. The number of the planets is 7 = 4 + 3; since it is also the product of 4 and 3 that gives the number of the signs, which is 12, it becomes clear that symbolically the planets are generated by the same archetypes as the signs.

[16] *EA*, p. 231.

[17] Burckhardt, *Clé spirituelle* . . ., p. 11.

[18] *EA*, p. 234.

body, psychology, architecture, religious and civil institutions.[19] For example, regarding the relation of the planets to the plant kingdom, al-Bīrūnī writes:

> Similarly the various organs of a plant are distributed to different planets. Thus, the stem of a tree is appropriated to the Sun; the roots to Saturn, the thorns, twigs and barks to Mars, the flowers to Venus, the fruit to Jupiter, the leaves to the moon, and the seed to Mercury. Even in the fruit of a plant like a melon the constituent parts are divided among several planets; the plant itself and the flesh of the fruit belong to the Sun, its moisture to the moon, its rind to Saturn, smell and color to Venus, taste to Jupiter, seed to Mercury and the skin of the seed and its shape to Mars.[20]

A similar relation exists with the members of the other kingdoms. As the macrocosmic manifestations of the Intellect, the planets must of necessity have a bearing upon all terrestrial beings which, like everything else in the cosmos, owe their existence to the Universal Intellect which in Islam is identified with the "light or reality of Muḥammad," *al-nūr al-muḥammadī* or *al-ḥaqīqat al-muḥammadīyah.*

With respect to the signs, the planets have a "domicile" as well as a place of exaltation (*sharaf*) and dejection (*hubūṭ*).[21] The domiciles where the planets have their maximum power are given in Figure 15.[22] Contrary to most Hindu astronomers and many Islamic ones, al-Bīrūnī does not consider the nodes of the Moon, or "head and tail of the dragon," to have the same effect as the planets nor does he discuss their cosmological symbolism.[23] He remains content with the seven regular planets. It is curious, however, that while rejecting the nodes al-Bīrūnī does give in the table of the places of exaltation the position of the "dragon's head" and "tail," making the scheme conform more to the Hindu and Muslim practice of his day.[24]

Table VI and the diagrams of Figures 15 and 16 indicate how the planets are related to the world of archetypes, or the signs, where they as well as all terrestrial beings find their origin and where alone

[19] *EA*, pp. 240–255. [20] *EA*, p. 236.

[21] Babylonian cuneiforms give a whole sign for the exaltation, and its opposite for the dejection, of each planet. For example, the Sun has his exaltation in Aries and dejection in the opposite sign Libra. In the late Egyptian papyri and Pliny's *Naturalis Historia*, as well as in most Muslim texts, the places of exaltation and depression are limited to single points rather than whole signs. See W. Hartner, "The pseudoplanetary nodes of the moon's orbit in Hindu and Islamic iconographies," *Ars Islamica*, 5:117 (1938).

[22] *EA*, p. 257.

[23] *EA*, p. 234. For an explanation of the symbolism of the nodes of the Moon, see W. Hartner, "The pseudoplanetary nodes . . .," pp. 113–154.

[24] *EA*, p. 258.

TABLE VI. THE EXALTATION AND DEPRESSION OF THE PLANETS

Saturn	21° of Libra
Jupiter	15° of Cancer
Mars	28° of Capricorn
Sun	19° of Aries
Venus	27° of Pisces
Mercury	15° of Virgo
Moon	3° of Taurus
Dragon's Head	3° of Gemini
Dragon's Tail	3° of Sagittarius

their significance can be understood. Without reference to the immutable realm of the signs, the motion of the planets remains without any significance; like all things, the planets find their meaning only when they are projected back to the Principle of which they are a manifestation.

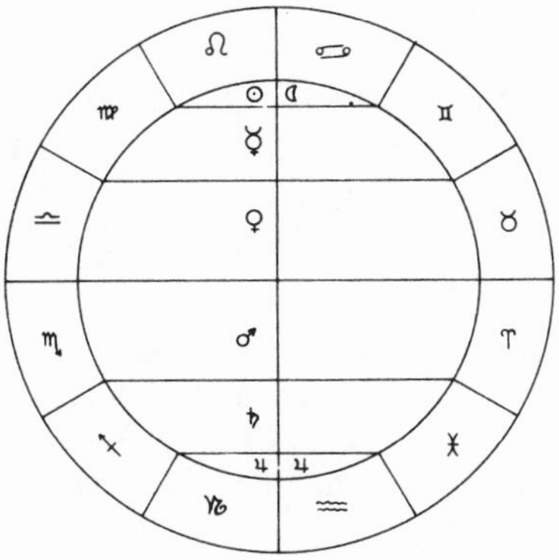

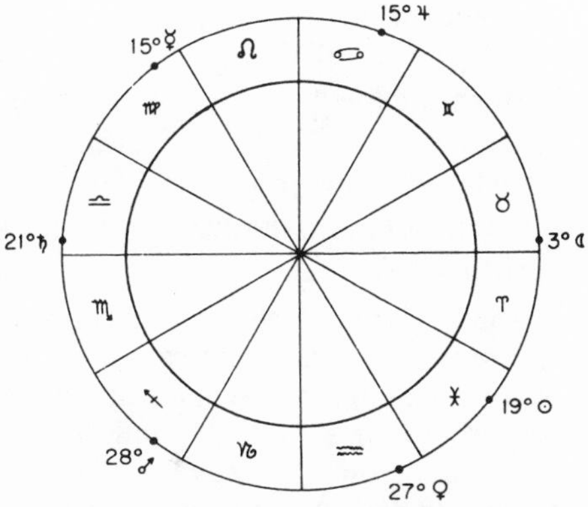

Figure 15 (left). The domiciles of the planets. Figure 16 (right). The exaltations and depressions of the planets. Whereas the symmetry of the domiciles in each figure is with respect to the main diameter, that of the exaltations and depressions is about the center of the Zodiacal circle. It is therefore less obvious although no less real than the axial symmetry of the domiciles.

Besides the Sun, the Moon is the only heavenly body whose motion around the Earth, traced by observation in the heaven of fixed stars, is a circle, or at least nearly so. The Moon as the symbol of the feminine principle of the Universe measures the heavens in a passive manner as the Sun does in a masculine and active way.[25] As

[25] "Le soleil mesure donc l'espace céleste d'une façon active, de même que l'acte essentiel de l'Intellect représente le *fiat lux* qui extrait le monde des ténèbres de l'indifférenciation potentielle; par contre, la lune mesure le ciel passivement en parcourant

the planet closest to the Earth, the Moon acts as the intermediary between all the heavens and the terrestrial domain so that the lunar mansions synthesize in themselves all the aspects of the Intellect which are manifested in the planetary spheres and the archetypal world of the signs. The numerical symbolism involved clarifies this relation. The number of the mansions of the Moon, which is 28, is equal to 7 + 6 + 5 + 4 + 3 + 2 + 1, that is, the sum of the number of planets.[26] Moreover, the 28 mansions are the macrocosmic counterparts of the 28 letters of the Arabic alphabet which form the language of the Divine Word and may be considered as the form or expression of the Divine Breath (*nafas al-raḥmān*) itself. Thus, the cosmos may also be considered, like the Revelation of God in his Sacred Book, as the manifestation of the Divine Word and a book in which the Divine mysteries are revealed. The significance of the lunar mansions in Islamic astrology is fundamental, particularly as it is related to the science of Divine Names in certain aspects of Sufism. The Moon itself, however, is not so important as in Hindu astrology where, in conformity with the structure of that civilization, the maternal aspect is given greater emphasis than in the more virile and patriarchal tradition of Islam. It must be mentioned, however, that in Islamic astrology the Moon does have a relation to terrestrial phenomena, particularly the growth and decay of things. As al-Bīrūnī writes:

> The students of physical sciences maintain that marrow and brain, eggs and most substances increase and decrease with the increase and decrease of the moonlight; that the wine in casks and jugs begins to move so as to get turbid with sediments; and that the blood during the increase of moonlight runs from the interior of the body towards the outer parts, whilst during its decrease it sinks back into the interior of the body.[27]

The Moon also influences meteorological phenomena. Al-Bīrūnī describes these influences fully; to give an example, he writes that "the term *anwā'* is associated with the rains, because the times of their occurrence are related to the setting of the mansions in the morning in the west, while that of *bawāriḥ* refers to the winds and is

---

le zodiaque solaire: elle subit à la fois les déterminations des directions de l'espace céleste et celles des directions des rayons solaires, double dépendance qui se traduit dans ses phases lumineuses et dans le rythme régulier de 18 ans, selon lequel leur cycle se déplace par rapport à celui du zodiaque." Burckhardt, *Clé spirituelle* . . ., p. 28.

[26] "Quant au nombre 28 des mansions de la lune, il s'obtient par la somme pythagoricienne des nombres de 1 à 7, ce qui signifie que le rythme lunaire développe ou expose en un mode successif toutes les possibilités contenues dans les archétypes et transmises, par la hiérarchie des intermédiaires, à la sphère qui entoure immédiatement le milieu terrestre." Burckhardt, *Clé spirituelle* . . ., p. 27.

[27] *Chronology of Ancient Nations*, p. 163.

related to other times of rain on the ascent of a mansion escaping from beneath the rays in the morning.[28]

The Moon possesses a double significance, first as the symbol of the female principle which governs the "maternal" processes on earth, such as the period of menstruation of the human female, and second as the "cosmic memory." Considered in this latter perspective, the Moon in its 28 mansions synthesizes the whole of the cosmos and therefore becomes the symbol of the Universal Man who is himself the archetype of the Universe. It is in this perspective that certain Ṣūfīs have identified the Moon with the Prophet Muḥammad—upon whom be peace—who in his inner reality is the Universal Man (*al-insān al-kāmil*) in whom all the cosmic qualities are unified and who is at once the origin and end of universal manifestation.

Al-Bīrūnī and His Attitude Toward Astrology

Much of the metaphysical basis of astrology, which we have tried to outline briefly above, does not appear explicitly in any of the extant writings of al-Bīrūnī; it may be debated, in fact, whether he was aware of the symbolic significance of astrology in the same way as Ibn 'Arabī and other Ṣūfīs, as can be seen by his opposition to alchemy, which, like astrology, is a major branch of Hermeticism. Yet, it is also certain that al-Bīrūnī was one of the greatest of Muslim astrologers and must therefore be considered as sympathetic to its point of view. "We know for certain that he remained attached to it to the end, even consulted it in his own troubles, and was reputed as the greatest astrologer."[29] It is true that al-Bīrūnī himself has little confidence in other astrologers when he says: "By the majority of people the decrees of the stars are regarded as belonging to the exact sciences, while my confidence in their results and in the profession resembles that of the least of them."[30] But here he is expressing his doubt about certain practitioners of the art, not astrology itself which he knew so well. To determine his attitude toward this subject therefore, it is best to turn to a passage of his own work where he describes the divisions and nature of astrology in detail:

There are as many divisions of astrology as there are elements in the Universe. These may be either simple or compound and on both the

[28] *EA*, p. 89. For an account of the relation of the moon to the life of man and other creatures, see *Alberuni's India*, I, 346–347.

For the meaning of *anwā'* and its use in Muslim meteorology and astrology, see Ibn Qutaibah, *Kitāb al-anwā'* (Hyderabad, 1956).

[29] Barani, "Al-Bīrūnī's scientific achievements," *Indo-Iranica*, 5:46 (1952).

[30] *EA*, p. 210.

influence of the planets is active. The former on the whole do not submit to such influence, nor to any change, except where they come into contact with each other, when, because they are mutually opposed and violent, they are always in strife. Such admixture does take place on the surface of the earth, but is only completed by the heat of the Sun's rays. So all four elements become united, and the surface is the place appointed for the action of the planets, which extends as far as the power of their rays penetrates by reason of the presence of interstices. Then these rays return by a contrary motion and carry with them the aqueous vapour which they have produced, and they rise from the earth until they reach a point where the power of such movement becomes weak. So this motion and agitation is the cause of all the vicissitudes and disasters of nature, the resultant phenomena being either permanent or temporary.

Anything therefore in the way of heat or cold or moderate temperature, of moisture or dryness, owing to movements of the atmosphere, or of the various forms of moisture carried by the winds such as cloud, rain, snow; everything that is heard in the air such as sharp claps and rolls of thunder; everything that is seen such as lightning, thunderbolts, rainbows, halos, meteors, also shooting stars, comets and similar atmospheric phenomena; everything that occurs in the earth in the way of tremors, and subsidences, and in the water as tempests and floods, and the flux and reflux of tides—all these form the subject matter of the first division of astrology. These phenomena are not permanent or rarely so; rain, snow, comets and earthquakes are those which have the longest duration; were they not sufficiently widespread their concentration in one spot would be disastrous.

A second division is that which is concerned with the mixed elements, such as occurs in plants and animals, and is of two kinds, affecting the whole of a population or only a part thereof. Famine may be taken as an example of the former, due to failure of crops or drought, and epidemics such as spread from country to country, like the plague and other pestilences which depopulate cities.

The latter variety is more localized and scattered in its appearances; it results from psychical phenomena, such as battles, struggle for power, change of dominion from one land to another, deposition of kings, revolutions, emergence of new religions and sects, so that this chapter is a long one and this variety the more important of the two.

The third division is specially concerned with the environment of the individual human or rather, the events which affect him in the course of his life, and the influences which remain behind him and in his progeny, while the fourth has to do with human activities and occupations. All of these are founded on beginnings or origins, "*mabādī*'," possibly trivial.

Beyond these there is a fifth division where such origins are entirely unknown. Here astrology reaches a point which threatens to transgress its proper limits, where problems are submitted which it is impossible to solve for the most part, and where the matter leaves the solid basis of universals for one of particulars. When this boundary is passed, where the astrologer is on one side and the sorcerer on the other, you enter a field of omens and divinations which has nothing to do with astrology although the stars may be referred to in connection with them.[31]

This passage speaks for itself; there is little need to try to prove al-Bīrūnī's belief in astrology after he himself divides the science into its constituent parts, some of which he considers to be true and others false. Moreover, we feel justified in identifying al-Bīrūnī with the astrological perspective since his *Elements of Astrology* was the standard text on the subject for many centuries. What remains perplexing, however, is al-Bīrūnī's rejection of alchemy which is the passive, or "earthly," aspect of Hermeticism of which the active, or "heavenly," aspect is astrology whose tenets he accepts fully.

The acceptance of astrology by al-Bīrūnī and, more generally, its integration into the Muslim perspective is due to the unitive point of view of this very ancient form of wisdom. This perspective is based on the idea of the polarization of Pure Being into the qualities of the signs of the Zodiac which are the archetypes for all cosmic phenomena. These archetypes are "transmitted" by the intermediate planetary spheres whose last sphere, that of the Moon, synthesizes all the cosmic qualities and as the "cosmic memory" transmits these qualities to the terrestrial domain. The qualities found here on earth are themselves the reflections of the heavenly archetypes which are the causes of all the diverse phenomena of Nature.

In astrology the whole cycle of manifestation, temporal and spatial, is seen as an unfolding of possibilities inherent in the unique Principle which itself lies above all manifestation. All multiplicity, all diversity, is deduced from Divine Unity, especially in Islamic astrology where this perspective of revealing the relation of the cosmos to its Unique Principle is of great importance. Therefore, although astrology, in placing intermediary causes between man and God, is opposed to a certain aspect of the Muslim perspective, its contemplative and symbolic side conforms closely to the basic spirit of Islam, which is to realize that all multiplicity comes from Unity and to seek to integrate the particular in the Universal. There can be little doubt that al-Bīrūnī did not only master the techniques of astrology but was also sympathetic to its perspective, since, like all genuine Muslim scholars and scientists, he was in search of the unifying principle behind the veil of the multiplicity of forms which the external aspect of Nature seems to display endlessly.

[31] *EA*, pp. 317–319.

CHAPTER 10

The Attitude of al-Bīrūnī Toward Philosophy and Learning

The paucity of philosophical writings by al-Bīrūnī makes it difficult to identify him with any of the well-known schools of his day. As we already know, few of his works on this subject have survived. From what remains of his writings, however, we can draw several conclusions of major importance. First of all, his intense interest in the Hermetical writings of al-Rāzī and others, and at the same time his frank criticism of some of their religious views, depict al-Bīrūnī as one who stands firm on his Islamic foundation and yet reaches for the elements of pre-Islamic forms of wisdom which would be conformable to his understanding of the Islamic spirit. It is also evident that al-Bīrūnī does not deal with the Hermetic-Neo-Pythagorean knowledge on the level of symbolic interpretation where it was integrated into certain dimensions of Islam.

Al-Bīrūnī was well acquainted with the philosophy of the Peripatetics as well as with that of the Alexandrian followers of Plato and Pythagoras. Although no direct works of his on this subject have been found, his letters to Ibn Sīnā, which have come down to us, represent one of the most acute Islamic criticisms of Aristotelian natural philosophy.[1] Much of the criticism against Aristotle in the Islamic world during the medieval period was not, as in Renaissance Europe, due to a lack of appreciation of Aristotelian ontology or dissatisfaction with his natural philosophy. Rather, such criticisms were usually made by the Ṣūfīs who considered Peripatetic philosophy as a "lesser truth" which hides its original metaphysical foundation by too great an emphasis upon rationalism, so that reason tends to obscure rather than to elucidate intellectual intuition. There were, however, two other sources of criticism of Peripatetic philosophy in Islam: the first by theologians like al-Ash'arī and, of course, Imām al-Ghazzālī, who completed the "destruction" of the

[1] *al-As'ilah wa'l-ajwibah*; 'A. A. Dehkhodā, *Sharḥ-i ḥāl-i nābighih-i shahīr-i Īrān . . .*, pp. 29–64.

rationalists a century after al-Bīrūnī; and the second which was less common, by those who attacked Aristotelianism either by pointing, by means of rational arguments, to the shortcomings of some aspect of its rational structure, as, for example, Ibn Sīnā's doctrine of motion criticizing that of the Stagirite, or by appealing to observation and the direct study of Nature to reject some aspect of Aristotle's physics. Al-Bīrūnī combines several of these lines of attack together, appealing to scripture, reason, and observation to show the weaknesses in certain aspects of Aristotle's philosophy; yet, at the same time, he displays great respect for the Stagirite. In fact, most often he criticizes not so much Aristotle himself as those of his followers who considered him infallible. As he writes:

> The trouble with these people is their extravagance in respect of Aristotle's opinions, believing that there is no possibility of mistakes in his views, though they know that he was only theorizing to the best of his capacity, and never claimed to be God's protected and immune from mistakes.[2]

The criticism of Aristotle by al-Bīrūnī is cosmological as well as astronomical and physical and involves questions which lie at the very heart of Peripatetic philosophy. Among these questions, the criticism of the eternity of the world has already been mentioned. Like the theologians, al-Bīrūnī considers the idea that the world is eternal as the most abhorrent of the Aristotelian doctrines and that which is most opposed to the Islamic perspective. He supports the criticism already made by John Philoponus (the Grammarian) against the Greeks on this subject. In one of his letters to Ibn Sīnā, Abū Raiḥān writes:

> God forbid that one should accuse John the Grammarian of falsification. If anyone deserves this title, it is Aristotle who has dressed his heresies in dissimulation and falsification. I think you have not seen the book of John dealing with the rejection of the views of Proclus regarding the eternity of the world and have not paused to see the book demolish and make absurd the deceits of Aristotle, nor have you read his commentaries upon the books of Aristotle. I object to Aristotle in that I see a beginning for time and motion. Aristotle, who himself considers any kind of infinite existence to be impossible, acknowledged this view, although, obeying the whim of his carnal soul (*nafs*), he later opposed his first view.[3]

[2] S. H. Barani, "al-Bīrūnī's scientific achievements," *Indo-Iranica*, 5:41 (1952). Al-Bīrūnī implies here the distinction between inspired writings which, like the sayings of the prophets and saints, have an ultimately Divine origin, and human knowledge based on reason which, even in the most favorable situation of Aristotelianism, does not transcend the purely human domain.

[3] *al-As'ilah* . . ., pp. 51–52; Dehkhodā, pp. 58–59. (The translations of these questions and answers are our own based on both the Arabic text and Dehkhodā's version.)

Al-Bīrūnī, in conformity with the Islamic perspective, as well as that of most other religions, believes in the possibility of many worlds and opposes the Aristotelian argument that there cannot be any other world than the one that is visible to us. In his fifth question put to Ibn Sīnā, he writes that:

A group of sages (*ḥukamā'*)[4] have been of the opinion that it is possible for another world to exist which differs from this world in nature. Aristotle has considered their views detestable, but his hatred is untimely and out of place. For we find information about natures and elements of things when we observe them with our eyes like a man born blind who can find out about sight only when he hears about its nature from other people. And if there were no faculty of hearing he would not know that in the world there is such a sense as sight, the fifth sense, by means of which colors and heights and shapes become visible and observable. To sum up, what harm can there be if there is a world which as we said differs in the directions of motion and is separated from this world by an isthmus (*barzakh*) so that each is hidden from the other?[5]

In the same correspondence with Ibn Sīnā, al-Bīrūnī discusses in several remarkable passages two basic aspects of the medieval sciences, namely, the gravity and levity of objects connected to their natural place in the Universe and the circular motion of the heavens. In his first question asked of Ibn Sīnā, he declares:

Since the heavens have no motion toward or away from the center, Aristotle has not acknowledged the gravity or levity of the heavens. However, this reasoning of Aristotle is not really aimed toward the desired end. It is possible to imagine in the realm of thought and possibility that the heavens do possess gravity which, however, does not cause them to move toward the center, because each part of the heavens resembles the other. After hypothesizing their having gravity, one may say that whenever by nature they are moved toward the center, their connected forms prevent them from doing so. And because of their forms, they remain stationary about the center. It is also conceivable that the heavens possess levity, but that levity does not cause them to move away from the center because this motion can only be conceived when the parts of the heavens become separated and dispersed from each other and when

[4] The word *ḥakīm* (plural *ḥukamā'*) is used in Arabic and Persian with two distinct meanings: the first refers to the followers of Greek philosophy, who tried to reach truth by means of rational demonstration. The second meaning implies wisdom, sagacity, and a knowledge (*ma'rifah*) which is *sapientia* rather than *scientia* and whose origin is ultimately Divine and not human. The most appropriate translation of *ḥakīm* would perhaps be "theosopher," as we have already indicated, if this term had not been colored by certain pseudo-spiritualist groups with whom it has become associated in recent years.

[5] *al-As'ilah* . . ., pp. 19–20; Dehkhodā, pp. 40–41.

a vacuum exists outside the heavens so that the parts move or become fixed in that vacuum. But because for us it has become proven and ascertained that the dispersal of the parts of the heavens is impossible and the existence of a vacuum absurd, therefore the heavens are themselves a hot fire limited and assembled in a place from which departure is impossible. As a result the levity or gravity of the heavens is not dependent upon the absurdities which he [Aristotle] has thought.[6]

We see that al-Bīrūnī is not criticizing the conclusions of Aristotle but the reasoning used to arrive at them.

In conjunction with the criticism of gravity and levity, Abū Raiḥān denies the Peripatetic notion of the natural place of the elements. He writes:

The presence of each element in its natural place is not certain because the natural place of gravity, that is, the base direction, is the center, and the natural place of levity, that is, the high direction, is the circumference. Yet, the center is nothing but a point, and a part of the earth, no matter how small we conceive it to be, cannot fit at the center . . . As for the boundary, it too is unable to hold any body so that light bodies may ascend to it, it being an imagined surface area. Besides, if we allow water to flow freely, taking away obstacles in its path, undoubtedly it will reach the center. Therefore, the claim that the natural place of water is above the earth has no basis. Consequently there is no natural place for any body.[7]

The Aristotelians, following the earlier Greek astronomers, considered circular motion to be natural to the heavens as rectilinear motion is natural to objects of the sublunary world. Al-Bīrūnī himself, in his astronomical works, always follows the Ptolemaic tradition, going back to Pythagoras, of analyzing the motion of the heavenly bodies in terms of circular motion. Yet he criticizes from the point of view of logic the doctrine of circular motion universally accepted in his time, without in any way implying its falsity. As before, he is more interested in criticizing the reasoning of the Aristotelians than their conclusions. He tells us:

As to there being only the possibility of circular motion for the heavens, it is possible that the heavens by essence and nature are the source of rectilinear motion, and by force and accident the source of circular motion, as is found in the stars which by nature move from east to west and by force from west to east. And if someone says that the stars have no accidental motion at all because they have no motion but the circular, and circular motion has no opposite to enable us to say that one is by nature

[6] *al-As'ilah* . . ., pp. 2–3; Dehkhodā, p. 29.
[7] *al-As'ilah* . . ., p. 51; Dehkhodā, p. 58.

and the other by force, we reply that falsification and concealment in such transverse sayings are obvious and clear.[8]

Abū Raiḥān goes so far as to imply that the heavens could have an elliptical motion without contradicting the tenets of medieval physics. Again, criticizing Aristotle on this point, he writes:

Aristotle has mentioned in his second article that the elliptical and lentil-shaped figures need a vacuum in order to have circular motion, and a sphere has no need of a vacuum. Such is not the case, however, for the elliptical figure is formed by the rotation of the ellipse about the major axis and the lentil-shaped figure by the rotation of that ellipse about the minor axis. Therefore, if in the process of revolving these ellipses which form these figures there be contradiction or infraction, what Aristotle has claimed does not occur. And there remain no necessary conditions for these figures other than those of the sphere, for if we make the axis of rotation of the ellipse the major axis and the axis of rotation of the lentil-shaped figure the minor axis, they will revolve like a sphere and have no need of a void. The objection of Aristotle, however, and his statement become true in the case where we make the minor axis the axis of the ellipse and the axis of rotation of the lentil-shaped figure . . . *I am not saying according to my belief that the shape of the great heavens is not spherical, but elliptical or lentil-shaped. I have made copious studies to reject this view, but I wonder at the logicians!*[9]

Al-Bīrūnī was much influenced by the atomistic theories of Muḥammad ibn Zakariyyā' al-Rāzī, and used many of his arguments against the Peripatetics.[10] As we noted in the Introduction, traditional atomism emphasizes the discontinuity between the finite and the Infinite, whereas the view which rejects atomism considers their aspect of continuity. These two views represent different aspects of the same truth, but on the level of logical discourse they are contradictory, so that historically many rationalistic criticisms have been made by one school against the other. Abū Raiḥān is aware of the many difficulties involved in the arguments of the various schools. He seems in fact more interested in showing that the "absurdities" of the followers of the Greek philosophers whom he calls the *ḥukamā'* were even greater than those of the Muslim theologians (*mutakallimūn*) whom they attacked. Al-Bīrūnī asks:

Why has Aristotle reproached the saying of the theologians that a body consists of invisible parts, and in what way has he chosen the saying of the philosophers who consider bodies to be indefinitely divisible, although the

[8] *al-As'ilah* . . ., p. 3; Dehkhodā, p. 30.

[9] *al-As'ilah* . . ., pp. 27–28; Dehkhodā, pp. 44–45 (italics ours).

[10] For the doctrines of atomism in Islam, especially the views of al-Rāzī, see S. Pines, *Beiträge zur islamischen Atomenlehre* (Berlin, 1936), pp. 34–93.

vices of the sayings of the philosophers are greater than the disgracefulness of the opinions of the theologians? For according to the saying of the philosophers who consider bodies to be connected and indefinitely divisible, it is necessary that a consequent rapidly moving body (*mutaḥarrik-i sarī'-i lāḥiq*) not touch the preceding slowly moving body (*mutaḥarrik-i baṭī'-i sābiq*). The touching of the preceding state by the consequent one is committed and determined if the consequent one traverses the intermediate distance so as to reach the preceding point; and the traversing of that distance requires the traversing of its parts. Since the parts of that distance are endless, how can one imagine that distance can be crossed? Therefore, no consequent state can reach the previous one.[11] It is necessary to give an example to prove this point. If there is a definite distance assumed between the Moon and the Sun, and both bodies move at that distance, it should be impossible for the Moon to reach the Sun although the motion of the Moon is much faster than that of the Sun. Such is not the case, however; by observation it is found that the Moon does overtake the Sun although such an event causes disgrace and turpitude to those who hold to the view of indefinite division as is well known and established among the geometers. What happens to the philosophers is more disgraceful than what happens to the theologians. How then can one escape what has befallen these two groups?[12]

To the reply of Ibn Sīnā that indefinite division exists potentially but cannot be carried out actually, al-Bīrūnī adds:

Abū 'Alī ibn Sīnā has learned this answer from Muḥammad ibn Zakariyyā' Rāzī . . . But that you say "actually"—I do not understand the meaning of this expression. For no matter how finely you grind collyrium you will never reach that part of which you speak because the actual division will be cut off before you reach that part. In any case, potentiality remains in its place. Also, according to your view it becomes necessary that the side of the square be equal to its diagonal; if you deny it you have opposed your own principles. Or you will say that between the parts there is a separation; in this case I ask if the separation is greater or smaller than the indivisible parts.[13]

[11] The arguments of Zeno are essentially repeated here.

[12] *al-As'ilah* . . ., pp. 17–18; Dehkhodā, p. 39.

[13] *al-As'ilah* . . ., p. 53; Dehkhodā, pp. 59–60. In this somewhat obscure argument, al-Bīrūnī is trying to show that if a square consists of indivisible parts, its sides and diagonal must have an equal number of parts.

If the indivisible parts are connected, the diagonal and side of the square should be equal, which, however, is impossible; while if the parts of the sides are connected but those of the diagonal separated, there must be space between the parts of the diagonal. Now if these empty spaces of the diagonal are equal to the indivisible parts, the diagonal will be twice the side, which is not the case; while if the spaces are smaller or larger than the indivisible parts, it is implied that those parts have quantity (*miqdār*) and can therefore be divided.

As a final example of the criticism of Aristotelian philosophy by al-Bīrūnī, we may consider the question of how change occurs. Abū Raiḥān himself asks:

In what way do change and vicissitude occur in certain objects and elements so that each of them changes into and becomes the other? Is this change because of the transition of one into another or because of the entrance of one into openings and ruptures of the other in such a way that after the mixture of the elements the original form remains and because of excessive mixing the subject appears as one?[14]

Ibn Sīnā, following Aristotle, answers these questions by saying that the *hylé*, which is capable of accepting all forms, throws off the form of one element and accepts that of another. For example, a jug full of water breaks when put into the fire because some of the *hylé* which had accepted the form of water now accepts the form of air which occupies a greater space.

Unsatisfied with this Aristotelian answer, al-Bīrūnī adds:

He who says that change consists in the dispersion of the elements of one thing in the parts of the elements of another does not say with respect to heating that the body seeks the wider space. On the contrary, he says that the element of fire enters the other bodies through its fissures and pores, and for this reason the element of fire has been added to it and by the addition of the two bodies the quantity of the sum increases; as when a jug of water is heated the element of fire enters into it, lengthens it, and breaks the jug. The reason for this occurrence is that we see whenever water leaves the form of the liquid and takes on the form of air again in the process of condensation it becomes converted to water. Therefore, if water were really converted to air, it would not convert to water in the case of condensation and it would not deserve to return to liquidity any more than any other air. Also, we say that it is necessary for you to give an explanation of the fact that a body lengthens due to heating; then that increase in length must cause a shortening in some other body to the same extent so that the occupied space will not be without an occupant. Otherwise how will that excess of length be removed?[15]

The several points already mentioned suffice to show the ingenuity of al-Bīrūnī as a critic of Aristotelian philosophy. He often accepts some cosmological tenet of the Peripatetics while at the same time attacking the reasoning upon which that tenet is based. For him there is a clear distinction between the syllogistic and rationalistic aspect of

This question is discussed in great detail by Khwājah Naṣīr al-Dīn al-Ṭūsī in his commentary upon the *Ishārāt* of Ibn Sīnā. See *Sharḥ al-ishārāt* (Tehran, 1378 [1958]), II, 9–36.

[14] *al-As'ilah* . . ., p. 34; Dehkhodā, p. 50.

[15] *al-As'ilah* . . ., pp. 55–56; Dehkhodā, pp. 61–62.

Aristotelianism and its cosmological doctrines, which he evaluates by direct appeal to the external manifestations of Nature, by the use of reason, and finally by means of the truths revealed in the Sacred Scriptures. These criteria permit him to adopt several of the main elements of Aristotelian cosmology without accepting many of the logical demonstrations and arguments used by the Peripatetics.

The Role of Learning in Islam

The devoutness of al-Bīrūnī as a Muslim has already been discussed. There is no doubt that he was orthodox and was penetrated deeply by the spirit of Islam. As a scholar and compiler he made studies which touch upon nearly every field of medieval learning, all of which he approaches as a Muslim. He fights vehemently against anything he believes to be against Islam, as, for example, the eternity of the world, while on the other hand he defends the virtues of acquiring knowledge in all domains as the duty of the Muslim. For example, with respect to the physical sciences he criticizes those who cover up their ignorance by appealing to God's wisdom and who make no effort to learn about the beauty of Nature through its study. As he says, "Many people attribute to God's wisdom all they do not know of physical sciences . . ."[16]

The study of creation as the handiwork of God is for al-Bīrūnī a natural and noble activity of man. Human reason, by the fact that it has its center in the Intellect, leads when unimpeded from the finite to the Infinite. As long as reason is tied to its principle, which is the Intellect, all of its activities acquire a "sacred" aspect because all learning which relates a domain to its principle partakes of this integrating and unitive function that belongs to the Intellect. There is for al-Bīrūnī no separation between "sacred" and "profane" learning. Whatever he studies, whether it be historical or physical sciences, takes on a religious character. Particularly the study of the visible world as the "signs" and creation of the Invisible, and of Nature as the creative power ordained by God to govern all things in the world, are for al-Bīrūnī characteristic features of the perspective of Islam. There is no legitimate domain outside of the spirit of Islam, least of all the domain of the manifestations of Nature, because the essence of this spirit is to integrate all particulars into the Universal, all divided knowledge into the unitive knowledge, or *ma'rifah*, which contains in principle the science of all things. Al-Bīrūnī, although not a gnostic (*'ārif*), shared that view in his approach

[16] *Chronology of Ancient Nations*, p. 253.

to all learning, and considered the pursuit of the traditional sciences as a religious activity. No better expression of al-Bīrūnī's attitude toward knowledge and the dependence of its verification upon God can be given than his own statement at the end of his *India* where he pleads for Divine help:

> We ask God to pardon us for every statement of ours which is not true. We ask Him to help us that we may adhere to that which yields Him satisfaction. We ask Him to lead us to a proper insight into the nature of that which is false and idle that we may sift it so as to distinguish the chaff from the wheat. All good comes from Him, and it is He who is clement toward his slaves. Praise be to God, the Lord of the worlds, and His blessings be upon the Prophet Muḥammad and his whole family![17]

The cosmos in which al-Bīrūnī lived and breathed is the handiwork of God in which all true science leads ultimately to the Creator and possesses truth which is guaranteed only when it is sanctioned by Him.

[17] *Alberuni's India*, II, 246.

The Essence of the First Absolute Light, God, gives constant illumination, whereby it is manifested and it brings all things into existence, giving life to them by its rays. Everything in the world is derived from the Light of His Essence and all beauty and perfection are the gift of His bounty, and to attain fully to this illumination is salvation.

Shaikh al-ishrāq Shihāb al-Dīn
al-Suhrawardī—*Ḥikmat al-ishrāq*

PART III

Ibn Sīnā

CHAPTER 11

The Life and Works of Ibn Sīnā and His Significance

Abū 'Alī al-Ḥusain ibn 'Abdallāh ibn Sīnā, or Avicenna, entitled al-Shaikh al-Ra'īs, or Ḥujjat al-ḥaqq by his compatriots, simply Shaikh by his disciples and the Prince of Physicians in the Occidental world, was born near Bukhārā in the year 370/980 during the reign of Amīr Nūḥ ibn Manṣūr al-Sāmānī. His father, originally from Balkh, had come to settle near Bukhārā as the governor of a village nearby.[1] At that time Bukhārā was the capital and intellectual center of the Sāmānid dynasty which ruled over much of eastern Persia in Khurāsān and Transoxiana, a rule which lasted until the rise of Turkish power during the reign of Maḥmūd of Ghazna.

When Ibn Sīnā was five years old he and his family moved to the city of Bukhārā itself where the young boy had a greater opportunity to study. At the age of ten he already knew grammar, literature, and theology as well as the whole of the Quran. His father, who was an Ismā'īlī and a sympathizer of the Fāṭimids, took great interest in his

[1] The most authentic and authoritative account of the life of Ibn Sīnā is that of his favorite disciple, 'Abd al-Wāḥid Abū 'Ubaid al-Juzjānī, who joined him in 403/1012 and remained with him until the end of Ibn Sīnā's adventurous life, and who completed parts of the *Dānishnāma-yi 'alā'ī*. See A. 'U. Juzjānī, *Sarguzasht-i Ibn-i Sīnā*, trans. Sa'īd Naficy (Tehran, 1331 [1952]); and W. E. Gohlman, *The Life of Ibn Sīnā* (New York, 1974).

For an account of the life and works of Ibn Sīnā based mostly on Juzjānī's account, see also Ibn Abī Uṣaibi'ah, *'Uyūn al-anbā' fī ṭabaqāt al-aṭibbā'*, II, 2–20; Ẓahīr al-Dīn al-Baihaqī, *Tatimmah ṣiwān al-ḥikmah*, pp. 38–62; Ibn al-Qifṭī *Akhbār al-ḥukamā'*, pp. 268–278; Shams al-Dīn Muḥammad al-Shahrazūrī, *Ta'rīkh al-ḥukamā'*, trans. Ḍiā' al-Dīn Durrī (Tehran, 1316 [1937]), pp. 126–137; Ibn Khallikān, *Wafayāt al-a'yān* (Cairo, 1310 [1892]), pp. 152–154; Niẓāmī 'Arūḍī, *Chahār maqālah*, pp. 150ff; Muḥammad Khwānsārī, *Rawḍāt al-jannāt* (Tehran, 1306 [1888]), pp. 241–246, and other traditional sources.

For modern accounts of his life, see Jalāl Homā'ī, "Ibn Sīnā," *Mihr*, 5:25–32, 147–154, 249–257 (1316 [1937]); Sayyid Ṣādiq Gawharīn, *Ḥujjat al-ḥaqq Abū 'Alī Sīnā* (Tehran, 1331 [1952]); Sa'īd Naficy, *Avicenna* (Tehran, 1333 [1954]); *Avicenna Commemoration Volume* (Calcutta, 1956), pp. 29–45 and Introduction; G. M. Wickens, ed., *Avicenna: Philosopher and Scientist* (London, 1952), chap. I; Y. A. al-Kāshī, *Aperçu sur la biographie d'Avicenne*, ed. Fu'ād al-Ahwānī (Cairo, 1952); and S. M. Afnan, *Avicenna, His Life and Works* (London, 1958), chap. II.

son's education. He sent Ibn Sīnā to study arithmetic with a vegetable seller, who was apparently the only teacher available at the time in the subject, and to learn jurisprudence (*fiqh*) from Ismā'īl al-Zāhid, Later, when the famous mathematician, Abū 'Abdallāh al-Nātilī, came to Bukhārā, he was invited to stay at the house of Ibn Sīnā in order to teach him mathematics. Under his tutelage Ibn Sīnā mastered the *Almagest*, the *Elements* of Euclid and some logic, all of which he soon knew better than his teacher.

Having mastered mathematics, he then turned his attention to physics, metaphysics, and medicine, which he probably studied under Abū Sahl 'Isā ibn Yaḥyā al-Masīḥī al-Jurjānī and perhaps Abū Manṣūr Ḥasan ibn Nūḥ al-Qamarī. By the time he was sixteen, Ibn Sīnā had mastered all the sciences of his day and was well known as a physician. In another two years, thanks to the commentary of al-Fārābī, he was also to complete his understanding of Aristotle's metaphysics which at first had presented considerable difficulty for him.

Worldly fame came to Ibn Sīnā in 387/997 when Nūḥ ibn Manṣūr al-Sāmānī fell seriously ill and was successfully treated by him. Henceforth, the doors of the palace library were open to the young Ibn Sīnā, and there, amidst one of the best collections of books on medieval learning, he saturated his mind with all that he was capable of mastering. As he said many years later to Juzjānī, "I now know the same amount as then but more maturely and deeply; otherwise the truth of learning and knowledge is the same."[2]

In 391/1001, at the age of twenty-one, Ibn Sīnā wrote his first books of which any knowledge has come to us. These works were the *Kitāb al-majmū'* on mathematics, *Kitāb al-ḥāṣil wa'l-maḥṣūl* in twenty volumes on all the sciences, and *Kitāb al-birr wa'l-ithm* on ethics.

The following year, amidst political turmoil and war, his father died. The combination of these conditions forced him to leave Bukhārā for Jurjānīyah, which was then the capital of the Khwārazmian dynasty. In the court of 'Alī ibn Ma'mūn Khwārazmshāh, Ibn Sīnā found much encouragement and a great patron in the person of the wazīr, Abu'l-Ḥasan Aḥmad ibn Muḥammad al-Suhailī, for whom he wrote the *Kitāb al-tadārik li anwā' al-khaṭā' fi'l-tadbīr* and *Qiyām al-arḍ fī wasaṭ al-samā'* on mathematics and astronomy. However, the growing power of Maḥmūd of Ghazna, for whom Ibn Sīnā had little love, was beginning to make itself felt even at the Khwārazmī court, so that once again Abū 'Alī had to flee.

This time he set out for Jurjān where the name of Shaikh al-Ma'ālī

[2] J. Homā'ī, "Ibn Sīnā," *Mihr*, 5:32 (1937).

Qābūs ibn Wushmgīr was celebrated as a lover of learning. By 403/1012, after possibly visiting the Ṣūfī sage, Abū Sa'īd ibn Abi'l-Khair, he reached the kingdom of Qābūs only to find that the king was already dead. Dejected by the loss of his expected patron, Ibn Sīnā returned to a village in Khwārazm and from there to Jurjān once again where he was joined by his lifetime companion, Juzjānī. It was at this time that Ibn Sīnā composed the *Kitāb al-mukhtaṣar al-awsaṭ*, the *Kitāb al-mabda' wa'l-ma'ād* and *al-Arṣād al-kullīyah*, along with chapters which were later to form parts of the *Najāt* and *Qānūn.*[3]

Sometime between 405/1014 and 406/1015 he went to Rai, where he cured the wife and son of Fakhr al-Dawlah al-Dailamī and wrote his *Kitāb al-ma'ād.* But the adventurous part in the life of Ibn Sīnā was not to end even here. He set out once again on a journey, going first to Qazwīn and then to Hamadān with the intention of meeting the famous Buwaihīd ruler, Shams al-Dawlah. Destiny was to make this encounter easy, for soon after his entrance into Hamadān, Ibn Sīnā was asked to treat Shams al-Dawlah who had just fallen ill. The mastery of Ibn Sīnā in curing the ruler was not only to make him a favorite at court, but was also to lead to his appointment as the wazīr, a position which was to create many political enemies for him. Until 411/1020, while he remained burdened with state duties, he nevertheless continued to write numerous works, including the masterpiece of Peripatetic philosophy, the *Kitāb al-shifā'*.

In 412/1021 Shams al-Dawlah died and was replaced by his son, Samā' al-Dawlah. The new ruler asked Ibn Sīnā to continue as wazīr, but by now, tired of the Hamadān court and hoping to join the circle of 'Alā al-Dawlah in Ispahān, Ibn Sīnā turned down the offer. The refusal was to have bitter repercussions. Tāj al-Mulk, who for a long time had been an enemy of Ibn Sīnā, took advantage of the situation and by intrigue imprisoned him in the Fardjān castle near Hamadān. Left to himself for four months, al-Shaikh al-Ra'īs composed several important treatises during his imprisonment, including *Kitāb al-hidāyah*, *Kitāb al-qūlanj*, and *Risālah Ḥayy ibn Yaqzān.*[4]

After the four-month interim, Ibn Sīnā took advantage of 'Alā'

[3] The word *Qānūn* in Arabic comes from the Greek *kanōn*, which means a set of principles (derived from the Pythagorean division of the musical chord) and not an encyclopedia as it is usually translated.

[4] He is also said to have composed sarcastically the verse:

دخولی باليقين كما تراه   وكلّ الشكّ فی امر الخروج

"My entrance is certain as thou canst see;
The whole uncertainty concerns the time of departure."

Ibn Abī Uṣaibi'ah, '*Uyūn al-anbā*', II, 6.

al-Dawlah's attack on Hamadān and escaped from his prison in the dress of a dervish and with Juzjānī reached Ispahān safely. The city under 'Alā' al-Dawlah had become a great center of learning, and Ibn Sīnā, treated with much honor and respect, found a haven for peaceful study and writing there. During the fifteen years of his quiet stay in Ispahān he wrote some of his most famous works, among them the *Najāt* and the *Dānishnāma-yi 'alā'ī* which he wrote in Persian and dedicated to his benevolent patron and ruler. He also began the construction of an observatory which was never completed.

Finally, even this long period of peace was disturbed. Mas'ūd, the son of Maḥmūd of Ghazna, attacked Ispahān, and in the pillaging many of the writings of the Shaikh were irretrievably lost. Weakened by an attack of colic and disturbed by all the unrest, Ibn Sīnā returned to Hamadān where he died during the Ramaḍān of 428/1037.

Despite the loss in part or *in toto* of several of his major works, such as the twenty-volume *Kitāb al-inṣāf* on the arbitration of "Eastern" and "Western" philosophy and the *Lisān al-'arab* in ten volumes, over two hundred and fifty books, treatises, and letters of Ibn Sīnā have survived.[5] They range from the voluminous *Kitāb al-shifā'* and *al-Qānūn fi'l-ṭibb* to treatises of only a few pages like *Risālat al-fi'l wa'l- infi'āl* and *Risālah fī sirr al-qadar*. Although most of the texts cover subjects which today would belong to the fields of philosophy, science, and religion at the same time, it is perhaps not incorrect to divide his works into four separate groups: the philosophical, religious, cosmological and physical, and finally the symbolical and metaphysical narratives. Needless to say, such a division is not precise, many works containing elements of all the four divisions.

The primarily philosophical works include the famous *Shifā'*, the *Najāt*, the *Dānishnāma-yi 'alā'ī*, *'Uyūn al-ḥikmah*, *al-Ishārāt wa'l-tanbīhāt*, and numerous small treatises on logic and various philosophical subjects. The religious works include several commentaries on the various *sūrahs* of the Quran, including *Sūrat al-ikhlāṣ*, *Sūrat*

[5] A comprehensive bibliography of Ibn Sīnā is given by Yaḥyā Mahdavī in his *Bibliographie d'Ibn Sīnā* (Tehran, 1954); see also G. C. Anawati, *Essai de bibliographie avicennienne* (Cairo, 1950) and O. Ergin, *İbin Sina Bibliografyasi* (Istanbul, 1956).

For the list of German books and articles on Ibn Sīnā see O. Spies, "Der deutsche Beitrag zur Erforschung Avicennas," in *Avicenna Commemoration Volume*, pp. 93–103.

The *Bibliographie* . . . of Y. Mahdavī contains also a fairly complete list of books and articles on Ibn Sīnā in Arabic, Persian, and the European languages (see pp. 401ff); also S. Naficy, *Bibliographie des principaux travaux européens sur Avicenne* (Tehran, 1953).

al-nās and *Sūrat al-a'lā*, the *Risālat al-nairūzīyah* and treatises dealing with pilgrimage and destiny.[6]

The cosmological works of Ibn Sīnā consist not only of what is today called natural science but also the principles underlying all "natural philosophy." The *ṭabī'īyāt* of the *Shifā'*, *Najāt*, and the *Dānishnāma-yi 'alā'ī* deal in great detail with this subject. There are, moreover, individual treatises on the hierarchy of being, the heavens, the intelligences, and similar questions. As part of his cosmological works must also be considered those texts dealing with the individual sciences—meteorology, psychology, music, and, of course, medicine on which he wrote not only the *Qānūn* but also *al-Urjūzah fi'l-ṭibb* and a large number of treatises on individual diseases.

Finally, there are several works of Ibn Sīnā which have a different character from the above texts. Unfortunately, large sections of the important *Kitāb al-ḥikmat al-m(a)shriqīyah*, in which he expounded his doctrines concerning the "science of the elite" (*'ilm al-khawāṣṣ*), seem to have been lost or, in any case, have not been located with certainty. However, most of the three visionary narratives or recitals, or, better, one narrative in three parts, *Ḥayy ibn Yaqẓān*, *Risālat al-ṭair*, and the account by Khwājah Naṣīr al-Dīn al-Ṭūsī of *Salāmān wa Absāl*, together with the *Risālah fi'l-'ishq* and a few smaller tracts have remained intact. The final chapters of the *Ishārāt wa'l-tanbīhāt* also belong to this last genre of writing, although the first part is mostly a concise summary of the philosophy of the *Shifā'*. These symbolic and metaphysical writings view Nature in a way which differs profoundly from that of the Peripatetic philosophers. In this study they will be treated separately because of the clarity with which they illustrate another perspective in Islam that we have not had occasion to discuss so far in this treatise.

Ibn Sīnā and the Islamic Religion

The position of Ibn Sīnā vis-à-vis the *Sharī'ah* is somewhat difficult to determine because although he was certainly a faithful Muslim and even went to the mosque to ask God's help in solving his philosophical and scientific problems, he has left in his works little trace

[6] In his Quranic commentaries Ibn Sīnā continued the attempt of al-Fārābī to reconcile religion and philosophy, or faith and reason. This goal was pursued in later centuries by a series of sages like Shaikh al-ishrāq Shihāb al-Din al-Suhrawardī, sometimes known as Shaikh al-ishrāq or "master of illumination," 'Alī ibn Turkah Iṣpahānī, and Mīr Dāmād, and found its most perfect solution in the hands of Ṣadr al-Din Shīrāzī, better known as Mullā Ṣadrā. See S. H. Nasr on the School of Ispahān and Mullā Ṣadrā, Vol. 2, *A History of Muslim Philosophy*, ed. M. M. Sharif (Wiesbaden, 1966).

of his exact beliefs. Like his contemporary al-Bīrūnī, Ibn Sīnā left himself uncommitted with respect to the Sunni-Shī'ah division. It is known that his father was Ismā'īlī but that from the beginning Ibn Sīnā was not attracted to that branch of Shī'ism.[7] Yet in certain of his treatises on numerical and alphabetical symbolism he shows clear sympathy for Ismā'īlī doctrines. As Massignon has stated: "En fait, Ibn Sīnā n'a pas innové son alphabet en s'inspirant d'une source hellénistique, mais a été guidé par une tradition orientale ismaëlienne."[8] Toward the end of his life Ibn Sīnā showed more sympathy toward Twelve-Imām Shī'ism, or perhaps it would be safer to say for the house of 'Alī ibn Abī Ṭālib—upon whom be peace. The subsequent influence of his doctrines upon the *Ishrāqīs* has in fact been confined mostly to the Shī'ah world. Suhrawardī, Quṭb al-Dīn al-Shīrāzī, Mīr Dāmād, Mullā Ṣadrā, and Ḥājjī Mullā Hādī Sabziwārī, all of whom took the *Ishrāqī* interpretations of Ibn Sīnā's philosophy seriously, have mostly come from the world of Twelve-Imām Shī'ism in Persia. They interpreted symbolically, or by *ta'wīl*, that the sage who guided Ibn Sīnā in his visionary narrative was 'Alī ibn Abī Ṭālib whom they considered to be to the other Companions of the Prophet as the intelligible world is to the sensible.[9] Still, there are many unanswered questions which make the exact identification of Ibn Sīnā with the various elements of Muslim orthodoxy difficult.

The faithfulness of Ibn Sīnā to Islam was questioned by many exoteric doctors of the law from the time of the spread of his teachings. Despite the sympathetic interpretations of many of his doctrines by the *Ishrāqīs*,[10] he was not accepted either by the doctors of the law or the branches of *taṣawwuf* existing outside of the Shī'ah world. Corbin has stated correctly:

It is certain that neither Avicenna nor Suhrawardī could be adopted either by the pure literalists (*ḥashwīyān*), or by the theologians of the type

[7] Barani, "Ibn Sina and Alberuni," in *Avicenna Commemoration Volume*, p. 7.

[8] L. Massignon, "La Philosophie orientale d'Ibn Sīnā et son alphabet philosophique," *Mémorial Avicenne* (Cairo, 1952), IV, 4.

[9] H. Corbin, *Avicenna and the Visionary Recital*, pp. 242ff. All English quotations from this work are from the translation of W. R. Trask, published by Pantheon Books (New York, 1960).

[10] We use the word *Ishrāqī* here not in its general meaning of "illuminationist" but in its technical sense as the school of the followers of Shaikh al-ishrāq Shihāb al-Dīn al-Suhrawardī. Although many of the masters of this school have been Ṣūfīs of the highest station (*maqām*), like Ibn Turkah, Ibn Abī Jumhūr, Sayyid Ḥaidar Āmulī, and Ṣadr al-Dīn Shīrāzī, there have been other members who have studied this particular form of wisdom only theoretically without the effective spiritual realization which in Islam depends upon the grace of the Prophet (*al-barakat al-muḥammadīyah*) and the spiritual chain (*silsilah*) issuing forth from him.

of Majlisī or by the pure Ṣūfīs. But it is doubtless the originality of Iranian Shī'ite Islam that, despite everything, it permitted the emergence of an Avicenno-Suhrawardian posterity.[11]

During his own lifetime, Ibn Sīnā was sensitive to charges of heresy brought against him and he considered himself a sincere Muslim despite the criticism of his contemporaries. In a famous poem he defends his religious beliefs in these terms:

> It is not so easy and trifling to call me a heretic;
> No belief in religion is firmer than mine own.
> I am the unique person in the whole world and if I am a heretic;
> Then there is not a single Musulman anywhere in the world.[12]

It is only in the Shī'ite world that the philosophy of Ibn Sīnā as interpreted by Suhrawardī became combined with the gnostic doctrines of Ibn 'Arabī and was integrated by Mullā Ṣadrā into the intellectual perspective of Shī'ism, thus having remained as a living tradition in Persia until today.

The *Shifā'* and the smaller Peripatetic treatises of Ibn Sīnā represent the basic texts of that school in Islam.[13] Greek philosophy in the eastern part of the Muslim world never found a more profound interpreter than Ibn Sīnā, who combined, in what he thought was Aristotelian philosophy, the doctrines of the Stagirite, his Alexandrian commentators, and especially the Neoplatonists, all of which he interpreted with intuitions of his own and in many instances in accordance with the monotheistic perspective.[14] His philosophy was to have a profound effect not only upon Latin Scholasticism but also upon Muslim philosophy of which it is the basis, and even upon

[11] Corbin, *Avicenna and the Visionary Recital*, p. 278.

[12] کفر چو منی گزاف و آسان نبود — محکمتر از ایمان من ایمان نبود
در دهر چو من یکی و آنهم کافر — پس در همه دهر یک مسلمان نبود

Translated by Barani, "Ibn Sina and Alberuni," *Avicenna Commemoration Volume*, p. 8.

[13] The *Shifā'* is undoubtedly the greatest encyclopedia of knowledge ever composed by an individual. It remains until today along with the *Sharḥ al-ishārāt* of Khwājah Naṣīr al-Dīn al-Ṭūsī, the *Asfār* of Mullā Ṣadrā and the *Sharḥ-i manẓūmah* of Ḥājjī Mullā Hādī Sabziwārī as the most important text on *ḥikmah*, or traditional theosophy, in Persia which has kept a continuous tradition alive from the time of Ibn Sīnā to the present day. See S. H. Nasr on Ḥājjī Mullā Hādī Sabziwārī in the *History of Muslim Philosophy*, vol. 2.

[14] For example, contrary to Ibn Rushd and the Greeks, who admitted physical proofs for the existence of God, Ibn Sīnā considered only metaphysical proofs as being valid. "Avicenne, au contraire (aux Grecs), représente la tradition juive la plus consciente d'elle-même, car son Dieu, qu'il nomme strictement et absolument le Premier, n'est plus le premier de l'univers, il est premier par rapport à l'être de l'univers, antérieur à cet être et, par conséquent aussi, hors de lui." E. Gilson, *L'Esprit de la philosophie médiévale* (Paris, 1932), p. 83.

Islamic theology, despite the attack against certain aspects of his thought by Imām al-Ghazzālī and Fakhr al-Dīn al-Rāzī. Ibn Sīnā has in fact been called the "first Scholastic,"[15] much of his terminology in ontology appearing in later texts of *kalām*, and his cosmology, which especially interests us here, influencing even al-Ghazzālī himself.

Ibn Sīnā, despite his great admiration for the Greek philosophers, always tried his best to make his philosophy conformable to the Islamic perspective.[16] It is true that in many of his writings he did not express the sense of the utter nothingness of the finite before the Majesty of the Divine which is characteristic of Islamic spirituality, but he did try to conform his ideas to the Quranic Revelation as much as the rationalistic approach in the Peripatetic school would permit.[17] He always kept before him the ideal of combining the philosophy of the Greeks with *ḥikmah*, or wisdom, which was originally the possession of the Hebrew prophets and later revealed in its fullness in Islam.[18] Out of this effort came the philosophy for which Ibn Sīnā has been famous in the West, a philosophy which is the finest expression of the Peripatetic school in Islam.[19]

[15] "Il trouve les matériaux préparés, et déjà un certain travail d'adaptation à l'Islam était commencé. Mais c'est lui qui fut le premier des scholastiques au sens exact du terme." A. M. Goichon, *Introduction à Avicenne* (Paris, 1933), Introduction, p. xvii.

[16] For a discussion of the relation of Ibn Sīnā to Islamic orthodoxy, see L. Gardet, "Quelques aspects de la pensée avicennienne dans ses rapports avec l'orthodoxie musulmane," *La Revue Thomiste*, 45:537–575 (1939).

Unfortunately, in this and similar articles the orthodoxy of Ibn Sīnā is always judged by the exoteric doctrines of the jurists and the theologians without consideration of the gnostic doctrines which are the ultimate criteria of orthodoxy in its universal sense and without consideration of the Shī'ite intellectual milieu in which the school of Ibn Sīnā was to find its future home.

[17] "Certes, Ibn Sīnā était avant tout un philosophe, un philosophe largement inspiré par la grande pensée hellénistique, à la fois aristotélicien et (sans le savoir) néoplatonicien, plus profondément néoplatonicien qu'aristotélicien au demeurant; ou si l'on préfère: croyant trouver dans la pseudo *Theologie d'Aristote* cet accord entre Aristote et Platon que Fārābī déjà avait voulu affirmer. Il est très vrai que l'adhésion à l'Islam ne semble point se présenter pour Ibn Sīnā avec l'absolue rigueur d'une adhésion de foi totale au mystère divin, à une Parole irréductible, émanée de la Volonté inscrutable de Dieu Très Haut, comme nous en trouvons le témoignage en certains ḥanbalites surtout, voire en certains ash'arites primitifs, et certains grands ṣūfīs. Sa non croyance en une résurrection corporelle le prouve. Mais, à notre sense, c'est très sincèrement et très spontanément qu'Ibn Sīnā, sur le plan philosophique même, voulut établir, à l'aide d'une exégèse allégorique, l'accord de ses propres conclusions et de données coraniques." L. Gardet. *La Pensée religieuse d'Avicenne* (*Ibn Sina*) (Paris, 1951), p. 202.

[18] "Il y a tout lieu de penser qu'Ibn Sina entendait réaliser ainsi une conciliation entre la philosophie grecque, *falsafah*, et la sagesse sémitique traditionnelle, *ḥikma*." Massignon, "La Philosophie orientale d'Ibn Sīnā . . ., " *Mémorial Avicenne*, IV, 1.

[19] "Le Néo-platonisme arabe, tel que nous le trouvons formulé dans les traités divers d'Avicenne et dans l'admirable *Philosophie* d'Al Gazāli, ne se présente pas à nous

Aristotelian philosophy, and in fact philosophy in general, was to have a very different role in the Western world from that in Islam. It can be said that philosophy, understood as a purely rationalistic system trying to encompass reality, is something peculiar to the Western world. In Islam it was an incidental and secondary development and did not touch the heart of the Tradition. Therefore, the purely rationalistic aspect of the writings of the Muslim philosophers—especially of Ibn Rushd, who was the most rationalistic among them—had a greater influence in the Latin world than in the Islamic. The Augustinian interpretation of Ibn Sīnā involved the acceptance of much of what was essentially philosophical and the rejection of his cosmology and angelology. The "banishing" of angels from the Avicennian Universe by authors like William of Auvergne helped to laicize the cosmos and prepare the Copernican Revolution.[20] In Islam, on the contrary, the philosophical doctrines of Ibn Sīnā were interpreted metaphysically by the *Ishrāqīs* and in this way became transformed into a doctrine, which, being composed of Peripatetic philosophy, Hermetic and ancient Persian ideas,[21] and Ṣūfī doctrines, served the purpose of leading reason from error to the vision of the truth and preparing the soul for catharsis (*tajrīd*) from the world of the senses, culminating in illumination and gnosis. What in the Western world became ultimately the battlefield of disputing philosophers and theologians became in the Islamic world, and especially in Persia, the guide which led the human soul from the debates of logic to the ecstasies of gnosis.

In connection with the study of the significance of Ibn Sīnā's philosophy, his "Oriental Philosophy" has produced the most bewildering array of opinions among scholars. It is the translation of the Arabic phrase *al-ḥikmat al-m(a)shriqīyah*[22] which Ibn Sīnā mentions in his symbolic writings. The Arabic word مشرقية from the root

---

comme une juxtaposition de théories disparates, mais comme une synthèse d'une extrême unité, où se coordonnait, suivant les principes d'une Métaphysique très définie et très pénétrante, la Théologie, la Psychologie, l'Astronomie et la Physique. Œuvre collective longuement préparée par les Ecoles d'Alexandrie et d'Athènes, dont le *Livre des Causes* et la *Théologie d'Aristote* ont transmis la Tradition aux Arabes, cette synthèse a, de la pensée musulmane, reçu son complet achèvement. En rigoureuse unité, en harmonieuse beauté, elle ne le cède guère à cette merveilleuse production du génie hellénique qu'est la Philosophie d'Aristote." P. Duhem, *Le Système du monde*, IV, 495.

[20] Corbin, *Avicenna and the Visionary Recital*, pp. 101ff.

[21] H. Corbin, "Le Récit d'initiation et l'hermétisme en Iran," *Eranos Jahrbuch*, 17:159 (1949).

[22] As mentioned above, Ibn Sīnā also wrote a work by this name as attested by himself as well as by Ibn Ṭufail in his *Ḥayy ibn Yaqẓān* and many later Muslim authors. There are presently three manuscripts of a work bearing this title and attributed to Ibn Sīnā, one in the Bodleian at Oxford (Pocock 181) written in Hebrew letters, the second

(*shrq*) can be vocalized either as *mashriqīyah* or *mushriqīyah*, the first meaning "Oriental" and the second "illuminative." Ever since the well-known article of Nallino,[23] however, it has become axiomatic for most European scholars to accept the *mashriqīyah* vocalization and consider the other as false.[24] Often they have overlooked the wisdom of the Arabic language itself in which "light," or "illumination," possesses the same root as "East" or "Oriental," conforming to the obvious solar symbolism.[25] In fact, this double meaning of the root (*shrq*) itself plays a major role in the whole plan of the visionary narratives where the East is identified with the realm of the spiritual and intelligible essences, or the realm of light, and the West with the material and corporeal world, or the realm of darkness.

In the *Manṭiq al-m*(*a*)*shriqīyīn*, which most likely is the section on logic of *al-Ḥikmat al-m*(*a*)*shriqīyah* that is now mostly lost, Ibn Sīnā "disowns" his own earlier Peripatetic works as being for the common crowd and announces that in his "Oriental Philosophy" he is going to expose his real views. Because of the great importance of this declaration we give a complete translation of the passage in which Ibn Sīnā presents his own view of his "science of the elite." He writes:

We have been inspired to bring together writings upon the subject matter which has been the source of difference among people disposed to argumentation and not to study it with the eye of fanaticism, desire, habit, or attachment. We have no fear if we find differences with what the people instructed in Greek books have become familiar with through their own negligence and shortness of understanding. And we have no fear if we reveal to the philosophers something other than what we have written for the common people—the common people who have become enamored of the Peripatetic philosophers and who think that God has not guided anyone but them or that no one has reached Divine Mercy except them.

Although we admit the wisdom of the most learned predecessor of these

---

in Nūr 'Uthmānīyah (no. 4894_{75}) in Istanbul, and the third in Aya Sophia (no. 2403) also in Istanbul. It cannot be said with certainty that this work is a section of the treatise to which Ibn Sīnā and Ibn Ṭufail had alluded. It is concerned with natural philosophy and seems to be mostly a summary of the natural philosophy of the *Shifā'*. See Mahdavī, *Bibliographie* . . ., p. 270.

The first Muslim to have spoken of "Oriental" and "Illuminationist" philosophy was Abū Ḥayyān al-Tawḥīdī in his *Fī kamāl al-naw' al-insānī*. See L. Massignon, "Contribution de la France à la commémoration d'Avicenne," *Millénaire d'Avicenne, Congrès de Bagdad* (Cairo, 1952). p. 80.

[23] A. Nallino, "Filosofia 'orientale' od 'illuminativa' d'Avicenna," *Rivista degli studi orientali*, 10:367–433 (1925).

[24] Unable to convey this double meaning in the Latin transliteration, we have chosen to write the word as *m*(*a*)*shriqīyah*, keeping the "a" in parentheses.

[25] In English and French, also, the double meaning of the word "Orient" points to the same symbolism.

philosophers [that is, Aristotle], and we know that in discovering what his teachers and companions did not know, in distinguishing between various sciences, in arranging the sciences in a better manner than before, in discovering the truth of many subjects . . . he was superior to those who came before him, the men who came after him should have brought to order whatever confusion had existed in his thought, mended whatever cracks they found in his structure, and expanded his principles. But those who came after him could not transcend what they had inherited from him. Bigotry over whatever he had not found out became a shield, so that they remained bound to the past and found no opportunity to make use of their own intellects. If such an opportunity did arise, they did not find it admissible to use it in increasing, correcting and examining the works of their predecessors.

When we turned our attention to their works, however, from the beginning the comprehension of these works became easy for us. *And often we gained knowledge from non-Greek sources.* When we began on this project, it was the beginning of our youth, and God shortened the time necessary for us to learn the works of our predecessors. Then we compared everything word for word with the science which the Greeks called logic, and it is not improbable that the Orientals had another name for it. Whatever was contrary by this means of comparison we rejected. We sought the reason for everything until the Truth became separate from error.

Since those who were the people of learning were strongly in favor of the Greek Peripatetics, we did not find it appropriate to separate ourselves and speak differently from everyone else. So, we took their side, and with those philosophers who were more fanatical than any of the Greek sects, we too became fanatical. Whatever they sought but had not found and their wisdom had not penetrated, we completed. We overlooked their faults and provided a leader and tutor for them while we were aware of their errors. If we revealed some opposition it was only in matters in which no patience was possible. But in most cases we neglected and overlooked their faults . . . We were forced to associate with people devoid of understanding who considered the depth of thought as innovation (*bid'ah*) and the opposition to common opinion as sin . . .

Under these conditions, we longed to write a book containing the important aspects of real knowledge. Only the person who has thought much, has meditated deeply, and is not devoid of the excellence of intellectual intuition can make deductions from it . . .

We have composed this book only for ourselves, that is, those who are like ourselves. As for the commoners who have to do with philosophy, we have provided in the *Kitāb al-shifā'* more than they need. Soon in the supplements we shall present whatever is suitable for them beyond that which they have seen up to this time. And in all conditions we seek the assistance of the Unique God.[26]

[26] Ibn Sīnā, *Manṭiq al-m(a)shriqīyīn* (Cairo, 1328 [1910]), pp. 2–4 (italics ours). In the *Dānishnāma-yi 'alā'ī*, for the first time in Islam, Ibn Sīnā begins with metaphysics

The views of modern scholars differ greatly as to what Ibn Sīnā means precisely by this passage and similar ones, in which he refers to this "Oriental Philosophy" meant for the elite. Among Europeans, an early author on Islamic philosophy, L. Gauthier, identifies the "Oriental Philosophy" with *taṣawwuf*, which he calls "la tendance mystique de l'Orient."[27] Among contemporary scholars, A. M. Goichon identifies "Orient" with the medical school of Jundishāpūr and therefore gives it a purely geographical significance. Moreover, she emphasizes the experimental tendencies of this school and believes that the "Oriental Philosophy" means the connection of experiment with reason and the acceptance of empirical causes as the middle term in a syllogism.[28]

The interest in experience and direct observation, however, does not mean necessarily that it must be connected with rationalism, as has been the case since the seventeenth century in the Western world. As Louis Gardet has justly remarked:

> Nous ne nierons point qu'en cette tradition à résonances ésotériques ne se puisse relever un goût prononcé pour les sciences expérimentales. Mais tout au cours de l'histoire, ne verrons-nous pas de forts courants platonisants liés maintes fois à un souci de recherches et d'expériences scientifiques? Ainsi déjà l'école de Chartres au moyen-âge latin, et plus encore le courant platonisant de la Renaissance du XVIe siècle. De ce point de vue, il nous semble que Mlle Goichon a trop aisément tendance à unir recherches expérimentales et "rationalisme." Les Giordano Bruno, Campanella et Jean Bodin, le grand amateur de kabbale, étaient tout autre chose que de purs "rationalistes."[29]

As for Gardet's own view on "Oriental Philosophy," he considers

---

(*ilāhīyāt*) and from there proceeds to natural philosophy (*ṭabī'īyāt*) in contrast to Aristotle and many Muslim authors like Abu'l-Barakāt al-Baghdādī (in his *Kitāb al-mu'tabar*) and Fakhr al-Dīn al-Rāzī (in his *al-Mabāḥith al-mashriqīyah*), who begin from natural philosophy and then proceed to metaphysics. Later Safavid and Qājār authors, among these Ṣadr al-Dīn Shīrāzī, Mullā Muḥsin Faiḍ, and Ḥājjī Mullā Hādī Sabziwārī, have followed the precedent of the *Dānishnāmah* . . .

[27] "La doctrine qui s'y trouve exposée sous forme d'allégories souvent abstruses mais parfois très belles n'est autre que le mysticisme des Soufis amalgamé avec la théorie aristotélicienne de l'intellect actif. Le soufisme, on le sait, représente moins une école qu'une tendance; c'est la tendance mystique de l'Orient, qui entrait déjà pour une part dans le péripatétisme alexandrin, et qui, dans la doctrine d'Avicenne, vient s'y mêler pour la seconde fois." L. Gauthier, *Introduction à l'étude de la philosophie musulmane* (Paris, 1900), pp. 52–53.

[28] "Il utilise toujours le syllogisme comme mode de raisonnement, mais il admet la cause empirique comme moyen terme, tandis qu'Aristote n'admettait là que la cause métaphysique." A. M. Goichon, "L'Unité de la pensée avicennienne," *Archives Internationales d'Histoire des Sciences*, no. 20–21 (1952), p. 300.

[29] Gardet, *La Pensée religieuse d'Avicenne*, p. 26.

it to mean a more Pythagorean, Platonic, Plotinian, and less Aristotelian philosophy. This tendency explains the adjective "Oriental" because, although all of these schools came from the West, the origin of the Pythagorean-Platonic school was the East.[30] The *Shifā'*, and *Najāt*, according to Gardet, are the doctrines of Ibn Sīnā in Aristotelian dress which he was to throw away in the later writings; the later works are "une prise de conscience plus nette et plus délibérée de son rapport personnel d'élaboration philosophique."[31] Gardet, like Goichon, admits that toward the end of his life Ibn Sīnā turned more toward experiment and observation but, contrary to Goichon, he writes:

> Il se peut qu'à la fin de sa vie, Ibn Sīnā ait envisagé de mettre un accent plus délibéré sur des recherches "expérimentales," entendons ici astronomie (et astrologie), magie naturelle, chimie, médecine; et que ces recherches aient activé sa réflexion philosophique. Mais nous ne voyons aucune raison pour penser qu'il s'agisse alors d'une ligne rationalisante.[32]

He considers on the contrary that the later tendency of Ibn Sīnā was "une gnose intellectualiste."

Massignon, in a general survey, mentions the use of the technical Ṣūfī term *'ishq* in place of *maḥabbah* and the alphabetical symbolism of *al-Risālat al-nairūzīyah* to point out that "Avicenne a un génie originel, une philosophie orientale profonde qui n'a pas reçu suffisamment d'attention jusqu'ici."[33]

In a notable study, Pines has reviewed this question, making use of hitherto unavailable fragments of Ibn Sīnā published by Badawī.[34] A treatise in this collection, the *Risālat al-kiyā*, discusses the arbitration between the "Oriental" and "Occidental" philosophers by Ibn Sīnā in his *Kitāb al-inṣāf* which itself was lost in the raid of Ispahān.[35] According to the interpretation of Pines, the term "Oriental" refers to Bukhārā, Ibn Sīnā's own city, and "Occidental" to Baghdād, and especially to the commentators of Aristotle like Abu'l-Faraj and 'Abdallāh ibn al-Ṭayyib who resided in that city. Although the latter's works have not survived, those of his student Mukhtār ibn al-Ḥasan, called Ibn Buṭlān, remain and are an indication of the doctrines of

[30] Gardet, *La Pensée religieuse d'Avicenne*, p. 27.

[31] L. Gardet, "Avicenne et le problème de sa 'philosophie orientale'," *La Revue du Caire*, 27:21 (1951).

[32] Gardet, *La Pensée religieuse d'Avicenne*, p. 27.

[33] L. Massignon, "Avicenne et les influences orientales," *La Revue du Caire*, 27:12 (1951).

[34] 'A. Badawī, *Arisṭū 'ind al-'arab* (Cairo, 1947), I, 121ff.

[35] S. Pines, "La Philosophie 'orientale' d'Avicenne et sa polémique contre les Bagdadiens," *Archives d'Histoire Doctrinale et Littéraire du Moyen Age*, 27:5–37 (1952).

this school. In his *al-Maqālat al-miṣrīyah* Ibn Buṭlān rejects the possibility of the existence of the soul without a body outside of God. Ibn Sīnā on the contrary emphasizes the immortality of the soul and therefore separates himself from the Christian commentators of Aristotle in Baghdād as well as the Greek commentators of Alexandria. This issue, according to Pines, must have been a central subject which distinguished the "Oriental Philosophy" from the Peripatetic school. He also thinks that the rejection of Aristotelian philosophy was a way for Ibn Sīnā to open the path for his personal reflection and was an illumination of his own intellect rather than an Oriental tradition. He may also have been influenced by a Persian "cultural nationalism" against the "Occidentals."

A modern Persian scholar, Qāsim Ghanī, like most other contemporary Persian authors, considers "Oriental Philosophy" to lie outside both Aristotelianism and the Neoplatonic schools. According to him, it perhaps refers to a Persian school of philosophy during the Sāssānid period which left its imprint upon Mānī, and even more upon Suhrawardī, the founder of the school of *Ishrāq*.[36] Another Persian scholar, Dhabīḥallāh Ṣafā, however, understands by the term "Oriental" the Baghdādī commentators of Aristotle in contrast to the Alexandrian disciples of the Stagirite.[37]

Finally, it is helpful to consider the views of H. Corbin, who, among Western scholars, has studied the question of *Ishrāq* most thoroughly and sympathetically. He writes regarding the relation between *Ishrāq* and Ibn Sīnā:

> Thus considered in the life of individual consciousness, the "Oriental philosophy" of the two masters [Ibn Sīnā and Suhrawardī] reveals what they have in common, far better than any theoretical discussions, or hypotheses deputizing for lost works, can do. For the two canons, that of the one and that of the other master, display this common trait: side by side with extremely solid systematic works, they both contain a cycle of brief spiritual romances, narratives of inner initiations, marking a rupture of plane with the level on which the potencies successively acquired by theoretical expositions are interconnected.[38]

Corbin considers the word "Oriental" as primarily a symbolic term signifying the realm of light and not just a geographical designation. "Oriental Philosophy" means the journey to the realm of the spirit and away from the prison of sense and matter.

[36] Qāsim Ghanī, *Ibn-i Sīnā* (Tehran, 1313 [1936]), pp. 45–46.

[37] Dhabīḥallāh Ṣafā, "al-Ḥikmat al-m(a)shriqīyah," *Mihr*, 8:36 (1331 [1952]).

[38] *Avicenna and the Visionary Recital*, p. 6; see also *ibid.*, pp. 271–278, where various studies on Ibn Sīnā's "Oriental philosophy" are discussed; and Suhrawardī, *Opera Metaphysica et Mystica*, ed. H. Corbin (Tehran, 1977), I, xxxvii–lxii.

A close study of the "esoteric" writings of Ibn Sīnā will reveal that the "Oriental Philosophy" is not at all a philosophy in the rationalistic sense, nor a system of dialectic to fulfill certain mental needs; rather, it is a form of wisdom or a "theosophy" which has for its purpose the deliverance of man from this world of imperfection to the "world of light." It is non-Greek in the sense that the specific "genius" of the Greeks of the historical period was dialectical. They even hid the Egyptian, Orphic, and Babylonian mysteries, upon which Pythagoreanism was based, under a veil of dialectics. The "Oriental Philosophy" removes this veil and seeks to present the *philosophia perennis* not as something to satisfy the need for thinking but as a guide, or at least doctrinal aid, for the illumination of man which arises from the inner experience of its author. Its language is therefore primarily symbolic rather than dialectical even if it begins with Aristotelian logic and employs some of the cosmological ideas of the Peripatetic philosophers.

What is difficult to determine is whether the "Oriental Philosophy" was only a theoretical formulation which borrowed its language of symbols from various ancient mysteries, or whether there was a living esoteric tradition which still possessed not only the doctrine but the grace and spiritual techniques necessary for an effective realization of theory. In the fourth Islamic century the latter possibility seems unlikely outside of the grace (*barakah*) of *taṣawwuf*, for it seems hardly conceivable that any small "candles of light" of pre-Islamic spirituality, as, for example, certain branches of Hermeticism, could remain intact and not be dissolved and integrated into the "sun" of Islamic spirituality as the Graeco-Roman mysteries were eventually integrated into Christianity. Even in the case of Shaikh al-ishrāq, his spiritual affiliation was certainly completely Islamic; where he differed from other Ṣūfīs was in the use of pre-Islamic—both Hermetic and Zoroastrian—symbols and a certain amount of Peripatetic philosophy in the formulation of his doctrines. For those who consider *taṣawwuf* to be equivalent with its verbal expression, the above distinction may seem all important, but the inner journey which depends absolutely upon the grace (*barakah*) issuing forth from the founder of the Tradition is one thing and its theoretical formulation another. We must ultimately, therefore, decide the inner meaning of the "Oriental Philosophy" in the light of Ibn Sīnā's relation to Islamic esotericism in general and *taṣawwuf* in particular.

The diversity of view of scholars regarding the meaning of Ibn Sīnā's "Oriental Philosophy" exists also in the problem of the connection of Ibn Sīnā with *taṣawwuf*, which is the esoteric aspect of

Islam, possessing not only a doctrine whose formulations may have been borrowed from external sources, but a "spiritual alchemy" and a grace whose origin can be traced to the Prophet Muḥammad—upon whom be peace.[39] *Taṣawwuf* is not identical with its theoretical formulations; there have been great Ṣūfīs who have not written a word about the theory of Islamic spirituality, as there have been authors outside of *taṣawwuf* who have written lucidly about certain aspects of its theoretical formulations. It is this distinction which makes the identification of Ibn Sīnā with *taṣawwuf* so difficult.

Western scholars who have been influenced, whether directly or indirectly, by the particular aspect of Christian spirituality as a way of love, have usually condemned the primarily gnostic character of Islamic spirituality as a form of "pantheism," "panentheism," and recently as "natural mysticism." Also, they have usually mistaken the theoretical formulations for the interior experience and have therefore postulated diverse origins for *taṣawwuf*, including Neoplatonism, Buddhism, and "the Aryan reaction against the Semites." Without attempting here to refute these many theories, all of which from the point of view of *taṣawwuf* are false, we base our definition of *taṣawwuf* upon the witness of the Ṣūfīs themselves. According to them, it is a set of doctrines, spiritual techniques, and finally a grace, or *barakah*, the totality of which constitutes the essence of Islam, the realization of Unity (*tawḥīd*).

Before turning to the testimony of Muslims speaking from within the Tradition, however, it is helpful to review the opinions of some Western scholars on the relation of Ibn Sīnā to *taṣawwuf*, bearing always in mind their concept of *taṣawwuf*, which is for the most part unacceptable to the authorities of that Tradition. A. M. Goichon, who emphasizes the observational interest of Ibn Sīnā during his later period, denies any real connection between Ibn Sīnā and the Ṣūfīs. She considers, on the contrary, "Ce ne sont donc pas des leçons de vie intérieure qu'il faut chercher auprès d'Avicenne. Son intérêt est lexicographique et philosophique seulement."[40]

[39] For a genuine account of the meaning of *taṣawwuf*, see Abū Bakr Sirāj ad-Dīn, "The origins of Sufism," *Islamic Quarterly*, 3:53–64 (1956); R. Guénon, "L'Esotérisme islamique," in *Islam et l'occident* (Paris, 1947), pp. 153–159; and T. Burckhardt, *Introduction to Sufi Doctrine*, trans. D. M. Matheson (London, 1976).

[40] *Introduction à Avicenne*, p. xxiv and Introduction. She also argues that it would be strange for a treatise on *taṣawwuf*, like *Manṭiq al-m(a)shriqīyīn*, to start with *manṭiq*, that is, logic, which for her implies the exact opposite of *taṣawwuf*. The word *manṭiq*, however, besides meaning logic, always bears an interior sense deriving from the root (*nṭq*) meaning to articulate a sound or speak, and therefore to be related to the Divine Word from which all things derive their being. The *Manṭiq al-ṭair* (usually translated as *Conference of the Birds*) by Farīd al-Dīn al-'Aṭṭār is one of the most celebrated Ṣūfī

Father J. Houben, following Massignon, distinguishes between early Ṣūfīs and the later ones who he calls "pantheistic" and classifies the gnosis (*ma'rifah*) of Ibn Sīnā as "a natural knowledge of God," implying therefore "natural mysticism."[41] Gardet takes a similar view and states: "Mais en fait, il s'agit chez Ibn Sīnā d'une réduction du *taṣawwuf* a un plan philosophique, par une interprétation appropriée."[42] Moreover, he identifies this "reduction of *taṣawwuf*" with natural mysticism. As he says: "Pour Ibn Sīnā donc, comme pour les *Upanishads*, c'est en se parachevant elle-même dans l'ordre de la nature que l'âme communique avec Dieu."[43] On another occasion he states that "l'élan mystique (mystique naturelle) plonge au contraire des racines profondes en ce système . . . il lui donne sa sève . . ."[44] Also: "Le système avicennien ne se peut comprendre, selon toutes ses dimensions existentielles, que grâce au mouvement initial de mystique naturelle qui le traverse."[45]

This "mysticism" is, according to Gardet, a combination of Plotinian intellectualism and the experience described by the great Ṣūfīs. Considering the indefiniteness and incorrectness of this definition of "mysticism," it is difficult to be satisfied with such a conclusion. We are guaranteed that Ibn Sīnā's system is profoundly dominated by natural mysticism, but then some of the greatest masters of *taṣawwuf*—Ibn 'Arabī, for example—have also been said to have had no other inspiration than natural mysticism. Therefore, how are we to distinguish between Ibn Sīnā and all the later Ṣūfīs who possess esoteric orthodoxy and a perfect regularity in their initiatic chain (*silsilah*)?

Muslim sources could perhaps give a clearer indication, for here we deal with authorities who speak from within *taṣawwuf*. In the account of the life of the well-known fourth-century Ṣūfī, Abū Sa'īd ibn Abi'l-Khair, in the *Asrār al-tawḥīd*,[46] there is an account of the

---

tracts and makes use of *manṭiq* in its symbolic rather than logical aspect. The title of *Manṭiq al-m(a)shriqīyīn*, therefore, does not condemn the work to a "rationalistic" plane. Moreover, many later works by Suhrawardī, Mullā Ṣadrā, and others, whose gnostic character all admit, begin with logic and terminate with Ṣūfī metaphysics.

[41] J. Houben, S. J., "Avicenna and mysticism," *Indo-Iranica*, 6:15 (1953).

[42] L. Gardet, "L'Expérience mystique selon Avicenne," *La Revue du Caire*, 27:64 (1951).

[43] *Ibid.*, p. 63. This point of view presupposes an absolute distinction between Nature and Supernature, forgetting that there is something "supernatural" in Nature as there is a "natural" aspect to Supernature. See F. Schuon, "Is there a natural mysticism?" in *Gnosis, Divine Wisdom*, trans. G. E. H. Palmer, pp. 35–44.

[44] L. Gardet, *La Connaissance mystique chez Ibn Sīnā et ses présupposés philosophiques* (Cairo, 1952), p. 62.

[45] *Ibid.*, p. 67.

[46] *Asrār al-tawḥīd fī maqāmāt al-Shaikh Abī Sa'īd* (Tehran, 1313 [1934]), 159–160.

meeting of Ibn Sīnā with the great Ṣūfī sage and their intimate discourse which lasted three days. Also, in traditional Muslim sources there is reference to a meeting between Abū Sa'īd and Ibn Sīnā in a bath house. According to these sources, Abū Sa'īd asked Ibn Sīnā if it were true that a heavy body seeks the center of the earth. Ibn Sīnā answered that this was absolutely true. Abū Sa'īd subsequently took up his metal vase and threw it into the air, whereupon instead of falling down it stayed up in the air. "What is the reason for this?" he asked. Ibn Sīnā answered that the natural motion would be the fall of the vase but that a violent force was preventing this natural motion. "What is this violent force?" asked Abū Sa'īd. "Your soul!" replied Ibn Sīnā, "which acts upon this." "Then purify your soul," Abū Sa'īd added, "so that you can do the same."[47]

Bahā' al-Dīn al-'Āmilī, known as Shaikh Bahā'ī, in his *Kashkūl* tells the story of Shaikh Majd al-Dīn al-Baghdādī, the famous Ṣūfī, who saw the Prophet in a dream and asked about the condition of Ibn Sīnā. The Prophet answered: "Ibn Sīnā wanted to reach God without me; so I touched his chest and he fell into the fire."[48]

There is also the story of another well-known Ṣūfī master, 'Alā' al-Dawlah al-Simnānī, who likewise saw the Prophet in a dream and asked: "What dost thou say on the subject of Ibn Sīnā?" The Prophet replied: "He is a man whom God has made to lose his way in knowledge." Again the Ṣūfī master asked: "What dost thou say regarding Suhrawardī Maqtūl?" He answered: "He also is a follower of Ibn Sīnā."[49] We see that all of these stories consider Ibn Sīnā outside of the tradition of *taṣawwuf* or at least outside the central element of Ṣūfī orthodoxy.

Among modern Persian scholars, as in the case of European authorities, there is some difference of opinion on this question. Naṣrallāh Taqawī, in his introduction to the *Ishārāt wa'l-tanbīhāt*, considers that Ibn Sīnā was an active Ṣūfī and possessed a spiritual station (*maqām*).[50] On the contrary, Badī' al-Zamān Furūzānfar, a leading contemporary Persian authority on *taṣawwuf*, points out that neither the journey of the soul in *Ḥayy ibn Yaqẓān* or *al-Ṭair* nor the union of the passive and Active Intellect are Ṣūfī doctrines, but that the *Risālat al-'ishq* and the last part of the *Ishārāt* . . . dealing with the grades of the spiritual life are in the tradition and language of

[47] See also Muḥammad Tunikābunī, *Qiṣaṣ al-'ulamā'* (Tehran, 1313 [1934]), p. 317.
[48] *Ibid.*
[49] Quoted in Corbin, *Avicenna and the Visionary Recital*, p. 244, n. 1.
[50] Ibn Sīnā, *al-Ishārāt wa'l-tanbīhāt*, trans. Naṣrallāh Taqawī (Tehran, 1316 [1937]), Introduction, p. ('*ain*).

taṣawwuf. According to Furūzānfar, al-Shaikh al-Ra'īs explained the secrets and difficulties of "The Path" in an excellent way and has been a defense for the Ṣūfīs against rationalism over the centuries. But he was too engrossed in the desires of this world to have participated in the "Muḥammadan poverty" (*al-faqr al-muḥammadī*), which requires a certain detachment from this world and its pleasures.[51]

From these passages it seems certain that Ibn Sīnā lies outside of the pure tradition of *taṣawwuf.* He is neither like a Ḥallāj, whom Western scholars consider as a "true mystic," nor like an Ibn 'Arabī or al-Jīlī, whom they label as "pantheist." From the exterior it seems that his life was too closely interwoven with the desires of the flesh and excess of sensual pleasures and differed markedly from the disciplined life of those traveling on "The Path" (*sālikūn*). Yet he probably spent three days alone with Abū Sa'īd in spiritual retreat (*khalwah*) and met other Ṣūfī masters like Abu'l-Ḥasan al-Kharraqānī.[52] Consequently he was most likely touched deeply by the *barakah* of *taṣawwuf* and even if not able to realize its aims in his life sympathized with it greatly and expressed many of its truths in his works.[53]

[51] Badī' al-Zamān Furūzānfar, "Abū 'Alī Sīnā wa *taṣawwuf*," in *Le Livre du millénaire d'Avicenne*, ed. Dhabīḥallāh Ṣafā (Tehran, 1953), II, 188.

The Egyptian scholar Abu'l-'Alā al-'Afīfī also considers Ibn Sīnā to be more of a philosopher with tendencies toward Sufism than a Ṣūfī in the truest sense of the word, although he believes that the philosophy of Ibn Sīnā is not simply a mixture of Aristotelian and Neoplatonic philosophy but is strongly influenced by Gnosticism, and especially Hermeticism, *Ḥayy ibn Yaqẓān* being an Arabic version of *Poimandres.* See 'Afīfī, "L'Aspect mystique de la philosophie avicennienne," *Millénaire d'Avicenne, Congrès de Bagdad*, pp. 399–449.

Another famous contemporary Arab scholar, Ibrāhīm Madkour, connects the Sufism of Ibn Sīnā with the tendencies and trends already found in al-Fārābī. See Madkour's *Fī'l-falsafat al-islāmīyah* (Cairo, 1947), pp. 48–54.

[52] It was after his meeting with al-Kharraqānī in Hamadān that Ibn Sīnā wrote the natural philosophy, or *ṭabī'īyāt*, of the *Shifā'*.

[53] An argument in favor of the view that Ibn Sīnā was not just a philosopher in the ordinary sense is his writing poetry along with philosophic prose. Usually the only background common to these two diverse types of activity is gnosis in which poetry is metaphysical as the expression of metaphysics is poetical. To clarify this matter further one must turn to the later Islamic centuries when in Persia three distinct schools can be discerned. These are the schools of pure gnosis represented by Ibn 'Arabī, Ṣadr al-Dīn al-Qunawī, 'Abd al-Razzāq al-Kāshānī, and 'Abd al-Karīm al-Jīlī; the school of Illumination combining philosophy with contemplation and intuition as in the case of Suhrawardī, Quṭb al-Dīn al-Shīrāzī, Ibn Turkah and later Mīr Dāmād and Mullā Ṣadrā; and finally the Peripatetic school. It can be safely said that Ibn Sīnā did not belong to the first school. But he cannot be limited to the third school either. There are elements in his writings, based on intellectual intuition (*dhawq*), which made it possible for the later *Ishrāqī* sages to interpret his writings in a direction diametrically opposed to the philosophy of Ibn Sīnā in the medieval Latin world, so that we can say that although not a Ṣūfī, Ibn Sīnā expresses certain views which make him not only a Peripatetic philosopher but a forerunner of the *Ishrāqīs* as well.

In the domain of cosmology, the late works of Ibn Sīnā possess many points of similarity with the conception of Nature of the gnostics (*'urafā'*). In both cases there is the concept of the interiorization of the cosmos, the journey through the Universe to what lies above it, and a symbolic interpretation of all natural phenomena. Therefore, whatever the effective realization and the spiritual station of Ibn Sīnā may have been, his theoretical consent to *taṣawwuf* and the expression of many Ṣūfī doctrines in the cosmology of his works on "Oriental Philosophy" permit us to study him in two distinct ways. Firstly, we may identify his early works, especially the *Shifā'* and the *Najāt*, as the most complete expressions of the philosophy of the Peripatetic school in Islam, a school that was much influenced, especially in the case of Ibn Sīnā, by the physics of Aristotle and Neoplatonic cosmology. Secondly, we may study the cosmology of his later works, especially the visionary narratives, as an early expression of the doctrines of the *Ishrāqī* school which were developed more fully in the following centuries and as a description of certain elements of the gnostic conception of Nature. We must not, however, identify Ibn Sīnā's treatment of Ṣūfī doctrines with the most universal exposition of Sufism which we find in the writings of such masters as Ibn 'Arabī, al-Qunawī, Maḥmūd Shabistarī, and al-Jīlī.

CHAPTER 12

The Anatomy of Being

Being and Its Polarizations

Ibn Sīnā is above all a "philosopher of Being"; all knowledge for him involves the analogy of the beings of particular things with Being itself which stands above and anterior to the Universe.[1] The highest form of knowledge, in fact, is the knowledge of Being itself, to which the knowledge of mathematics and of the physical world are subordinated.[2] To understand his cosmological ideas, therefore, it is necessary to discuss briefly the relation of Being to the Universe and its hierarchy, though without going into the details of this question since it belongs to the "First Philosophy," or metaphysics, and so lies outside the scope of this study.[3]

Being in itself is the cause of all particular existents without being reduced to a genre common to all of them.[4] Being is above all

[1] A. M. Goichon, "L'Unité de la pensée avicennienne," *Archives Internationales d'Histoire des Sciences*, no. 20–21 (1952), pp. 290ff.

[2] Ibn Sīnā considers the hierarchy of knowledge to start with metaphysics, then mathematics, and finally natural science. *Dānishnāma-yi 'alā'ī, Ilāhīyāt* (Tehran, 1331 [1952]), p. 3. For him, as for Christian Platonists like St. Augustine and in contradiction to Aristotle, sensible knowledge does not precede the intellectual.

[3] There are several well-known studies in European languages on the philosophical aspect of Ibn Sīnā's ontology. Among these works may be included A. M. Goichon, *La Distinction de l'essence et de l'existence d'après Ibn Sīnā* (*Avicenne*) (Paris, 1937); Dj. Saliba, *Etude sur la métaphysique d'Avicenne* (Paris, 1926); and E. Gilson, *Avicenne et le point de départ de Duns Scot* (Paris, 1927). The most comprehensive and thorough study of the philosophy of Ibn Sīnā, interpreted in a Peripatetic fashion that we have encountered is *Ḥikmat-i Bū 'Alī* (Tehran, 1375–1377 [1955–1957]), by 'Allāmah Ḥā'irī Māzandarānī. This work, in three volumes, written from within the tradition of *ḥikmah* by one of the leading *ḥakīms* of present-day Persia, gives a thorough exposition of the thought of Ibn Sīnā, especially his ontology, as understood by those who have preserved his school as a continuous living tradition in Persia until today.

[4] "Bien qu'en effet l'être ne soit pas un genre réellement commun à tous les êtres, il doit y avoir un certain point de vue, duquel tout ce qui est, au même sens et de la même façon. L'être de la substance n'est pas celui de l'accident, mais, du fait même qu'il n'y a pas d'idée antérieure à l'idée d'être, on doit nécessairement accorder que l'une et l'autre viennent se ranger sous cette idée commune et que, d'un certain point de vue, l'accident et la substance reçoivent le nom d'être selon la même signification . . . L'être peut s' affirmer de tout selon le même sens, mais non pas aussi immédiatement de tous

distinctions and polarizations and yet the cause of the world of multiplicity, casting its light upon the different and distinct quiddities (*māhīyāt*) of all things. Being is the reality of each thing, as it is the source of all goodness and beauty as well as the cause of all perception, the quiddities constituting no more than the limitations of being.[5]

There are two major distinctions which underlie the philosophy of Ibn Sīnā, one an ontological distinction between quiddity, or essence (*māhīyāh*),[6] and existence (*wujūd*), and the other tripartite division between the Necessary (*wājib*), contingent (*mumkin*) and impossible (*mumtani'*) beings. Only in the Necessary Being (*wājib al-wujūd*), or God, are essence and existence inseparably united, while for all other beings unity and existence are only accidents added to their essence or quiddity. The Necessary Being whose essence and existence

---

les êtres" (Gilson, *Avicenne et . . . Duns Scot*, p. 111). And further on Gilson writes: "L'Être, cause de tous les êtres, nous a doués d'une lumière naturelle faite à sa ressemblance" (*ibid.*, p. 117).

Regarding the question of Being and quiddities in Muslim philosophy see S. H. Nasr, "The Polarization of Being," *Pakistan Philosophical Journal*, 3:8–13 (October, 1959).

The Muslim Peripatetics, following Ibn Sīnā, considered being to be real and principial and the quiddities to be the limitations of the existence of things abstracted by the intellect. In later centuries the debate as to whether essence or existence is principial became a central issue, especially with Mīr Dāmād and Mullā Ṣadrā. See S. H. Nasr on Mullā Ṣadrā in the *History of Muslim Philosophy*.

[5] "فالواجب الوجود له الجمال والبهاء المحض وهو مبدأ جمال كل شيء وبهاؤه هو ان يكون على ما يجب له فكيف جمال ما يكون على ما يجب في الوجود الواجب وكل جمال وملائمة وخير ومدرك فهو محبوب معشوق ومبدأ ذلك كله ادراكه اما الحسي واما الخيالي واما الوهمي واما الظني واما العقلي."

Ibn Sīnā, *Kitāb al-shifā'* (Tehran, 1305 [1887]), p. 598;

"وكل واجب الوجود بذاته فهو حق محض لان حقيقة كل شيء خصوصية وجوده الذي يثبت له فلا حق اذاً احق من الواجب الوجود."

al-Najāt (Cairo, 1938), p. 229.

[6] The notion of essence, or quiddity, according to Ibn Sīnā corresponds to the question *quid est*. If one knows the essence of something, one knows all its attributes. (See Dj. Saliba, *La Métaphysique d'Avicenne*, pp. 80–81.) "L'essence, considérée en elle-même, comprend ce qui est nécessaire à une chose pour pouvoir exister comme telle. Elle s'exprime donc par l'énoncé des caractères qui constituent cette nature, cette quiddité, à l'exclusion de ses accidents, et même des particularités découlant de tel ou tel de ses traits constitutifs; en effet, celles-ci n'ajouteraient rien d'essentiel" (A. M. Goichon, *La Distinction de l'essence et de l'existence* . . ., p. 49). As for existence, it is not a constitutive attribute of essence but a necessary one added accidentally to the essence. The existence of something does not have its principle in the essence of that thing but derives its principle from the Being whose essence is the same as its existence, that is, the Necessary Being.

are one is pure Truth as It is pure Goodness;[7] It is the source and origin of all existence.

As for the contingent beings (*mumkin al-wujūd* or *mumkināt*), they are further divided into two classes:

(1) Those that are necessary in the sense that they could not not be. They are contingent by themselves but receive from the First Cause the quality of being necessary. These beings are the simple substances (*mujarradāt*), that is, the Intelligences and angelic substances.

(2) Those that are only contingent, that is, the composed bodies of the sublunary region which come into being and pass away.[8]

The first category of possible beings is the eternal effect of the Creator and must therefore always be, while the second category contains in itself the principle of "non-eternity" and therefore has a beginning and an end. Substance, in the context mentioned above and as used generally by Ibn Sīnā, means that which exists by itself without being supported by or existing in any subject, in contradistinction to accident, which exists in a subject and is supported by

[7] «ان الواجب الوجود هو الموجود الذي متى فرض غير موجود عرض منه محال وان الممكن الوجود
هو الذي متى فرض غير موجود او موجودا لم يعرض منه محال والواجب الوجود هو الضروري
الوجود والممكن الوجود هو الذي لا ضرورة فيه بوجه اي لا في وجوده ولا في عدمه.»

Ibn Sīnā, *Najāt*, pp. 224–225.

«وكل واجب الوجود بذاته فانه خير محض وكمال محض والخير بالجملة هو ما يتشوقه كل
شيء ويتم به وجوده...»

Ibid., p. 229. In his commentary on the *Theology of Aristotle*, Ibn Sīnā defines being as a "category" above the division of possible and necessary. He considers that in all existents outside of the First Being there are three distinct elements: (1) Its being *qua* being referred to nothing but Being itself and standing above the division of possible and necessary; (2) Its being as much as it derives from the First Being and refers to it; (3) Its being as related to its quiddity (*māhīyah*) or its intelligible principle of definition which is carefully distinguished from its essence (*dhāt*). See G. Vajda, "Les Notes d'Avicenne sur la 'Théologie d'Aristote,'" *La Revue Thomiste*, 51:346–406 (1951); L. Gardet, "En honneur du millénaire d'Avicenne," *ibid.*, p. 336.

[8] Ibn Sīnā, *Dānishnāmah . . . Ilāhīyāt*, pp. 7–11, *Najāt*, pp. 224–225; Gardet, *La Pensée religieuse d'Avicenne*, p. 45; S. Munk, *Mélanges de philosophie juive et arabe* (Paris, 1859), p. 358. In the *Ilāhīyāt* of the *Dānishnāmah . . .*, and in apparent contrast to his other writings, Ibn Sīnā implies that only the Necessary Being is eternal while all other things are created and new (*muḥdath*), pp. 76–83. Islamic philosophers usually distinguish between two kinds of *imkān*, *imkān al-'āmm* and *imkān al-khāṣṣ*, the first meaning all that is not impossible (*mumtani'*) and the second that of which neither existence or non-existence is necessary. The first is usually translated as possibility and the second as contingency although sometimes possibility is used for both kinds of *imkān*.

a substance.[9] Substance is divided according to species; the ten categories as defined by Aristotle, of which substance itself is a category, become so many species of being,[10] while potentiality and act, unity and multiplicity, cause and effect, remain but accidents with respect to Pure Being.

The three simple substances which comprise the first category of contingent beings are irreducible to one another according to the definition of substance just given. One cannot be reduced to the other in an ontological sense because of the basic distinction that Ibn Sīnā makes between them:

(1) The substance whose being is one, which possesses contingency (*mumkin*) and is completely separate (*mujarrad*) from all matter and potentially is called Intellect (*'aql*).

(2) The substance whose being is one but accepts the form of other beings is divided into two categories:

(a) That which does not accept divisibility and, although separate from matter, has need of a body in its action is called Soul (*nafs*).

(b) That which accepts divisibility, and has the three divisions of length, width and depth is called Body (*jism*).[11]

These three substances, Intellect, Soul, and Body, although all partaking of the light of Being, remain in the domain of cosmology separate entities, the knowledge of the interrelation of which is the aim of all sciences dealing with the cosmos.

The separate substances themselves form the first class in the list of beings which "have a right to exist," that is, which possess a rank in the hierarchy of being. The order of this scale may be given as follows:[12]

1. Separated substances
2. Form
3. Body
4. Matter

As the separate substances, or angels, stand highest in this scale, matter stands lowest in the hierarchy and possesses an inferior degree of reality with respect to form, contrary to the view of Aristotle.

[9] Ibn Sīnā, *Najāt*, pp. 324ff.

[10] For a description of the ten categories which follows closely the teachings of the Stagirite, see *Dānishnāmah . . .*, *Ilāhīyāt*, p. 36.

[11] Ibn Sīnā, *Dānishnāmah . . .*, *Ilāhīyāt*, p. 115.

[12] Ibn Sīnā, *Najāt*, p. 338; Saliba, *La Métaphysique d'Avicenne*, p. 68.

The anatomy of being just described forms the basis of all the hierarchies which exist in the Universe since the cosmos is nothing but the manifestation and effusion of Being. Any particular being increases in its degree of reality, beauty, and goodness according to how closely it approaches the Necessary Being.[13] Whatever is more perfect and more true is closer to the Necessary Being, which is the source of all perfection and Truth.[14] Using the symbolism of light, Ibn Sīnā often compares the particular beings of the cosmos to points in the rays of the Sun which receive illumination from this source of all light and rise in the scale of being to the degree in which they approach this source. All creatures, in fact, find their happiness and felicity in union with this source of all existence which is Pure Being, upon which they utterly depend and without which they are literally nothing.

Closely related to the science of the anatomy of being is the question of universals, because ultimately it determines the quality of knowledge which can be gained in the study of any domain. The science of things, according to Ibn Sīnā, is not innate to the human soul. Our intelligence receives the intelligibles by turning toward the Active Intellect after being excited by the senses in contact with the external world. In the Divine Intellect alone do the intelligible essences exist independent of all potentiality as universals. In the Intellect everything has an existence as a universal even before the coming into being of any plurality. In the realm of plurality it becomes material form to be raised once again in the intellect of man to the domain of the universal.[15]

Ibn Sīnā has often been accused of nominalism because he considers universals as accidents added to the essence. This accusation is not just, however, because he upholds the existence of separate intelligences and the universals in the Active Intellect which is transcendent with respect to man. Man receives the intelligibles as an illumination by the Active Intellect; all knowledge in the ultimate

[13] For example, besides dividing all beings into the Necessary and possible, Ibn Sīnā also distinguishes between three types of beings according to whether they are pure goodness (God, or Necessary Being), both good and evil, or pure evil. Ibn Sīnā, *Dānish-nāmah . . ., Ilāhīyāt*, pp. 118–119.

[14] *Ibid.*, p. 112. The Necessary Being may also be considered as pure necessity and all beings considered as standing in the hierarchy of Being according to their degree of necessity. "La nécessité diminue dans l'existence proportionnellement à la distance qui sépare l'être de son principe" (Saliba, *La Métaphysique d'Avicenne*, p. 101).

[15] "Prior to any plurality, everything has an existence in the mind of God and of the angels; then as material form it enters upon plurality, to be raised finally in the intellect of man to the universality of the Idea . . ." Tj. de Boer, *History of Philosophy in Islam*, trans. E. R. Jones (London, 1933), 135.

sense is in fact an illumination.[16] The hierarchy of being is understood only by the "Ideas" which reside eternally in the Divine Intellect
and which return to the realm of the Universal in the process of
intellection through which man comes to know the anatomy of being.
Particular beings are all united in that they issue from Being, or God,
who stands transcendent with respect to the Universe. Being is not
identical with its differentiation but remains totally independent of it;
yet multiplicity, or the polarization of Being which constitutes the
cosmos, is absolutely dependent upon Pure Being without which it
would cease to have an external reality.

The Generation of the Universe

The cosmogony of Ibn Sīnā is closely connected with the ontological
hierarchy already described. If in his ontology, however, emphasis is
placed upon the transcendence of Being, or God, above all particular
beings or creatures, in cosmogony, on the contrary, accent is placed
upon the relation of generated beings to Being and their effusion
(faiḍ) from the source of all things. The Universe in this perspective
is compared to the rays of the Sun, and God to the Sun itself. The
rays of the Sun are not the Sun but also they are nothing other than
the Sun. This perspective is alien to the exoteric element of monotheistic traditions in which the absolute distinction between the
Creator and the creature is preserved. In Islam the doctrine of
emanation, or effusion, therefore, can be understood and integrated
only in the esoteric aspect of the Tradition. The doctrine of the
Unity of Being (waḥdat al-wujūd) of Ibn 'Arabī and the majority of
Ṣūfīs after him does not state that the Universe is God or that God
is the Universe. The Ṣūfīs join Ibn Sīnā on this point to say that there
cannot be two independent orders of reality so that the being of the

---

[16] "Cultivate the self with learning in order to progress and leave all else; for knowledge is an abode of all things. The self is like glass, the knowledge, like a lamp, and the
wisdom of God, like oil. When your self is illuminated you are alive, and when there is
darkness, you are dead."

هذّبِ النَّفسَ بالعُلوم لِترقَى .   وذرِ الكلَّ فهى للكلِّ بيتْ

إنّما النَّفسُ كالزجاجة والعلمُ   سِراجٌ وحكمةُ الله زيتْ

فاذا اشرقت فانّك حَيٌّ ،   واذا اظلمتْ فانّكَ مَيتْ .

This poem by Ibn Sīnā is quoted by Ibn Abī Uṣaibi'ah (II, 15) and translated by
A. Muid Khan in "Some aspects of the Arabic writings of the philosopher Ibn Sīnā,"
Islamic Culture, 25:42 (1951).

Universe cannot be other than Pure Being. The Plotinian cosmogony which Ibn Sīnā follows in a similar manner derives the hierarchy of creatures from Pure Being itself without in any way destroying the absolute transcendence of Being with respect to the Universe which it manifests.

The principles according to which the manifestation of the cosmos takes place are as follows:

(1) Division of beings into necessary and contingent.
(2) From Unity only unity can come into being (*ex uno non fit nisi unum*).[17]
(3) Intellection of God is the cause of existence.[18]

The First Intellect (*al-'aql al-awwal*) is contingent in essence and necessary by virtue of the "Cause of Causes," (*'illat al-'ilal*) or the Necessary Being Itself. But because the First Intellect is contingent, it generates multiplicity within itself. By intellection of the Divine Essence, it gives rise to the Second Intellect, and by intellection of its own essence to two beings which are the Soul of the first heaven and its body. One may say that the First Intellect has three forms of knowledge:

(1) Knowledge of the Essence of the Necessary Being.
(2) Knowledge of its own essence as a being necessary by virtue of another being (*wājib bi'l-ghair*).
(3) Knowledge of its own essence as a contingent being.

It is these three forms of knowledge which give rise respectively to the Second Intellect, the Soul of the first heaven, and its body.[19] The Second Intellect through intellection generates in a similar manner the Third Intellect, the Soul of the second heaven and its body. This process continues until the ninth heaven and the Tenth Intellect, which governs the sublunary region, are generated.[20] This

[17] «الواحد لا يصدر عنه الا الواحد.»

[18] See introduction by Mūsā 'Amīd to Ibn Sīnā, *Risālah dar ḥaqīqat wa kaifīyat-i silsila-yi mawjūdāt wa tasalsul-i asbāb wa musabbabāt* (Tehran, 1952), p. 8. Also Gardet, *La Pensée religieuse d'Avicenne*, p. 48.

The authenticity of the *Risālah dar ḥaqīqat wa kaifīyat* . . . has been doubted by some authorities, but there is no question that it summarizes Ibn Sīnā's views on the chain of being found with greater elaboration in the *Shifā'* and other works.

[19] *Najāt*, pp. 256–257; Saliba, *La Métaphysique d'Avicénne*, pp. 128–132.

[20] This scheme is a systematization of the Plotinian cosmology; Ibn Sīnā's First Being, First Intellect, and Soul correspond to the Plotinian hypostases. For a detailed account of the hierarchy of intelligences and souls and generation from the Necessary Being, see *Shifā'*, *Ilāhīyāt*, pp. 618ff.

scheme corresponds to the planetary spheres in the following manner:[21]

TABLE VII. THE HEAVENS AND THEIR GENERATING INTELLECTS ACCORDING TO IBN SĪNĀ

No. of Heavens	*Name of Heaven*	*No. of Generating Intellect*
9	"Heaven of heavens" (*falak al-aflāk*)	1
8	Heaven of signs of Zodiac (*falak al-burūj*)	2
7	Saturn	3
6	Jupiter	4
5	Mars	5
4	Sun	6
3	Venus	7
2	Mercury	8
1	Moon	9

The heavens, therefore, are generated by a series of intellections, each Intellect actually bestowing existence upon that which it generates.[22] In his commentary on the *Theology of Aristotle*, certain nuances of this scheme are changed or accentuated. The ontological degree of the Intelligences is clearly distinguished from the celestial Souls, and the Intelligences who are the angels are made definitely separate substances and the source of all forms.[23] The knowledge which the Intelligences have of the First Cause is, moreover, the prototype of all gnosis and all epiphany.[24]

The generation of the Universe must also be described in terms of the powers and functions of the beings that comprise it and which are responsible for its life and activity. The First Intellect, the highest of all beings, has only one power (*qudrah*), that of knowledge (*'ilmīyah*), which it receives from the command (*amr*) of the Divine Truth (*Ḥaqq*). The Soul (*nafs*), which is closest to it, possesses not only the power of knowledge which it receives from the Intellect, but also that of desire, or love (*shawqīyah*), which comes directly from the Divine Command. From the Soul in turn the Universal Nature (*al-ṭabī'at*

[21] Ibn Sīnā, *Risālah dar ḥaqīqat wa kaifīyat . . .*, p. 23.

[22] "L'être qui vient après l'Intelligence (séparée) est d'une part pensé par elle, et reçoit d'autre part son être d'elle, en tant qu'émané d'elle, non pas en tant que l'Intelligence l'a reçu d'un autre." Gardet, *La Pensée religieuse d'Avicenne*, p. 49.

[23] "Nous disons que la forme de toute chose, universelle ou particulière, se réalise dans ce monde-là (le monde des substances séparées); tout particulier y est appréhendé suivant le mode dont il dérive de ses causes, et ce mode fait du particulier un universel." Vajda, "Les Notes d'Avicenne . . .," *La Revue Thomiste* 51:346–406 (1951). The text therein is referred to as *Gloses* (p. 48).

[24] "Il faut plutôt dire qu'elle se pense elle-même comme existente en pensant sa Cause, et c'est là le vrai mode de la saisie intellectuelle." Vajda, *Gloses*, p. 60.

al-kullīyah)[25] and the Universal Element (*al-'unṣūr al-kull*) are brought into being.

Universal Nature is a force which moves the Element toward that perfection which is possible for it. Nature, whose essence derives from that aspect of the Soul coming from the Divine Command, however, has no knowledge of the conditions of this action but acts rather for the sake of subjugating the Element. The Element itself which receives the action of Nature is a force which comes from that aspect of the Soul having its origin in the Intellect.[26]

Being the third principle in the hierarchy of being, after the Intellect and the Soul, Nature has three powers:

(1) The power of putting into motion (*quwwat al-taḥrīk*) which comes from the world of Divine Command.
(2) The power of guidance (*quwwat al-hidāyah*) from the world of the Intellect.
(3) The power of inclining toward movement (*quwwat al-mail ila'l-taḥrīk*) from the world of the Soul.[27]

Nature and the Element are complementary and cannot exist without each other. Although both are generated by the Soul and are passive with respect to it, they are created so as to interact with each other. Nature exists in order to put into motion the Element. The Element on the other hand is given the ability to accept motion, or the act of Nature. Also coming after Nature, it has four defined effects (*āthār*) corresponding to the four worlds which lie above it: the world of the Divine Command, Intellect, Soul, and Nature.

Ibn Sīnā mentions that the first Element (*'unṣur*) in the world was *in principia* the point which, acted upon by Nature, was extended to a line, plane, and finally a three-dimensional body (*jism*). Having become a body, it was then acted upon by the force of motion (*taḥrīk*) of Nature and the power of ordering (*tadbīr*) of the Soul. The body formed in this way, going through the geometrical shapes from the most perfect circle, then triangle, and finally square, was purified, and out of the part with the greatest degree of purity (*ṣafā'*) the highest heaven was formed, to which the Intellect and Soul became attached. Out of the less pure the next heaven was formed, and the process continued until in the heaven of the Moon most of the purity was exhausted, and gravity and opaqueness (*kathāfah*) and impurity

[25] Ibn Sīnā uses "Nature" with several meanings, of which this is the most universal. In all the meanings the term contains, the sense of dynamism, power or principle of change similar to that found in the doctrines of the Hellenistic cosmologists is present.

[26] Ibn Sīnā, *Risālah dar ḥaqīqat wa kaifīyat . . .*, pp. 14–19.

[27] *Ibid.*, p. 19.

(*kudūrah*) became dominant so that the body could no longer accept a heavenly form but became the world of generation and corruption.[28]

The world of generation and corruption, which is the sublunary region, was not only prepared to receive form by the Intelligences symbolized by the celestial bodies, but received its very being from them.[29] Once having been brought into being, the sublunary region was moved by the power of Nature.[30] From this motion a great deal of heat was generated, and from the heat the separation of the body of this region was brought about. The separation in turn caused dryness; hence a substance called fire, possessing the qualities of heat and dryness, came into being. Whatever remained of the body fell away from the heavens toward the center. Unable to move, it became cold; the cold quality caused opaqueness and subsequently dryness. Out of these qualities of dryness and cold the element earth was formed. Whatever of the body remained was bound by the earth below and fire above. The half near the fire became warm without there being any separation among its parts, since the heat was not excessive. Therefore, a new element comprised of the qualities of heat and moisture, called air, came into being. The other half near the earth became cold, but since this coldness was not excessive it did not condense, so that an element consisting of the qualities of moisture and cold, called water, was formed. In this way the four principles (*arkān*) of all sublunary bodies were generated.[31]

The progressive "coagulation" of the Universal Element terminates with extreme differentiation, and the process of emanation, or effusion (*faiḍ*), reaches its terminal point. Henceforth the movement is no longer a drawing away from the principle but a return to it, not a *faiḍ* but an *'ishq*, or love, by which all things are attracted to the source of all Being. The elements in mixing together reach a degree of

[28] Gardet believes that limiting the Intelligences to ten is purely *a posteriori* (*La Pensée religieuse d'Avicenne*, p. 53). The number 10, however, by its completion of the cycle of numbers, symbolizes quite naturally the totality of the intelligible hierarchy.

[29] *La Pensée religieuse d'Avicenne*, p. 49.

[30] Nature as the cause of motion of the elements was a well-known Peripatetic doctrine. We see here that in his cosmogony, however, Ibn Sīnā makes Nature not only the cause of change of the four elements which lie in the sublunary region, but also the force which caused the body of all the heavens to be formed from the originally undifferentiated body (*jism*).

[31] Ibn Sīnā, *Risālah dar ḥaqīqat wa kaifīyat . . .*, pp. 24–25. In this treatise, at least, Ibn Sīnā seems to be making the four qualities the principles of the four elements, in agreement with the school of Jābir ibn Ḥayyān and contrary to the doctrines of Aristotle. Moreover, Ibn Sīnā always emphasizes the positive existence of all the four qualities—that is, that cold is not just the absence of heat, and so on, but that it has a reality of its own. In other works, however, he implies the importance of the four elements above that of the qualities, and the dependence of the qualities upon the elements. See *Shifā'*, *Ṭabī'īyāt*, pp. 209ff.

harmony which permits the descent of the lowest form of Soul upon them. This descent brings into being the minerals which form the lowest kingdom of the physical domain. In the mineral kingdom itself, purity increases until in the jewels, the highest members of this domain, the "fire of the Soul" is much stronger than in stones or mud.

In the coral, the first stage of the plant kingdom is reached. The increase in purity of the mixture of elements permits a new soul, or more precisely a new faculty, of the Universal Soul to descend upon it. This new faculty, and not the elements or their manner of combination, is responsible for the characteristics which distinguish the plant world from the mineral. In the plant kingdom, also, there is a hierarchy in which purity increases, reaching its highest degree in the palm, which already possesses certain features of animals.

With increasing purity in the mixing of the elements, again a new faculty of the Soul—this time called the animal soul—enters the stage of the cosmic play and manifests itself in ever greater degree from the lowly snail to the monkey, which even resembles man in certain of his features.[32]

The hierarchy of being rises with the degree of purity to the stages of man, the demons and devils of the first, second, sixth, and seventh climatic zones, and then the higher form of humanity of the third, fourth, and fifth zones. In each case a new soul, or a faculty of the Soul, comes into play. There are also stages above that of humanity, including the stage of the Sacred Spirit (*al-rūḥ al-qudsī*) through which the Active Intellect is reached, and finally the highest stage, that of the saints and prophets, which itself comprises numerous angelic worlds.[33] The end of the whole cosmic process is Pure Being itself where all things began. Creation therefore comes from God and returns to Him.[34]

[32] It is instructive to note that Ibn Sīnā, like al-Bīrūnī, considers the monkey as the highest of animals in opposition to the Ikhwān al-Ṣafā' who believe the elephant to be the most intelligent animal and therefore the terminal link in the animal kingdom.

[33] Ibn Sīnā, *al-Ishārāt wa'l-tanbīhāt*, pp. 483ff, *Risālah dar ḥaqīqat wa kaifīyat . . .*, pp. 30–31. Ibn Sīnā quotes from the Quran (XXXVII, 164): "There is not one of Us [revealing angel speaking in first person] but hath his known position."

„وَمَا مِنَّا إِلَّا لَهُ مَقَامٌ مَعْلُومٌ . . "

[34] *Risālah dar ḥaqīqat wa kaifīyat . . .*, p. 31, Ibn Sīnā quotes in this context the verses of the Quran (X, 35):

„اللَّهُ يَبْدَؤُا الْخَلْقَ ثُمَّ يُعِيدُهُ . . "

"Allah produceth Creation, then reproduceth it" and Quran (XI, 125):

„وَإِلَيْهِ يُرْجَعُ الْأَمْرُ كُلُّهُ . . "

"And unto Him the whole matter will be returned."

The intuition of the unity and interrelatedness of the parts of the Universe which underlies the description of the generation of the cosmos given above is dressed in the syllogistic language of Peripatetic philosophy, which perhaps hides rather than clarifies its true nature in the mind of the modern reader unaccustomed to this mode of thought. As so often occurs with the Peripatetics, basic intuitions which are metaphysical rather than merely philosophical are enclosed within a rationalistic system whose interest is more in satisfying the thirst for causality than in leading to the direct contemplation of the Truth. In a sermon on unity (*al-Khuṭbat al-gharrā'*) delivered by Ibn Sīnā on the praise of God and made famous in its Persian translation by 'Umar Khayyām, for an instant the usual syllogistic veil is partly cast aside and the contemplative aspect of his cosmogony revealed. The reader catches a glimpse not of the rationalistic aspect of Ibn Sīnā's thought which, as shown by Imām al-Ghazzālī, contradicted certain aspects of the spirit and letter of Islam, but of his metaphysical vision of the view of Nature in which Nature appears as a unified domain and the Universe as the manifestation of the Divine Principle in conformity with the essence of Islam. The movement of the cosmos from the highest heaven to the earth, and on earth through the three kingdoms, is described as a drawing away from the Principle and a return to It in such a manner as to convey that every particle and every movement displays the wisdom of the Creator and serves his purpose. Ibn Sīnā writes:

Above the heavens there are two spheres: One of the Equinox and the other of the Zodiac. If the heavens were without stars, there would not have been change of Time, efficacious for the growth of animals and plants. Similarly, had there been all stars without heaven, the lights would have vanished and with them the causes of existence and annihilation. Had not the (Zodiacal) Sphere been "inclined" towards the Sphere of Equinox, the seasons would have been equal and the state of surroundings and environments would have been monotonous. Thou Holy (God) the possessor of infinite power, whose bounty has left nothing out of it while granting existence! It is impossible that an infinite being can exist jointly, as it can only exist separately and not in company with others. So Thou didst create (by Order) the Primal Matter *possessing infinite power in Passivity, inasmuch as Thou possessest power in Activity.* Thou didst know that Generation and Corruption are effected by means which are contracting and expanding, susceptible of receiving (impression) and controlling corruption. Hence Thou createdst Heat expanding in its essence, Cold contracting in its qualities, Moisture for preserving the bodies from being decomposed. From these (humours), Thou createdst the primal elements, and the hottest of them hast stationed on the higher space (i.e. the heavens) which, were it Cold, would have been heated by the heavenly motion and no being had remained but perished, on account of the Heat spread over all the elements in potentiality and space. Thou createdst the higher (heavenly) elements (i.e. Fire, Air, Water) naturally transparent, otherwise no luminous ray could have passed through them. Thou didst create the Earth dust-coloured, otherwise the light, which is the cause of the Instinctive Heat, active in creating physical forms, would not have paused over it (but would have passed through). So Thou createdst from the Earth, Minerals, Vegetables, and Animals of different kinds, which became generator and corruptor, begetter and begotten. The principal object of this (process) was the creation of Man, *from whose residues Thou createdst all beings*, so that no being may be deprived of its elements and one being may not be weakened by another negative (being). Thou didst create Man possessing an intelligent Soul, which if purified through the knowledge of good deeds, becomes like the Substances of the First Causes (i.e., angels). Whenever the temperament of Man is equable and without contraries, it becomes like the "Seven strong Heavens"; and whenever it is devoid of the receiving forms (i.e., Matter), it resembles the First Causes (i.e., angels). Thou Sustainer and Lord of lords: We desire Thee, pray and fast for Thee. Thou art the First Origin. From thee we ask for succour and warning to guard us against our negligence, and guide us in our doubts. Thou art the perfector and originator of these (doubts). Praise be to God who alone is deserving of it! And His blessings be upon His messenger Muḥammad, best of all His creatures, and on all his companions.[35]

In a fashion very similar to certain esoteric schools in Islam, especially to some branches of Ismā'īlism, Ibn Sīnā in his *al-Risālat al-nairūzīyah* symbolizes the stages of the generation of the cosmos by letters of the Arabic alphabet.[36] He first divides created beings into: the hierarchy of pure Intelligence, or angels, which are separated completely from matter and which are above change and multiplicity; the animated world of Intelligences not completely divorced from matter but "dressed" by the stable matter of the heavens and causing the celestial motion; the world of physical Nature (*al-ṭabī'ah*) comprising the forces which circulate in bodies, which are completely bound to

[35] K.A.M. Akhtar, "A tract of Avicenna," *Islamic Culture*, 9:221–222 (1935). For the original Arabic text of the sermon and its Persian translation by Khayyām, see S. Naficy, *Avicenna*, Tehran (1954), pp. 260–266.

[36] *Al-Risālat al-nairūzīyah* . . ., in *Tis' rasā'il* (Cairo, 1908), pp. 134–141. Ibn Sīnā, however, does not follow the Ismā'īlī scheme completely [for the Ismā'īlī scheme in *Gushāyish wa rahāyish*, see the Introduction by H. Corbin to the *Kashf al-maḥjūb* of Abū Ya'qūb al-Sijistānī (Tehran, 1949), p. 11, n. 2]; but he makes several revisions to bring the meaning of the letters and the order of their emanation into conformity with his philosophic conception of generation derived from Neoplatonism. In assigning numerical values to the letters, he follows the traditional *abjad* system.

Regarding the changes brought about by Ibn Sīnā, see L. Massignon, "La Philosophie orientale d'Ibn Sīnā . . .," *Mémorial Avicenne* (Cairo, 1952), IV, 5.

matter and which are the source of all movement;[37] and finally the corporeal world itself.[38]

Having made this general division, Ibn Sīnā follows the science of *jafr* in establishing a correspondence between the hierarchy of the Universe and the letters of the Arabic alphabet in the following manner:

A = 1 = *al-Bārī'*: Creator.
B = 2 = *al-'aql*: Intellect.
J = 3 = *al-nafs*: Soul.
D = 4 = *al-ṭabī'ah*: Nature.
H = 5 = *al-Bārī' (bi'l-iḍāfah)*: Creator in relation to what is below it.
W = 6 = *al-'aql (bi'l-iḍāfah)*: Intellect in relation to what is below it.
Z = 7 = *al-nafs (bi'l-iḍāfah)*: Soul in relation to what is below it.
Ḥ = 8 = *al-ṭabī'ah (bi'l-iḍāfah)*: Nature in relation to what is below it.
T = 9 = *al-hayūlā'*: material world having no relation to anything below it.
Y = 10 = 5 × 2 = *al-ibdā'*: the plan of the Creator.
K = 20 = 5 × 4 = *al-takwīn*: Structure transmitted to the created realm.
L = 30 = 5 × 6 = *al-amr*: the Divine Commandment.
M = 40 = 5 × 8 = *al-khalq*: the created Universe.
N = 50 = M + Y = the twofold aspect of *wujūd* (being).
S = 60 = M + K = the double relation to *khalq* and *takwīn*.
'ayn = 70 = L + M = *al-tartīb*: chain of being impressed upon the Universe.
Ṣ = 90 = L + M + K = the triple relation to *amr*, *khalq*, and *takwīn*.
Q = 100 = 2Y = S + Y = *ishtimāl al-jumlah fi'l-ibdā'*: The assembly of all things in the plan of the Creator.

[37] Among followers of Hellenistic cosmology in Islam, Nature is usually the common ground or substance of the four natural qualities and elements and of all the changing forms brought into being by them. In the ultimate sense, Nature for them, as for the Greeks, is the principle of change, while for the Ṣūfīs it is the "Breath of God" (*al-nafas al-ilāhī*) or the Breath of the Compassionate (*nafas al-raḥmān*), and the feminine, passive or "motherly" aspect of the Divine act of creation. We see that in this respect both Ibn Sīnā and the Ikhwān al-Ṣafā' are followers of Hellenistic cosmology without, of course, being necessarily opposed to the Islamic perspective. As we mentioned earlier, it was not so much the pre-Islamic (*awā'il*) sciences, but the rationalistic tendencies of the Peripatetics against which the Islamic world reacted.

[38] Goichon, *La Distinction entre l'essence et l'existence . . .*, pp. 243–244.

R = 200 = 2Q = the return of all things to the One, which is their principle and entelechy.[39]

This table, which associates the three hypostases of Intellect, Soul, and Nature with the Creator to form a tetrad, limits the stages of manifestation to the number 9. It is connected to the adjacent magic square which came originally from China, being associated with the Ming Tang, the first magic square of Yū, and which was integrated into Islamic alchemy by Jābir ibn Ḥayyān and used by later authors like al-Ghazzālī and the Ismā' īlī Aḥmad al-Khayyāl.[40] With this

D 4 د	Ṭ 9 ط	B 2 ب
J 3 ج	H 5 ه	Z 7 ز
Ḥ 8 ح	A 1 ا	W 6 و

Figure 17. The first magic square.

system of alphabetical symbolism, Ibn Sīnā, in the last section of the *Risālat al-nairūzīyah*, seeks to interpret the meaning of the letters at the beginning of the *sūrahs* Maryam (XIX) and al-Shawrā (XLII) of the Quran. Despite certain differences in Ibn Sīnā's procedure from the usual interpretation of these letters by various traditional authorities, his attempt is of great interest. Firstly, as we have seen, Ibn Sīnā is attempting in this treatise to combine Greek philosophical notions with the Oriental tradition of *ḥikmah* and certain Islamic sacred

[39] *Tis' rasā'il*, pp. 138–140; Massignon, "La Philosophie orientale d'Ibn Sīnā," p. 3. See also Carra de Vaux, *Les Penseurs de l'Islam*, IV, 38–42.

[40] Ibn Sīnā's scheme is related to the magic square of Fermat, in that it is limited to nine stages corresponding to the nine "letters of Adam"; all the other letters are formed by the addition and multiplication of the first nine principial "states."

For an explanation of the meaning of this magic square in Chinese civilization see R. Guénon, *La Grande Triade* (Paris, 1946), chap. XVI.

There are many books in Arabic and Persian on magic squares and the numerical symbolism of letters connected with them (*'ilm al-wifq wa'l-a'dād*), such as the *Shams al-āfāq fī 'ilm al-ḥurūf wa'l-awfāq*, *Baḥr al-wuqūf fī 'ilm al-ḥurūf*, and *Shams al-ma'ārif al-kubrā* by Muḥyī al-Dīn al-Būnī and *Kunh al-murād fī wifq al-a'dād* of Ya'qūb ibn Muḥammad al-Ṭāwūsī.

sciences which have their basis in the Quran and the Arabic language. Secondly, by use of alphabetical symbolism he tries once more to demonstrate that all things come from the One and return to It. Moreover, the analogy of cosmic entities with the sacred language of Islamic Revelation is the framework within which the study of Nature becomes also the study of "the macrocosmic Book," which is the counterpart of the sacred text, so that all sciences of the Universe may be considered as so many works of "exegesis of the cosmic text."

The Relation between God and the Universe

We saw how in his ontology Ibn Sīnā clearly separates Being from all particular beings, while in his cosmogony he considers the Universe as an effusion (*faiḍ*) of Being. This apparent contradiction, and more generally the whole question of creation, or manifestation, has always remained among the most debated aspects of Ibn Sīnā's philosophy and the one which has been attacked most severely. The Islamic perspective can be said to have its particular *raison d'être* in integrating the particular in the Universal and in leveling into nothingness all that is creaturely before the absolute transcendence of the Divine Principle.[41] Therefore it could not accept the Greek notion of the eternity of the heavens or any other order of reality which might detract from the transcendence of God, and reacted to the notion of creation held by philosophers like Ibn Sīnā in the spirit which is most conformable to the essence of Islam.[42]

Ibn Sīnā uses four words to designate the creation or generation of the Universe:

iḥdāth—production of contingent beings, whether they be eternal or temporal.

[41] "Conformément à ce qui fait la raison d'être particulière de l'Islam, à savoir l'idée de la transcendance absolue du Principe divin, transcendance qui nivellera tout ce qui est 'créature,' du 'verbe fait chair' jusqu'au dernier grain de poussière . . ." F. Schuon, *L'Œil du cœur* (Paris, 1950), p. 148.

[42] ". . . on peut dire qu'il y a là, dans le créationisme occasionaliste des ash'arites et dans le panenthéisme des philosophes mystiques (Soufis), comme deux aspects extrêmes d'un même sentiment qui est peut-être le plus puissant et le plus constant de l'Islam: la non-existence absolue de ce qui n'est pas Dieu. Les théologiens orthodoxes anéantissent le créé devant le Créateur; les mystiques hétérodoxes intègrent la création en Dieu, et le *fanā'* est pour eux l'entrée dans la vie mystique. Ibn Sīnā, semble-t-il, s'est efforcé de réaliser un moyen terme: repoussant l'anéantissement ontologique de la créature, et sauvegardant cependant la contingence essentielle du créé, et donc, en un sens, sa distinction avec le Créateur." Gardet, *La Pensée religieuse d'Avicenne*, p. 68.

ibdā'—production without intermediary of incorruptible and eternal beings, whether they be corporeal or not.
khalq—production, with or without intermediaries, of corporeal beings, whether they be corruptible or incorruptible.
takwīn—production with intermediaries of corruptible beings.[43]

According to Ibn Sīnā, creation itself is intellection by God of His own Essence. It is this intellection (*ta'aqqul*) and the knowledge (*'ilm*) of His own Essence that brings all things into being. This act of intellection is limitless (*lā yatanāhā*), and the manifestation of the Universe is God's eternal knowledge of Himself.[44] Creation is at the same time the giving of being by God and the shining of the rays of intelligence so that each creature in the Universe is related to its Divine Source by its being and its intelligence.[45] In some of Ibn Sīnā's more esoteric works, in fact, God is identified with the source (*al-manba'*) of the overflowing of light (*fayaḍān al-nūr*) which fills all things.[46] So, one can say that Creation is the realization of the intelligible essences and existence the theophany (*tajallī*) of these essences, so that being and light are ultimately the same. To give existence to creatures is to illuminate them with the Divine Light which is the ray emanating from His Being.[47]

In the perspective of Ibn Sīnā the invisible world depends for its subsistence upon the Divine Intellect, and even the physical domain can be said to be dependent not only upon God's Will but also His Being. The existence of everything in the physical domain derives ultimately from the Divine Essence. Ibn Sīnā writes:

Le premier est trop élévé dans sa majesté pour qu'aucun motif l'entraîne, qu'aucune impulsion l'emporte, et nulle chose extrinsèque à son être n'est assez bonne (de soi) pour mériter d'exister. Tout au contraire, l'être de tout chose procède de Lui de cette façon, et son intellection de sa propre

[43] Gardet, *La Pensée religieuse d'Avicenne*, p. 65. See also Goichon, *La Distinction de l'essence et de l'existence . . .*, pp. 249–255.

[44] See Ibn Sīnā, *Risālah dar ḥaqīqat wa kaifīyat . . .*, pp. 8–9.

[45] "C'est une pensée des plus hautes et d'une rare plénitude de vérité, que de faire de la création à la fois le don de l'être et le rayonnement de l'intelligence" (Goichon, *La Philosophie d'Avicenne et son influence en Europe médiévale* [Paris, 1944], p. 41). Also: "La création est en même temps transmission de l'être et rayonnement de l'intelligence" (Goichon, "L'Unité de la pensée avicennienne," *Archives Internationales . . .* [1952], p. 296).

[46] See, for example, Ibn Sīnā's "discourse" with the Ṣūfī master Abū Sa'īd ibn Abi'l-Khair on the effect on the soul of visiting places of pilgrimage in A. F. von Mehren, *Traités mystiques d'Abou Ali al-Hosain b. Abdallah b. Sīnā ou d'Avicenne* (Leiden, 1889), p. 45.

[47] "La création est la réalisation des intelligibles. L'être est donné avec la lumière; ou plutôt l'être est une lumière. C'est pourquoi le flux créateur envisagé sous cet angle, est appelé rayonnement, *tajallī*." Goichon, *La Philosophie d'Avicenne . . .*, p. 42.

essence est l'essence par laquelle l'être de toute chose est possible, alors qu'est nécessaire l'intellection qui les a pour objet.[48]

It is neither in his unified vision of the cosmos nor in the doctrine of Divine intellection that Ibn Sīnā differs from the Islamic perspective. It is more in limiting the power of God to a predetermined logical structure and in diminishing the sense of awe of the finite before the Infinite that he came to be criticized by certain authorities of the Islamic Tradition. The nothingness of man and his limited knowledge before the Divine is hidden by the veil of a rationalistic system in which Ibn Sīnā clothes his basic intuitions. In the Muslim perspective, God, as the source of all qualities, must not only be absolute determination and necessity but also absolute freedom. His Will must transcend all systems which try to limit it to the domain of finiteness. The philosophers like Ibn Sīnā, especially when they followed the Neoplatonists, began with metaphysical intuitions of the profoundest order which are more or less direct applications of the first *Shahādah* of Islam. It was when they hid these intuitions within an excessively rationalistic system that they moved away from the domain of gnosis, which is the meeting-ground of faith and science, to that of reason, which is the battleground of their conflict. In the case of Ibn Sīnā we also find an oscillation between doctrines both metaphysical and cosmological in nature which, being in conformity with the Islamic perspective, became integrated into its viewpoint. Moreover, we also encounter ideas that belong more strictly to philosophy understood in a purely rationalistic sense, and have always remained on the periphery of Islamic civilization.

[48] Ibn Sīnā, *Gloses*, pp. 63–64, in Vajda, "Les Notes d'Avicenne," in *La Revue Thomiste* (1951).

CHAPTER 13

Principles of Natural Philosophy

Natural philosophy (*ṭabīʿīyāt*) is, according to Ibn Sīnā, that aspect of wisdom which deals with the domain that moves and changes.[1] It is the study, at once quantitative and qualitative, of that which is an accident (*ʿaraḍ*) and constitutes along with mathematics and metaphysics the domain of speculative philosophy. The branches of natural philosophy constitute all the sciences of the sublunary region and are enumerated in the following manner:[2]

1. *ṭibb*—medicine
2. *nujūm*—astrology
3. *firāsah*—physiognomy
4. *taʿbīr*—oneiromancy
5. *ṭalismāt*—natural magic (drawing celestial forces upon terrestrial ones)
6. *nairanjīyāt*—theurgy (employing terrestrial forces to produce effects which appear as supernatural)
7. *kīmiyā'*—alchemy

The sciences of geometric astronomy, geography, geodesy, mechanics, statics, optics, and hydraulics, although also pertaining to the study of the physical domain as understood today are classified by Ibn Sīnā under the mathematical sciences.[3]

Natural philosophy depends upon certain principles such as the notions of matter and form, time and space, and the varieties of motion which serve as the basis for all the sciences of Nature in the

[1] "حكمة تتعلق بما في الحركة والتغير وتسمى حكمة طبيعية." Ibn Sīnā, *ʿUyūn al-ḥikmah*, ed. Badawī (Cairo, 1954), p. 17. The object of natural philosophy is "ce qui est dans le mouvement et la transformation en tant que tel" (L. Gardet, *La Pensée religieuse d'Avicenne*, p. 30). In his *Fann-i samāʿ-i ṭabīʿī*, from *al-Shifā'* (trans. M. A. Foroughi, Tehran, 1316 [1937], p. 12), Ibn Sīnā compares the relation of the study of Nature to that of metaphysics with the study of a particular science to the universal science.

[2] See Ibn Sīnā, *Aqsām-i ʿulūm-i ʿaqlīyah* in *Rāhnamā-yi ḥikmat* (Tehran, 1372 [1952], pp. 12–13).

[3] See A. F. von Mehren, "Les Rapports de la philosophie d'Avicenne avec l'Islam," *Le Muséon*, 2:565 (1883).

Peripatetic sense. To ask why in natural philosophy means to inquire into the causes of something in terms of the four Aristotelian causes and in the context of the above principles.[4] As for giving proofs of principles in natural philosophy, this is not so easy in terms of natural philosophy itself because proofs of essentials, like the existence of a power called Nature capable of changing things, belongs to the realm of metaphysics alone. "One cannot prove the principles of a science by that science itself."[5]

Before probing into the meaning of the principles which underlie the study of natural philosophy, we must understand the meaning or meanings which Ibn Sīnā gives to the word Nature (*ṭabī'ah*). The Aristotelians, whom he follows in this branch of learning more than in other fields, use the word nature with four meanings: as *natura generatio*, *natura essentia*, *natura substantis simplex* and *natura rei corporeae*.[6] Aristotle himself defines Nature as "a certain principle and cause of motion and rest to that in which it is primarily inherent, essentially and not according to accident."[7]

Ibn Sīnā also uses the word "Nature" with several meanings, of which the most essential is the force responsible for moving the elements. "The form of an element is a Nature which is known by action but not felt or seen by the senses."[8] It is this Nature which keeps the element at rest if it is in its right place and makes it move toward its correct position if it is out of its natural place.

Using the word "Nature" in a somewhat different sense, it can be said that the tendencies of lightness and heaviness are due to Nature, which here implies the form of the elements, the form which gives them the particular qualities that they possess. "Therefore, each of the four elements possesses a nature," writes Ibn Sīnā, "which is its lot and its form (*ṣūrah*); fire has one, water another, air another and earth another. And these qualities are accidents which come from that nature and that form."[9] In this sense the nature of water, for example, is that by virtue of which it is water. If water is considered with respect to the motions and actions it performs, it is studied in its

[4] Ibn Sīnā, *Shifā'*, *Ṭabī'īyāt*, pp. 33–44.

[5] *Ibid.*, p. 41.

[6] Ibn Gabirol, *Fons Vitae*, ed. C. Baumker (Monasterii, 1895), pp. 492–494.

[7] Aristotle, *Physics*, trans. T. Taylor (London, 1912), vol. II, pt. 1, pp. 20–23.

[8] Ibn Sīnā, *Dānishnāma-yi 'alā'ī*, *Ṭabī'īyāt*, (Tehran, 1952), p. 53.

[9] *Ibid.*, p. 55. Ibn Sīnā believes, therefore, that the form of the elements is the cause of their natural motion. "According to this view, therefore, the cause of the natural motion of the elements abides within the elements themselves. The form is the cause of the motion of the elements just as the soul is the cause of motion of animals. The elements are therefore said to be moved by themselves *hyph' auton*, in the same way as animal beings." H. A. Wolfson, *Crescas' Critique of Aristotle* (Cambridge, Mass., 1929), p. 673.

nature, and if with respect to the substance from which it derives its being, then it is considered in its form.

In considering the relation of Nature to motion and rest, Ibn Sīnā begins with the most general consideration of change. All objects in this world, according to him, must be moved (that is, changed)[10] by an outside cause, as in the case of the heating of water, or by an inner cause which belongs to their essence, as in the case of the growth of a seed into a plant or a sperm into an animal. The force causing change can be classified in the following manner:

1. Single motion { (a) involuntary—like falling of stones; (b) voluntary—like motion of the Sun }

2. Several motions { (c) involuntary—like motion of plants; (d) voluntary—like motion of animals }

Ibn Sīnā calls force (a) in this classification Nature, (b) the heavenly soul (*al-nafs al-falakīyah*), (c) the vegetative soul (*al-nafs al-nabātīyah*), and (d) the animal soul (*al-nafs al-ḥayawānīyah*).[11] In this perspective, therefore, Nature becomes, along with the various souls, one of the forces (*quwwah*) responsible for motion in the Universe. But it is also the power which can keep something at rest. Its function is not only dynamic but "regulatory"; it is not only a power coming from the essence of something which brings about all qualitative and quantitative changes in it, but also the power which keeps it at rest and makes it remain what it is.[12]

[10] Motion for Ibn Sīnā, as for Aristotle, means not only a locomotion but changes of quantity, quality, and posture as well.

« فالأول من الأقسام كما للحجر في هبوطه ووقوفه في الوسط ويسمى طبيعة والثاني
كما للشمس في دورانها عند محصّل الفلاسفة ويسمى نفسا فلكية والثالث كما للنبات
في تكونه ونشوئه ووقوفه فانها يتحرك لا بالارادة حركات الى جهات شتى تفريعا او
تشعيبا للاصول وتعريضا ويسمى نفسا نباتية والرابع كما للحيوان ويسمى نفسا حيوانية
وربما قيل اسم الطبيعة على كل قوة يصدر عنها فعلها بلا ارادة. »

Shifā', *Ṭabī'iyāt*, p. 13.

[11] Ibn Sīnā, *Fann-i samā'-i ṭabī'ī*, pp. 39–40.

[12] "La *ṭabi'a* est par essence principe premier du mouvement de ce en quoi elle est essentiellement et de son repos essentiel; bref, elle est principe premier de tout changement et de toute stabilité essentiels." Goichon, *La Distinction de l'essence et de l'existence . . .*, p. 45.

Ibn Sīnā, aware of the many uses of the word "Nature," writes:

But the expression *ṭabī'ah* is used with many meanings. What is mentionable is the following three meanings:

1. Nature in the sense we already gave to it (as form of simple elements).
2. Nature as that from which the substance of something is formed.
3. Nature as the essence of things.[13]

To this list he adds the meaning of Nature as the power which preserves the cosmic order.

Nature can be considered as particular (*juz'ī*) or universal (*kullī*). Particular Nature is confined to each individual while Universal Nature can be considered as belonging to the intelligible order and being the immaterial source from which the total order emanates. If we accept a single Universal Nature, this Nature is the first sphere of the heavens which preserves the cosmic order.[14]

It is in keeping with these diverse meanings of the philosophical concept of the word "Nature" and the purpose and goal of natural philosophy that we must approach the study of time and space and form and matter as the primary conditions of terrestrial existence. The final aim of this study is to understand motion which in medieval philosophy always means change in terms of principles belonging to a domain which is itself above change, remembering that the principles of the traditional sciences of Nature do not lie in these sciences themselves but in metaphysics.

Form and Matter

The basic intuition of hylomorphism which underlies Aristotelian doctrines is to be found nearly everywhere in medieval philosophy, even though the meaning given to form and matter is not always that given by the Stagirite himself. This is also true in the case of Ibn Sīnā, who bases his natural philosophy upon the doctrine of form and matter without following completely the teachings of Aristotle. Form, according to Ibn Sīnā, is "the quality of quiddity (*māhīyah*) by which a body (*jism*) is what it is," whereas matter "is that which supports (*ḥāmil*) the quality or form."[15] Matter can only exist by the form imparted to it by the Intellect; without form it would be pure

[13] Ibn Sīnā, *Fann-i samā'-i ṭabī'ī*, p. 48.

[14] *Ibid.*, p. 52. We see once again how Ibn Sīnā, while expounding Peripatetic doctrines, steps outside the boundary of their philosophy.

[15] *Fann-i samā'-i ṭabī'ī*, p. 46.

receptivity deprived of reality. That is why prime matter cannot be found by itself.[16] Moreover, "matter is [created] for form and its purpose is to have form imposed upon it, but form is not [created] for matter."[17]

Body (*jism*), which is made up of form and matter, is that which possesses the possibility of receiving division.[18] Inasmuch as it possesses a corporeal form it is in act, and inasmuch as it is capable of receiving it is in potentiality.[19] A body may then be considered as a substance which possesses on the one side actuality and on the other potentiality. The first named aspect is its form and the second its matter, or *hylé*.

The complex notion of matter in Ibn Sīnā is derived from several sources, Aristotelian as well as Neoplatonic. For Aristotle, generation and corruption mean a transition from existence in potentiality to existence in act and vice versa, not from non-being to matter. Matter for him exists in potentiality, which means that already it possesses a kind of being. In a substance, the part that is actual is form, and the part which is potential matter, the two being wedded together inseparably in all things which do not exist in pure actuality. Matter for him has clearly two separate meanings, one as *hylé* which means that which is in potentiality, and the other as *tò hypocheimenon*, meaning the substratum which subsists permanently through generation and corruption.

Neoplatonists also use the word *hylé* but with the meaning of non-being *tò mē hon*. *Hylé* for them does not have an existence in potentiality as it does with Aristotle; it has no existence at all. There is therefore no material cause or creation of matter because matter does not even exist.[20]

Ibn Sīnā rejects the Aristotelian idea of existence *in potentia* and

[16] Ibn Sīnā, *Le Livre des directives et remarques* (*Kitāb al-išārāt* . . .), trans. A. M. Goichon (Beirut, 1951), p. 266. (We have made use of M. Goichon's translation of Ibn Sīnā's *Kitāb al-ishārāt* . . . in this and following chapters.) See also Gardet, *La Pensée religieuse d'Avicenne*, p. 61.

[17] Ibn Sīnā, *Shifā'*, *Ṭabī'īyāt*, p. 33, and *Fann-i samā'-i ṭabī'ī*, p. 96.

[18] "La corporéité, en tant qu'elle est la corporéité, n'est pas autre que la possibilité de recevoir la division. Il est dans la nature de la corporéité d'être susceptible de division." P. Duhem, *Le Système du monde*, IV, 470.

[19] Ibn Sīnā emphasizes the receptive nature of the body and its inability to cause anything. "That which causes—is in every case a Power, a Form, or a Soul, the Spirit operating through such instrumentality. In the realm of the Physical there are accordingly countless powers, the chief grades of which, from the lower to the higher, are—the Forces of Nature, the Energies of Plants and Animals, Human Souls and World-Souls" (Tj. de Boer, *The History of Philosophy in Islam*, p. 139).

[20] For an excellent analysis of these notions and their comparison with the views of Ibn Sīnā, see Duhem, *Le Système du monde*, IV, 454ff.

admits only existence in act. The Aristotelian divisions into the contradictory, in potentiality and in act, are for Ibn Sīnā the classes of the impossible, contingent, and necessary. Therefore, whereas for the Peripatetics matter is eternal and the *hylé* does not admit or require a cause but is necessary, according to Ibn Sīnā the *hylé* has need of multiple causes for its existence in act. Matter, or *hylé*, in fact is brought into existence by the form which is given by the Intelligence of the tenth sphere that governs the sublunary region. In his doctrine of matter, Ibn Sīnā implicitly assumes the "original matter" of the Ikhwān al-Ṣafā' without, however, mentioning it. He considers the *hylé* as the subject of corporeality and that to which corporeal form (*ṣūrah jismīyah*) is added to make a general body. The body is in fact the sum of corporeal form and matter.

Matter is also the principle of individuation, that which permits the multiplicity of forms.[21] But in itself, it has only a "negative existence" and the capability (*qābilīyah*) of accepting division upon which the form of corporeality is imposed. It is deprived of all perfection and beauty because it is non-being, or that which is farthest away from Being which is the source of all perfection and beauty. Matter is also pure passivity; it does nothing on its own but remains always the subject upon which celestial influences act. It is the influence of the Intelligences which prepares matter to receive form and then imposes various forms upon it, the form of matter being its *raison d'être*. Unlike Aristotle, for whom both matter and form have their own reality, Ibn Sīnā emphasizes the ontological inequality of the two. Form, according to him, is the principle of matter, or what links it to Being; without form, matter would have no existence at all.

Ibn Sīnā rejects the various forms of atomism as held by al-Naẓẓām, al-Shahrastānī, and other theologians and philosophers and the corollary belief in the existence of the vacuum by arguments which are metaphysical and logical as well as experimental.[22] He gives most of the Aristotelian arguments against the vacuum—for example, that a body having a finite speed in water or air would have

[21] "Le principe de l'individuation est la matière marquée d'une quantité déterminée" (A. M. Goichon, *La Philosophie d'Avicenne* . . ., p. 47). "La matière est rendue existante par une cause fondamentale et un déterminant qui agit en faisant suivre la forme. Quand elles se réunissent, l'être de la matière est achevé et, par elle, la forme est individualisée, tandis qu'elle-même est encore individualisée par la forme d'une manière qui supporterait une explication autre que ce résumé" (Ibn Sīnā, *Le Livre des directives et remarques* . . ., p. 271).

[22] Ibn Sīnā, *'Uyūn al-ḥikmah*, pp. 24–25. For a detailed discussion of the various forms of atomism in the Muslim world and the reason for their rejection by Ibn Sīnā, see Khwājah Nāṣir al-Dīn al-Ṭūsī, *Sharḥ al-ishārāt*, II, 8ff.

infinite speed in a vacuum.[23] He also gives experimental evidence of the jug which, although inverted, does not lose its water, and suction plates which, although pulled away from each other, refuse to separate. In both cases, he argues that the cause is that Nature does not want to create a vacuum.[24]

In discussing the composition of bodies, Ibn Sīnā rejects the views of both the ancient atomists and those like al-Naẓẓām who consider that it is possible actually (*bi'l-fi'l*) to divide a body indefinitely. He discusses the problems of indefinite division posed by Zeno and answers them in an Aristotelian fashion, and criticizes severely Democritus and the other atomists who believed that bodies are actually composed of indivisible particles which themselves are bodies.[25] Moreover, he rejects the school that considered the composition of bodies to be dependent upon objects which themselves are not bodies.[26]

His arguments against atomism include the well-known one that anything which occupies space can be divided by virtue of the fact that space has a beginning, middle, and end and can itself be divided.[27] He also gives certain geometrical arguments similar to those discussed already in the correspondence between himself and al-Bīrūnī. For example, Ibn Sīnā states that if the existence of an atom be accepted, and this atom be placed between two others, it must either touch them in two distinct parts, in which case it would no longer be geometrically indivisible, or it would touch them in all parts, in which case it would become one with them and there would no longer be a distinction between them. Or it would not touch other atoms at all, in which case one could not compose a body from atoms. Since all these three possibilities are excluded, the existence of atoms is also rejected. The atomist might also argue that movement proceeds by

[23] "Puisqu'on a vu clairement que la dimension continue ne subsiste pas sans matière, et non moins clairement que les dimensions relatives au volume ne se compénètrent pas, à cause de leur spatialité, c'est donc qu'un vide qui serait distance pure n'existe pas. Quand les corps suivent la voie de leurs mouvements, ce qui est entre eux s'éloigne d'eux; il ne demeure pas pour eux de distance en solution de continuité. Il n'y a donc pas de vide." Ibn Sīnā, *Le Livre des directives et remarques* . . ., p. 275.

[24] Ibn Sīnā, *Dānishnāmah* . . ., *Ṭabī'īyāt*, p. 23.

[25] Not only does Ibn Sīnā reject the notion of Democritus that everything is made of matter and motion, he also refutes the possibility of the world's having come into being through chance. Ibn Sīnā, *Shifā'*, *Ṭabī'īyāt*, pp. 29–30; *Fann-i samā'-i ṭabī'ī*, p. 88. He likewise rejects the view attributed to Empedocles and his followers that particulars and matter are accidental and the imposing of form upon matter essential, and that Nature is without an end or entelechy. He asserts on the contrary that accidents occur in Nature only with respect to particulars, the Universal being always determined (*Fann-i samā'-i ṭabī'ī*, p. 90).

[26] *Ibid.*, pp. 251–256.

[27] Ibn Sīnā, *Dānishnāmah* . . ., *Ilāhīyāt*, 23.

instantaneous bounces, but this, according to al-Shaikh al-Ra'īs, would also cause difficulty, because according to this assumption a square formed of regularly disposed points would have its diagonal equal to its side since there are the same number of points in the diagonal as in the sides. But inasmuch as this is not true geometrically, the distances between the atoms would have to be greater or less than a unit or atom, and the atom would therefore be divisible. He applies this argument also to the shadow of the gnomon cast by the Sun where, if the shadow were to make jumps from one atom of the ground to the next, the Sun would have to make a bigger jump.[28]

Ibn Sīnā's own position with respect to this difficult question is to accept the division of a body at every point no matter how far this is carried out—that is, to claim that a body is always indefinitely divisible potentially but not actually. This position rejects both atomism and the geometric arguments of Zeno. Although a body is indefinitely divisible potentially, in actuality the process of division cannot be carried out.[29] Actually, all bodies are composed of form and matter, corporeal form being in essence continuity (*ittiṣāl*), and matter being the capability of accepting both continuity and division, or discontinuity (*infiṣāl*), these two traits—that is, essential continuity and the possibility of division—being characteristic of all corporeal objects.

All bodies, besides consisting of form and matter, exist in the corporeal state by virtue of time and space. In Peripatetic natural philosophy, the heart of which is the problem of motion, the parameters of time and space in terms of which motion is described become of paramount importance. Time and space, however, are never considered as realities independent of bodies, but as two conditions of corporeal manifestation. It is the equating during the seventeenth century, of abstract geometrical space, or "absolute space," with "physical space," in which bodies are placed that separates modern physics so distinctly from its medieval predecessor. For Ibn Sīnā, the idea of the existence of space and time independent of bodies is absurd, so that the question asked centuries later by Kant, among others, about what lies beyond the Universe if space be finite, would be meaningless for him. There is no space if there is no corporeal existence, because

[28] Ibn Sīnā, *Dānishnāma-yi 'alā'ī* (Tehran, 1315 [1936]), I, 77–81; Carra de Vaux, *Les Penseurs de l'Islam*, IV, 28.

[29] The difficulties brought about by applying numbers as pure quantity to the physical domain, as in the arguments of Zeno, are the best indication that physical space is not pure quantity and that its reduction to pure quantity is at the expense of overlooking its qualitative nature which is an integral and essential aspect of it.

space is a condition of this state of manifestation and not an independent reality.

Al-Shaikh al-Ra'īs emphasizes that the body comes before geometrical space, as he writes:

D'après cela, tu sais que le corps est avant la surface dans l'existence, la surface avant la ligne et la ligne avant le point; les scrutateurs l'ont prouvé. Quant à ce qu'on dit inversement, que le point par son mouvement engendre la ligne, puis la ligne la surface ensuite la surface le corps, c'est pour faire comprendre, concevoir, imaginer.[30]

The notion of space is closely tied to the natural place of things in the Universe. According to the Peripatetics, whom Ibn Sīnā follows in this matter, each simple element, that is, fire, air, water, and earth, has its natural place in concentric spheres with the earth below and fire above.

Il y a donc dans sa nature le principe de cette obligation. Le [corps] simple a un lieu unique exigé par sa nature, et le composé a ce qu'exige [l'élément] qui prédomine en lui, soit absolument, soit selon son lieu ou selon ses conditions d'existence quand les forces luttant en sens contraire s'équilibrent. Tout corps a donc un seul lieu. Et il est nécessaire que la figure qu'exige le corps simple soit circulaire, sans quoi, dans une matière unique, ses dispositions diverses l'empêcheraient de constituer une force unique.[31]

In the light of this doctrine, the place of a body becomes the boundaries which surround it—for example, the place of fire being within the heavens and of air within fire. Or water, which is in a container, is surrounded by the surfaces of the vessel which together form its place (*makān*).[32] The place of an object, or what seems to us as the space surrounding it, is therefore nothing but the boundary of that which contains the object.[33]

The notion of space is closely allied to that of direction and orientation, which in all traditional sciences have an extremely important role to play. Hierarchy implies direction and orientation; and since medieval science is always based on the notion of hierarchy, the significance of direction becomes central. We have already had occasion to refer to the relation of this aspect of the science of space with sacred rites and religious architecture. In the Peripatetic works of Ibn

[30] Ibn Sīnā, *Le Livre des directives et remarques* . . ., p. 273.

[31] *Ibid.*, pp. 283–284.

[32] Ibn Sīnā, *Najāt*, pp. 116–124; *Fann-i samā'-i ṭabī'ī*, pp. 176–180.

[33] « فالمكان هو السطح الذى هو نهاية الجسم الحاوى . » *Shifā'*, *Ṭabī'īyāt*, p. 62.

Sīnā which we are discussing here, the more metaphysical aspects of spatial symbolism are not considered, yet the meaning that is given to the up and down directions and the hierarchy that derives from it is considered to be absolute and independent of any subjective relativity.[34]

Ibn Sīnā correlates the six directions of space with the left and right, front and back, and up and down directions of the human body. The left and right and front and back are, however, relative, whereas the up and down are absolute, corresponding to heaven and earth.[35] Since bodies in rectilinear motion cannot determine direction, it is for the heavenly spheres, which possess no translational motion, to specify the high and low directions in an absolute sense. The center of the sphere of the cosmos is the downward direction and its circumference the upward. Moreover, the heavens possess an east–west direction corresponding to the places of the rising and setting of the stars, and an up-and-down direction corresponding to the place of the noonday sun and the horizon of the earth, a forward-and-backward direction corresponding to the direction of motion of the heavens (*aflāk*) and its opposite, and finally a left-and-right direction, right being East and left West. By virtue of this correspondence, the heavens are like an animal which faces the North Pole.[36]

By this differentiation of space, the world possesses the three basic dimensions of length, breadth and thickness. Length is the plane between the two Poles, width between the right and left, and depth between front and back. Curiously enough, the South Pole is considered as the upward direction and the North as the downward because, as Ibn Sīnā states, "If a person lies down, facing the heavens with his right hand toward the East his head will be toward the South."[37] One sees, therefore, that direction and orientation depend essentially upon the heavens and have a nominal and not a real existence if considered only with respect to the world of the elements. It is only with reference to the heavens that the indefiniteness of space can be crystallized into its basic directions, which give space a qualitative aspect of fundamental importance.

Time has a more qualitative nature than space and is not so easily defined or measured. Whereas space can be measured directly by means of a chosen unit, man possesses no faculty by which he can make the same type of direct measurement of time. The measurement

[34] Ibn Sīnā, *Le Livre des directives et remarques . . .*, pp. 275–277.

[35] Ibn Sīnā, '*Uyūn al-ḥikmah*, pp. 20–21; *Fann-i samā'-i ṭabī'ī*, pp. 313–314.

[36] *Fann-i samā'-i ṭabī'ī*, p. 325. The indication of the microcosm-macrocosm analogy in spatial orientation is quite evident.

[37] *Ibid.*, pp. 325–326.

of time depends upon motion; time is, in fact, defined by Ibn Sīnā as the quantity, or measure, of motion.[38] Time is therefore, dependent completely upon change; "if there is no change and no motion there is no time."[39] Consequently, as bodies do not exist in a uniform space but space is a condition of corporeality, so motion does not take place in an abstract, uniform time, but time is one of the characteristics of movement (which in its most general sense means change). Likewise, if there were no coming into existence and passing away of things there would be no before or after, because an object comes before another if it exists while the other is in a state of nonexistence (*‘adam*).

Time, according to al-Shaikh al-Ra'īs, is a continuous quantity which can be divided indefinitely without ever reaching "the atom of time."[40] The proof of its existence, in fact, lies in the observation of two bodies which, starting from the same point, do not keep pace with each other but fall one behind the other. This proof of the existence of time itself depends upon the continuity of motion and therefore implies indirectly the continuity of time.[41] As a continuous entity, however, time, like space, must have a division (*faṣl*) which Ibn Sīnā calls the moment (*ān*). This moment does not have an actuality, as in the doctrine of the Ash‘arites, who believe in "atomic time," but exists only potentially (*bi'l-quwwah*) and "imaginatively" (*bi'l-tawahhum*). Just as any line, no matter how short, can be further divided, likewise any moment, no matter how brief its duration, can also be divided into parts.

A point in space may be considered either as the indivisible part of a line when it is divided indefinitely or that geometrical entity whose locus (motion) generates a line. The moment of time can also be conceived in two ways: either as the instant which is a part of time and whose existence depends upon time or as the instant from whose flow time comes into being. But for Ibn Sīnā the spatial point, as well as temporal moment, has only an "imaginary" (*tawahhumī*) existence, not a real (*ḥaqīqī*) one. The unreality of the moment, however, does

[38] "Time is the measure of motion." «فالزمان عدد الحركة.» *Shifā'*, *Ṭabī‘īyāt*, p. 73.

Ibn Sīnā, *‘Uyūn al-ḥikmah*, p. 27. «وهو مقدار الحركة في المتقدم والمتأخر.»

[39] Ibn Sīnā, *Fann-i samā‘-i ṭabī‘ī*, p. 204.

«لا يتصور الزمان الا مع الحركة ومتى لم يحس الحركة لم يحس بزمان.» Ibn Sīnā, *Najāt*, p. 116.

[40] For arguments against both atomic time and atomic space, see Ibn Sīnā, *Dānish-nāmah . . .*, *Ilāhīyāt*, p. 128.

[41] *Fann-i samā‘-i ṭabī‘ī*, p. 200.

not nullify the reality of time itself, which depends upon the Universal Soul[42] and the circular motion of the heavens. If there were no heavenly motion (or rotation) there would be no time, as there would be no directions of space nor any type of motion.[43] The heavens therefore define space and time, as well as permit the existence of the rectilinear motion of the sublunary region.

Motion

The problem of motion becomes important in natural philosophy only after Nature has ceased to be alive, when a distinction has been made between living beings and "dead matter." The question of how a living creature moves never presents itself to the human mind in the same way as that of bodies which are considered to have no innate movement. That is why in Aristotelian physics, where the live Universe of the ancients had already been deprived of some of its life, the problem of motion became central. It was also the "Achilles' heel" of Peripatetic natural philosophy, so that with a further secularization of the Universe during the Renaissance it became the point of attack and the weak spot through which the structure of medieval physics was destroyed.

In the contemplative, or gnostic, view of Nature, there is no distinction between "dead" and "alive." All natural phenomena and all terrestrial beings are symbols of the spiritual world, becoming more central in the degree that they ascend in the ontological hierarchy. The "problem of motion" therefore does not exist, and, if treated, it remains peripheral. That is why in the gnostic works of Ibn Sīnā, which view Nature symbolically, the question of motion is hardly of any importance. In his Peripatetic writings, however, motion becomes a central topic; he treats it with great generality, in a way which includes qualitative and teleological aspects of change as well as the consideration of motion as change of place.[44]

[42] "The soul is the cause of the existence of time." «فالنفس علة وجود الزمان.»

Ibn Sīnā, *'Uyūn al-ḥikmah*, p. 29.

[43] Ibn Sīnā, *Fann-i samā'-i ṭabī'ī*, pp. 214–217.

[44] Ibn Sīnā mentions four types of motion:

(1) From one quantity to another.
(2) From one quality to another.
(3) From one place to another.
(4) From one substance to another.

By this last-named process is meant only generation and corruption which involve sudden and not gradual substantial change (*al-ḥarakat al-jawharīyah*). Substance was

Motion, according to Ibn Sīnā, who here follows Aristotle, is "going from potentiality to actuality in time either in a continual or a non-immediate manner."[45] When an object is between potentiality and act it is in motion. Motion may also be considered as the first entelechy (*kamāl*) of that which is in potentiality and the gradual actualization, depending upon time, of what is potential.[46] An object moves because it still has something potential and therefore imperfect in it, because it seeks perfection as part of the total purpose of the Universe. Motion depends not only upon the mover and moved, time and space, but also upon an origin and an end. Any discussion of change which does not include the end in view does not consider all the factors involved.

There are three types of motion:

1. Accidental—*bi'l-'araḍ*
2. Violent—*bi'l-qasr*
3. Natural—*bi'l-ṭab'*

Accidental motion occurs in the case of a body being within another body which moves, as, for example, clothing in a box would move accidentally if the box were moved. Violent motion is one which is not caused by the essence of the object moved but by an outside force, as, for example, the throwing of an object or the burning of it. Natural motion, on the other hand, comes from the body itself, as, for example, the rising of fire and air.[47] The distinction between natural and violent motion depends upon the Aristotelian distinction between the heavens where motion is circular and the sublunary region where the natural motion is rectilinear.[48] Ibn Sīnā rejects the views of those who consider the motion of the four elements as violent, and despite his criticism of other aspects of Aristotelian dynamics he remains faithful to this school on the rigorous division of motion into the natural and violent categories

Ibn Sīnā also uses another classification of quantitative motion or

---

made a category of motion seven centuries after Ibn Sīnā by Mullā Ṣadrā. *Fann-i samā'-i ṭabī'ī*, pp. 123–136. Motion therefore includes, as in Aristotelian physics, all change and not only the change of position as is the case in modern physics.

[45] *Ibid.*, p. 102. «انّ الحركة هى فعل و كمال اوّل للشئ الذى بالقوة من جهة المعنى الذى هو له بالقوة.»

Ibn Sīnā, *Najāt*, p. 105. "Motion is the actuality of that which is in potentiality in so far as it is in potentiality." Aristotle, *Physics*, vol. III, pt. 1, 20/a, pp. 10–11.

[46] S. Pines, "Etudes sur Awḥad al-Zamān Abu'l-Barakāt al-Baghdādī," *La Revue des Etudes Juives*, 3:37 (1936).

[47] Ibn Sīnā, *Dānishnāmah . . .*, *Ṭabī'īyāt*, p. 10.

[48] Ibn Sīnā, *Fann-i samā'-i ṭabī'ī*, pp. 401–402; *Najāt*, pp. 138–139.

change which covers a wider field than that of dynamics. Motion in this view is divided into four classes:[49]

- Quantitative motion
  - by nourishment
    - *growth* (food is assimilated so as to become like him who eats it)
    - *withering* (body diminishes because of percolation and filtration)
  - not by nourishment
    - *compression* (motion toward diminution without addition of outside body)
    - *expansion* (motion toward increase without addition of foreign body)

This classification exemplifies the wide scope of medieval physics which treats the question of motion in the most general sense. Ibn Sīnā, however, does not confine himself to this type of study. He considers also the difficulties of projectile motion which from the time of John Philoponus had become the major point of criticism of Aristotelian physics. Ibn Sīnā rejects the views of three previous schools regarding the motion of a projectile.[50]

1. The Aristotelian theory of antiperistasis.
2. The other Aristotelian theory according to which the air receives an impulsion from the mover as does the projectile; the latter, however, being pushed more rapidly than the air, involves it in its movement.
3. The Muʿtazilite view of motion according to which it is in the nature of motion to engender another motion after it, as it is in the nature of a "support" (that is, that upon which one relies) (*iʿtimād*) to engender another *iʿtimād*.[51]

Ibn Sīnā himself adopts the view that a moving body borrows or receives (*istifādah*) from the mover an *inclinatio*, or inclination (*mail*), which permits the continuation of violent motion.[52] The intermediary called *mail* transmits all the force which keeps a body moving, but it

[49] *Dānishnāmah . . .*, *Ṭabīʿīyāt*, p. 8.

[50] *Shifāʾ*, *Ṭabīʿīyāt*, pp. 153ff.

[51] "Ce concept dénote soit une propension à un mouvement dans une direction déterminée, soit l'impulsion que le corps ayant une telle propension fait subir aux corps contigus qui font obstacle au mouvement en question." Pines, "Etudes sur Awḥad al-Zamān Abu'l-Barakāt . . .," p. 46.

[52] "Le *mayl* est la chose (*al-maʿnā*) qui est perçue par les sens dans le corps en mouvement; même si celui-ci est immobilisé de force, on perçoit en lui le *mayl*, comme si au moyen de celui-ci, le corps immobilisé—et malgré son immobilité—résistait (à ce qu'il l'immobilise), cherchant à se mouvoir." Pines, *Etudes . . .*, p. 50.

differs from the moving force (*quwwah muḥarrikah*) itself which may continue to exist even after the motion has ceased. The *mail* provides force for the motion until the resistance of the milieu exhausts it, thus bringing motion to an end.

Ibn Sīnā defines three kinds of *mail*: *mail nafsānī* (psychic *mail*), *mail ṭabī'ī* (natural *mail*), and *mail qasrī* (violent *mail*). This division, as well as the word *mail* itself which also means desire, implies that the study of motion is not only that of dead things. By identifying this *mail* with the love which pervades the whole Universe,[53] Ibn Sīnā returns to the very ancient view of a live cosmos in which all change is due to the love and sympathy of things for each other and the love of the Universe for God.

All motion, whether accidental, natural, or violent, is, according to Ibn Sīnā, due to a power (*quwwah*) which exists in the mover. The existence of this force leads through a series of arguments to the existence of the Prime Mover who moves the heavenly spheres,[54] and for whose love all the heavenly spheres move. It is also the *mail*, or desire, of beings for the Prime Mover that overcomes all the obstacles in the way of motion. Ibn Sīnā also argues that since both natural motion and forced motion must eventually come to an end, the perpetual motion of the heavens must be due to the will (*irādah*) of the Souls which reside at each heavenly sphere and which cause motion because of their love for the First Cause or Prime Mover.[55] He emphasizes that it is the Souls and not the Intelligences which are directly responsible for the motion of the heavens.[56]

The relation of the mover to the moved, whether in the heavens or the sublunary region, is either like that of a beloved to a lover or of the soul to the body. The heavens exemplify both these relations, inasmuch as they are moved by the heavenly Souls and by the desire for the Beloved who is the Creator.[57]

On Causes

The Sunnī theological attitude in Islam toward causality is the absorption of the finite, immediate causes of things into the Transcendent

---

[53] Ibn Sīnā, *Risālah fi'l-'ishq*, trans. E. Fackenheim, *Medieval Studies* (Toronto, 1946), pp. 208-228.

[54] ‏« المحرّكات في كل طبيعة تنتهي الى محرّك اوّل لا يتحرّك ... »‏   Ibn Sīnā, *'Uyūn al-ḥikmah*, p. 29.

[55] With regard to the perpetual motion of the heavens, Ibn Sīnā writes that motion cannot begin temporally because as long as time has existed so has motion. Therefore, it cannot be said that motion has a beginning (*ibtidā'*) in time, although it has been created and is new and is not eternal in the sense of being uncreated.

[56] Ibn Sīnā, *Dānishnāmah . . ., Ilāhiyāt*, p. 145.   [57] *Ibid.*

Cause so that God is considered directly as the Cause of all things. Fire burns not because it is its nature to do so but because God has willed it. A parallel view can be seen in the Ṣūfī doctrine of the continuous creation of the Universe. At every moment the Creator destroys and re-creates the cosmos so that every being at every moment of time is utterly dependent upon Him. Ibn Sīnā in his Peripatetic works does not adopt this point of view. On the contrary, he follows the Aristotelian doctrine of the four causes which considers not only the final cause of things but also the immediate ones.

There are, according to Ibn Sīnā, once again following Aristotle, four causes for each natural event, these being the efficient (*fā'ilī*), material (*māddī*), formal (*ṣūrī*), and final (*ghā'ī*).[58] The efficient cause is that which is the source of motion in something other than itself. The material cause is the support for an action other than itself. An object contains matter (*māddah*) by the fact that matter accepts existence (*kawn*), by the change of state (*istiḥālah*), by assembling and combining (*ijtimā' wa tarkīb*), or finally by assembling and change of state (*ijtimā' wa istiḥālah*).

The formal cause, like the material one, is used with a variety of meanings. Form (*ṣūrah*) means:

1. A state (*hai'ah*) which, when present in matter, causes the coming into being of a species (*naw'*).
2. The species itself.
3. Shape (*shakl*).
4. The state of an assembly (like that of an army).
5. Preserved order (like *sharī'ah*).
6. A state (*hai'ah*) no matter of what type.
7. The truth (*ḥaqīqah*) of anything, whether that be substance or accident.

As for the final cause, it is the purpose for which form is produced in matter. The four causes are interrelated and can be essential or accidental, remote or near, particular or universal, potential or actual. The efficient and final causes are usually the remote (*ba'īd*) ones while the formal and material causes are those that are near (*qarīb*). The causes that are near act without an intermediary, as in the case of motion of a part of the body by the muscles, while remote causes act by means of intermediaries, such as the motion of the parts of the body by the soul.[59]

[58] *Shifā'*, *Ṭabī'iyāt*, pp. 20–23.

[59] For various types of causality, see *ibid.*, pp. 72–78. In his study of causality, Ibn Sīnā does not exclude from the cosmos the direct act of God (*al-fi'l al-ilāhī*).

In the light of this analysis of causality, there is no place for chance or probability in Nature. All events occur either necessarily (*wājib*), having a permanent (*dā'imī*) cause, or occur possibly (*mumkin*) or rarely (*nādir al-wuqū'*). In the first instance there is no possibility of chance, and even in the second category it is the hindrances and obstacles (*'ā'iq wa māni'*) placed before the permanent causes which make the events occur occasionally and not all the time. Therefore, even here there is no question of chance.

The need for causality depends upon the psychic and mental structure of each society and usually increases not with the knowledge of things but with the lack of it. The Peripatetic analysis of causality did not correspond in every respect to the Islamic spirit which is based on the reintegration of all multiplicity into Unity and the absorption of all particular causes into the Universal and Transcendent Cause. Yet, by considering the interrelatedness of natural events and studying the immediate in the light of the ultimate purpose of things, the Peripatetic notion of causality did find a place in the Islamic world view. Although not a direct result of the essence of that tradition, Ibn Sīnā's notion of causality was not completely opposed to the Islamic perspective, because it sought to demonstrate the interrelatedness and final purpose of things and consequently the unicity of Nature and the meaning of its existence. It is always to the degree in which a science of Nature is capable of demonstrating this unicity that it is capable of being in conformity with the Islamic perspective and able to be integrated into it. It was this underlying intuition of the "unicity of all that exists" in the Aristotelian philosophy of Nature which, despite its syllogistic and rationalistic character and its placing of intermediate causes between God and the world, permitted the integration of many of its cosmological elements into the Islamic world view.

Ibn Sīnā and the Study of Nature

For Ibn Sīnā the approach toward the study of Nature depends completely upon the purpose for which Nature was created. Nature is the domain where everything possesses a meaning and an end and where the wisdom of the Creator is everywhere manifest.[60] "L'Univers porte dans son ensemble les marques d'un plan qui a pour objet la

[60] "Considère la sagesse de l'Artisan (*al-bārī'*). Il commença par créer les fondements, puis d'eux, il créa les mixtes distincts les uns des autres et prépara chaque mixte pour une espèce. Il se mit à faire provenir les mixtes de l'équilibre, pour faire provenir les espèces de la perfection; et il disposa le mixte de l'homme afin d'en faire un nid à son âme raisonnable." Ibn Sīnā, *Le Livre des directives et remarques* . . ., p. 302.

réalisation du Bien et s'accorde dans son ordre réel avec la prescience de l'Eternel."[61] The providence of God implies

la pleine compréhension, par la science du Premier, du tout et de la nécessité pour le tout de reposer sur lui de manière à être selon l'ordre le meilleur. [Il comprend pleinement aussi] que cela vient nécessairement de lui et de la saisie totale qu'il en a. L'être correspond donc à ce qui est connu selon l'ordre le meilleur, sans que le Premier, le Vrai, suggère un dessein ni suscite une recherche. La science qu'a le Premier de la modalité d'une juste manière d'agir pour organiser l'être du tout, est donc source du débordement du Bien dans le tout.[62]

Nature moves all things according to a natural purpose (*qaṣd ṭabīʻī*). The ends and purpose which Nature intends are always toward goodness and perfection if obstacles are not placed in its way. Even what seems like evil, as, for example, the decay of a flower, is for the purpose of a greater good. All things move toward goodness, whether they be the elements, plants, animals, or the human body. In the human body, for example, illness which is due to the excess of some force is overcome by Nature, which tends to re-establish the equilibrium and order. If there is evil or ugliness (*qubḥ*) in Nature from the human point of view, it is not due to Nature, whose action is toward goodness, but due to matter and the shortcoming of the action of Nature upon it.[63] Inasmuch as Nature acts upon matter, it guides matter toward its purpose, but because of the possibility and potentiality which are synonymous with matter, Nature cannot act upon all of it. As for death, which appears as an evil everywhere in Nature, it too has a purpose with regard to the totality. The death of man, for example, serves the purpose of freeing the soul to complete and perfect itself.[64]

[61] A. F. von Mehren, "La Philosophie d'Avicenne," *Le Muséon*, 1:409 (1882).

[62] Ibn Sīnā, *Le Livre des directives et remarques . . .*, p. 458.

[63] "Si le beau, le laid, le juste et le mal étaient aux yeux de Dieu ce qu'il sont aux yeux des hommes, il n'aurait pas créé le lion redoutable, aux dents dialoguées et aux jambes tortues, dont la faim n'est satisfaite qu'en mangeant la chair à demi gâtée et sanglante du cheval, de la brebis et de la vache; ses mâchoires, ses griffes, ses tendons solides, son cou imposant, sa nuque, sa crinière, ses côtes et son ventre, la forme de tous ses membres excitent en nous l'étonnement, quand nous considérons que tout cela lui est donné pour atteindre le bétail fugitif, le saisir et le déchirer. Il n'aurait pas non plus créé l'aigle aux griffes crochues, au bec recourbé, avec ses ailes soupples et divisées, son crâne chauve, les yeux pénétrants, son cou élevé, ses jambes si robustes; et cet aigle n'a pas été créé ni pour cueillir des baies, ni pour mâcher ses aliments et brouter des herbes, mais pour saisir et déchirer sa proie. Dieu en le créant n'a pas eu le *même* égard que toi aux sentiments de compassion, ni suivi les mêmes principes d'intelligence." Ibn Sīnā, *Risālat al-qadar*, trans. A. F. von Mehren in *Traités mystiques d'Avicenne . . .* (Leiden, 1889–1891), pp. 47–48.

[64] Ibn Sīnā, *Shifāʼ*, *Ṭabīʻiyāt*, p. 32.

Nature also has the purpose of keeping the order, equilibrium, and harmony which govern the Universe.

La Nature, qui est une manifestation de Dieu dans les êtres matériels, veille à que ces êtres se perpétuent. Elle règle leurs fonctions de façon que tout ordre établi se conserve, et que tout tende vers un ordre. Ainsi, chez les animaux, l'espèce se conserve par la reproduction. La reproduction est assurée par l'accouplement, et l'accouplement par le rapprochement. Ce rapprochement n'est cependant pas continu, l'animal ayant d'autres besoins qui exigent divers mouvements et déplacements.

Le besoin impérieux de la reproduction de l'espèce incite les animaux à se retrouver, à se rejoindre pour s'accoupler après qu'ils se sont séparés. La Nature leur a donné, à cet effet, le moyen de s'appeler, de se signaler leur présence; ils emploient aussi ce moyen dans d'autres circonstances, comme pour se signaler un danger ou demander du secours. La poussin, le lionceau, le jeune animal, en impressionera un autre à distance, qui viendra à son aide, ou fuira un danger dont il n'avait pas notion. Ce sont là des choses évidentes, confirmées par l'expérience; on ne saurait en douter, quand *on connaît le soin que le Créateur prend de son oeuvre.* Dieu, dans sa Prévoyance, a, en effet, pourvu aux besoins de ses créatures et leur a donné tout ce qui leur est nécessaire ou utile.[65]

The study of Nature, in which the purpose and wisdom of God is manifested, leads ultimately to the knowledge of the source of all beings. Inasmuch as all creatures by the fact that they exist derive their existence from the Creator who is Pure Being, all sciences of Nature have for their purpose the knowledge of the essence of things in relation to their Divine Origin. The essences of things, in fact, come from and have their existence in Him. As Ibn Sīnā writes:

Sais tu ce qu'est le Roi? Le Roi véritable c'est le Riche véritable au sens absolu, et nulle chose ne peut en rien se passer de lui. A lui est l'essence de toute chose, parce qu'elle vient de lui, ou de ce qui vient de lui. Toute chose autre que lui est donc en sa possession, et il n'a besoin d'aucune d'elles.[66]

Therefore, to explain something or to have veritable knowledge or science of it means to be able to relate it to Being itself, to relate all of the properties and qualities of that particular being to its ontological status.[67] What is found by means of observation and logical infer-

[65] Ibn Sīnā, *Shifā', Riyāḍīyāt*, chap. XII, art. I, trans. R. D'Erlanger in *La Musique arabe* (Paris, 1935), II, 107–108. (Italics ours.)

[66] *Le Livre des directives et remarques . . .*, p. 398.

[67] Ibn Sīnā's conception of true science is expressed aptly by F. Brunner, a contemporary author: "La science véritable suspend la connaissance du monde à la connaissance de Dieu pour le monde dans son intégrale réalité et pour constituer l'expression légitime, au niveau du monde, de l'intellection transcendante qui est la fin de l'homme" (*Science et réalité*, Paris, 1954, p. 13).

ences from it does not lead to the "metaphysical secrets" of things but rather to the discovery of certain aspects of their outward manifestation or to the relation of phenomena. True science is to relate these phenomena to their inner aspect, or noumena, which is the essence and the center relating them to Pure Being.

The study of Nature is not just a study of phenomena, seeking by a "mental plastic continuity" to explain things away, but basically a study of phenomena in relation to noumena, a search to discover the relation of each particular to the Universal. Therefore, the sciences of Nature always possess a sense of mystery which accompanies the metaphysical, and even rational, explanation of things. For example, with regard to the determination of corporeal forms, Ibn Sīnā writes:

> Mais au contraire il (forme corporelle) a besoin, en ce dont les dispositions sont diverses, de choses déterminantes et de dispositions concordantes provenant de l'extérieur, par lesquelles sont délimitées la quantité et la figure qui sont nécessaires. *Ceci est un mystère par lequel tu apprendras à connaître d'autres mystères.*[68]

To explain is not to explain away; to relate the particular to the Universal or the realm of Nature to Being is to bring into focus the sense of mystery which resides in Universal Existence itself.

The end of all knowledge is that of Pure Being and the relation of particular beings to this Being which is their origin and principle. The acquisition of this knowledge depends essentially upon metaphysics and intellectual intuition. Cosmology is in fact an application of metaphysical principles to the cosmic domain. But once the principles have been established, both reason and observation, or experiment, serve as aids to complete the knowledge of the particular aspects of things. Both reason and the senses have a legitimacy on their own level. The science which derives from them, however, finds its meaning and legitimacy only in the light of the wisdom, or *sapientia*, which lies above the domain of the senses as well as that of reason. Ibn Sīnā therefore makes use of observation, experiment, and reasoning in trying to understand the various manifestations of Nature in the light of cosmological principles which derive from intellectual intuition.

In the *Qānūn*, for example, after establishing the principles of medicine upon cosmic analogies and other cosmological doctrines based upon metaphysics, he proceeds to use observation and inductions based upon them in a way not unlike the methods used for

[68] *Le Livre des directives et remarques*, p. 266 (italics ours).

establishing modern "experimental laws."[69] Likewise, in the field of meteorology, within the general context of the doctrine of the four elements, which again is based neither on the senses nor upon reason, he uses observation of the diffraction of light by water particles created at the time of the watering of gardens and in a bathhouse in order to try to understand the phenomena of the rainbow.[70] In astronomy also, in which he became interested toward the end of his life, Ibn Sīnā makes use of observation. He is even said to have constructed an instrument in order to read in an easy way in minutes and seconds of arc the positions of stars.[71] In geology he uses observation continuously, comparing sedimentary rocks to the drying of clay on the banks of the Oxus River and the iron of a meteorite to iron found in regular mines.[72]

The range of natural sciences with which Ibn Sīnā deals varies from his treatise on simple machines,[73] which involves nothing other than the knowledge of the sensible domain and logical conclusions based upon it, to his symbolic narratives and treatises on what today are called "the occult sciences."[74] The study of Nature for him entails the physical and subtle domain and the use of the senses, the reason and the faculty of intellectual intuition. All these "ways of knowing" possess a legitimacy and lead to a form of knowledge of Nature whose scope depends upon the inherent limitation of each faculty. The only universal faculty whose essence is above all limitation is the intellectual one by means of which the diverse aspects of Nature are reintegrated into their universal prototype and all becoming re-absorbed into Being. The facts of Nature discovered through the senses remain isolated and meaningless until by means of the intelligence they are integrated into the totality of manifestation, where alone they find their meaning. The sciences of Nature are veritable only to the extent that they make intelligible the order of Nature by showing the dependence, both existential and intellectual, of all things upon the Divine Source of all existence.

[69] A. M. Goichon, "L'Unité de la pensée avicennienne," *Archives Internationales*. . ., (1952), p. 300.

[70] M. von Horten, "Avicennas Lehre von Regenbogen nach seinem Werk al-Shifā'," *Meteorologischen Zeitschrift*, 11:533–544 (1913).

[71] E. Wiedemann, "Über ein von Ibn Sina (Avicenna) hergestelltes Beobachtungsinstrument," *Zeitschrift für Instrumentkunde*, 6:269–275 (1925), and "Avicennas Schrift über ein von ihm ersonnenes Beobachtungsinstrument," *Acta Orientalia* 5:81–167 (1926). For a general discussion of the use of observation and experiment by Ibn Sīnā, see A. Sayili, "Rawish-i 'ilmī-i Abū 'Alī Sīnā," *Le Livre du millénaire d'Avicenne*, 2:403–412.

[72] *Shifā', Ṭabī'īyāt*, pp. 247–249; E. J. Holmyard, *Avicennae de congelatione et conglutinatione lapidum* (Paris, 1927).

[73] *Mi'yār al-uqūl* (Tehran, 1331 [1952]).

[74] *Kunūz al-mu'azzimīn* (Tehran, 1331 [1952]).

CHAPTER 14

The Universe, Man, and their Relation

The Heavens

The classification of beings by Ibn Sīnā into the four classes of separate Intelligences (angels), celestial Souls, celestial bodies, and sublunary bodies forms the basis for his division of the cosmos. The ontological distinction between simple substances (*mujarradāt*) and bodies in generation and corruption is made to correspond to the cosmological and astronomical difference between the heavens and the sublunary region. The Universe consists of nine spheres, the eight of Ptolemaic astronomy and the starless heaven added by Muslim astronomers which stands above the heaven of the fixed stars and symbolizes the transition between becoming and Being.[1] Each heaven is governed by an intellect or group of angels, moved by a soul, or group of souls, and composed of a body generated by the being which stands above it in the hierarchy of creation.[2]

Contrary to Aristotelian cosmology, in which God as the Prime Mover moves only the outer sphere, Ibn Sīnā emphasizes that the motion of the heavens as a whole is due to God. He moves all the heavens together but not any one individually.[3] As a result, the

[1] Despite his deviation from Ptolemaic astronomy in adding this heaven to the cosmos of the Greeks, Ibn Sīnā, like other Muslim Peripatetics, follows the Greeks in insisting on the fact that the spheres of heaven as a whole form a single body. "The natural shape of each body is circular; since if these bodies disperse they will create a vacuum between them and since the presence of a vacuum is impossible, therefore the totality of the world is one body." Ibn Sīnā, *al-Najāt*, p. 136.

[2] In the *Shifā'*, *Ilāhīyāt*, pp. 615–616, and other Peripatetic works, Ibn Sīnā describes both the Ptolemaic and Aristotelian system of planetary spheres without showing a preference for either system. On the other hand, he shows a definite preference, in the visionary narratives, for the Aristotelian cosmos with its 55 spheres. "On ne peut admettre que les [substances] intellectuelles soient rangées dans l'ordre qu'elles occupent et que le corps céleste découle nécessairement de la dernière d'entre elles, parce que chaque corps céleste n'est que l'intermédiaire d'un [autre] corps céleste. Il faut donc que les corps célestes entrent dans l'existence pendant qu'une continuité demeure entre les substances intellectuelles, en tant que leur existence découle tandis qu'elles gardent, en l'acquérant, un ordre, décroissant et que, simultanément, décroissent les [sphères] célestes" (Ibn Sīnā, *Le Livre des directives et remarques* . . ., p. 427).

[3] P. Duhem, *Le Système du monde*, IV, 447–448.

heavens have a simple and multiple motion at the same time, receiving their unity from God and multiplicity from the Intelligences and Souls. The movement of the heavens is not natural or innate but is due to the will of the soul of each sphere. The Intelligences are the real causes of motion, but the Souls act as the intermediaries and immediate movers, moving the heavenly bodies because of the love (*'ishq*) which impels them toward the realization of what has not been realized within them.[4] All motion in the Universe in fact, is due to the desire to actualize what is potential, to bring to perfection what is imperfect.

The heavens, however, have nothing potential in their form or being. They possess circularity, which is the most perfect of forms, and nobility of being, which manifests itself in their luminosity. There remains but one thing which the heavens do not possess in act, and that is place or location. They do not have one place which is more appropriate for them than another. Since it is impossible for them to possess all places at once, they therefore move from one point to another in succession and in such a manner that there is the least change possible. That is why they move in circular motion which, unlike rectilinear motion, can proceed in a permanent and unchanging manner.[5]

The heavenly regions, being uncorruptible and made of the element ether, which is superior to the elements of the sublunary world, move like a live and animated being. The heavenly Souls have the same relation to their bodies as human souls have to man's body. In each case, motion is by the will of the soul, which in the case of the heavens possesses the perfection of the angelic state. The heavens exist in a world of "pre-eternity" in a stability which is above the vicissitudes of the world of generation and corruption. They move according to an order which comes from Divine prescience and in turn give order to the sublunary region.[6]

[4] "Dès lors, elle est atteinte par le désir, l'amour qui la porte vers ce qui n'est pas encore réalisé en elle, vers son principe de perfection. C'est pour y atteindre qu'elle mettra en mouvement le Corps qui est en sa dépendance." L. Gardet. *La Pensée religieuse d'Avicenne*, p. 55.

[5] "Le corps du ciel s'est donc appliqué à ce que l'espèce des situations qu'il peut occuper demeurât éternellement en lui d'une manière effective; par là, il s'est rendu, autant qu'il lui a été possible, semblable aux substances nobles." Duhem, *Le Système du monde*, p. 448.

[6] "Si tu cherches comment échapper [à cela], tu ne trouves pas d'issue, sinon en ce sens de la représentation de l'ordre universel dans la prescience [divine], y compris son moment nécessaire, convenable, cet ordre débordant en un flux, avec son organisation poussée dans tous ces détails, Intelligibles. Et c'est la Providence." Ibn Sīnā, *Le Livre des directives et remarques . . .*, p. 401.

The cosmology and astronomy of Ibn Sīnā, especially as they have been subsequently understood and interpreted in the Muslim world, are wed in an inseparable fashion to angelology and can therefore provide the appropriate setting for the religious vision of the cosmos. Religious cosmology must in the end be connected to angelology, for in the religious perspective angels are the prototypes upon whose model man is made and toward whom he aspires in his life on earth. We find this aspiration toward union with the angelic state not only in Islam but also in Christianity, where the order of monks is considered as being based upon the life of the angels. The role of angels in the cosmos becomes central in Ibn Sīnā's symbolic works and the later commentaries written upon them. Yet, even in his popular, Peripatetic writings, the angels play a basic role as movers of the heavens, the angels themselves being moved by God.[7]

The angels influence this world either according to their will, or the nature and force of their bodies, or finally by means of communion (*shirkah*) with terrestrial beings. They include the assembly of the Intelligences and Souls in the heavens; yet their action is not confined to the celestial world. They fulfill many functions in the daily religious life of man as well as preserving the order of the cosmos.[8] It is ultimately the angels who guide man to his final beatitude and who thereby bring to fruition the purpose of creation.

Although in certain short treatises which are attributed to Ibn Sīnā and which it seems most likely, though not absolutely certain, were written by him, there is a description and defense of astrology,[9] there are also several of his works which attack violently many of its elements, equating it with magic and the "occult sciences."[10] Prediction of events, according to him, is to be made only by the prophets and saints who receive this power as a special gift from God. He also

[7] A. F. von Mehren, "Vues d'Avicenne sur l'astrologie et le destin," *Le Muséon*, 2:399 (1883).

[8] Ibn Sīnā, *Risālat al-ziyārah*, in *Traités mystiques d'Avicenne . . .*, trans. A. F. von Mehren, p. 33.

[9] See, for example, Ibn Sīnā, *Kunūz al-mu'azzimīn* (Tehran, 1952), pp. 4–5. This and other similar short treatises have been traditionally attributed to Ibn Sīnā. Although certain modern scholars have doubted their authenticity, there has been no positive proof against Ibn Sīnā's authorship of these works.

[10] "L'autre espèce, au dessus de laquelle le savant sérieux se sent trop élevé pour s'en occuper, est d'un ordre bas et infime; telle qu'est par exemple la magie, les prédictions qui se font à l'inspection des omoplates et de tremblement des intestins d'animaux tués, etc. Le savant qui se respecte ne trouve aucune de ces matières digne de son attention. Il en est de même de l'astrologie. Pour tout savant qui a quelque profondeur de vue et solidité de connaissance, il est clair, que tout ce qui appartient à cette espèce de science, n'a aucune base solide . . ." (von Mehren, "Vues d'Avicenne sur l'astrologie . . .," p. 386).

argues that since prophets cannot contradict each other, the Quranic verse (XXVII, 65): "None in the heavens and the earth knoweth the Unseen save Allah . . ." must nullify whatever has been attributed to the prophet Idrīs regarding astrology.[11]

Ibn Sīnā also gives several physical and astronomical arguments against astrology. For example, he mentions that since the heavens are not made of the four elements, but of ether, they cannot possess the four qualities according to which the signs are divided, or that since the heavens are simple they cannot be divided into four regions each having a different nature. Another astronomical reason he gives is that there are many bodies in the heavens like those in the Milky Way whose effects cannot be studied and calculated. In fact, just as Ibn Sīnā compares the astronomy of the *Almagest* to anatomy in medicine and the science of astronomical tables to that of remedies, he equates judicial astrology with "the practice of quack doctors and charlatans."[12]

The attack of Ibn Sīnā upon astrology is primarily upon its claim to predict future events; he does not attack the cosmological foundations upon which astrology is based. On the contrary, he describes the relation of the heavens and the sublunary region in a way that is conformable to the astrological perspective. As has been already mentioned, the sublunary region represents the lowest state in the ontological as well as the cosmological scale. It receives its very being from the tenth Intelligence and remains utterly dependent upon and completely passive with respect to celestial influences. All the changes which occur in the world of generation and corruption are due to the influence of the heavens, which regulate all things and give order to generation and corruption in this world.[13]

Without the influence of the heavens, there would be complete chaos in the sublunary region, and without the last heavenly Intelligence there would be no sublunary world at all, because the sphere of the Moon and the Intelligence connected with it are the ontological link between the world of generation and corruption and the rest of the cosmos. Ibn Sīnā attacks the astrologers not because they believe in the importance of celestial influences on events on earth, but because they claim to be able to predict exactly the future events

[11] von Mehren, "Vues d'Avicenne . . .," p. 395. [12] *Ibid.*, p. 398.

[13] According to Ibn Sīnā, the celestial bodies have an influence on the bodies of this world by the qualities which are proper to them and which are diffused in this world. (Goichon, *La Distinction de l'essence et de l'existence* . . ., p. 242; Ibn Sīnā, *Dānish-nāma-yi 'alā'ī, Ilāhīyāt*, p. 165.) Ibn Sīnā also mentions the influence of some stars on men (*ibid.*, p. 118). These influences are in addition to the more obvious effects of the Sun and Moon on terrestrial phenomena such as the tides and the ripening of fruit.

which these heavenly forces will cause to happen in the world of change.

The World of Generation and Corruption

The world of generation and corruption, which coincides with the sublunary region, is the realm of beings in whom form and matter are inseparably united. In contrast to the heavens where separate forms like the Intelligences or angels can exist without matter, the condition of existence in the sublunary world requires the existence of matter for every form and form for all matter. In fact, it is this necessity which causes continuous change; matter is made to discard one form and accept another in a ceaseless process.[14] The sublunary region also differs from the heavens in possessing rectilinear motion rather than the circular movement of the celestial orbs. Moreover, all beings in the world of generation and corruption are made from the four elements (*'anāṣir*), fire, air, water, and earth, each of which possesses a pair of the fundamental natural qualities.[15] Fire is warm and dry, air, warm and moist, water, cold and moist, and earth, cold and dry.[16] Other properties of objects derive from the four basic qualities, for example, softness from moisture and hardness from dryness.[17]

The four elements out of which all sublunary beings are composed consist basically of the same matter which on different occasions accepts different forms. They are therefore transformed into each other continuously.[18] This transformation is accomplished by the rejection of one form and the acceptance of a new one. These changes, however, are not autonomous or independent. They are brought

[14] *Dānishnāmah . . .*, *Ilāhīyāt*, pp. 134–135.

[15] Ibn Sīnā follows the Peripatetic school in distinguishing the sublunary region of the four elements and the celestial region, in contrast to the Hermetic school where the cosmos is considered as a united whole composed of the same fundamental qualities.

[16] "Le corps qui atteint par nature à la plénitude de la chaleur, c'est le feu; et celui qui atteint par nature à la plénitude du froid, c'est l'eau; à la plénitude de la fluidité, c'est l'air; à la plénitude de l'épaississement, c'est la terre." Ibn Sīnā, *Le Livre des directives et remarques . . .*, p. 293.

[17] Ibn Sīnā, *Dānishnāmah . . .*, *Ṭabī'īyāt*, pp. 27–28.

[18] "Les récipients se refraîchissent parfois par la condensation, due à une rosée venue de l'air; toutes les fois que tu la recueilles elle s'étend à n'importe quelle limite que tu désires. Et cela ne se produit pas seulement dans un endroit où il y a suintement; cela ne se produit d'ailleurs pas à partir de l'eau chaude, qui est plus subtile et plus susceptible de suinter. C'est donc l'air changé en eau. De même la sérénité règne quelque fois au sommet des montagnes, puis l'intensité du froid saisit l'air qui les surmonte et condense un nuage, sans que celui-ci soit venu d'ailleurs se ranger autour d'elles, ni provienne d'un amoncellement de vapeur ascendante. Puis on voit ce nuage tomber en neige et la sérénité revient; ensuite cela recommence . . ."

"Ces quatre sortes de corps peuvent être transmués l'un en l'autre, ils ont donc une matière première commune." Ibn Sīnā, *Le Livre des directives et remarques . . .*, pp. 295–296.

about by the tenth Intelligence, which gives order to all activities in the sublunary region and which is also the principle of the plant, animal, and the human kingdoms. As Ibn Sīnā states:

> Il faut donc que la matière du monde des éléments fasse suite à la dernière intelligence, et rien n'empêche que les corps célestes apportent en ceci une sorte de secours; mais cela ne suffit pas pour établir qu'elle en découle tant que les formes ne lui sont pas jointes.
>
> Quant aux formes, elles débordent aussi de cette intelligence, mais elles sont diverses dans leur matière, selon que celle-ci les mérite diversement, d'après ses préparations variées. Il n'y a pas à sa diversité d'autre principe que les corps célestes, par la division qu'ils apportent entre ce qui avoisine la région centrale et ce qui avoisine la région périphérique, ainsi que par des dispositions dont les détails sont trop délicats pour être saisis par les estimations, bien que tu en comprennes l'ensemble. Là, se trouvent les formes des éléments, et en ceux-ci, selon leurs rapports dus aux corps célestes et à ce qu'ils envoient, sont nécessités des mélanges de préparations variées, opérées par certaines forces qui les disposent. Et là, les âmes végétales, animales et raisonnables débordent de la substance intellectuelle qui est proche de ce monde. A l'âme raisonnable s'arrête la hiérarchie de l'être des substances intellectuelles. Elle a besoin d'être perfectionnée par les organes corporels et les effusions d'en haut qui l'avoisinent.[19]

Following Aristotle, Ibn Sīnā considers each element in the sublunary region to have a natural place dependent upon the elements of which it is composed. All motion in this region is in fact due to the desire of bodies to return to the place which corresponds to their nature.[20] In their natural order, water exists above the earth, air consisting of a lower moist region and an upper pure region above the water, and pure fire which does not glow by itself above the air. Changes in the atmosphere and on earth are due to the disruption of the original equilibrium which has taken each element out of its natural place and which has brought into existence various bodies seeking constantly to regain the place conforming to their natures.

In the study of meteorology as understood in Aristotelian physics, Ibn Sīnā, like most Muslim authors, follows closely the teachings of Aristotle in trying to explain the diverse events occurring between the surface of the earth and the Moon by an interplay of the four elements. The air is divided into four layers:

(1) The layer right above the earth composed of vapors and the heat which the earth receives from the earth and transmits to this layer.

[19] Ibn Sīnā, *Le Livre des directives et remarques . . .*, pp. 431–433.
[20] *Shifā'*, *Ṭabī'īyāt*, p. 145; also, *Fann-i samā'-i ṭabī'ī*, p. 384.

(2) A layer which still possesses vapor but has more heat.
(3) A layer of clear and pure air.
(4) A layer of exhalation which has come forth from the mountains and has risen to this height.

Above these four layers lies the sphere of fire which in itself is colorless but becomes colored in the presence of exhalations.

The vapor rising from the earth under the influence of the heavens reaches a point where the cold air condenses it, similar to the case of opening the door of a hot bathhouse. The condensation causes the formation of clouds which become particularly dense in mountainous regions where there is more vapor. Once the clouds are formed one of three conditions occurs:

(1) There is only a little condensation which is then scattered by the rays of the Sun.
(2) There is a large amount of condensation which the Sun cannot scatter. In that case, with the help of winds the clouds become heavy and dense and descend once more as rain; or, if it is cold enough to condense the clouds before the drops become too large, then they descend as snow. If, on the other hand, heat surrounds the condensation so that the cold remains inside it, then frost will occur.[21]
(3) There is moisture in the air through which the Sun shines as in a mirror, and its light is mixed with the darkness of the vapor. In this case a single or double rainbow can result; it is a circular band of colors with the Sun at the center of the circle. The colors are due to the reflection of the rays of the Sun by the individual water particles.[22]

There are, according to Ibn Sīnā, seven causes for thunder: the striking of two clouds against each other like the clapping of hands; wind entering a cloud and causing sound as it does in a cave; the element of fire entering the moist cloud, causing sound like that caused when the smith places hot iron in water; wind striking against a frosty and icy cloud as it does against a scroll of paper; wind blowing into a hollow rain cloud as a butcher blows into an intestine; wind blowing through a cloud and clearing it away as one blows through a

[21] Ibn Sīnā does not consider the material causes of these phenomena as sufficient without the help of God. As he states: "When the Sun approaches the earth it causes evaporation which in turn in the cooler atmosphere condenses into clouds and rain . . . But the material necessity (*ḍarūrīyah māddīyah*) is not sufficient. Divine action (*al-fi'l al-ilāhī*) also acts upon matter." *Fann-i samā'-i ṭabī'ī*, p. 95.

[22] *Dānishnāmah . . .*, *Ṭabī'īyāt*, pp. 65–70; Muḥammad al-Shahrastānī, *al-Milal wa'l-nihal* (Tehran, 1944), pp. 535–537. Ibn Sīnā admits that he does not know the reason for the presence of the colors.

bladder by means of a tube; and two rough clouds rubbing against each other as one rubs two molar teeth against one another.

As for lightning, he considers it to be due to four causes: the striking of two clouds giving off fire like two stones which give off sparks; the rubbing of two clouds which, like the rubbing of two pieces of wood, causes fire; the extinguishing of fire by the humidity of the cloud which gives off sparks, as in the case of the smith placing hot iron in water; and the squeezing of certain clouds containing fire which causes the fire to come out, as the squeezing of a sponge forces the water inside to trickle out. As for the thunderbolt, it is a windy fire caused by winds present in the cloud.[23]

Higher in the sphere of air the vapour which arises from the surface of the earth becomes transformed into exhalation and ascends to the fiery region where it burns. If the exhalation is not subtle (*laṭīf*) but has fire within it, then it begins to glow like a star and becomes a meteor. If there is much exhalation, the meteor may have a tail which then burns with a brilliant glow.[24]

Drawing analogies from daily experience and observation, Ibn Sīnā explains each of the meteorological phenomena, which for him include all the apparently changing aspects of the regions above the earth, in terms of the four qualities and elements of his cosmology. As in so many other instances, he makes free use of direct observation and comparison by analogy between two natural phenomena, but this is done always in the context of his cosmology and in a Universe where the same cosmic agents which are pawns in the hands of the celestial Intelligences and Souls bring about all the diverse manifestations of the physical domain.

Meteorological phenomena, like other aspects of Nature, are dependent not only upon the four elements but also upon heat and light, which directly or indirectly come from the Sun, so that the Sun plays a dominant role in sublunary events. Heat can come by friction, by contact with a hot body, or from a luminous body. As for light, Ibn Sīnā does not accept the notion that light is a body or a stream of corpuscles. Light in his physics is not a substance but an accident so that there is for him no question of constructing a Plotinian "physics of light," at least not in his Peripatetic works.[25] Only in the later *Ishrāqī* school of interpreters of Ibn Sīnā does the symbolism of light become the key to the understanding of the Universe.

From a study of meteorology, Ibn Sīnā turns to a study of changes

[23] *Risālah fī asbāb al-ra'd* (Hyderabad, 1935), pp. 2–3.
[24] *Dānishnāmah . . .*, *Ṭabī'īyāt*, pp. 70–73; also *Shifā'*, *Ṭabī'īyāt*, pp. 235–236.
[25] *Dānishnāmah . . .*, *Ṭabī'īyāt*, pp. 42–43.

occurring at or near the surface of the earth, that is, geology. It is particularly in the study of physical changes on and near the crust of the earth that the observational and experimental aspects of the approach of Ibn Sīnā become evident. Not only did he make careful and long observations on the formation of river deposits, structure of mountains, fossils, that is, the petrified remains of animals and plants, and so on, but he also analyzed meteorites to compare their composition to rocks of terrestrial origin. The fifth section of the physics of his *Shifā'*, which gives the most complete treatment of geology and its related fields known in the medieval period, was long considered in the Latin world as a work of Aristotle completing the treatment of the three kingdoms. But it is in fact only in the *Shifā'* that the study of all three domains, the animal, plant, and mineral, becomes complete. Ibn Sīnā in this domain of study follows closely the attitude of Aristotle in relying upon detailed observation of natural phenomena within the framework of the teleological Universe of the ancient and medieval sciences. In the *Shifā'* he appeals directly to Nature, but the questions he asks and the formulation of the answers he receives both depend upon the cosmological principles which underlie all of his studies of Nature.

Ibn Sīnā gives an account of the formation of stones which coincides with that of the sedimentary group in modern geology. "In general," he writes, "stone is formed in two ways only: (a) through the hardening of clay, and (b) by the congelation [of waters]."[26] He narrates his own experience as a young man observing on the banks of the Oxus River the deposition of clay which gradually congealed into a soft stone.[27] As for congelation from water, he considers it to be due to the presence of a solidifying "virtue." He states:

> We know therefore that in that ground there must be a congealing, petrifying virtue which converts the liquid to the solid . . . In short, it is in the nature of water, as you know, to become transformed into earth through a predominantly earthy virtue; you know, too, that it is in the nature of earth to become transformed into water through a predominantly aqueous virtue.[28]

[26] E. J. Holmyard, *Avicennae de congelatione et conglutinatione lapidum* (Paris: Geuthner, 1927), p. 18. Regarding Ibn Sīnā's geological ideas, see also M. Sate' al-Hosri, "Les Idées d'Avicenne sur la géologie," in *Millénaire d'Avicenne, Congrès de Bagdad* (1952), pp. 454–463.

[27] Ibn Sīnā perhaps also made a study of clays on the bottom of the bodies of water, for he writes: "As to the bottom of the sea, its clay is either sedimentary or primaeval, the latter not being sedimentary. It is probable that the sedimentary clay was formed by the disintegration of the strata of mountains." Holmyard, *Avicennae de congelatione* . . ., p. 31.

[28] Holmyard, p. 20.

Larger stones are formed by two processes. "As for the formation of large stones, this may occur all at once by intense heat acting suddenly upon a large mass of clay, or little by little with the passage of time."[29] These bodies, due to the difference of hardness, may be eroded in different degrees by the wind, thereby causing differences in elevation on the surface of the earth, differences which, if great enough, become known as mountains.

> Mountains have been formed by one [or other] of the causes of the formation of stones, most probably from agglutinative clay which slowly dried and petrified during ages of which we have no record. It seems likely that this habitable world was in former days uninhabitable and, indeed, submerged beneath the ocean. Then, becoming exposed little by little, it petrified in the course of ages the limits of which history has not preserved; or it may have petrified beneath the waters by reason of the intense heat confined under the sea. The more probable of these two possibilities is that petrifaction occurred after the earth had been exposed, and that the condition of the clay, which would then be agglutinative, assisted the petrifaction.[30]

Ibn Sīnā also attributes the formation of mountains to the forces of earthquakes which have deformed the surface rocks. He considers the cause of the earthquakes to be the vapors which, having formed under the influence of the heavens, have been locked up inside the earth without any means of escape except eruption and violence.

Ibn Sīnā's belief in the inundation of present land masses makes the explanation of fossils easy for him. He refers to fossils as petrifaction of animals and plants caused by the rise of "a powerful mineralizing and petrifying virtue which arises in certain stony spots, or emanates suddenly from the earth during earthquakes and subsidences."[31] He attributes fossils which he found in mountainous regions not to just one flood but to a series of inundations which over long ages have covered and shaped the mountains. He admits, however, that he is not able to distinguish between the successive floods, each of which must have left its record in the rocks.

When the four elements mix to a certain degree of perfection and purity, the mineral soul (*rūḥ ʿaqdī*) possessing the faculty of preserving forms becomes attached to the mixture. From this wedding results the formation of the lowest domain of beings on earth consisting of the whole of the mineral kingdom. Ibn Sīnā adopts the Aristotelian vapor and exhalation theory to explain the formation of the mineral world. Exhalations and vapors locked up inside the earth

[29] Holmyard, p. 26. [30] *Ibid.*, p. 28. [31] *Ibid.*, p. 22.

become the cause of minerals. Each mineral contains some amount of exhalation or vapor and different proportions of the four qualities. In some minerals, sulphur and sal-ammoniac, for example, the exhalation exceeds, while in beryl and rubies the vapor is dominant.[32] Precious stones are formed also from exhalations and vapors which fall under the influence of the stars. Some of them even acquire special powers like that of regeneration by virtue of the celestial influences existing in them.

Ibn Sīnā divides minerals into four groups: stones (*aḥjār*), fusible substances (*dhā'ibāt*), sulphurs (*kabārīt*), and salts (*amlāḥ*).[33] The difference in them is due to the difference in the strength of the substance from which they are made. For example:

The material of malleable bodies is an aqueous substance united so firmly with an earthy substance that the two cannot be separated from one another. This aqueous substance has been congealed by cold after heat has acted upon it and matured it.[34]

With respect to vitriols he writes: "The vitriols are composed of a salty principle, a sulphureous principle and stone, and contain the virtue of some of the fusible bodies."[35]

To explain the formation of metals, Ibn Sīnā relies exclusively on the sulphur-mercury theory of Jābir ibn Ḥayyān and speaks about the union (*ittiḥād*) of sulphur and mercury.[36] Sulphur for Ibn Sīnā is a principle rather than a chemical element in the modern sense, so that he can even refer to a substance as sulphureous.[37] He defines the sulphurs as a group in this manner: "In case of the sulphurs, their aquosity has suffered a vigorous leavening with earthiness and aeriness under the leavening action of heat, so far as to become oily in nature; subsequently it has been solidified by cold."[38]

All metals are formed from mercury and sulphur in different proportions and degrees of purity.

If the mercury be pure, and it be commingled with the solidified virtue of a white sulphur which neither induces combustion nor is impure, but on the contrary is more excellent than that prepared by the adepts, then the product is silver. If the sulphur besides being pure is even better than that just described, and whiter, and if in addition it possesses a tinctorial,

[32] *Dānishnāmah . . .*, *Ṭabī'iyāt*, pp. 73–76; *'Uyūn al-ḥikmah*, pp. 34–35.

[33] Holmyard, p. 33.

[34] *Ibid.*, p. 34. Ibn Sīnā follows Jābir in the theory that metals are formed from an aqueous and earthy substance.

[35] *Ibid.*, p. 36.

[36] Ibn Sīnā, *Risālat al-iksīr*, ed. A. Ateş (Istanbul, 1953), p. 42.

[37] Holmyard, p. 36.

[38] *Ibid.*, p. 36.

fiery, subtle and non-combustive virtue—in short, if it is superior to that which the adepts can prepare—it will solidify the mercury into gold.[39]

Other metals like copper, iron, tin, and lead are likewise explained as combinations of mercury and gold, but with various defects.

Despite his fame as an alchemist and magician in medieval Europe, Ibn Sīnā was firmly opposed to the possibility of the transformation of one metal into another by human agency, and wrote many paragraphs ridiculing the alchemists. In a well-known passage in the *Shifā'*, he writes:

> As to the claims of the alchemists, it must be clearly understood that it is not in their power to bring about any true change of species. They can, however, produce excellent imitations, dyeing the red metal white so that it closely resembles silver, or dyeing it yellow so that it closely resembles gold. They can, too, dye the white metal with any colour they desire, until it bears a close resemblance to gold or copper; and they can fire the lead from most of its defects and impurities. Yet in these the essential nature remains unchanged; they are merely so dominated by induced qualities that errors may be made concerning them, just as it happens that men are deceived by salt, *qalqand*, sal-ammoniac, . . .[40]

Much like al-Bīrūnī, Ibn Sīnā accepts the cosmological principles of alchemy and the Jābirian theory for the formation of metals while rejecting the possibility of transmutation because of the lack of evidence. His basic refusal to accept alchemical transformation of metals is that "there is no way of splitting up one combination into another."[41] He is not interested in the symbolic aspect of alchemy, at least not in his Peripatetic works, nor is he interested in making physical gold by a literal interpretation of alchemical texts like the group that the true alchemists called the "charcoal burners." Despite his acceptance of the sulphur-mercury theory and his description of chemical processes in terms of the four elements and qualities, Ibn Sīnā has a very experimental approach in describing the preparation of dyes and other mineral compounds.[42] In these matters he must be classified much more with the medieval predecessors of modern chemists than with the alchemical tradition either in its esoteric and

[39] Holmyard, p. 39.

[40] *Ibid.*, p. 41. For the views of Ibn Sīnā on alchemy, see also L. Madkour, "Avicenne et l'alchimie," *La Revue du Caire*, 27:120–129 (1951), and J. Ruska, "Die Alchemie des Avicenna," *Isis*, 21:14–51 (1934). Referring to al-Rāzī and Jābir, Ibn Sīnā states: "Ce sont des absurdités; car pour tout ce que Dieu a créé moyennant la force de la nature, l'imitation artificielle est impossible; comme au contraire les productions artificielles et scientifiques n'appartiennent d'aucune manière à la nature" (von Mehren, "Vues d'Avicenne sur l'astrologie . . .," *Le Muséon*, 3:387 [1884]).

[41] Holmyard, p. 41.

[42] *Risālat al-iksīr*, pp. 35–42.

symbolic aspect or in its branch connected with the making of objects and the craft guilds.

With a further mixing of the elements, the establishment of a higher degree of purity and a closer approach to equilibrium, a new faculty of the World Soul or, one may say, a new soul, joins the world of the elements to form the plant kingdom. This vegetative soul (*al-nafs al-nabātīyah*) has the three powers of feeding (*ghādhīyah*), growth (*nāmīyah*), and reproduction (*muwallidah*), in addition to all the powers of the mineral kingdom.[43] It is in terms of these faculties that Ibn Sīnā explains the life of plants.

Plants possess sexuality in the sense that the female accepts the seed of the male and makes it grow within itself, but "in plants the two powers are united in one member."[44] The planting of seeds in the earth, however, differs from the insertion of the male sperm in the female animal because the female provides food as well as the power of the soul (*nafs*) while the earth provides only food. The sexual parts of plants do have a certain resemblance to the animal, and even the seed of plants resembles the egg of birds in having a part which is the center of life, the source of the masculine and feminine principles, as well as a section which is used as food. Plants also have a certain resemblance in their generating processes to some of the lower animals which do not possess separate organs for the sensitive and digestive functions. In both cases the male and female organs may exist together, and the new generation may be reproduced without being separated from the old. The branches of trees which can be cut and planted are like a new generation which grows without being separated from its parents. The fruit of plants is also similar in many ways to the animal seed, although not every part of it is essential to reproduction as in the case of the seed. The seed of the plant contains some food within itself which is used up until a shoot grows out of

[43] Ibn Sīnā, *Risālah-i nafs*, ed. M. 'Amīd (Tehran, 1952), p. 14; *La Psychologie d'Ibn Sīnā* (*Avicenne*) *d'après son œuvre aš-Šifā'*, ed. and trans. J. Bakoš (Prague, 1956), I, 53–59.

Ibn Sīnā defines these powers in the following manner: "La première est la faculté de se nourrir; elle est servie par celle qui attire la nourriture, celle qui se saisit de l'objet attiré pour que la force qui digère et qui altère l'assimile, et celle qui repousse le résidu.

"La seconde est la [faculté] de croître qui tend à l'achèvement de la croissance; car grandir est autre chose qu'engraisser.

"La troisième est la faculté d'engendrer un semblable à soi. Elle s'éveille après que les deux autres facultés ont agi et se sert d'elles deux. Mais la faculté de grandir s'arrête d'abord; ensuite celle d'engendrer se fortifie pendant un temps, puis s'arrête aussi. La faculté de se nourrir reste [seule] active, jusqu'à ce qu'elle s'affaiblisse [à son tour]; alors arrive la fin" (*Le Livre des directives et remarques . . .*, p. 343).

[44] Ibn Sīnā, *Shifā'*, *Ṭabī'īyāt*, pp. 368–378, where the physiology, manner of generation, and growth of plants are discussed.

the seed into the earth. Once this stage is reached the nutritive faculty of the plant awakens and is able then to assimilate food from the earth like a child who, once torn from his mother's womb, can then be fed through the mouth. The assimilation of food by the roots of the plant is also like the attraction of food to the liver through the many veins of the body.

The life of plants, like that of all other beings, depends upon the imposing of form upon matter, which, according to Ibn Sīnā, requires the presence of moisture. Also, the assimilation of food which is then converted into the form of the plant makes the presence of water an essential condition for the life of all plants. Besides moisture, there is need of heat which all living creatures need in order to assimilate their food. Moisture and heat, therefore, are the basic needs of all plants and animals, and the death of these creatures occurs when the opposite qualities of dry and cold become dominant.[45]

Plants possess primary and secondary organs similar to those of animals. The essential organs are the root, trunk, branches, bark, wood and pith, or core; and the secondary ones are the fruit, leaves, and blossoms which Ibn Sīnā compares to the hair of animals. The size and importance of these organs differ among various plants. For example, trees in which the earthy element predominates need a greater instrument to attract food, so that they dig their roots deeper; on the contrary, trees with a warm nature need to attract the airy and fiery elements, so that their roots are close to the surface of the earth. The many roots of plants are to enable them to find food in one place if not another, just as animals are given the power to move around in search of food.

The life of plants fulfills its purpose in the hierarchy of being as the link between the mineral and animal worlds. Plants have certain parts, like roots, whose function is to maintain plant life, but also certain features such as beautiful patterns and colors, symmetry and smell, which are created to be appreciated and contemplated by beings other than the plants and by faculties both sensual and intellectual which the plants themselves do not possess.

The animals are also composed of the four elements but with a higher degree of perfection and purity. When the mixture of the elements approaches even closer to equilibrium, the animal soul (*al-nafs al-ḥayawānīyah*) becomes attached to it. The animal, besides all the powers of the minerals and plants, possesses additional faculties which it gains by virtue of the coming into play of this new soul, or new faculty of the World Soul. The faculties of the animal soul consist

[45] *Shifāʾ*, *Ṭabīʿīyāt*, p. 47.

of the power of motion (*muḥarrikah*) and the power of comprehension (*mudrikah*).[46] The totality of the animal faculties may be outlined in the following manner:[47]

- Animal soul (*al-nafs al-ḥayawānīyah*)
  - power of motion (*muḥarrikah*)
    - power of desire (*shawqīyah*)
      - power of lust (*shahwah*)
      - power of anger (*ghaḍab*)
    - power of motion of body (*nāqilah*)
  - power of comprehension (*mudrikah*)
    - five exterior senses
    - five interior senses

The five internal senses consist of the common sense, that is, *sensis communis*, (*al-ḥiss al-mushtarak*), the power of retaining forms (*muṣawwirah*), imagination (*takhayyul*), apprehension (*wahm*), and memory (*ḥāfizah*). These faculties are developed in different degrees in various animals and are by no means present in their totality in all members of the animal kingdom. The animals, by virtue of these faculties added to those of the plant and mineral kingdoms, are able to perform the various biological functions which belong to their nature. They constitute a degree in the scale of being between the plant world and man, and through their physical and psychic qualities form a bridge between man and the rest of the terrestrial environment.

The three kingdoms on earth, which lead in an ascending order to man, all consist of the same four elements which act as the ground, or substance, of manifestation and of the faculties of the World Soul

[46] "Quant aux mouvements soumis au choix, ils se rattachent davantage à l'âme. Ils ont un principe qui veut, qui décide, subissant docilement l'action de l'imagination, de l'estimative ou de l'intelligence. Par elle est suscitée une faculté irascible repoussant ce qui est nuisible, ou une faculté concupiscible conduisant à ce qui est nécessaire ou utile par rapport à l'animal. A cela obéissent les forces motrices dispersées dans les muscles et servant ces facultés dirigeantes." Ibn Sīnā, *Le Livre des directives et remarques . . .*, pp. 344–345. See also *La Psychologie d'Ibn Sīnā . . .*, trans. J. Bakoš, pp. 157–189. Also *Dānishnāmah . . .*, *Ṭabī'īyāt*, pp. 80–82; *Risālah-i nafs*, pp. 15–16; M. Winter, *Über Avicennas Opus Egregium de Anima* (Munich, 1903), pp. 25–32.

[47] For a discussion of the faculties of the soul according to Ibn Sīnā, see also A. Siassi, *La Psychologie d'Avicenne et ses analogies dans la psychologie moderne* (Tehran, 1954), pp. 58ff, and M. 'Amīd, *Essai sur la psychologie d'Avicenne* (Génève, 1940), pp. 151ff.

In the *Shifā'*, *Ṭabī'īyāt* (pp. 381–520), Ibn Sīnā discusses in great detail the science of zoology, assembling there all that was known in the medieval period about physiology, embryology, and so forth, in the context of the faculty psychology outlined here.

which manifests a different faculty at each level of existence.[48] The union of a particular faculty of the Soul to a combination of the elements is not as a compound but *ad extra* and by way of a nexus. It is brought about when the correct proportion of the elements, reaching a new degree of purity and approaching closer to perfect equilibrium and harmony, attracts to itself a faculty of the World Soul.

The concept of equilibrium, or justice, as the necessary condition for the wedding of the Soul and the mixture of the elements, is widespread in Islam and is far from being confined to Ibn Sīnā.[49] According to this view, once the harmony and correct proportion of the elements has been reached, the Soul cannot but be attracted toward it because of the inner sympathy which exists between the invisible and the visible. Justice, the mean, equilibrium, harmony, are so many expressions of the same basic idea which dominates the Universe and preserves the wedding of "heaven" and "earth." It is the mingling of substances in the compound bodies which accounts for their ability to receive life. The commingling of the components so modifies their contraries as to produce an ensemble in which all the various contraries are blended harmoniously. The more harmonious the blending, the more suitable is the resultant compound to be the vehicle, not merely of life in general, but of a very particular kind of life. Perfect equilibrium and perfect balance render possible the manifestation of the perfect intellectual life which celestial beings possess but which may be also enjoyed by man.[50]

The Constitution of the Microcosm

As one of the masters of the art of medicine and one in whom the traditions of Hippocrates and Galen met, Ibn Sīnā has written much

[48] For a summary treatment of the faculties of the Soul according to Ibn Sīnā, see E. Gilson, "Les Sources gréco-arabes de l'augustinisme avicennisant," *Archives d'Histoire Doctrinale et Littéraire du Moyen Age*, 4:5–149 (1929).

[49] Referring to the bond between the soul and the body, Maḥmūd Shabistarī writes.

Not that bond which subsists between the compound and its parts,
(For spirit is free from the attributes of corporeity)
But when water and clay are purified altogether,
Spirit is added to them by "The Truth".
When the parts, to wit, the elements attain equilibrium,
The beams of the spirit world fall upon them.
The Spirit's rays shining on the body at the time of equilibrium,
Are like the rays of the sun shining upon the earth.
(*Gulshan-i rāz*, trans. E. H. Whinfield, London: 1880, p. 61.)

[50] Ibn Sīnā, *A Treatise on the Canon of Medicine, Incorporating a Translation of the First Book*, trans. and commented on by O. C. Gruner (London: Luzac & Co., 1930), p. 535, hereafter cited as *TCM*.

about man as a spiritual, psychical, and physical entity whose body he studies by observation and whose illnesses he seeks to cure by experimental means.[51] His medicine, however, is plunged deeply into his metaphysical view of man as the microcosm in whom creation returns to its source. The principles of his medicine provide, therefore, the last link in the cycle of his cosmology and a key for the understanding of the macrocosm. It is in man that the elements are best mixed and all the faculties of the Soul assembled.

For Ibn Sīnā the study of the body of man is intricately related to that of the human soul because, in his words, "The body and soul form one complete whole—one single being."[52] The science of the human body, therefore, is also connected with and leads to the science of the origin of things.

One must presuppose a knowledge of the accepted principles of the respective sciences of origins, in order to know whether they are worthy of credence or not; and one makes inferences from the other sciences which are logically antecedent to these. In this manner one passes up step by step until one reaches the very beginnings of all knowledge—namely pure philosophy; to wit, metaphysics.[53]

The study of the human body by Ibn Sīnā is not that of dead matter to which life has been added.

Modern medicine is based on the conception of the universe as a conglomeration of dead matter out of which, by some unexplainable process, life may become evolved in forms. To Avicenna the whole of the universe is the manifestation of a universal principle of life, acting through the instrumentality of forms. Or, again, in modern medicine, the forms are the source of life; to Avicenna they are the product of life.[54]

Life, according to Ibn Sīnā, pervades the whole Universe.

Life and every perfection and every good for which creatures are destined, comes from nothing but the Prime Most High Truth—the source of all good, and from the Strong Desire ever proceeding therefrom.[55]

This pervading life principle exists not only in the human, animal, and plant worlds, but in all beings outside of the four elements which are the principles of physical manifestation.

All corporeal bodies may receive life except the four first principles, and whatever is of like nature to them. For these are non-living bodies, and are also of negligible bulk. In fact their bulk is infinitesimal compared with the

[51] For a list of Ibn Sīnā's medical writings see Maḥmūd Najmābādī, "Kutub wa mu'allafāt-i ṭibbī-i Ibn-i Sīnā," *Jahān-i Pizishkī*, 2:1–7 (1327 [1948]), pp. 1–7.

[52] *TCM*, p. 12.

[53] *TCM*, pp. 31–32.

[54] *TCM*, p. 9

[55] *TCM*, p. 534.

planets, and still more strikingly so compared with some of the fixed stars. Indeed it can be shown that these first-principles in their totality have not as much bulk as a point compared with the body of Saturn; how much less then are they when compared with the higher bodies?[56]

The same four principles of which minerals, plants, and animals are comprised, constitute the human body,[57] and through their combination give rise to the humors and qualities. Their relation may be represented in the manner shown in Figure 18.[58]

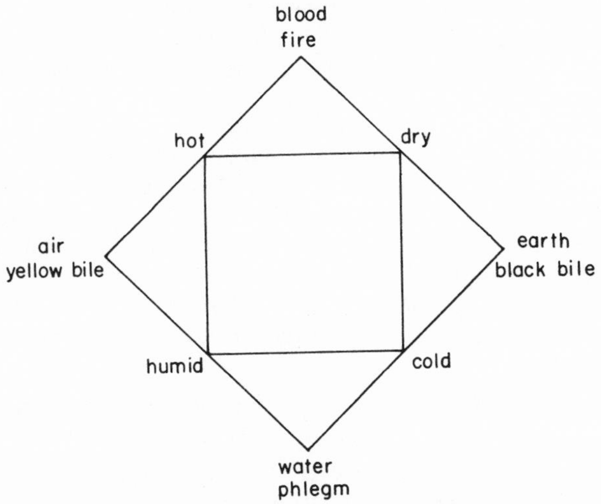

Figure 18. The four humors and the elements and natures.

The four elements, manifest in their admixture all the qualities which the human body displays.

The earth is an "element" normally situated at the center of all existence. In its nature it is at rest, and all others naturally tend toward it, at however great a distance away they might be. This is because of its intrinsic weight. It is cold and dry by nature, and it appears so to our senses as long as it is not interfered with by extraneous agencies, and obeys its own peculiar nature. It is by means of the earthy element that the parts of our body are fixed and held together into a compacted form; by its means the outward form is maintained.

[56] *TCM*, p. 534.

[57] "The elements are simple bodies. They are the primary components of the human being throughout all its parts, as well as of all other bodies in their varied and diverse forms. The various orders of being depend for their existence on the intermixture of the elements." *TCM*, p. 34.

[58] Ibn Sīnā, *Poème de la médecine—Urǧūzah fi'ṭ-ṭibb* (Paris, 1956), p. 13.

The water is a simple substance whose position in nature is exterior to the earth, and interior to the air. This position is owing to its relative density. In nature it is cold and moist. It appears to our senses as long as there are no influences to counteract it. Its purpose in creation lies in the fact that it lends itself readily to dispersion, and consequently assumes any shape without permanency. In the construction of things, then, it provides the possibility of their being moulded and spread out and attempered. Being moist, its shapes can be readily fashioned and as easily lost . . .

Air is a simple substance, whose position in nature is above the sphere of water, and beneath that of fire. This is due to its relative lightness. In nature it is hot and moist, according to the rule which we have given. Its effect, and value, in (the world of) creation is to rarefy, and render things finer, lighter, more delicate, softer, and consequently better able to move to the higher sphere.

Fire is a simple substance, which occupies a position in nature higher than that of the other three elements—namely the hollow of the sublunary world, for it reaches to the heavens. All things return to it. This is because of its absolute lightness. In nature it is hot and dry. The part which it plays in the construction of things is that it matures, rarefies, refines, and intermingles with all things. Its penetrative power enables it to traverse the substance of air; by this power it also subdues the sheer coldness of the two heavy cold elements; by this power it brings the elementary properties into harmony.[59]

The interaction of the qualities of the four elements determines the temperament of the human being.[60] The temperament is equable when the contrary qualities are in perfect equilibrium, and out of harmony and inequable when the temperament tends toward a particular quality. Ibn Sīnā, like other Muslim physicians and such ancient Greeks as Alcmeon of Croton, considers all disease, in fact, to be due to the destruction of this equilibrium by the excess of some quality, and all cure an attempt to re-establish the harmony between opposites.

The temperament of each individual is unique and equable only with respect to the race and geographic region to which he belongs; climate has a major effect upon the human being not only in a "naturalistic" manner but also because of the close relationship which exists always between man as the microcosm and the cosmic milieu.[61] The fourth climatic zone, which is the most equable one on

[59] Ibn Sīnā, *TCM*, pp. 35–37.

[60] "Temperament is that quality which results from the mutual interaction and interpassion of the four contrary primary qualities residing within the imponderable elements." *TCM*, p. 57.

[61] "The Hindus, in health, have a different equability than the Slavs, and so on. Each is equable in regard to their own race, but not in regard to others. So if a Hindu were to develop the temperament of a Slav he would probably fall ill, and might even die. So,

earth, is therefore the home of people who are more attempered than occupants of other zones. The temperament is also influenced by such cyclic phenomena as the change of seasons during each of which the body reaches a new equilibrium.

Each animal and each organ of the body has a temperament of its own.

> Allah Most Beneficent has furnished every animal and each of its members with a temperament which is entirely the most appropriate and best adapted for the performance of its functions and passive states. The proof of this belongs to philosophy and not to medicine.
>
> In the case of man, He has bestowed upon him the most befitting temperament possible of all in this world, as well as faculties corresponding to all the active and passive states of man.[62]

The growth and decay of the body of man is dependent upon the human temperament. Growth depends upon the heat contained in the sperm, which is gradually used up.[63] Meanwhile, the moisture lessens in quantity and quality, thus preserving the innate heat at a constant level up to the age of senescence.[64] Ultimately, however, the moisture of the body comes to an end, and the innate heat is extinguished, thus causing the death to which everyone is destined and which depends upon the original temperament of the human body.

The basic qualities combine together to generate the humors.

> One must not forget that the most fundamental agents in the formation of the humours are heat and cold. When the heat is equable, blood forms; when heat is in excess, bilious humour forms; when in great excess, so oxidation occurs, atrabilious humour forms. When the cold is equable, serous humour forms; when cold is in excess, so that congelation becomes dominant, atrabilious humour forms.[65]

---

too, if the temperament of a Slav should come to be that of the Hindu, for the state of his body is contrary. So it seems that the various inhabitants of the earth have received a temperament appropriate for the conditions of their particular climate, and in each case there is a corresponding range between two extremes." *TCM*, p. 60.

62 *TCM*, p. 65.

63 "The human being takes its origin from two things—(1) the male sperm, which plays the part of 'factor'; (2) the female sperm [menstrual blood], which provides the matter.

"Each of these is fluid and moist, but there is more wateriness and terrene substance in the female blood and female sperm, whereas air and igneity are predominant in the male sperm. It is essential that at the outset of the congelation of the two components there should be moisture, even though earth and fire are found in the product. The earth provides the firmness and rigidity; the fire provides the maturing power." *TCM*, p. 359.

64 "Moisture is the material cause of growth and only changes in virtue of a formative power acting upon it. As a matter of fact this formative power is the 'soul' or 'nature'—that which is in the decree of Allah (*amr allāh*)." *TCM*, p. 71.

65 *TCM*, p. 90.

These humors affect profoundly the function of the body and are themselves influenced by the motion and rest, or excited and peaceful states, of the human being.

The humors in turn act as the constituent elements for the members of the body which "are derived primarily from the commingling of the humors, just as the humors are derived primarily from the commingling of the aliments, and the aliments are primarily composed of commingled 'elements.'"[66] The members are divided into simple ones having homogeneous parts such as flesh, bones, and nerves, and compound members such as the hands and face. The members are the instruments by which the passions and actions of the mind are achieved and act as its servants.

The body also possesses faculties which originate the functions of various organs. The faculties are (1) the vital (*ḥayawānīyah*), responsible for preserving the integrity of the breath, sensation, and movement of the heart; (2) the natural (*ṭabī'īyah*) governing the nutritive powers of the liver and the reproductive powers of the generating organs; and (3) the animal (*nafsānīyah*) controlling the brain and the rational faculty. Ibn Sīnā believes that "the heart is the source of all these functions, though they are manifested in several principal organs."[67]

The powers of the various members are due to the vital faculty which provides the body with its inner force.

> Hence it is clear that there is something else preparing (the members of those powers), something akin in temperament to itself—and this something is the vital faculty. This is that faculty which appears in the breath at the very moment at which the breath develops out of the rarefied particles of the humours.[68]

The breath acts as the link between the physical and the psychic and spiritual worlds, and plays a basic role not only in the physiological functions of the human being but also in his deliverance from the life of the body.

With regard to the central role of the breath, Ibn Sīnā writes:

> Allah the Most High created the left side of the heart, and made it hollow in order that it should serve both as a storehouse of the breath [its psychic aspect] and the seat of manufacture of the breath. He also created

[66] *TCM*, p. 93. See pp. 93ff for a detailed description of the members.

[67] *TCM*, pp. 110–111. Ibn Sīnā gives in these pages a thorough account of the faculties in the individual and the race and their relation to the qualities, elements, and the accompanying mental processes.

[68] *TCM*, p. 120.

the breath to enable the faculties of the "soul" to be conveyed into the corresponding members. In the first place the breath was to be the rallying-point for the faculties of the soul, and in the second place it was to be an emanation into the various members and tissues of the body.

Now He produced the breath out of the finer particles of the humours, and out of igneity; and at the same time produced the tissues themselves out of the coarser and terrene particles of these humours. In other words, the breath is related to the attenuated particles as the body is related to the coarser particles of the same humours . . .

The beginning of the breath is as a divine emanation from potentiality to actuality proceeding without intermission or stint until the form is completed and perfected.[69]

There is in principle but one breath, just as originally there was but one member from which all the other members of the body were formed.

There is one single breath which accounts for the origin of the others; and this breath, according to the most important philosophers, arises in the heart, passes thence into the principal centers of the body, lingering in them long enough to enable them to impart to it their respective temperamental properties . . .[70]

It is this principal breath associated with the heart that is identified with the force of life itself and is the link between the corporeal and the subtle and spiritual aspects of man's being. It is the human breath which renders possible the perfect equilibrium and balance of the elements, the necessary condition for the manifestation of the Intellect.

The breath, then, is that which emerges from a mixture of first-principles, and approaches towards the likeness of celestial beings. It is a luminous substance. It is a ray of light.

This accounts for the fact that the wind rejoices when it looks toward the light, and is depressed when exposed to darkness. Light is in harmony with the breath. Darkness is in discord with it.[71]

The manifestation of the Intellect on the microcosmic level depends upon the hierarchy of the faculties which man possesses, including those of the kingdoms below him in the hierarchy of cosmic existence. The human soul (*al-nafs al-nāṭiqah*), which is given to each human

[69] *TCM*, pp. 123–124. Ibn Sīnā distinguishes three breaths (natural, animal, and vital), each with its own temperament.

[70] *TCM*, p. 124.

[71] *TCM*, p. 535. Ibn Sīnā is here expounding the physiological and microcosmic significance of the basic Ṣūfī technique of invocation (*dhikr*) which reintegrates man into his own Origin by the use of the breath.

being by the Active Intellect, has, in addition to the powers of the vegetative and animal souls, the faculties of action (*'amal*) and speculation (*naẓar*) which stand between the world of form and matter and the world of pure forms and which are able to turn toward both this world and the next.[72] Man stands between the sensible and the intelligible worlds. Through his senses he receives impressions which by means of various faculties of the animal soul reach the level of ratiocination.[73] He also possesses the rational soul, which, with the aid of the Active Intellect, can lead him beyond this world to the angelic realm of the pure Intelligences. Ibn Sīnā interprets the Quranic verse (*āyat al-nūr*)[74] symbolically to describe the faculties of the soul:

Parmi les facultés de l'âme, il y a aussi ce qu'elle possède pour autant qu'elle a besoin de parachever sa substance en la rendant intelligence en acte. La première est une faculté qui la prépare à se tourner vers les intelligibles, certains l'appellent intelligence matérielle et elle est la niche. Celle-ci est suivie par une autre faculté qui vient à l'âme lors de la mise en acte en elle des premières intelligibles. Par cette nouvelle faculté, [l'âme] se dipose à acquérir les seconds; soit par la réflexion, qui est l'olivier, si elle demeure faible, soit par l'intuition intellectuelle, qui est de plus l'huile, si l'intuition est plus forte que la réflexion; elle s'appelle intelligence *habitus* et elle est le verre. Et la faculté noble, mûrie, est une faculté sainte, "dont l'huile est presque allumée." Un peu plus tard, lui viennent en acte

[72] In his many treatises on the soul (*nafs*), Ibn Sīnā insists on the unity of the soul, its creation with the body (*ḥudūth*), and its survival after the death of the body because of the nature of the soul as an intellectual substance. "Cette substance est unique en toi; plutôt, elle est toi, on le vérifie. Elle a des ramifications, des facultés dispersées dans tes organes . . ." (*Le Livre des directives et remarques* . . ., p. 311). See also Madkour, *Fi'l-falsafat al-islāmīyah*, pp. 224ff.

[73] The faculties of the animal soul as described by al-Shaikh al-Ra'īs are classified by O. C. Gruner (*TCM*, p. 139) in the following manner:

Higher	5. ratiocinative faculty	
	3. cogitative faculty	4. memory
	3. apprehensive faculty	
	2. imagination	
Lower	1. common sense	

[74] "Allah is the Light of the heavens and the earth. The similitude of His light is as a niche wherein is a lamp. The lamp is in a glass. The glass is as it were a shining star. (This lamp is) kindled from a blessed tree, an olive neither of the East nor of the West, whose oil would almost glow forth (of itself) though no fire touched it. Light upon light, Allah guideth unto His light whom He will. And Allah speaketh to mankind in symbols, for Allah is knower of all things." Quran: XXIV, 35.

une faculté et une perfection. La perfection consiste en ce que les intelligibles lui sont donnés en acte, en une intuition qui les représente dans l'esprit, et c'est "lumière sur lumière." Et la faculté consiste en ceci qu'il lui appartient de réaliser l'intelligible acquis, porté ainsi à son achèvement, comme est l'objet de l'intuition dès qu'elle le veut, sans avoir besoin de l'acquérir [à ce dernier instant], et c'est la lampe. Cette perfection s'appelle intelligence acquise, et cette faculté s'appelle intelligence en acte. Ce qui la fait passer de l'*habitus* à l'acte parfait, et aussi de l'intelligence matérielle à l'*habitus*, c'est l'Intellect Actif. Il est le feu.[75]

Man contains within himself the nature of minerals, plants, and animals as well as, potentially, the nature of the angels or Intelligences.[76] Just as the Universe has as its highest principle the Intellect, below which exist the other domains of being, so does man as the microcosm possess all the levels of existence within himself and have the Intellect as the inner principle of his being. The complex faculties of the various souls within man are so many stages between the vegetative and angelic life.

The human soul stands between the earthly and heavenly worlds. Its felicity lies in uniting itself with the Intellect and in leaving the sensible world in favor of the Intelligible.[77] This is its entelechy and deliverance. As the Universe is generated by God's contemplation and intellection of Himself, so does it become integrated in its Divine archetype in the act of intellection within man which results in the return of the sensible world to the intelligible one. Ibn Sīnā describes the human soul as a wanderer in this world who has lost his home and forgotten his original abode. It is for him to remember once again from where he came and to return once again to his original dwelling place. In his well-known *al-Qaṣīdat al-ʿainīyah* he asks:

> Why then was she [the soul] cast down from her high peak
> To this degrading depth? God brought her low;
> But for a purpose wise, that is concealed
> E'en from the keenest mind and liveliest wit.

[75] Ibn Sīnā, *Le Livre des directives et remarques . . .*, pp. 324–326.

[76] "L'homme, créé après la plante, l'animal et les éléments, comme aussi après les sphères, les étoiles, les âmes célestes et les intelligences suprêmes, est la dernière création de tout l'univers; Dieu ayant commencé la création par l'Intellect actif, et l'ayant finie par l'être doué de l'âme raisonnable, l'homme est l'être le plus élevé de l'espèce, comme l'Intellect tient le premier rang dans le genre." A. F. von Mehren, "Vues théosophiques d'Avicenne," *Le Muséon*, 4:606–607 (1885).

[77] "Quant à l'âme rationnelle, sa véritable perfection consiste à devenir un monde intellectuel, dans lequel doit se retracer la forme de tout ce qui est, l'ordre rationnel qu'on aperçoit dans tout, le bien qui pénètre tout . . ." Ibn Sīnā, *Shifāʾ*, *Metaphysics*, Book IX, ch. 7; trans. S. Munk, in *Mélanges de philosophie juive et arabe* (Paris, 1859), pp. 364–365.

And if the tangled mesh impeded her,
The narrow cage denied her wings to soar
Freely in heaven's high ranges, after all
She was a lightning-flash that brightly glowed
Momently o'er the tents, and then was hid
As though its gleam was never glimpsed below.[78]

Sympathy between Man and the Universe

The correspondence between the microcosm and the macrocosm is based upon an inner sympathy and harmony which exist between them. The sympathy, which is hidden to most men, becomes more evident as the soul increases in purity until in the case of the prophets the inner harmony between man and the cosmos becomes universally manifested.[79] The performance of religious rites increases the sympathy which exists between the microcosm and macrocosm and permits man to receive more fully the influx of the spiritual forces from the celestial spheres. Rites, and particularly prayer, also interiorize the order of the world within the being of man. It is for this reason that "sacrifice possesses a great utility and especially prayers which ask for rain and other similar events."[80]

The soul of man can also act upon the world in the degree that it can purify itself and concentrate its energies. In most people the soul is weak and confined to the body so that it is unable to act upon the outside world. Some souls, however, by the power of apprehension (*wahm*) can act upon other human beings of a weaker nature, and others of even greater powers can act upon the world of the elements.

[78] A. J. Arberry, "Avicenna: his life and times," in G. M. Wickens, *Avicenna, Scientist & Philosopher* (London, 1952), p. 28. Or, as the Turkish Abu'l-Sa'ūd wrote, basing his words on the *Ode* of Ibn Sīnā:

"Tu es parvenu à réaliser tous tes vœux dans ce monde. Les puissances, les prospérités et les bienfaits de toute sorte, possibles et imaginables se sont soumis à toi. Mais sache bien qu'aucun de ceux-ci n'a aucune valeur. Que ceux-ci ne t'attachent pas à ce monde. Allons ramasse ta tente. Passe ton temps lentement et marche vers les sphères célestes d'ou tu es venu.

"As-tu oublié tes frères et tes amis avec lesquels tu vivais là-bas? Jusqu'à quand séjourneras-tu dans ce monde si matériel? Toi, tu as vu les circonstances de toutes sortes de ce monde matériel, qu'il est impossible de définir et dont l'horreur n'a pu empêcher personne d'y pénétrer."

See also A. S. Unver, "Supplément aux commentaires de Ibn Sīnā," *La Revue du Caire*, 27:168 (1951).

[79] "C'est que le prophète, de par la perfection de sa nature, est apte à recevoir une illumination plus directe de l'Intellect et de l'Ame universelle; il est apte, donc, à pénétrer et à vivre l'harmonie secrète qui relie l'homme au cosmos—cette harmonie que précisément l'observance des actes religieux cultuels (*'ibādāt*) tend sans cesse à actualiser." L. Gardet. *La Pensée religieuse d'Avicenne*, p. 129.

[80] Ibn Sīnā, *Najāt*, p. 301.

This action by the soul is, according to Ibn Sīnā, the source of miracles and unnatural events.[81] All extraordinary manifestations of Nature and "occult sciences" are based upon the disposition of the soul, the properties of the elementary bodies, and the celestial forces which may interrupt the ordinary functions of Nature.[82] The will of man, however, does not upset the order of the cosmos but is always in conformity with its laws. For example, when a pure soul asks for rain it is the World Soul which grants the prayer. As for the prophet, he possesses a sacred soul (*nafs qudsīyah*) which is attached to the world of the angels and therefore has knowledge of things without having need of a teacher or books. As the vicegerent (*khalīfah*) of God on earth, he can perform miracles by the influence of his angelic soul upon the *hylé* of the world.

The sympathy between man and the Universe is based upon the love (*'ishq*) which pervades the cosmos.[83] God Himself is the Lovable, Lover, and Beloved and thus the Origin and End of the cosmos. The love which He has for the world traverses the whole Universe, manifesting itself in a different way at each stage of the ontological hierarchy.

In his *Risālah fi'l-'ishq*, Ibn Sīnā considers love as the very cause of existence. He writes:

Every being which is determined by a design strives by nature toward its perfection, i.e., that goodness of reality which ultimately flows from the reality of the Pure Good, and by nature it shies away from its specific defect which is the evil in it, i.e., materiality and non-being,—for every evil results from attachment to matter and non-being. Therefore it is obvious

[81] Ibn Sīnā, *Dānishnāmah* . . ., *Ṭabī'īyāt*, pp. 138–140.

[82] "Certes les choses extraordinaires sont envoyées dans le monde de la nature sous l'impulsion de trois principes. Le premier est la disposition de l'âme déjà mentionnée; le second, les propriétés des corps élémentaires, telles que l'attrait exercé par l'aimant sur le fer grâce à une force qui lui est propre; le troisième, ce sont des forces célestes; entre elles et les mélanges des corps terrestres, qui sont particulièrement disposés pour occuper une position, ou bien entre elles et les forces des âmes terrestres particulièrement douées d'états angéliques, actifs ou passifs, il y a une convenance qui amène furtivement à l'existence des effets extraordinaires. La magie noire est de la première catégorie, mais les prodiges faits dans un but d'apologétique, les miracles gracieux et les pratiques de la magie blanche appartiennent à la seconde, les talismans à la troisième." *Le Livre des directives et remarques* . . ., pp. 523–524.

[83] "Le cosmos avicennien, le monde sensible et le monde intelligible, est tout entier traversé et vivifié par un élan ascendant d'amour, *'ishq*, l'*eros* qui répond au mouvement descendant, et le moteur même du mouvement ascendant des lumières" (L. Gardet, *La Connaissance mystique chez Ibn Sīnā et ses présupposés philosophiques*, Cairo, 1952, pp. 36–37). See also Ibn Sīnā, *Risālah fi'l-'ishq* (Tehran, 1318 [1939]), pp. 2ff, and "Risālah fi'l-'ishq," trans. E. L. Fackenheim in *Medieval Studies*, 7:208–228 (1945), where Ibn Sīnā considers *'ishq* as the inner force connecting all realms of existence from the minerals and plants to the angels.

that all beings determined by a design possess a natural desire and an inborn love, and it follows of necessity that in such beings love is the cause of their existence.[84]

The perfection which each being possesses and toward which it strives is due to the innate love of that being, which is a gift of Divine Wisdom. Even in "inanimate" objects the universal love manifests itself, for example, as the force which attracts form to matter or as that which enables a being to preserve the perfection adhering to its nature. Likewise, each of the vegetative and animal faculties possesses a particular kind of love corresponding to its function. The desire to maintain food in the body or increase the size of the body to fit its proportion, or natural and voluntary love of animals, all come from the cosmic love pervading all creatures. "Every entity which receives the manifestation does so with the desire to become assimilated to It to the full extent of its capacity."[85]

The sympathy between the microcosm and macrocosm is itself a manifestation of the love of God for His own Perfection and for all of creation. What attracts the various beings to Nature and to each other, and the pure soul of man toward the celestial Intelligences, is an expression of the sympathy of God for Himself, a sympathy which is the very reason for the manifestation of the Universe.

Because It (Absolute Good), by Its very nature, loves the Being of what is caused by It, It desires to manifest Itself. And since the love of the Most Perfect for Its own perfection is the most excellent love, It has as Its true object the reception by others of Its manifestation, and this is most properly Its reception by those divine souls which have reached the highest degree of assimilation to It.[86]

[84] "Risālah fi'l-'ishq," p. 212.
[85] *Ibid.*, p. 227.
[86] *Ibid.*, p. 228.

CHAPTER 15

Nature and the Visionary Recitals

Background and Setting of the Narrative Cycle

Ibn Sīnā wrote three visionary narratives, or recitals, which form the parts of a great cycle differing in point of view from his better-known Peripatetic works. These writings constitute, along with the *Risālah fi'l-'ishq* and the last chapters of the *Ishārāt* . . ., most of what remains of his "esoteric philosophy."[1] These works were commented upon and explained throughout the succeeding centuries by many sages (*ḥukamā'*) of the *Ishrāqī* school, including Suhrawardī himself, and are the basic testament of that aspect of the doctrines of Ibn Sīnā according to which the later sages interpreted his philosophy and in the light of which he has been studied during the past millennium in Persia.

These narratives are the records of the intellectual visions of the author described in a symbolic language which itself constitutes an integral aspect of the visions and which is not simply an allegory more or less made up by the author.[2] In these narratives Ibn Sīnā has a vision of the Universe as a vast "cosmos of symbols" through which the initiate seeking Divine Knowledge, or gnosis (*ma'rifah*), must travel. The cosmos, instead of being an exterior object, becomes for the gnostic (*'ārif*) an interior reality; he sees all the diversities of Nature reflected in the mirror of his own being.[3] Thanks to the

[1] The cycle consists of *Ḥayy ibn Yaqẓān*, *Risālat al-ṭair*, and *Salāmān wa Absāl*; of the latter work only fragments have survived, these being recorded in the commentary of Khwājah Naṣīr al-Dīn al-Ṭūsī upon the *Ishārāt* of Ibn Sīnā.

[2] "Trop souvent l'on confond allégorie et symbole. Nous avons ici des symboles, mais non pas des symboles artificiellement construits; ce sont au témoignage de l'auteur, des symboles montrés en une vision intérieure, une vision qui ne pouvait être donnée qu'en symboles, et ces symboles à leur tour ouvrent la vision." H. Corbin, *Avicenne et le récit visionnaire*, I (Tehran, 1954), Introduction, p. vi.

The nature of the symbol differs profoundly from that of an allegory. A symbol is the "reflection" in a lower order of existence of a reality belonging to a higher ontological status, a "reflection" which in essence is unified to that which is symbolized, while allegory is a more or less "artificial figuration" by an individual having no universal existence of its own.

[3] "Hence the cosmos is no longer the external object, the distant model, of descriptions, of theoretical inventories, of deductive explanations; it is experienced and shown

transformation of the physical and astronomical elements of the Universe, the traveler (*sālik*) on his journey toward gnosis is able to realize the progressive interiorization of the cosmos within himself until finally he ascends above and beyond the "cosmic crypt" itself.[4]

Just as the logical coherence of everyday phenomena of Nature depends upon the ordinary consciousness of mankind, so does the symbolic vision of all cosmic realities and their transformation into "shadows of the spiritual world" depend upon the new, illuminated consciousness of the gnostic. It is the realization of superior states of being that enables the gnostic to "see" all manifestations of Nature integrated into their celestial archetypes.[5]

At the end of the *Ishārāt*, Ibn Sīnā describes the categories of those who know and the special qualities of the gnostic who is the traveler in the visionary narratives. There are, according to al-Shaik al-Ra'īs, three classes of knowers: the *zāhid*, who practices asceticism and is pious, the *'ābid*, who turns his thought to the sanctity of the Divine, and the *'ārif*, who knows through illumination and ecstasy.[6] The sole aim of the *'ārif* is to know and to become identified with the Truth. His life begins with affirmed will, then asceticism and piety, occasional tastes of union (*ittiṣāl*) and finally habitual union with the Divine. His journey through these stages corresponds to his journey through

---

as the succession of the stages of a more or less perilous exodus upon which one is about to enter or which one has essayed." H. Corbin, *Avicenna and the Visionary Recital*, trans. W. Trask, p. 33.

Throughout this chapter we have made use of quotations from the English translation of Corbin's *Avicenna and the Visionary Recital* by W. Trask with the permission of the publishers, Pantheon Books, New York.

[4] "C'est une intériorisation du firmament et des Sphères qui se produit: l'astre prend un sens intérieur analogue à celui de *l'astrum* ou *sidus* chez Paracelse. Ici, à chaque astre et à sa sphère correspond une faculté de l'âme. L'émergence hors du cosmos, hors de la Sphère des Sphères, est pour le mystique la représentation physique de son émergence hors des Cieux intérieurs à chacun desquels correspond une faculté de l'âme." Corbin, "Le Récit d'initiation et l'hermétisme en Iran," p. 141.

[5] "Ainsi existe-t-il un monde du rêve comme un monde de l'éveil où, non seulement la relation de la conscience et des objets est différente de la relation maintenue, *collectivement*, dans le monde de la veille mais où, encore, le déterminisme phénoménal de celui ci ne semble plus cohérent ni valable. Une conception scientifique de l'Univers ne représente donc que la conception d'un univers dans l'Univers. Le consentement commun ne saurait suffire à établir l'autorité, la vérité et la validité générales des lois.

"Les efforts incessants qu'exigeait l'élaboration du Grand-Œuvre semblent donc avoir été destinés à produire, d'une part, la 'projection' de la conscience de l'état de veille sur le plan d'un état transrationnel d'éveil, et, d'autre part, l'ascension de la matière jusqu'à la lumière ignée qui en constitue la limite." R. Alleau, *Aspects de l'alchimie traditionnelle*, p. 134.

[6] Ibn Sīnā, *Le Livre des directives et remarques . . .*, pp. 485–486.

the cosmos. He leaves the world of illusions for the world of Reality, and when his journey is complete he becomes himself the mirror in which Truth and its cosmic manifestation are reflected.[7] The whole being of the gnostic is transformed by the Truth he has realized in the center of his being; not only is his soul illuminated by It but even his body becomes immune to disorder and illness because of the presence of the spiritual light within the tabernacle of his heart.[8] By virtue of this same inner illumination he is able to gain knowledge from superior worlds, including knowledge of future events which ordinary men cannot achieve. He is also able to see things not in their usual opacity but in their essence as intelligible and transparent symbols of the spiritual world.

The journey of the gnostic begins in the *Ḥayy ibn Yaqẓān* where he is initiated into the world of pure forms symbolized by the Orient, which is the domain of the archangels of light, in opposition to the Occident, which symbolizes this earth, and the extreme Occident, which corresponds to the world of pure matter. The sage and spiritual master (*pīr*), Ḥayy ibn Yaqẓān, the "living son of the awake," appears to the adept, or *sālik*, as an angel and describes to the initiate the Universe through which he must journey, the Universe in which all physical realities are transformed into symbols. He invites the adept to undertake the journey across this cosmos of symbols to the Orient of pure light. In the *Risālat al-ṭair* the adept, accepting to undertake this journey, awakens from his slumber of daily life and breaks through the valleys and chains of the cosmic mountain (*qāf*) in the company of the angel.[9]

The *Salāmān wa Absāl* describes the last part of the journey of the adept in which the soul of the traveler is transformed into the

[7] *Le Livre des directives et remarques*, p. 495.

[8] "Le *'ārif* possède, tout autant que le malade de quoi détourner sa nature de la matière et il a, de plus, deux avantages: celui d'être dépourvu de dissolvant semblable au mal qui atteint le mélange chaud, et d'être dépourvu de maladie s'opposant à la force. Il possède encore une troisième donnée: le repos corporel, les mouvements du corps étant interrompus. C'est un bienfait de Celui qui aide. Ainsi, le *'ārif* est plus apte [que le malade] à conserver sa force.

"Ce qui t'est raconté là n'est en opposition avec aucune loi de la nature." *Ibid.*, p. 505.

[9] Ibn Sīnā here describes the journey of the soul as the flight of a bird. The use of the bird as a symbol of the soul is universal. As Plato says in the *Phaedrus*: "The wing is the corporeal element which is most akin to the divine and which by nature tends to soar aloft and carry that which gravitates downwards into the upper region, which is the habitation of the gods. The divine is beauty, goodness, and the like; and by these the wing of the soul is nourished and grows apace; but when fed upon evil and foulness and the opposite of good, wastes and falls away." (*Dialogues of Plato*, trans. B. Jowett, London, 1892, I, 452–453.)

angelic state.[10] From the fragments of this work given in Khwājah Naṣīr al-Dīn al-Ṭūsī's commentary upon the *Ishārāt*, the outline of the story can be detected. Salāmān and Absāl were half-brothers, Absāl being the younger of the two. He was brought up by his elder brother, Salāmān, who was the ruler of the kingdom, and became a very intelligent and handsome young man. The wife of Salāmān fell in love with her brother-in-law but could not have her love satisfied because of Absāl's complete refusal to comply with her wish. Unable to quench her desire, she decided to have her sister marry Absāl, and on the wedding night took her place. Just before the consummation of the marriage, lightning struck, revealing to Absāl the identity of the woman he had assumed to be his wife. Horrified by the situation, the noble Absāl fled from the house and in fact during the next day with a group of soldiers left the kingdom of his brother altogether.

Absāl wandered with his army all over the world, like Alexander of Macedon, conquering each land that he had crossed. Finally, after a long period of absence he returned home and gave the world that he had conquered to his brother. Upon returning, however, he once again became the object of the infatuations of Salāmān's wife but as before refused to satisfy her desire. This time she paid his soldiers not to fight with him during the next battle; as a result he was wounded and assumed dead. However, the animals of the forest picked him up, took care of him, and brought him back to health so that he was once again able to return to his homeland.

Salāmān's wife, seeing that her plans had failed, now decided to poison Absāl with the help of his servants. This time the plan succeeded, and Absāl died. Salāmān, grieved by the passing away of his noble brother, saw in a dream the real cause of his death and forced his own wife and the servants to drink of the same poison.[11]

The death of Absāl, who symbolizes the gnostic (*'ārif*), signifies the irreversibility of the process of illumination. The journey toward the Orient of pure light is a journey without return. Once the gnostic has become divorced from the world of matter and is allowed to enter the realm of pure forms, the domain of the angels, he does not fall back into the darkness of this world, just as in alchemy once the gold is made it cannot be unmade into a base metal.

The journey of the gnostic through the cosmos, the many dangers he encounters on the way, and his final death, which signifies a

[10] *Salāmān wa Absāl* was originally the name of a Hermetical work translated by Ḥunain ibn Isḥāq, and later transformed and orchestrated in a famous poem by 'Abd al-Raḥmān Jāmī.

[11] Corbin, *Avicenna and the Visionary Recital*, trans. W. Trask, pp. 224–226. Hereafter this work will be cited as *AVR*.

spiritual rebirth, complete the program of the cycle of visionary narratives. In this cycle Nature plays a double role, one negative and obscure, the other positive and transparent. When the consciousness of the adept becomes awakened by the visit from the angel, when he stops being an "ordinary" man and begins on the path as a "traveler" (*sālik*), then the cosmos becomes for him a crypt, a prison from which he must escape. However, as his consciousness becomes transformed and illuminated and as the escape from the cosmic crypt becomes actualized, then Nature itself becomes transformed from fact to symbol, from obscurity to light, and begins to aid him in his spiritual journey.[12] Cosmogony becomes important in his spiritual realization and illumination because it makes it possible for the gnostic to orient himself with respect to the cosmos across which he is to journey.[13]

The journey of the gnostic is from the world of matter to the world of pure forms, from the Occident to the Orient. The Orient, being the place of the rising Sun, symbolizes the domain of pure forms, which is the domain of light, while the Occident, where the Sun sets, corresponds to the darkness of matter. All beings in this world contain within themselves these symbolic worlds of the Orient and Occident inasmuch as they are composed of form and matter. Form in the visionary cycle is the essence, or "idea" (*ḥaqīqah*), of a thing, that by which "a thing is what it is." The gnostic's journey takes him from matter to pure form, from the Occident of darkness to the Orient of light; he traverses the realm of pure matter, the material body, the mixed region of the three kingdoms and the imagination, the world of the intelligibles, and finally the angelic world.

The sojourn which signifies the illumination of the consciousness of the gnostic and the transformation of the cosmos from fact to symbol cannot be told but in terms of symbols, in the language of what Ibn Sīnā calls the "science of the elite" (*'ilm al-khawāṣṣ*).[14]

[12] "The cosmological schema doubtless persists (it is recognizable in the *Recital of Ḥayy ibn Yaqẓān*, the *Recital of the Bird*, the *Recital of Occidental Exile*, etc.), but what is modified and changed completely is man's situation in this cosmos. The astronomical or psychic processes are henceforth perceived only under their symbolic form." *AVR*, p. 33.

[13] "The cosmogonic myth that returns with variants in all Gnosis propounds an *interpretatio mundi*—that is, a mode of comprehension, a fundamental and initial interpretation that goes beyond and precedes all external perceptions. Rather, this initial interpretation is what makes possible and orients all these perceptions, because it begins by situating the interpreter in a world, in the world that he interprets to himself; it is this interpretation that initially determines his experience of cosmic space." *AVR*, p. 17.

[14] "For modern 'sciences' the examples alleged, and all others similar to them, generally represent merely so many aberrations and 'superstitions.' But in fact it is not even certain that the mass of 'observations' and 'properties' mentioned in '*ilm al-khawāṣṣ* are called upon to constitute as it were a chapter in a history treating of a

Only he whose consciousness has been transformed, or who at least has been given certain "conceptual dimensions," can understand this science. For the rest, it remains either a fanciful story or a superstition. The "science of the elite," moreover, depends upon the symbolic interpretation (*ta'wīl*) of the Sacred Scriptures whose tradition goes back to the Prophet, an interpretation which likewise stands above the common religious law as it is meant for all men.[15]

The gnostic begins his journey in the *Ḥayy ibn Yaqẓān* after the encounter with the guiding angel, the sage who has been identified by later commentators with 'Alī ibn Abī Ṭālib—upon whom be peace. There appear two orders of angels before the "traveler," one being the Intelligences who are the Cherubim, and the other the Souls moving the celestial orbits who originate from the Cherubim. The tenth Intellect, which is also the Active Intellect, is identified with the Holy Spirit and the Archangel Gabriel.[16] The angels together play a central role in guiding the gnostic toward his ultimate goal.

In beginning the journey upon the path, the sage Ḥayy ibn Yaqẓān describes to the traveler the vast desert which lies before him. To be able to cross this obstacle, the adept must drink of the fountain of life which runs near "the permanent Source of Life."[17] To drink this water means to gain the knowledge of the discourse, or "logic" (*manṭiq*), which is the secret language of the birds to which the prophet Solomon was initiated (Quran, XXVII, 16). The angel describes to the adept the fountain of life in these words:

Thou hast heard of the Darkness that forever reigns about the pole. Each year the rising sun shines upon it at a fixed time. He who confronts that Darkness and does not hesitate to plunge into it for fear of difficulties will come to a vast space, bound and filled with light. The first thing he sees

---

continuous development of the natural sciences, if we tacitly understand the latter in the sense in which they are understood today. If it is already true that the operations and formulas of alchemy have a meaning that is far more precise (and of today) as psychic operation and technique than they would have for a contemporary laboratory that attempted to reproduce them, the same condition determines the horizon of all these ancient sciences. It is the phenomenon of the world as such that has changed. Essentially, the perception of correspondences and sympathies that they presuppose cannot, as psychic event, find a place in the schema of our sciences, which are based on causality." *AVR*, p. 290, n. 2.

[15] "It is necessary that in the religious Law a part of its declarations should speak according to appearance, and another part speak under the veil of symbols, so that the Sages shall meditate and reflect upon this secret and thus raise themselves to a higher rank in Real Knowledge." *AVR*, p. 314.

[16] All of Ibn Sīnā's cosmology derives from angelology because "both the cosmic process and the process of knowledge mark the soteriological function of the Angel. . ." *AVR*, p. 117.

[17] *AVR*, p. 321.

is a living spring whose waters spread like a river over the *barzakh* [isthmus]. Whoever bathes in that spring becomes so light that he can walk on water, can climb the highest peaks without weariness, until finally he comes to one of the two circumscriptions by which this world is intersected.[18]

The *barzakh* is the *intellectus materialis*, or *al-'aql al-hayūlānī*, which with respect to the intelligible forms acts as *materia prima*. But the use of the Aristotelian language of form and matter is here transposed into the spiritual domain to symbolize the inner experiences of the traveler.

Having drunk from the spring of life, the traveler is prepared to undertake the journey across the Occident into the Orient.

At the uttermost edge of the Occident there is a vast sea which in the Book of God is called the *Hot* (and Muddy) *Sea*. It is in those parts that the sun sets. The streams that fall into that sea come from an uninhabited country whose vastness none can circumscribe. No inhabitant peoples it, save for strangers who arrive there unexpectedly, coming from other regions. Perpetual Darkness reigns in that country Those who emigrate there obtain a flash of light each time that the sun sinks to its setting. Its soil is a desert of salt.[19]

The warm sea symbolizes non-being, the uninhabited country, matter, the setting of the Sun, the imposing of form upon non-being, and the desert of salt, the sublunary region where everything is always changing. The Sun symbolizes the macrocosmic Intellect which gives form to all things.

The first world to be crossed is the sublunary region, or the realm of "terrestrial matter."

All kinds of animals and plants appear in that country; but when they settle there, feed on its grass, and drink its water, suddenly they are covered by outsides strange to their Form. A human being will be seen there, for example, covered by the hide of a quadruped, while thick vegetation grows on him. And so it is with other species. And that clime is a place of devastation, a desert of salt, filled with troubles, wars, quarrels, tumults; joy and beauty are but borrowed from a distant place.[20]

In the first stage of the journey, the traveler must pass through several domains:

(1) A region in which there are no inhabitants, either mineral, vegetable, animal or human, but a vast desert symbolizing elementary air.

[18] *AVR*, p. 324. [19] *AVR*, pp. 327–328. [20] *AVR*, p. 331.

(2) The world of the elements and their exhalations which combine to form the mineral kingdom and the mountains, winds, clouds and so on.
(3) The world in which elements are better mixed and in which all species of plants appear in addition to what had appeared before.
(4) The world of all living beings not possessed with reason or "logos," including all kinds of animals which come into being through a better mixing of the elements.

After crossing these domains, the traveler turns toward the rising Sun, toward the Orient of light. But first he must cross the human state itself, the domain which Ibn Sīnā compares to a city possessing its king, soldiers, travelers, streets, walls, and so on. The human being possesses a *sensus communis* located in the middle of the anterior cavity of the brain; memory in the posterior cavity; and the active imagination in the intermediary cavity. These faculties are channels leading from the world of the senses to that of forms.

Know further that the sense organs—as the eye, the ear, the nose, the mouth, the hand, and the foot—are all like avenues by way of which entrance can be found into the city that is the sensible faculty itself, until the *sensus communis* itself is reached. And these five senses are like the men-at-arms who take prisoner whoever passes near them—in other words, "apprehend" him. The *sensus communis* is their chief, and it is through his intermediation that the captives come to the other faculties, as we explained earlier. Thus the sensible forms and figures are like captives entrusted to the Treasurer who keeps them—that is, to the representative Imagination. The significances of these forms are like the information contained in a letter, which the messenger does not know and which is intended for the King.[21]

The soul has two "troops" of faculties, one guiding it toward the world of forms and the other toward matter. The soul, moreover, has contact with beings made of pure fire called genis (*jinns*), or *parīs*, which exist in a realm below the terrestrial angels. It also has a pair of guardian terrestrial angels, the one on the right side leading it to gnosis and light and the other on the left attaching it to the darkness of the world of the senses.

In traveling "across" the three kingdoms and the human state and in leaving the sublunary region, the traveler has not yet left the Occident, or world of matter; the celestial spheres still belong to the Occident because they are also composed of form and matter. Matter

[21] *AVR*, pp. 351–352.

in the heavens, however, is incorruptible and subtle and is generated by the intellection of the cherubim.[22] Celestial matter, unlike that of the sublunary region, remains wed to one form instead of changing ceaselessly one form for another. The Oriental knowledge of the heavens, therefore, is not identical with the astronomical but must deal with a domain that is beyond the visible heavens.

The journey of the traveler through the visible heavens is a passage across the nine celestial spheres of Islamic astronomy and the fifty-five orbs of the Aristotelian system. He passes through nine domains:

(1) *The Moon.* The climate inhabited by a people with short trunks and rapid motion. These cities are nine in number.[23]

(2) *Mercury.* A kingdom occupied by people of even shorter trunks but whose motion is slower. They love the art of writing, the sciences of stars, theurgy, magic; they have also a taste for subtle and profound actions. Their cities are ten in number.

(3) *Venus.* A region whose inhabitants are extremely beautiful and lovable, who like gaiety and possess no worries. They have a refined taste for music and beauty and are ruled by a woman. They have nine cities.

(4) *Sun.* A kingdom whose inhabitants have very large bodies and are very handsome. Their nature is to have great bounty for all that is distant from them. The number of their cities is five.

(5) *Mars.* A kingdom where there dwell a people who bring destruction to earth. They love to wound, to kill, to mutilate, and are ruled by a king who is red in color and who always inclines toward doing evil. He is said to have been seduced by the female ruler already mentioned and to have been inspired by a passionate love. The cities of this kingdom are eight in number.

(6) *Jupiter.* A vast realm whose inhabitants have great wisdom, temperance, and piety and who spread their virtues to all parts of the Universe. They have great compassion for those who are near and far, for those who know them, and for those who are ignorant of their existence. They are of extraordinary radiance and beauty. They have eight cities.

(7) *Saturn.* A kingdom whose people tend toward evil but if inclined toward the good go to the extremes of goodness. They

[22] *AVR*, pp. 333–334.

[23] The number of cities in each domain refers to the number of secondary orbs in each sphere according to Aristotelian astronomy. Although in the *Shifā'* Ibn Sīnā shows no preference between the Ptolemaic and Aristotelian systems, in the narrative cycle his preference for the Aristotelian system is obvious.

do not hasten in their actions and are accustomed to long delays. They have eight cities.

(8) *Heaven of the Zodiacal Signs.* A kingdom of vast space with numerous inhabitants some of whom live alone outside cities. This realm is divided into twelve regions and twenty-eight stations. No group hastens to invade the station of another until that station has been abandoned. All the expatriated travelers described already journey across this realm and revolve about it.

(9) *The Starless Heaven.* A realm at the limit of the cosmos which no one has attained or seen until today. There are no cities, towns, or places of refuge in it, nor anything which can be seen by the eyes of the body. Its inhabitants are spiritual angels, and no human being can have access to it or live in it. From here descends the Divine Imperative and Destiny for all beings existing below it. Above it there is no longer a land which is occupied. The heavens and the earth which make up the left side of the Universe, the Occident, here come to an end.[24]

Having described the many levels of existence of the "cosmic mountain," the sage, Ḥayy ibn Yaqẓān, turns the attention of the adept toward the Orient which lies beyond all the physical heavens. There appears beyond the heavens the world of the highest angels:

He who is taught a certain road leading out of this clime and who is helped to accomplish this exodus, such a one will find an egress to what is beyond the celestial spheres. Then, in a fugitive glimpse, he describes the posterity of the Primordial Creation, over whom rules as king the One, the Obeyed.[25]

The King of the Universe is surrounded by two hosts of angels, the first the Cherubim who dwell in his proximity and the second a lower order which dwells near the boundary of the highest heaven, content to carry out the orders of the King. The King of the Universe is himself Absolute Beauty, whose contemplation is the highest of all beatitudes.

Among them all the King is the most withdrawn into that solitude. His beauty obliterates the vestiges of all other beauty. His generosity debases the worth of all other generosity. Whoever perceives a trace of His beauty fixes his contemplation upon it forever; never again, even for the twinkling of an eye, does he let himself be distracted from it.[26]

[24] *AVR*, pp. 336–342. The astrological symbolism of this description of the heavens is quite evident. The inhabitants of the cities most likely refer to the angels connected with each orb.

[25] *AVR*, p. 362.

[26] *AVR*, pp. 372–373.

Having described the whole of formal and, one might say, informal, manifestation from the desert of matter to the splendor of the Presence of the King of the Universe, the sage invites the adept to undertake with him the journey through the cosmic mountain to the throne of the Divine Being.

Were it not that in conversing with thee I approach that King by the very fact that I incite thy awakening, I should have to perform duties toward Him that would take me from thee. Now, if thou wilt, follow me, come with me toward him. Peace.[27]

In the *Risālat al-ṭair*, the second of the three treatises comprising the *Visionary Recital*, the adept accepts the invitation of the sage and begins his journey across the Universe in the form of a bird flying toward its original home.[28] He must acquire the virtues inherent in the nature of other animals in order to be able to overcome the many obstacles on the way.[29] Still he falls into the net of hunters and is unable to free himself. One day a flock of birds passing by take pity upon him and promise to take him to a land where he will never again be beset by dangers of traps if he promises to follow them. He accepts their aid and with their guidance flies above the valleys and pitfalls of the cosmic mountain until he emerges out of the cosmos.

Our flight led us between the two flanks of a mountain, through a green and fertile valley. We flew pleasantly on, until we had passed all the snares, paying no heed to the whistling of any hunter. Finally, we reached the summit of the first mountain, whence we saw eight other summits, so high that eye could not reach them . . .[30]

He flies over each summit until he reaches the heaven of the fixed stars.

There we saw green gardens, beautiful places, charming pavilions; there were fruit trees, streams of living water. So many delights refreshed our eyes! Our souls were confounded, our hearts troubled, by so much beauty.[31]

[27] *AVR*, p. 379.

[28] "Know, O Brothers of Truth, that a party of hunters went into the desert. They spread their nets, set out their lures, and hid in the thickets. For my part, I was one of the troop of birds." *AVR*, p. 188.

[29] "Brothers of Truth! Strip yourselves of your skins as the snake casts his. Be like the scorpion that ever bears its weapon at the end of its tail, for it is from behind that the demon seeks to surprise men. Take poison, that you may remain alive. Love death, that you may still live . . . Be like the salamander that lets itself be wrapped in flame, at ease and confident. Be like the bats that never come out by day . . ." *AVR*, p. 187.

[30] *AVR*, p. 189.

[31] *AVR*, p. 190.

Therein he encounters the other birds, the other souls, which have already made the journey safely. They welcome him and tell him of the city of the King of the Universe which lies before him and in which he will find the consummation and final purpose of his long journey.

The adventure of the gnostic in the *Salāmān wa Absāl* and his ultimate death symbolize the final stage of the journey from the "roof of the cosmos" to the Divine Presence, and union with God. In leaving the cosmos, the gnostic has integrated within himself all that is positive in the world of manifestation. In order to be able to pass through the cosmic mountain, he has had to possess the "virtues" of all the domains of the cosmos including the celestial spheres; he has been allowed to fly beyond the cosmos on the condition of having integrated the cosmos within his own being. His spiritual death, which means the return of his soul to its Divine Source, is therefore also the return of the cosmos to its Origin. The gnostic asks permission to enter the city of the King of the Universe in the name of the whole creation. The cosmos prays with him before the Divine Presence and shares with him in the beatitude of the contemplation of the Divine Beauty. The gnostic who has journeyed beyond the cosmos becomes the norm of the Universe and the channel through which all of Nature receives Divine grace. In his union with God, the whole Universe becomes once again integrated into its Transcendent Principle, as his life is the life of the cosmos and his prayers before the Divine throne, the prayer of all of Nature before the Divine artisan.

Conclusion

From the study undertaken in the foregoing chapters it becomes clear that in Islam, as in other traditional civilizations, the cosmological sciences came into being in the matrix of the traditional conception of the cosmos and were molded and conditioned by the principles of the Islamic revelation. The "material" of the various sciences came into the hands of the Muslims from diverse sources during the first three centuries of Islamic history, and then gradually all these elements became integrated and absorbed into the unitary perspective of Islam.

During the fourth and fifth centuries interest in the natural and mathematical sciences reached its peak and the cosmological sciences became formulated in a manner that was to have a lasting influence upon the whole of Muslim history. The writers of this period laid the foundation for the study of the sciences and determined the direction which various schools of Islamic philosophy and science were to follow during the later centuries.

Among the writers of this most prolific and fruitful period, the Ikhwān al-Ṣafā', al-Bīrūnī, and Ibn Sīnā are of special significance not only because of the extent of their influence but also because together they represent nearly all the important perspectives followed in the cosmological sciences in Islam. In studying their doctrines, therefore, one meets with most of the basic ideas which constitute Islamic cosmological doctrines as such.

The Ikhwān al-Ṣafā', whose perspective may be identified with the general Shī'ite view and more specifically with Ismā'īlism, and whose cosmological doctrines are shared by many later Ṣūfīs, present the study of Nature as a part of a more general program for the education of mankind. Through considerations of a metaphysical order they relate their vision of the cosmos to its Divine Origin and consider the study of the Universe and its parts as a valid and necessary step toward the knowledge of Divine realities.

Al-Bīrūnī represents the point of view of the scholar and compiler as well as that of the mathematician and astronomer. As a very competent scientist, historian, and general observer and commentator on the civilizations of mankind, he approaches the study of Nature as a devout Muslim who sees the world as the handiwork of God and considers the observation and study of Nature as a religious duty. In his writings, certain elements of the Hindu cosmological sciences, especially concerning the concept of time and cosmic cycles, become combined with knowledge derived from Greek sources, and the whole is viewed in the light of the Muslim attitude toward Nature as a purposeful domain in which the power and wisdom of the Creator is manifested.

As for Ibn Sīnā, his works may be divided into an "official," or "exoteric," philosophy and a more hidden or "esoteric" set of doctrines. The "exoteric" philosophy represents the most masterly expression of the philosophy of the Peripatetic school in Islam, a school which itself drew its principles from the teachings of Aristotle, his Alexandrian commentators, the Neoplatonists, and the monotheistic perspective of Islam. In his Peripatetic works, Ibn Sīnā seeks to study the world of becoming in terms of the Aristotelian categories, relating becoming to Being and particulars to Universals. He considers the science of any object in the Universe as the science of its being and a realization of its ontological status in the great chain of Being. The Universe at all levels of its existence emanates from Pure Being and ultimately returns to it.

In the "esoteric" philosophy, which in many ways is akin to the later school of *Ishrāqī* theosophy, Ibn Sīnā considers knowledge as "operative" and as a process by which the being of the knower is transformed. In this phase of his writings, which in its cosmological aspect also resembles the doctrines of the Ṣūfīs, knowledge of the cosmos is reached by means of the effective journey through it. All natural phenomena become interiorized within the being of the gnostic until, having come to know the whole of the cosmos in principle, he is able to transcend formal manifestation itself and reach the Divine Presence. Nature in this perspective provides the background for the gnostic's journey and the knowledge of it, the means of reaching spiritual deliverance.

The various authors whom we have considered have employed diverse means to reach the ultimate goal of the realization of the unicity of Nature, these means ranging from contemplation and intellection to ratiocination and finally observation and experiment. There is no one method to be employed to the exclusion of others. Rather, these "ways of knowing," if used correctly and with an understanding of the limitation inherent in modes of knowledge connected with the sensible and rational domains, lead to the assertion of the interrelatedness of all parts of the cosmos, because this unicity lies in the nature of things.

Despite the differences in perspective and emphasis, however, the general accounts of the sciences of Nature given by most Muslim writers, including those we have described, seem like so many exegeses of the same cosmic text. These authors all deal with a Universe created and sustained by God, in which there is hierarchy, an ontological dependence upon the Creator, an order governing things, and a purpose toward which things strive. They consider space, which one may say "contains" formal manifestation, as finite, implying that outside the Divine Being all things partake of the nature of finiteness and limitation. They believe that the order of the cosmos is due to the constant intervention in the world by the Creator or His agents who are the angels, or faculties of the World Soul, and in one way or other assert that there is an interrelation between all things in the Universe and also between man and the cosmic milieu.

Finally, it must be remembered that all of the authors whom we have studied here, like other Muslim scientists and scholars, consider the study of Nature not as an end in itself but as a means to an end, as a *scientia* which leads to *sapientia* because it is always cultivated in the bosom of a wisdom which lies above the purely human domain of reason. Nature is not to be studied for mere curiosity nor just for the sake of itself and as an end in itself. Rather, the reason why they consider the pursuit of the natural sciences to be legitimate is that the purpose of man's life and his entelechy is to gain knowledge of the Creator Whose wisdom is reflected in His creation in such a way that the study of this reflected wisdom leads to the knowledge of the Creator Himself.

Muslim authors also share with each other and with the general point of view of medieval science the belief that the coordinate which determines knowledge of Nature is ultimately the Divine Intellect and not just the mind of man. Inasmuch as God is the source of being for both the Universe and man, all knowledge of the cosmos must be able to relate the Universe to Him Who is its ontological origin. Among authors whose writings we have considered in this treatise, this point of view is less emphasized in the writings of al-Bīrūnī, at least the works of his that have survived, than in the works of Ibn Sīnā and the Ikhwān; yet, even in al-Bīrūnī's writings, where the knowledge of immediate causes of things is given greater emphasis, Nature and the study of it are considered always with respect to the Creator. To have the complete science of something is to know it as it exists in the Divine Mind.

The major perspectives presented in the writings of the Ikhwān al-Ṣafā', al-Bīrūnī, and Ibn Sīnā, for whom the study of the cosmos implies either the application of metaphysical principles, or the projection of the microcosm upon it, or the observation and contemplation of the handiwork of God, are to be found among many other Muslim authors as well. In fact, these perspectives constitute the dominant points of view in Islamic cosmological doctrines. These views are to be found in one form or another in the writings of other important figures of the 4th/10th and 5th/11th centuries, such as Abū Ḥayyān al-Tawḥīdī, Abū Sulaimān al-Manṭiqī, Abu'l-Barakāt al-Baghdādī, 'Umar Khayyām, Nāṣir-i Khusraw, Ibn al-Haitham, al-Ghazzālī, the encyclopedists, and various Ṣūfī sages like Ḥakīm al-Tirmidhī who wrote on cosmological questions.

During the later centuries, interest in the natural and mathematical sciences gradually diminished while at the same time the intellectual and spiritual life of Islam became dominated by the gnostic doctrines of Ibn 'Arabī and the *Ishrāqī* theosophy of Suhrawardī, both of whom made use of the cosmological views of the earlier authors and especially those whom we have studied here. The treatises of the Ikhwān al-Ṣafā' were spread into Andalusia by al-Kirmānī and, along with other Ismā'īlī writings, had some influence on certain aspects of Ibn 'Arabī's works. Ibn 'Arabī integrated into his gnostic vision of the cosmos Alexandrian cosmology as found in the writings of the Ikhwān, the pseudo-Empedoclean cosmology of Ibn Masarrah, as well as certain astronomical and astrological works of al-Bīrūnī, and elevated Hermetic doctrines, of which traces are also to be found in the *Rasā'il*, to the highest level of their meaning.

Likewise, Suhrawardī, whose *Ishrāqī* school became a dominant aspect of the intellectual life of the eastern part of the Islamic world and especially Persia after the 6th/12th century, made use of Hermeticism both as he found it in earlier writings, like those of Jābir ibn Ḥayyān and the Ikhwān, and in the more recent cosmology of Ibn Sīnā, especially that of his "esoteric" works. Suhrawardī's *Story of the Occidental Exile* (*Qiṣṣat al-ghurbat al-gharbīyah*) continues the theme of the visionary recitals of Ibn Sīnā, and it was the master of *Ishrāq* who translated the *Risālat al-ṭair* into Persian and praised Ibn Sīnā for having begun to tread upon the path which led to *Ishrāqī* theosophy, although he never succeeded in unveiling all of its mysteries. In any case, Ibn Sīnā's doctrines served as one of the main components and the immediate background of the synthesis achieved by Suhrawardī nearly two centuries later. Moreover, there has always existed a living tradition in Persia which has interpreted the philosophy of Ibn Sīnā itself on *Ishrāqī* lines and taken this aspect of his philosophy seriously. The great Safavid sage, Mullā Ṣadrā, who succeeded in unifying the gnostic doctrines of Ibn 'Arabī, *Ishrāqī* theosophy, and Peripatetic philosophy considered Ibn Sīnā in many ways as the predecessor of Suhrawardī.

During the centuries following Ibn Sīnā many metaphysical doctrines which surpassed his formulations in their profundity and lucidity were expounded by both the gnostics and the *Ishrāqīs*, who criticized Ibn Sīnā on more than one point in metaphysical and philosophical questions. Yet, so far as cosmological doctrines and natural philosophy are concerned, these later authors followed the formulations of Ibn Sīnā and other earlier authorities, among them those we have discussed in the preceding chapters. In many pages of the writings of Ibn 'Arabī and Suhrawardī, as well as those of Mullā Ṣadrā a few centuries later, one meets with ideas found in the *Rasā'il* or the Avicennian corpus transformed and synthesized into another perspective and therefore in a new guise beneath which one can discern the older patterns and modes.

Moreover, whenever and wherever in the Muslim world the natural and mathematical sciences continued to be cultivated after the 5th/11th century—as, for example, after the Mongol invasion in Marāghah by Khwājah Naṣīr al-Dīn al-Ṭūsī and his students; or in the 8th/14th century in Samarqand under Ulugh Beg by Ghiyāth al-Dīn Jamshīd al-Kāshānī, Qāḍī-zādah, and others; or in Safavid Persia by Bahā' al-Dīn al-'Āmilī—the example set by the early masters was followed and the tradition of the cosmological sciences preserved. As a result, the influence of the Ikhwān al-Ṣafā', al-Bīrūnī, and Ibn Sīnā remained a lasting one far transcending the immediate time and place in which their works were composed. Rather, their doctrines, being molded in the light of the general spirit and perspective of Islam which is based on Unity (*al-tawḥīd*), became guiding principles for the study of the cosmological sciences throughout Islamic history.

There is a deep intuition in Islam, and in fact in most Oriental doctrines, that the aim of knowledge is not the discovery of an unknown which lies in an unexplored domain outside the being of the seeker of knowledge or beyond the "boundary of the known," but a return to the Origin of all things which lies in the heart of man as well as within "every atom of the Universe." To have a knowledge of things is to know from where they originate, and therefore where they ultimately return. Muslim authors, who have been generally imbued with the central Islamic doctrine of Unity, have been fully aware of this basic intuition of the ultimate return of all things to their Origin and the integration of multiplicity into Unity. That is why they have believed that the return of man to God by means of knowledge and purification, which is the reverse tendency of cosmic manifestation, conforms to the nature of things and their entelechy. Creation is the bringing into being of multiplicity from Unity, while gnosis is the complementary phase of the integration of the particular in the Universal.

The natural sciences cultivated by the Muslims in general and by the authors we have studied in this book in particular, like other ancient and medieval cosmological sciences, are so many expressions of the unicity of Nature, of the dependence of all things upon each other and upon their Divine Source. All the doctrines that the Muslims borrowed from Greek as well as Babylonian, Egyptian, Persian, and Indian sources became integrated into their general perspective, which has always been dominated by this central idea.

Besides considering all knowledge with respect to God, Islamic cosmological sciences, as outlined in the present study, also consider the logical coherence of natural events as they present themselves to man. This coherence is accepted as the passive reflection of the absolute freedom of the Divine Act, a freedom whose passive and feminine pole appears as the determined and bound matrix of cause and effect. The key to all cosmology is, in the last analysis, the distinction between the active and passive, or masculine and feminine, principles which govern all things. The coherence of cosmic events is due to the passivity of all things before the Divine Act which preserves its freedom with respect to creation. The determination and ordering of all terrestrial events by the Intelligences and the faculties of the World Soul, as described, for example, by the Ikhwān and Ibn Sīnā, symbolize the passivity of all things before the active pole of the Universe, which can be considered either as the Divine Act or as the Divine Intellect.

The main approaches to the study of Nature by such Muslim authors as the Ikhwān, al-Bīrūnī, and Ibn Sīnā—that is, the consideration of cosmology as a branch of metaphysics, the study of the macrocosm in analogy with the microcosm, and the observation of Nature as the handiwork of God and as an order that is completely dependent upon Him—are all legitimate from the Islamic perspective. The reason for this legitimacy and the possibility of the integration of cosmological sciences based upon their perspectives within the Islamic world-view is that they share in common the condition by which the legitimacy of all sciences in Islam is judged, namely, the expression of the interrelatedness and unicity of the whole of creation and the absolute dependence, and one might say nothingness, of all beings before the Divine Unity. A science in conformity with the spirit of Islam must have for its final goal the integration of all particulars in the Universal. The examples of cosmological sciences which we have attempted to study in this work can be called Islamic in that they are faithful to the basic Islamic doctrine of Unity in its many levels of meaning, and are therefore so many interpretations, possessing different degrees of profundity, of the principle that "the world consists of the unity of the unified, whereas the Divine Independence resides in the unity of the Unique." *Wa'Llāhu a'lam.*

Appendix
Bibliography
Index

APPENDIX

The Symbols of the Planets and the Divisions of the Zodiac

The Planets

Saturn	♄
Jupiter	♃
Mars	♂
Sun	☉
Venus	♀
Mercury	☿
Moon	☾

The Divisions of the Zodiac

Aries	♈	ϒ
Taurus	♉	ا
Gemini	♊	ب
Cancer	♋	ج
Leo	♌	د
Virgo	♍	ه
Libra	♎	و
Scorpio	♏	ز
Sagittarius	♐	ح
Capricornus	♑	ط
Aquarius	♒	ي
Pisces	♓	يا

A Selected Bibliography

General

Ahmad, N., "Muslim contribution to geography during the Middle Ages," *Islamic Culture* (Hyderabad–Deccan), 17:241–264 (1943); 18:167–186 (1944).

Ali Shah, I., "Arab occult writers," *Islamic Culture* (Hyderabad–Deccan), 6:401–408 (1932).

Alleau, R., *Aspects de l'alchimie traditionnelle*, Paris: Editions de Minuit, 1953.

Āshtiyānī, Mīrzā Mahdī, *Asās al-tawḥīd*, Tehran: University Press, 1947.

Badawī, 'Abd al-Raḥmān, *Arisṭū 'ind al-'arab*, vol. I, Cairo: Maktabat al-nahḍat al-miṣrīyah, 1947.

Baihaqī, Ẓahīr al-Dīn, *Tatimmah ṣiwān al-ḥikmah*, Lahore: 1351 (1932).

Balāghī, 'Abd al-Ḥujjat, *Kitāb maqālāt al-ḥunafā' fī maqāmāt Shams al-'urafā'* Tehran: Maẓāhirī Press, 1948.

Barthold, W., *Turkestan Down to the Mongol Invasion*, trans. and rev. by author and H. A. R. Gibb, London: Luzac & Co., 1928.

Béroukhim, M., *La Pensée iranienne à travers l'histoire*, Paris: A. Marchand, 1938.

De Boer, Tj., *The History of Philosophy in Islam*, trans. E. R. Jones, London: Luzac & Co., 1933.

Brockelmann, C., *Geschichte der arabischen Litteratur*, 2 vols., Weimar: E. Felber, 1898–1902; *Supplement*, 3 vols., Leiden: E. J. Brill, 1937–1942.

Browne, E. G., *A Literary History of Persia*, 4 vols., London: T. Fisher Unwin, 1902–1930.

Burckhardt, T., *Clé spirituelle de l'astrologie musulmane d'après Mohyiddin ibn Arabi*, Paris: Les Editions Traditionnelles, 1950.

——— "Considérations sur l'alchimie," *Etudes Traditionnelles* (Paris), 49:288–300 (1948); 50:116–125 (1949).

——— *Principes et méthodes de l'art sacré*, Lyons: Derain, 1958.

——— *Introduction to Sufi Doctrine*, trans. D. M. Matheson, Lahore: Muḥammad Ashraf, 1959; London: Thorsons, Publishers Ltd. 1976.

——— "Nature de la perspective cosmologique," *Etudes Traditionnelles* (Paris), 49:216–219 (1948).

Campbell, D., *Arabian Medicine*, 2 vols., London: Kegan Paul, Trench, Trübner & Co., 1926.

Carmody, F. J., *Arabic Astronomical and Astrological Sciences in Latin Translation*, Los Angeles: University of California Press, 1956.

Carra de Vaux, B., *Les Penseurs de l'Islam*, 5 vols., Paris: P. Geuthner, 1921–1926.

Christensen, A., "Un Traité de métaphysique de 'Omar Khayyām,' " *Le Monde Oriental* (Uppsala), 1:1–16 (1906).

Corbin, H., *L'Imagination créatrice dans le soufisme d'Ibn 'Arabi*, Paris: Flam-

marion, 1958; new edition, Paris: Flammarion, 1977.
——— "Le Livre du Glorieux de Jābir ibn Ḥayyān," *Eranos Jahrbuch* (Ascona), 18:47–114 (1950).
——— "Le Récit d'initiation et l'hermétisme en Iran," *Eranos Jahrbuch* (Ascona), 17:121–188 (1949).
——— "Sympathie et théopathie chez les 'Fidèles d'Amour' en Islam," *Eranos Jahrbuch* (Ascona), 24:199–301 (1958).
Cornford, F. M., *Principium Sapientiae*, Cambridge University Press, 1952.
Cruz Hernandez, M., *Historia de la filosofía española. Filosofía hispano-musulmana*, 2 vols., Madrid: Domicilio de la Asociación, 1957.
Dehkodā, 'Alī Akbar, *Lughat-nāmah*, Tehran: Dawlatī Iran, 1325 (1946) on.
DeLacy O'Leary, D., *Arabic Thought and Its Place in History*, London: Kegan Paul, 1922.
——— *A Short History of the Fatimid Caliphate*, London: Kegan Paul, 1923.
Dugat, G., *Histoire des philosophes et des théologiens musulmans*, Paris: Maisonneuve, 1878.
Duhem, P. *Etudes sur Léonard de Vinci*, 3 vols., Paris: Hermann, 1906–1913.
——— *Le Système du monde*, 10 vols., Paris: Hermann, 1913–1959.
Eliade, M., *Forgerons et alchimistes*, Paris: Flammarion, 1958.
The Encyclopaedia of Islam, ed. M. Th. Houtsma, A. J. Wensinck, *et al.*, 4 vols., Leiden: E. J. Brill, 1911–1938.
Gandz, S., "Artificial fertilization of date-palms in Palestine and Arabia," *Isis*, 23:245–250 (1935).
Gardet, L., "La Mention du nom divin en mystique musulmane," *La Revue Thomiste* (Paris), 52:642–679 (1952); 53:197–216 (1953).
——— "Le Problème de la 'philosophie musulmane,' " in *Mélanges offerts à Etienne Gilson*, Paris: J. Vrin, 1959.
——— "Raison et foi en Islam," *La Revue Thomiste* (Paris), 42–43:437–478 (1937); 444:145–167, 342–378 (1938).
——— *Introduction à la théologie musulmane*, Paris: J. Vrin, 1948.
Gauthier, L., *Introduction à l'étude de la philosophie musulmane*, Paris: Editions Ernest Leroux, 1900.
Ghoraba, H., "The dilemma of religion and philosophy in Islam," *Islamic Quarterly* (London), 2:241–251 (1955); 3:4–15 (1955); 3:73–87 (1956).
Gibb, H. A. R., "The structure of religious thought in Islam," *The Muslim World*, 38:17–28, 113–123, 185–197, 280–291 (1948).
Gilson, E., *L'Esprit de la philosophie médiévale*, Paris: J. Vrin, 1932.
——— *History of Christian Philosophy in the Middle Ages*, New York: Random House, 1955.
Goldziher, I., *Le Dogme et la loi de l'Islam*, trans. F. Arin, Paris: Paul Geuthner, 1920.
Ḥājjī Khalīfah, *Kashf al-ẓunūn*, 2 vols. and supplements, Istanbul: Maarif Matbaasi, 1941–1947.
Hartner, W., "The pseudoplanetary nodes of the moon's orbit in Hindu and Islamic iconographies," *Ars Islamica*, 5:113–154 (1938).
——— "Quand et comment s'est arrêté l'essor de la culture scientifique dans l'Islam?" in *Classicisme et déclin culturel dans l'histoire de l'Islam*, ed. R. Brunschvig and G. E. von Grunebaum, Paris: Besson & Chantemerle, 1957, p. 319–337.

Homā'ī, Jalāl al-Dīn, *Ghazzālī-nāmah*, Tehran: Majlis Press, 1936.
von Horten, N., *Die Philosophie des Islam*, Munich: Ernst Reinhardt, 1923.
——— *Die Religiöse Gedankwelt des Volkes in Heutigen Islam*, 2 vols., Halle: Max Niemayer, 1917–1918.
Ibn Abī Uṣaibi'ah, *'Uyūn al-anbā' fī ṭabaqāt al-aṭibbā'*, 2 vols., Cairo: Wahhābīyah Press, 1299 (1881).
Ibn al-Qifṭī, *Akhbār al-ḥukamā'*, Leipzig: Dieterich, 1903; Cairo: Sa'ādah Press, 1326 (1908).
Ibn Khaldūn, *The Muqaddimah*, trans. F. Rosenthal, 3 vols., New York: Pantheon, 1958.
Ibn Khallikān, *Ibn Khallikān's Biographical Dictionary*, trans. W. M. de Slane, Paris: Oriental Translation Fund, 1842–1871.
Ilāhī Qumshahī, Mahdī, *Ḥikmat-i ilāhī*, 2 vols., Tehran: University Press, 1335–1336 (1956–1957).
Iqbal, M., *The Development of Metaphysics in Persia*, London: Luzac, 1908.
al-Jurjānī, Mīr Sayyid Sharīf, *Kitāb al-ta'rīfāt*, ed. G. Flügel, Leipzig: Guilielmi Vogelii, 1835.
al-Kāshānī, Afḍal al-Dīn, *Muṣannafāt*, 2 vols., ed. Mujtabā Mīnovī and Yaḥyā Mahdavī, Tehran: University Press, 1952–1958.
Khayyām, 'Umar, "Az nathr-i fārsī-yi Khayyām," *Sharq* (Tehran), 1:167–168 and 641–660 (1309–1310 [1930–1931]).
Khwānsārī, Muḥammad, *Rawḍāt al-jannāt* (Lithograph), Tehran, 1306 (1888).
Kraus, P., *Jābir ibn Ḥayyān*, 2 vols., Cairo: l'Institut Français d'Archéologie Orientale, 1942–1943.
Lane-Poole, S., *The Mohammadan Dynasties: Chronological and Genealogical Tables with Historical Introductions*, Paris: P. Geuthner, 1925.
——— *Studies in a Mosque*, 2nd ed., London: Sydney, Eden, Remington & Co., 1893.
Leclerc, L., *Histoire de la médecine arabe*, 2 vols., Paris: Librairie des Sociétés Asiatiques, 1876.
Levi della Vida, G., *Studi orientalistici in onore di Giorgio Levi della Vida*, 2 vols., Rome: Istituto per l'Oriente, 1956.
Levy, R., *The Social Structure of Islam*, Cambridge University Press, 1957.
MacDonald, D. B., *Development of Muslim Theology, Jurisprudence and Constitutional Theory*, New York: Scribner's, 1903.
Madkour, I., *Fi'l-falsafat al-islāmīyah*, Cairo: Dār Iḥyā' al-kutub al-'arabīyah, 1947.
Masqati, J., "Theory of 'matter' and 'spirit' and its influence on the Egyptian poetry of the Fatimid period," *Islamic Culture* (Hyderabad–Deccan), 23:108–116 (1950).
Massignon, L., "L'Arithmologie dans la pensée islamique primitive," *Archeion* (Rome), 14:370–371 (1932).
——— *Essai sur les origines du lexique technique de la mystique musulmane*, Paris: J. Vrin, 1954.
——— "L'Homme parfait en Islam, et son originalité eschatologique," *Eranos Jahrbuch* (Ascona), 15:287–314 (1947).
——— "L'Inventaire de la littérature hermétique arabe," in A. J. Festugière and A. D. Nock, *La Révélation d'Hermès Trismégiste*, vol. I, App. III, Paris: Librairie Lecoffre, 1950.

Massignon, L., "La Nature dans la pensée islamique," *Eranos Jahrbuch* (Ascona), 14:144–148 (1946).

——— *La Passion d'al-Ḥallāj*, Paris: P. Geuthner, 1914–1921.

——— "Le Temps dans la pensée islamique," *Eranos Jahrbuch* (Ascona), 20:141–148 (1952).

Michell, R. L. N., *An Egyptian Calendar for the Koptic Year 1617* (*1900–1901, A.D.*) *Corresponding to the Mohammadan Years 1318–1319*, London: Luzac, 1900.

Mieli, A., *La Science arabe et son rôle dans l'évolution scientifique mondiale*, Leiden: E. J. Brill, 1938; also new edition, Leiden: Brill, 1966.

Nallino, C. A., *'Ilm al-falak, ta'rīkhuhu 'ind al-'arab fi'l-qurūn al-wusṭā*, Rome: Carlo de Luigi, 1911.

——— *Raccolta di scritti editi e inediti*, Rome: Istituto per l'Oriente, vol. V (1944) and vol. VI (1948).

Nasr, S. H., "The polarization of Being," *Pakistan Philosophical Journal* (Lahore), 3:8–13 (October 1959).

——— *Science and Civilization in Islam*, Cambridge, Mass.: Harvard University Press, 1968; New York: Mentor Books, 1970.

Nicholson, R. A., *A Literary History of the Arabs*, Cambridge University Press, 1956.

Niẓāmī 'Arūḍī, *Chahār Maqālah*, Tehran: University Press, 1334 (1955).

Obermann, J., "Das Problem der Kausalität bei den Arabern," in *Festschrift Joseph R. von Karabaček*, Vienna: Holder, 1916, pp. 15–42.

Pines, S., *Beiträge zur islamischen Atomenlehre*, Berlin: A. Heine Gmb. H. Gräfenhainichen, 1936.

——— *Nouvelles études sur Awḥad al-Zamān Abu'l-Barakāt al-Baghdādī*, Paris: Durlacher, 1955.

——— "Quelques tendances antipéripatéticiennes de la pensée scientifique islamique," *Thalès* (Paris), 3–4:210–220 (1937–1939).

——— "Some problems of Islamic philosophy," *Islamic Culture* (Hyderabad–Deccan), 11:66–80 (1937).

Quadri, G., *La Philosophie arabe dans l'Europe médiévale*, Paris: Payot, 1947.

Rahman Khan, M. A., "A survey of Muslim contributions to science and culture," *Islamic Culture* (Hyderabad–Deccan), 16:2–20, 136–152 (1942); and Lahore: Muḥammad Ashraf, 1946.

Rosenthal, F., "On the knowledge of Plato's philosophy in the Islamic world," *Islamic Culture* (Hyderabad–Deccan), 14:387–422 (1940).

Ṣafā, Dhabīḥallāh, *Tārīkh-i adabīyāt dar Īrān*, 3 vols., Tehran: Ibn Sīnā Press, 1338 (1959 onwards).

——— *Tārīkh-i 'ulūm-i 'aqlī dar tamaddun-i islāmī*, vol. I, Tehran: University Press, 1331 (1952).

Sarton, George, *Introduction to the History of Science*, vols. I and II, Baltimore: Williams and Wilkins, 1927–1931.

Schmölders, A., *Essai sur les études philosophiques chez les arabes*, Paris: Firmin Didot Frères, 1842.

Schuon, F., *Comprendre l'Islam*, Paris: Gallimard, 1961; also Paris: Editions du Seuil, 1976.

——— *Gnosis, Divine Wisdom*, trans. G. E. H. Palmer, London: John Murray, 1959.

——— *L'Œil du cœur*, Paris: Gallimard, 1950; and Paris: Dervy-Livres, 1974.

Schuon, F., *Stations of Wisdom*, trans. G. E. H. Palmer, London: John Murray, 1961.
al-Shahrastānī, Muḥammad, *al-Milal wa'l-nihal*, trans. Ibn Turkah Iṣfahānī, Tehran: 'Ilmī Press, 1944.
al-Shahrazūrī, Shams al-Dīn Muḥammad, *Ta'rīkh al-ḥukamā'*, trans. Ḍiyā' al-Dīn Durrī, 2 vols., Tehran: Danesh Bookstore, 1316 (1937).
Sharif, M. M., ed., *History of Muslim Philosophy*, 2 vols., Wiesbaden: O. Harrassowitz, 1963–1966.
Siddiqui, M. R., "The contribution of Muslims to scientific thought," *Islamic Culture* (Hyderabad–Deccan), 14:33–44 (1940).
Sirāj al-Dīn, A., *The Book of Certainty*, London: Rider & Co., 1952; also New York: Samuel Weiser, Inc., 1970.
——— "The Islamic and Christian conceptions of the march of time," *Islamic Quarterly* (London), 1:229–235 (1954).
Spirit and Nature, Papers from the Eranos Yearbooks, vol. I, New York: Pantheon, 1954.
Suter, H., *Die Mathematiker und Astronomer der Araber und ihre Werke*, Leipzig: H. G. Teubner, 1900.
Ṭabāṭabā'ī, Muḥammad Ḥusain, *Uṣūl-i falsafah*, with commentary by Murtaḍā Muṭahharī, Qum: Dar al-'ilm Press, 1379 (1959) on.
al-Tahānawī, Muḥammad 'Alī, *Kashshāf iṣṭilāḥāt al-funūn*, Istanbul: Iqdām Press, 1317 (1899).
Tunikābunī, Muḥammad, *Qiṣaṣ al-'ulamā'*, Tehran: 'Ilmīyah Islāmīyah Press, 1313 (1934).
Validi Togan, A. Z., "Considérations sur la collaboration scientifique entre l'orient islamique et l'Europe," *La Revue des Etudes Islamiques* (Paris), 9:249–271 (1935).
Walzer, R., "Islamic philosophy", in *History of Philosophy, Eastern and Western*, ed. S. Radhakrishnan, London: Allen and Unwin, 1953, II, 120–148.
Winter, H. J. J., "Science in Medieval Persia," *Journal of Iran Society* (London), 1:55–70 (1951).
Wolfson, H. A., *Crescas' Critique of Aristotle*, Cambridge, Mass.: Harvard University Press, 1929.

IKHWĀN AL-ṢAFĀ'

(Primary Sources)

Ikhwān al-Ṣafā', *Dispute between Man and the Animals*, trans. J. Platts, London: W. H. Allen, 1869.
——— *Khulāṣat al-wafā' fī ikhtiṣār rasā'il Ikhwān al-Ṣafā'*, Leipzig and Berlin: J. C. Heinrichs'sche, 1886.
——— *Kitāb Ikhwān al-Ṣafā' wa Khullān al-Wafā'*, 4 vols., Bombay: Nukhbat al-Akhbar Press, 1888.
——— *Rasā'il*, 4 vols., Cairo: 'Arabīyah Press, 1928.
——— *Rasā'il Ikhwān al-Ṣafā'*, 12 vols., Beirut: Dār Bairūt, 1957.
——— *Risālah jāmi'at al-jāmi'ah*, ed. 'Ārif Tāmir, Beirut: Dār al-Nashr li'l-jāmi'īn, 1959.
——— *al-Risālat al-jāmi'ah*, 2 vols., ed. Dj. Saliba, Damascus: al-Taraqqī Press, 1949.

(Secondary Sources)

'Abd al-nūr, Jabbūr, *Ikhwān al-Ṣafā'*, Cairo: Dar al-Ma'ārif Press, 1954.
Apollonius of Tyana, "Le Livre du secret de la créature par le sage Bélinous,"

trans. M. S. de Sacy in *Notices et Extraits des Manuscrits* (Paris), 4:107–158 (1798).

'Awā 'A., *L'Esprit critique des 'Frères de la Pureté.' Encyclopédistes arabes du IVe/Xe siècle*, Beirut: Imprimerie Catholique, 1948.

Casanova, P., "Alphabets magiques arabes," *Journal Asiatique* (Paris), 17–18:37–55 (1921); 19–20:250–262 (1922).

——— "Une Date astronomique dans les Epîtres des Ikhwān aṣ-Ṣafā," *Journal Asiatique* (Paris), IIme série, 5:5–17 (1915).

Chaignet, A. E., *Pythagore et la philosophie pythagoricienne*, 2nd ed., 2 vols., Paris: Didier, 1874.

Corbin, H., "Epiphanie divine et naissance spirituelle dans la gnose ismaélienne," *Eranos Jahrbuch* (Ascona), 23:141–250 (1954).

——— "Rituel sabéen et exégèse ismaélienne du rituel," *Eranos Jahrbuch* (Ascona), 19:181–246 (1950).

——— "Le Temps cyclique dans le mazdéisme et dans l'ismaélisme," *Eranos Jahrbuch* (Ascona), 20:149–218 (1951).

Dānishpazhūh, Muḥammad Taqī, "Ikhwān-i Ṣafā," *Mihr* (Tehran), 8:353–357, 605–610, 709–714 (1331 [1952]).

DeLacy O'Leary, D., *A Short History of the Fatimid Khaliphate*, London: Kegan Paul, 1923.

Dieterici, F., *Die Abhandlungen der Ichwān es-Sefā in Auswahl zum ersten Mal aus arabischen Handschriften herausgegeben von Fr. Dieterici*, Leipzig: J. C. Heinrichs'sche, 1886.

——— *Die Philosophie der Araber*, 16 vols., Leipzig and Berlin: J. C. Heinrichs'sche and Nicolai'schen, 1858–1891.

Fabre d'Olivet, A., *The Golden Verses of Pythagoras*, New York: Putnam, 1917.

Fackenheim, E. L., "The conception of substance in the philosophy of the Ikhwān aṣ-Ṣefā (Brethren of Purity)," *Medieval Studies* (Toronto), 5:115–122 (1943).

Farrukh, U., *Ikhwān al-Ṣafā'*, 2nd ed., Beirut: Manimnah Press, 1953.

al-Fārūqī, Ismā'īl, "On the Ethics of the Brethren of Purity," *Muslim World*, 50:109–121 (April 1960); 50:193–198 (July 1960); 50:252–258 (October 1960); 51:18–24 (January 1961).

Flügel, G., "Über Inhalt und Verfasser der arabischen Encyclopädie," *Zeitschrift der Deutschen morgenländischen Gesellschaft* (Wiesbaden), 13:1–43 (1859).

Goldziher, I., "Über die Beneinung der Ichwān al-Safā," *Der Islam* (Berlin), 1:22–26 (1910).

Guttmann, J., *Die Philosophie des Salomon ibn Gabirol dargestellt und erläutert*, Göttingen: Vandenboeck and Ruprecht, 1889.

al-Hamdānī, H. F., "A compendium of Ismā'īlī esoterics," *Islamic Culture* (Hyderabad–Deccan), 2:210–220 (1937).

——— "Rasā'il Ikhwān aṣ-Ṣafā' in the literature of the Ismā'īlī Ṭaiyibī Da'wat," *Der Islam* (Berlin), 20:281–300 (1932).

Haneberg, D. B., *Abhandlung über das Schul- und Lehrwesen der Muhammadaner im Mittelalter*, Munich: J. G. Weiss, 1850.

Ivanov, V. A., *The Alleged Founder of Ismailism*, Bombay: Ismaili Publishing Society, 1946.

——— *A Guide to Ismaili Literature*, London: Royal Asiatic Society, 1933.

——— *Studies in Early Persian Ismailism*, Leiden: E. J. Brill, 1948.

Job of Edessa, *Encyclopaedia of Philosophical and Natural Sciences as Taught in*

Baghdad about A.D. 817 or Book of Treasures, trans. A. Mingana, Cambridge, England: W. Heffer, 1935.

Kaufmann, D., *Studien zur Salomon ibn Gabirol*, Budapest: Pressburg, A. Alkalay, 1899.

Lane-Poole, S., *The Brotherhood of Purity*, Lahore: Muḥammad Ashraf, 1960.

Massignon, L., "Sur la date de composition des Rasā'il," *Der Islam* (Berlin), 4:324 (1913).

Nicomachus Gerasenus, *Introduction to Arithmetic*, trans. M. L. D'Ooge in *Great Books of the Western World* (Chicago: Encyclopedia Britannica, 1952), II, 807–848.

Ṣafā, Dhabīḥallāh, *Ikhwān al-Ṣafā'*, Tehran: University Press, 1330 (1951).

Sprenger, A., "Notices of some copies of the Arabic work entitled Rasāyil Ikhwān al-Çafā," *Journal of the Asiatic Society of Bengal* (Calcutta), (i) 17:501–507 (June 1848); (ii) 17:183–202 (August 1848).

Stern, M., "The authorship of the Epistles of the Ikhwān aṣ-Ṣafā," *Islamic Culture* (Hyderabad–Deccan), 20:367–372 (1946).

Strothmann, R., *Gnosis Texte der Ismailiten*, Göttingen: Vandenboeck and Ruprecht, 1943.

Tāmir, A., *La Réalité des Ikhwān aṣ-Ṣafā' wa Khullān al-Wafā'*, Beirut: Imprimerie Catholique, 1957.

Tannery, P., *Mémoires scientifiques*, vol. II, Toulouse: J. L. Heiberg and H. C. Zeuthen, 1912.

al-Tawḥīdī, Abū Ḥayyān, *al-Imtā' wa'l-mu'ānasah*, 3 vols., Cairo: Junnah Press, 1939–1944.

Taylor, T., *The Commentaries of Proclus on the Timaeus of Plato in Five Books; Containing a Treasury of Pythagoric and Platonic Physiology*, 2 vols., London: A. J. Valpy, 1820.

——— *The Philosophical and Mathematical Commentaries of Proclus on the First Book of Euclid's Elements*, 2 vols., London: T. Payne & Sons, 1792.

Ṭibāwī, A. L., "The idea of guidance in Islam," *Islamic Quarterly* (London), 3:139–158 (1956).

——— "Ikhwān aṣ-Ṣafā and their Rasā'il," *Islamic Quarterly* (London), 2:28–46 (1956).

——— "Jamā'ah Ikhwān aṣ-Ṣafā'," *Journal of the American University of Beirut*, 1–80 (1930–1931).

Zakī, Aḥmad, *Etudes bibliographiques sur les encyclopédies arabes*, Bulāq: Amīrī Press, 1308.

Abū Raiḥān al-Bīrūnī
(*Primary Sources*)

al-Bīrūnī, *al-Āthār al-bāqiyah*, trans. A. Dānāsirisht, Tehran: Khayyām Bookstore, 1941.

——— *Alberuni's India. An Account of the Religion, Philosophy, Literature, Geography, Chronology, Astronomy, Customs, Laws and Astrology of India*, 2 vols., trans. E. C. Sachau, London: Kegan Paul, Trench, Trübner & Co., 1910.

——— *al-Bīrunī on Transits*, trans. Mohammad Saffouri and Adnan Ifram, with a commentary by E. S. Kennedy, Beirut: American University of Beirut Oriental Series, No. 32, 1959.

al-Bīrūnī, "The chapter on pearls in the book on precious stones," trans. F. Krenkow, *Islamic Culture* (Hyderabad–Deccan), 5:399–421 (1941); 6:21–36 (1942).

——— *Chronology of Ancient Nations*, trans. E. C. Sachau, London: W. H. Allen, 1879.

——— *Die Einleitung zur al-Birunis Steinbuch. Mit Erläuterungen Übersetzt von Taḳi ed-Din al-Ḥilali*, Leipzig: Harrassowitz, 1941.

——— *Elements of Astrology*, trans. R. Ramsay Wright, London: Luzac, 1934.

——— *Epître de Beruni contenant le répertoire des ouvrages de Muḥammad Zakariya al-Razi*, trans. and ed. P. Kraus, Paris: A. Maisonneuve, 1936.

——— *Fī taḥqīq mā li'l-Hind min maqūlatin maqbūlatin fi'l-'aql aw mardhūlatin*, ed. E. C. Sachau, Leipzig: O. Harrassowitz, 1925.

——— *al-Kanun-ul-masudi* (*Canon Masudicus*), trans. and ed. M. Farooq, Aligarh: Muslim University Press, 1929.

——— *Kitāb al-āthār al-bāqiyah 'an al-qurūn al-khāliyah*, ed. E. C. Sachau, Leipzig: Deutsche Morgenländische Gesellschaft, 1878.

——— *Kitāb al-jamāhir fī ma'rifat al-jawāhir*, Hyderabad: Dāiratu'l Ma'ārif'l-Osmānia, 1935.

——— *Kitāb istikhrāj al-awtār fi'l-dā'irah*, trans. H. Suter, *Bibliotheca Mathematica*, 2:11–78 (1910).

——— *Kitāb al-tafhīm li awā'il ṣinā'at al-tanjīm*, ed. Jalāl al-Dīn Homā'ī, Tehran: Majlis Press, 1938–1940; new edition, Tehran: Bahman Press, 1973.

——— *al-Qanūn al-mas'ūdī* (*Canon Masudicus*), 3 vols., Hyderabad: Dāiratu'l Ma'ārif'l-Osmānia, 1954–1955.

——— *Rasā'ilul-Bīrūnī Containing Four Tracts. Based on the Unique Compendium of Mathematical and Astronomical Treatises in the Oriental Public Library, Bankipore* (Hyderabad: Dāirat'ul Ma'ārif'l-Osmānia, 1948), comprising the following:

Istikhrāj al-awtār fi'l-dā'irah
Ifrād al-maqāl fī amr al-ḍalāl
Tamhīd al-mustaqarr lī taḥqīq ma'na'l-mamarr
Rāshikāt al-Hind

——— *Das Vorwort zur Drogenkunde des Beruni*, trans. and with preface by Max Meyerhof, Berlin: J. Springer, 1932.

Ritter, H., "Al-Bīrūnī's Übersetzung des Yoga-Sūtra des Patañjali," *Oriens*, 9:165–200 (1956).

Validi Togan, A. Z., *Biruni's Picture of the World*, in *Memoirs of the Archeological Survey of India*, vol. 53 (Calcutta, 1937–38).

(*Secondary Sources*)

Ahmad, Z., "al-Bīrūnī, his life and his works," *Islamic Culture* (Hyderabad–Deccan), 5:343–351 (1931).

——— "al-Bīrūnī's researches in trigonometry," *Islamic Culture* (Hyderabad–Deccan), 6:363–369 (1932).

Barani, S. H., "al-Bīrūnī's scientific achievements," *Indo-Iranica* (Calcutta), 5:37–48 (1952).

——— "Kitabut-taḥdid (an unpublished masterpiece of al-Biruni on astronomical geography)," *Islamic Culture* (Hyderabad–Deccan), 3:165–177 (1957).

al-Biruni Commemoration Volume, Calcutta: Iran society, 1951.

Boilot, D. J., "L'Œuvre d'al-Bērūnī. Essai bibliographique," *Institut Dominicain d'Etudes Orientales du Caire, Mélanges* (Cairo), 2:161–256 (1955).

Clément-Mullet, J. J., "Pesanteur spécifique de diverses substances minérales, procédé pour l'obtenir d'après Abou'l Raihan Albirouny. Extrait de l'Ayin Akbery," *Journal Asiatique* (Paris) 11:379–406 (1858).

Dehkhodā, 'Alī Akbar, *Sharḥ-i ḥāl-i nābighi-yi shahīr-i Īrān Abū Raiḥān Muḥammad ibn Aḥmad Khwārazmī-i Bīrūnī*, Tehran: Majlis Press, 1945.

Haschmi, M. J., *Die Quellen des Steinbuches des Bērūnī*, Bonn: Druck von C. Schülze, 1935.

Kennedy, E. S., and A. Muruwwa, "Bīrūnī on the solar equation," *Journal of Near Eastern Studies*, 17:112–121 (1958).

Krenkow, F., "Abu'R-Raiḥan al-Beruni," *Islamic Culture* (Hyderabad–Deccan), 6:528–534 (1932).

Leslie, M., "Bīrūnī on rising times and daylight lengths," *Centaurus* (Copenhagen), 5:121–141 (1957).

Memon, M. M., "al-Beruni and his contribution to medieval Muslim geography," *Islamic Culture* (Hyderabad–Deccan), 33:213–218 (October 1959).

Meyerhof, M., "The article on aconite from al-Bīrūnī's Kitāb aṣ-Ṣaidana," *Islamic Culture* (Hyderabad–Deccan), 19:323–328 (1945).

——— "Etudes de pharmacologie arabe tirées de manuscrits inédits," *Bulletin de l'Institut d'Egypt* (Cairo), 22:133–152 (1939–40).

Mieli, A., *Pagine di storia della chimica*, Rome: Casa Editrice "Leonardo da Vinci," 1922.

Minorsky, A., (trans.), *Ḥudūd al-'ālam*, E. J. W. Gibb Memorial Series, No. XI, (London: Oxford University Press, 1937).

Naficy, Sa'īd, "Āthār-i chāpshudih-i Abū Raiḥān," *Indo-Iranica* (Calcutta), 5:1–4 (1952).

Pines, S., "La Théorie de la terre à l'époque d'al-Biruni," *Journal Asiatique* (Paris), 244:301–306 (1956).

de Sacy, A. I. S., *Chrestomathie arabe*, Paris: Imprimerie Impériale, 1806.

Ṣafā, Dhabīḥallāh, "Barkhī az naẓarhā-yi falsafī-yi Abū Raiḥān wa mukhtaṣarī dar munāqishāt-i 'ilmī-yi ū wa Ibn-i Sīnā," *Indo–Iranica* (Calcutta), 5:5–12 (1952).

Schoy, C., "Original Studien aus al-Bīrūnī's al-Qanūn al-Mas'ūdī," *Isis*, 5:51–74 (1923).

Suter, H. and E. Wiedemann, "Über al-Biruni und seine Schriften," *Beiträge zur Geschichte der Naturwissenschaften. Sitzungsberichten der physikalisch-medizinischen Sozietät in Erlangen*, no. 1–69, Erlangen: Kommissionsverlag von Max Mencke, 1902–1929.

Validi Togan, A. Z., "al-Bīrūnī wa ḥarikati 'arz," *Islam Tetkikleri Enstitüsü Dergisi* (Istanbul), 1:90–94 (1953).

——— "Islam and the science of geography," *Islamic Culture* (Hyderabad–Deccan), 8:511–528 (1934).

Wilczynski, J. Z., "On the presumed Darwinism of Alberuni eight hundred years before Darwin," (pt. 4) *Isis*, 50:459–466 (December 1959).

Yusuf Ali, A., "al Biruni's India," *Islamic Culture* (Hyderabad–Deccan) 1:31–35, 223–230, 473–487 (1927).

Ibn Sīnā
(*Primary Sources*)

Holmyard, E. J., trans., *Avicennae de congelatione et conglutinatione Lapidum*, Paris: Paul Geuthner, 1927.

von Horten, M., trans., *Die Metaphysik Avicennas. Metaphysik: enthaltend die Metaphysik, Theologie, Kosmologie und Ethik*, Halle a.S.: Rudolf Haupt, 1909.

Ibn Sīnā, *Aḥwāl al-nafs. Risālah fi'l-nafs wa baqā'uhu wa ma'āduhu*, ed. Fu'ād al-Ahwānī, Cairo: Dār al-Iḥyā' al-Kutub al-'arabīyah, 1952.

——— *Avicenna on Theology*, trans. A. J. Arberry, London: John Murray, 1952.

——— *Avicenna's De Anima*, ed. F. Rahman, London: Oxford University Press, 1959.

——— *Avicenna's Psychology*, trans. F. Rahman, London: Oxford University Press, 1952.

——— *Dānishnāma-yi 'alā'ī*, vol. I, ed. Aḥmad Khurāsānī, Tehran: Markazī Press, 1315 (1936).

——— *Dānishnāma-yi 'alā'ī (Ilāhīyāt)*, ed. Muḥammad Mo'in, Tehran: Anjuman-i āthār-i millī, 1331 (1952).

——— *Dānishnāma-yi 'alā'ī (Ṭabī'īyāt)*, ed. Sayyid Muḥammad Mishkāt, Tehran: Anjuman-i āthār-i millī, 1331 (1952).

——— *al-Fawā'id al-durrīyah*, comprising *al-Risālat al-'arshīyah* and *Risālah sirr al-qadar*, trans. Ḍiyā' al-Dīn Durrī, Tehran Markazī Press, 1318 (1939).

——— *Ḥayy ibn Yaqẓān*, ed. Aḥmad Amīn, Cairo: Dār al-ma'ārif Press, 1952.

——— *Ḥayy ibn Yaqẓān*, trans. A. M. Goichon, Paris: A. Maisonneuve, 1959.

——— *al-Ishārāt wa'l-tanbīhāt (Ṭabī'īyāt, Ilāhīyāt)*, trans. Naṣrallāh Taqawī, Tehran: Majlis Press, 1937.

——— *al-Ishārāt wa'l-tanbīhāt*, with the commentary of Naṣīr al-Dīn al-Ṭūsī, 3 vols., ed. Sulaimān Dunyā, Cairo: Dār al-ma'ārif, 1959.

——— *Jāmi' al-badāyi'*, Cairo: 1335 (1916).

——— *Kunūz al-mu'azzimīn*, ed. Jālal al-Dīn Homā'ī, Tehran: Anjuman-i āthār-i millī, 1331 (1952).

——— *Le Livre de science*, trans. M. Achena et H. Massé, 2 vols., Paris: Les Belles Lettres, 1955–1958.

——— *Le Livre des directives et remarques (Kitāb al-Išārāt wa l-Tanbīhāt)*, trans. with introduction and notes by A. M. Goichon, Beirut: Commission Internationale pour la Traduction des Chefs d'œuvres, 1951.

——— *Majmū'at Ibn Sīnā al-kubrā fi'l-'ulūm al-rūḥānīyah*, Damascus: Madāris Press (n.d.).

——— *Majmū'at al-rasā'il*, Cairo, Kurdistān al-'Ilmīyah Press, 1328 (1910).

——— *Majmū' rasā'il al-Shaikh al-Ra'īs* (Hyderabad: Dairatu'l Ma'ārif'l-Osmānia, 1935), comprising the following:

Risālat al-fi'l wa'l-infi'āl
Risālah fī dhikr asbāb al-ra'd
Risālah fī sirr al-qadar
al-Risālat al-'arshīyah fi'l-tawḥīd
Risālah fi'l-baḥth 'ala'l-dhikr
Risālah fi'l-mūsīqā

——— *Manṭiq al-m(a)shriqīyīn*, Cairo: Salafīyah Press, 1328 (1910).

Ibn Sīnā, *Mi'rāj-nāmah*, ed. Mahdī Bayānī, Tehran: Anjuman-i dūstdārān-i kitāb, 1331 (1952).

——— *Mi'yār al-'uqūl*, ed. Jalāl al-Dīn Homā'ī, Tehran: Anjuman-i āthār-i millī, 1331 (1952).

——— *al Najāt*, Cairo: Muḥyī al-Dīn al-Kurdī Press, 1938.

——— *Panj risālah*, ed. Ehsan Yarshater, Tehran: Anjuman-i āthār-i millī, 1332 (1953), comprisng the following:

Risālah fi'l-lughah
Tafsīr sūrat al-tawḥīd
Tafsīr sūrat al-falaq
Tafsīr sūrat al-nās
Risālat ba'ḍ al-afāḍil

——— "Le Poème de l'âme," trans. H. Massé, *La Revue du Caire* (Cairo), 27:7–9 (1951).

——— *Poème de la médecine-urğūza fi'ṭ-ṭibb*, ed. and trans., H. Jahier et A. Noureddine, Paris: Les Belles Lettres, 1956.

——— *Psychologie v Jehe díle aš-Šifā'*, 2 vols., ed. and trans. J. Bakoš, Prague: Académie Tchécoslovaque des Sciences, 1956.

——— *Qurāḍa-yi ṭabī'īyāt*, ed. Ghulâm Ḥusain Ṣadīqī, Tehran: Anjuman-i āthār-i millī, 1332 (1953).

——— *Rāhnamā-yi ḥikmat*, trans. Ḍiyā' al-Dīn Durrī, Tehran: Ḥaidarī Press, 1372 (1952).

——— *Risālah aḍḥawīyah*, ed. Sulaimān Dunyā, Cairo: I'timād Press, 1949.

——— *Risālah faiḍ-i ilāhī*, trans. Ḍiyā' al-Dīn Durrī, Tehran: Markazī Press, 1318 (1939).

——— *Risālah fi'l-'ishq*, trans. E. L. Fackenheim, *Medieval Studies* (Toronto), 7:208–228 (1945).

——— *Risālat al-iksīr*, ed. A. Ateş, Türkiyat Mecmuasi, 1953.

——— *Risālah dar ḥaqīqat wa kaifīyat-i silsila-yi mawjūdāt wa tasalsul-i asbāb wa musabbabāt*, ed. Mūsā 'Amīd, Tehran: Anjuman-i āthār-i millī, 1331 (1952).

——— *Risāla-yi jawdīyah*, ed. Maḥmūd Najmābādī, Tehran: Anjuman-i āthār-i millī, 1330 (1951).

——— *Risāla-yi nafs*, ed. Mūsā 'Amīd, Tehran: Anjuman-i āthār-i millī, 1331 (1952).

——— *al-Shifā'* (*Ṭabī'īyāt* and *Ilāhīyāt*) lithograph, Tehran: 1303–1305 (1885–1887).

——— *Tis' rasā'il* (Cairo: Hindīyah Press, 1908), comprising the following:

Fi'l-ṭabī'īyāt min 'uyūn al-ḥikmah
Fi'l-ajrām al-'ulwīyah
Fi'l-quwwat al-insānīyah wa idrākātihā
Fi'l-ḥudūd
Fī aqsām al-'ulūm al-'aqlīyah
Fī ithbāt al-nubuwwah wa ta'wīl rumūzihim wa amthālihim
al-Nairūzīyah fī ma'āni'l-ḥurūf al-hijā'īyah
Fil-'ahd
Fī 'ilm al-akhlāq

——— *A Treatise on the Canon of Medicine, Incorporating a Translation of the First Book by O. C. Gruner*, London: Luzac, 1930.

——— *al-'Urjūzah fi'l-ṭibb*, Paris: al-Faransiyah Jan Japi wa A. Nūreddīn, 1907.

Ibn Sīnā, *'Uyūn al-ḥikmah*, ed. 'Abd al-Raḥmān Badawī, Cairo: L'Institut Français d'Archéologie Orientale, 1954.

von Mehren, A. F., *Traités mystiques d'Abou Ali al-Hosain b. Abdallah b. Sīnā ou d'Avicenne; texte arabe avec l'explication en français*, Leiden: E. J. Brill, 1889–1891.

Naṣīr al-Dīn al-Ṭūsī, Khwājah, *Sharḥ al-ishārāt*, 3 vols. Tehran: Ḥaidarī Press, 1378 (1958).

(*Secondary Sources*)

al-Ahwānī, Fu'ād, *Ibn Sīnā*, Cairo, Dār al-Ma'ārif Press, 1958.

——— "La Théorie de la connaissance et la psychologie d'Avicenne," *La Revue du Caire* (Cairo), 27:23–43 (1951).

Akhtar, K. A. M., "A tract of Avicenna," *Islamic Culture* (Hyderabad–Deccan), 9:218–235 (1935).

Alonso, M., "El 'Liber de causis'," *Al-Andalus* (Granada–Madrid), 9:43–69 (1944).

d'Alverny, M. T., "Anniya-Anitas," in *Mélanges offerts à Etienne Gilson*, Paris: J. Vrin, 1959.

'Amīd, M., *Essai sur la psychologie d'Avicenne*, Geneva: A. Kundig, 1940.

Anawati, G. C., *Essai de bibliographie avicennienne*, Cairo: Edition al-Maaref, 1950.

Anawati, M. M., "La Tradition manuscrite orientale de l'œuvre d'Avicenne," *La Revue Thomiste* (Paris), 51:415–440 (1951).

Avicenna Commemoration Volume, Calcutta: Iran Society, 1956.

Ben Yahia, B., "Avicenne médecin. Sa vie, son œuvre," *La Revue d'Histoire des Sciences* (Paris), 5:350–353 (1952).

Bloch, E., *Avicenna und die aristotelische Linke*, Berlin: Rütten and Loening, 1952.

Brown, J. W., *Enquiry into the Life and Legend of Michael Scott*, Edinburgh: D. Douglas, 1897.

Carra de Vaux, B., *Avicenne*, Paris: F. Alcan, 1900.

——— "La kacidah d'Avicenne sur l'âme," *Journal Asiatique* (Paris), 14:157–173 (1899).

Corbin, H., *Avicenna and the Visionary Recital*, trans. W. Trask, New York: Pantheon, 1960.

——— *Avicenne et le récit visionnaire*, 3 vols., Tehran–Paris: Institut Franco-Iranien and A. Maisonneuve, 1952–54.

Cruz Hernandez, M., *La metafísica de Avicena*, Granada: Universidad de Granada, 1949.

——— *Sobre la metafísica de Avicena. Textos anotados*, Madrid: Revista de Occidente, 1950.

Ergin, O., *Ibni Sina Bibliografyasi*, Istanbul: Osman Yalsin Matbaasi, 1956.

d'Erlanger, R., *La Musique arabe*, vol. II, Paris: Paul Geuthner, 1935.

Forget, J., "Un Chapitre inédit de la philosophie d'Avicenne, *La Revue Néoscolastique* (Louvain), 1:19–38 (1894).

Gardet, L., "Avicenne et le problème de sa 'philosophie orientale,' " *La Revue du Caire* (Cairo), 27:13–22 (1951).

——— *La Connaissance mystique chez Ibn Sīnā et ses présupposés philosophiques*, Cairo: Institut Français d'Archéologie Orientale du Caire, 1952.

Gardet, L., "En honneur du millénaire d'Avicenne," *La Revue Thomiste* (Paris), 51:333–345 (1951).

——— "L'Experience mystique selon Avicenne," *La Revue du Caire* (Cairo), 27:56–67 (1951).

——— "La Mystique avicennienne," *La Revue Thomiste* (Paris), 45:693–742 (1939).

——— *La Pensée religieuse d'Avicenne* (*Ibn Sina*), Paris: J. Vrin, 1951.

——— "Quelques aspects de la pensée avicennienne dans ses rapports avec l'orthodoxie musulmane," *La Revue Thomiste* (Paris), 45:537–575 (1939).

Gawharīn, Sayyid Ṣādiq, *Ḥujjat al-Ḥaqq Abū 'Alī Sīnā*, Tehran: Iran Bookshop, 1331 (1952).

Ghanī, Qāsim, *Ibn Sīnā*, Tehran: Farhangistān Press, 1936.

al-Ghazzālī, Abū Ḥāmid, *Maqāṣid al-falāsifah*, Cairo: Dār al-Ma'ārif Press, 1961.

Ghurābah, Ḥammūdah, *Ibn Sīnā bain al-dīn wa'l-falsafah*, Cairo: Islamīyah Press, 1949.

Gilson, E., *Avicenne et le point de départ de Duns Scot*, from *Extrait des Archives d'Histoire Doctrinale et Littéraire du Moyen Age*, T. 2, 1927.

——— "L'Etude des philosophies arabes et son rôle dans l'interprétation de la scolastique," *Proceedings of the Sixth International Congress of Philosophy* (Harvard University, 1926), New York: Longmans Green, 1927, pp. 592–596.

——— "Les Sources gréco-arabes de l'augustinisme avicennisant," *Archives d'Histoire Doctrinale et Littéraire du Moyen Age*, Paris, 4:5–149 (1929).

Goichon, A. M., *La Distinction de l'essence et de l'existence d'après Ibn Sina* (*Avicenne*), Paris: Desclée, de Brouwer, 1937.

——— *Lexique de la langue philosophique d'Ibn Sina* (*Avicenne*), Paris: Desclée, de Brouwer, 1938.

——— *La Philosophie d'Avicenne et son influence en Europe médiévale*, Paris: A. Maisonneuve, 1944.

——— "L'Unité de la pensée avicennienne," *Archives Internationales d'Histoire des Sciences*, Paris, nos. 20–21, 1952, pp. 290–308.

——— *Vocabulaires comparés d'Aristote et d'Ibn Sina*, Paris: Desclée, de Brouwer, 1939.

Ḥā'irī-i Māzandarānī, 'Allāmah Mīrzā Ṣāliḥ, *Ḥikmat-i Bū 'Alī*, 3 vols., Tehran: Shirkat-i Sahāmī-yi Chāp, 1335–1337 (1956–1958).

Ḥaqq al-Yaqīn, Sayyid, *Sharḥ-i ḥaqq al-yaqīnī-yi Shifā'-i Bū 'Alī*, Tehran: Sa'ādat-i Bashar Press, 1316 (1937).

Hırschberg, J. and J. Lippert, *Die Augenheilkunde des Ibn Sina*, Leipzig: von Veit, 1902.

Homā'ī, Jalāl al-Dīn, "Ibn Sīnā," *Mihr*, 5:25–32, 147–154, and 249–257 (1316 [1937]).

von Horten, M., "Avicennas Lehre von Regenbogen nach seinem Werk al-Shifā'," *Meteorologische Zeitschrift*, Berlin, 11:533–544 (1913).

Houben, J., S. J., "Avicenna and mysticism," *Indo-Iranica*, 6:1–18 (1953).

Ibn Gabirol, *Fons Vitae*, ed. C. Baumker, Monasterii: Druck und Verlag der Aschendorffachen Buchhandlung, 1895.

Jazā'irī, Sayyid Ni'matallāh, *Sharḥ-i 'ainīya-yi Ibn-i Sīnā*, ed. Ḥusain 'Alī Maḥfūẓ, Tehran: Ḥaidarī Press, 1954.

al-Juzjānī, Abū 'Ubaid, *Sarguzasht-i Ibn-i Sīnā*, trans. Sa'īd Naficy, Tehran: Anjuman-i dūstdārān-i kitāb, 1331 (1952).

Kaiwān, Shaikh 'Abbās 'Alī, *Kunū al-fawā'id* (lithograph), Tehran: 1308 (1890),

Karam, Y., "La Vie spirituelle d'après Avicenne," *La Revue du Caire* (Cairo). 27:44–55 (1951).

al-Kāshī, Yaḥyā ibn Aḥmad, *Aperçu sur la biographie d'Avicenne*, edited by Fu'ād al-Ahwānī, Cairo: Institut Français d'Archéologie Orientale du Caire, 1952.

Ley, H., *Avicenna*, Berlin: Aufbau Verlag, 1953.

Lokotsch, K., *Ein Beitrag zur Geschichte des Mathematik. Avicenna als Mathematiker*, Bonn: Phil. Diss. v. 28, 1912.

Madkour, I., "Avicenne et l'alchimie," *La Revue du Caire* (Cairo), 27:120–129 (1951).

——— *L'Organon d'Aristote dans le monde arabe, ses traductions, son étude et ses applications*, Paris: Les Presses Modernes, 1934.

Mahdavī, Yaḥyā, *Bibliographie d'Ibn Sīnā*, Tehran: Bank Millī Press, 1954.

Massignon, L., "Avicenne et les influences orientales," *La Revue du Caire* (Cairo), 27:10–12 (1951).

——— "La Philosophie orientale d'Ibn Sīnā et son alphabet philosophique," *Mémorial Avicenne*, 4:1–18 (Cairo: Institut Français d'Archéologie Orientale du Caire, 1952).

von Mehren, A. F., "L'Allégorie mystique Hāy ben Yaqzān," *Le Muséon* (Louvain) 5:411–426 (1885).

——— "L' Oiseau, traité mystique d'Avicenne," *Le Muséon* (Louvain), 6:383–393 (1887).

——— "La Philosophie d'Avicenne," *Le Muséon* (Louvain), 1:389–409, 506–522 (1883).

——— "Les Rapports de la philosophie d'Avicenne avec l'Islam," *Le Muséon* (Louvain), 2:460–471, 561–574 (1883).

——— "La Traité d'Avicenne sur le destin," *Le Muséon* (Louvain), 4:35–50 (1885).

——— "Vues d'Avicenne sur l'astrologie et le destin," *Le Muséon* (Louvain), 3:383–403 (1884).

——— "Vues théosophiques d'Avicenne," *Le Muséon* (Louvain), 4:594–599 (1885); 5:52–67 (1886).

Meyer, E. H. F., *Geschichte der Botanik*, vol. III, Königsberg: Gebrüder Bomtäger, 1856.

Millénaire d'Avicenne, Congrès de Bagdad, Cairo: Imprimerie Misr S. A. E., 1952.

Mishkāt, Sayyid Muḥammad, "Muqaddimah bar risāla-yi 'ishq-i Bū 'Alī," *Mihr*, 2:155–159, 233–237, 313–320, 376–382 (1321 [1942]).

Mo'in, Muḥammad, "Ḥikmat-i ishrāq wa farhang-i Īrān," *Āmuzish wa Parwarish* (Tehran), 24: no. 2, 1–8, no. 3, 9–16, no. 4, 17–24, no. 5, 25–32, no. 6, 33–40 (1328 [1949]); no. 7, 9–16, no. 8, 8–19 (1329 [1950]).

Muid Khan, A., "Some aspects of the Arabic writings of the philosopher Ibn Sina," *Islamic Culture* (Hyderabad–Deccan), 28:27–42 (1951).

Munk, S., *Mélanges de philosophie juive et arabe*, Paris: A. Frank, 1859.

Naficy, Sa'īd, *Avicenna: His Life, Works, Thought and Time*, Tehran: Danesh Bookstore, 1333 (1954).

Najātī, M., *al-Idrāk al-ḥissī 'ind Ibn Sīnā*, Cairo: Dār al-Ma'ārif Press, 1948.

Nallino, A., "Filosofia 'orientale' od 'illuminativa' d'Avicenna," *Rivista degli studi orientali* (Rome), 10:367–433 (1925).

Nasr, S. H., "Cosmologies of Aristotle and Ibn Sina," *Pakistan Philosophical Journal* (Lahore), 3:13–28 (January 1960).

Ozden, A. M., "Avicenne médecin," *La Revue du Caire* (Cairo), 27:107–119 (1951).

Pārsīnizhād, A., *Ibn-i Sīnā*, Arāk: Farwardīn Press, 1332 (1953).

Pines, S., "Etudes sur Awḥad al-Zamān Abu'l-Barakāt al-Baghdādī," *La Revue des Etudes Juives* (Paris), 3:3–64 (1938); 4:1–33 (1938).

——— "La 'Philosophie orientale' d'Avicenne et sa polémique contre les Bagdadiens," *Archives d'Histoire Doctrinale et Littéraire du Moyen Age* (Paris), 27:5–37 (1952).

Pope, A. U., "Avicenna and his cultural background," *Bulletin of the New York Academy of Medicine*, 31:318–333 (1955).

al-Rāzī, Fakhr al-Dīn, *al-Mabāḥith al-mashriqīyah*, Hyderabad–Deccan: Dā'iratu'l Ma'ārif'l-Osmānia, 1343 (1924).

Ronald-Gosselin, M. D., *Le "De Ente et Essentia" de St. Thomas d'Aquin*, Le Saulchoir: Bibliothèque Thomiste, 1926.

——— "Sur les relations de l'âme et du corps d'après Avicenne," *Mélanges Mandonnet*, 2 vols., Paris: J. Vrin, 1930, II, 47–54.

Ruska, J., "Avicennas Verhältnis zur Alchemie," *Fortschritte der Medizin* (Berlin), 52:836–837 (1934).

——— "Die Alchemie des Avicenna," *Isis*, 21:14–51 (1934).

Ṣafā, Dhabīḥallāh, "al-Ḥikmat al-m(a)shriqīyah, "*Mihr* (Tehran), 8:33–38 (1331 [1952]).

Saliba, Dj., *Etude sur la métaphysique d'Avicenne*, Paris: Les Presses Universitaires de France, 1926.

Sauter, C., *Avicennas Bearbeitung der aristotelischen Metaphysik*, diss., Munich, 1904; Freiburg: Herder, 1912.

Sayili, A., "Ibni Sīnā' nin ilim zihniyeti (The scientific method of Ibn Sina)," *Türk Tarih Kurumu Basimevi* (Ankara), 12:145–152 (1954).

Siāssī, 'Alī Akbar, "Nafs wa badan wa rābiṭa-yi ānhā bā yikdīgar dar naẓar-i Ibn-i Sīnā wa dīgarān," *La Revue de la Faculté des Lettres* (Université de Téhéran), 1:12–32 (1332 [1953]).

——— "Naẓar-i 'irfānī-yi Ibn-i Sīnā dar ḥuṣūl-i ma'rifat wa wuṣūl-i bi ḥaqq," *La Revue de la Faculté des Lettres* (Université de Téhéran), 1:1–17 (1333 [1954]).

——— *La Psychologie d'Avicenne et ses analogies dans la psychologie moderne*, Tehran: University Press, 1954.

Smith, S. J. C., "Avicenna and the possibles," *New Scholasticism*, 17:340–357 (1943).

Soubiran, A., *Avicenne prince des médecins*, Paris: Librairie Lipschutz, 1935.

Suhrawardī, Shihāb al-Dīn, *Opera Metaphysica et Mystica*, 2 vols., ed. with introduction by H. Corbin; vol. I (Istanbul: Bibliotheca Islamica 16, 1945); vol. II (Tehran–Paris: Institut Franco-Iranien, A. Maisonneuve, 1952); Tehran: Imperial Iranian Academy of Philosophy, 1977.

Ṭāliqānī, Sayyid Maḥmūd, "Tarjuma-yi yikī az mabāḥith-i ṭabī'īyāt az kitāb-i Shifā'," *Āmuzish wa Parwarish*, 12:40–52 (1321 [1942]); 13:34–49 (1322 [1943]), 14:435–441 (1323 [1944]).

Théry, G., *Tolède, grande ville de la renaissance médiévale*, Oran: Heintz frères, 1944.

al-Ṭuraiḥī, Muḥammad Kāẓim, *Ibn Sīnā (Avicenna)*, Najaf: al-Zahrā' Press, 1950.

Unver, A. S., "Supplément aux commentaires et Imitations de l'"Elégie Spirituelle' d'Avicenne," *La Revue du Caire* (Cairo), 27:166–169 (1951).

Vajda, G., "Les Notes d'Avicenne sur la 'Théologie d'Aristote'," *La Revue Thomiste* (Paris), 51:346–406 (1951).

Wickens, G. M., ed., *Avicenna, Scientist and Philosopher: a Millenary Symposium*, London: Luzac, 1952.

Wiedemann, E., "Avicennas Schrift über ein von ihm ersonnenes Beobachtungsinstrument," *Acta Orientalia* (Leiden), 5:81–167 (1926).

——— "Einleitung zu dem astronomischen Teil des Kitāb al-Shifā' (Werk der Genesung) von Ibn Sīnā," *Sitzungsberichte der Physikalisch-medizinischen Sozietät in Erlangen*, 58–59:225–237 (1926–27).

——— Über ein von Ibn Sīnā (Avicenna) hergestelltes Beobachtungsinstrument," *Zeitschrift für Instrumentkunde* (Berlin), 45:269–275 (1925).

Wilczynski, J., "Contribution oubliée d'Ibn Sina à la théorie des êtres vivants," *Archives Internationales d'Histoire des Sciences* (Paris), no. 33 (1954), pp. 35–45.

Winter, M., *Über Avicennas Opus Egregium de Anima*, Munich: C. Wolf & Sohn, 1903.

Wolfson, H. A., "The amphibolous terms in Aristotle, Arabic philosophy and Maimonides," *Harvard Theological Review*, 31:151–173 (1938).

——— "Goichon's three books on Avicenna's philosophy," *Moslem World*, 31:29–38 (1941).

Supplementary Bibliography

Since we prepared the bibliography for the first edition of this book, many works have appeared which have a bearing on the subject with which it deals. This is particularly so in the case of works on al-Bīrūnī, to whom numerous studies have been devoted since 1973 when a worldwide celebration was held to commemorate the millennium of his birth. In the supplementary bibliography which follows, we have sought to list the most important works which have been written in the East and the West since the compilation of the main bibliography on various cosmological aspects of Islamic doctrines, as well as on those facets of the writings and teachings of the Ikhwān al-Ṣafā', al-Bīrūnī and Ibn Sīnā which touch upon cosmology and the study of nature. The supplementary bibliography is divided into four sections as in the main bibliography, but because of the small number of primary sources which have appeared during this period the sections on the Ikhwān, al-Bīrūnī and Ibn Sīnā have not been further divided into primary and secondary sources.

GENERAL

Anawati, G.C., *Etudes de philosophie musulmane*, Paris: J. Vrin, 1974.

Ardalan, N., and L. Bakhtiyar, *The Sense of Unity: The Sufi Tradition in Persian Architecture*, Chicago and London: The University of Chicago Press, 1973.

Arkoun, M., *L'Humanisme arabe au IVe-Xe siècle: Miskawayh, philosophe et historien*, Paris: J. Vrin, 1982.

Arnaldez, R., L. Massignon, and A.P. Youschkevitch, "*La science arabe*," R. Taton (ed.), *Histoire générale des sciences. I.,La Science antique et médiévale*, Paris: Presses Universitaires de France, 1957, 440–525.

Baffioni, C., *Atomismo e antiatomismo nel pensiero islámico*, Naples: Istituto Universitari Orientale, 1982.

Bakar, O., "The Question of Methodology in Islamic Science," *Muslim Education Quarterly*, 21: 16–30 (1984).

Bausani, A., "Cosmologia e religione nell'Islam," *Scientia*, 108: 723–767 (1973).

Burckhardt, T., *Alchemy, Science of the Cosmos, Science of the Soul*, trans. W. Stoddart, London: Stuart and Watkins, 1967: also Baltimore: Penguin Books, 1971.

______ *Art of Islam, Language and Meaning*, trans. J.P. Hobson, London: World of Islam Publishing Company and Thorsons Publishers Ltd., 1976.

______ *Mirror of the Intellect*. ed. W. Stoddart, Cambridge: Islamic Text Society and Albany (N.Y.): State University of New York Press, 1987.

Corbin, H. (with the collaboration of S.H. Nasr and O. Yahya), *Histoire de la philosophie islamique*, Paris: Gallimard, 1986.

______ *Cyclic Time and Ismaili Gnosis*, London: Kegan Paul, 1983.

______ *En Islam iranien*, 4 vols., Paris: Gallimard, 1971–1972.

Craig, W.L., *The Kalam Cosmological Argument*, London: McMillan Press, 1979.

Critchlow, K., *Islamic Patterns, An Analytical and Cosmological Approach*, London: Thames and Hudson, 1976.

Cruz Hernández, M., *Historia del pensamiento en el mundo islamico.* 2 vols., Madrid: Alianza Editorial, 1981.

______ *La filosofia árabe*, Madrid: Revista de Occidente, 1963.

Daffa, A. and Stroyls, J.J., *Studies in the Exact Sciences in Medieval Islam*, Chichester: Wiley, 1984.

Davison, H.A., *Proofs for Eternity, Creation and the Existence of God in Medieval Islamic and Jewish Philosophy*, London and New York: Oxford University Press, 1987.

Dictionary of Scientific Biography, ed. C. Gillispie, New York: Charles Scribner's Son, 1970 on.

Druart, T.A. (ed.), *Arabic Philosophy and the West: Continuity and Interaction*, Washington, D.C.: Center for Contemporary Arab Studies, Georgetown University, 1988.

Dunlop, D.M., *Arabic Science in the West*, Karachi: Pakistan Historical Society, 1958.

Encyclopaedia of Islam, new edition, ed. H.A.R. Gibb, T.H. Kramer, E. Lévi Provençal et al., Leiden: E.J. Brill, 1960 on.

Fakhry, M., *A History of Islamic Philosophy*, New York and London: Columbia University Press, 1983.

La filosofia della natura nel medioevo, Milan: Societa Editrice Vita e Pensiero, 1966.

de Fouchécour, C.H., *La Description de la nature dans la poésie lyrique persane du XI siècle, Inventaire et analyse des thèmes*, Paris: Librairie C. Klincksieck, 1969.

Goichon, A.M., and M.S. Khan, *The Philosophy of Avicenna and Its Influence on Medieval Europe*, Delhi: Motital Banarsidass, 1969.

Goldstein, B.R., *Theory and Observation in Ancient and Medieval Astronomy.* London: Variorum, 1985.

Guénon, R., *Aperçus sur l'ésotérisme islamique et le Taoisme*, Paris: Gallimard, 1973.

Hartner, W., *Oriens-Occidens*, Hildesheim: Georg Olms Verlagsbuchhandlung, 1968.

Hourani, G., *Essays on Islamic Philosophy and Science*, Albany: State University of New York Press, 1978.

Izutsu, T., *The Key Philosophical Concepts in Sufism and Taoism*, 2 vols., Tokyo: The Keio Institute of Cultural and Linguistic Studies, 1966–1967.

Kennedy, E.S., *Studies in the Islamic Exact Sciences*, Beirut: American University of Beirut, 1983.

King, D., *Islamic Mathematical Astronomy*, London: Variorum, 1986.

Kraemer, J.L., "Humanism in the Renaissance of Islam: a preliminary study," *Journal of the American Oriental Society*, 104: 135–164 (1984).

______ *Philosophy in the Renaissance of Islam: Abū Sulaymān al-Sijistānī and His Circle*, Leiden: E.J. Brill, 1986.

Massignon, L., *Opera Minora*, 3 vols., collected, arranged and presented with a bibliography by Y. Moubarac, Beirut: Dar al-Maaref, 1963.

______ *The Passion of al-Hallāj-Mystic and Martyr of Islam*, trans. H. Mason, Princeton: Princeton University Press, 1982.

Mieli, A., *Panorama general de historia de la ciencia, II, El mundo islámico y el occidente medieval cristiano*, Buenos-Aires, Mexico: Espasa-Calpe Argentina, S.A., 1952.

______ *La Science arabe et son rôle dans l'évolution scientifique mondiale*, additional bibliography with subject index by A. Mazahéri, Leiden: E.J. Brill, 1966.

Morewedge, P. (ed.) *Islamic Philosophical Theology*, Albany: State University of New York Press, 1979.

Murata, S., *The Tao of Islam*, Albany: State University of New York Press, 1992.

Naqvi, S.S.N., "The evolution of cosmology in the hands of Muslims up to the time of al-Bīrūnī," *Al-Biruni Commemoration Volume*, Karachi, 1979, 558–577.

Nasr, S.H., *An Annotated Bibliography of Islamic Science*, 3 vols., Tehran: Imperial Iranian Academy of Philosophy, 1975–1991.

______ "Islamic Cosmology", in A.H. Al-Hassan and M. Ahmed (eds.), *Science in Islam*, Paris: UNESCO (forthcoming).

______ *Islamic Science: An Illustrated Study*, London: World of Islam Festival Publishing Company and Thorsons Publishers Ltd., 1976.

______ *Islamic Life and Thought*, Albany: State University of New York Press, 1981.

______ (ed.). *Islamic Spirituality*, New York: Crossroad Publications, 1987.

______ "Life sciences, alchemy and medicine," *The Cambridge History of Iran*, vol. 4, R.N. Frye (ed.), Cambridge: Cambridge University Press, 1975, 396–418.

______ *Knowledge and the Sacred*, Albany: State University of New York, Press, 1989.

______ *Man and Nature, The Spiritual Crisis of Modern Man*, London: Harper Collins, 1989.

______ *The Need for a Sacred Science*, Albany: State University of New York Press, 1993.

______ "Philosophy and Cosmology," *The Cambridge History of Iran*, vol. 4, 419–441.

______ *Science and Civilization in Islam*, new ed., Cambridge, Islamic Text Society, 1987.

______ *Sufi Essays*, London: George Allen and Unwin, 1972; Albany: State University of New York Press, 1991.

______ "Theology, Philosophy and Spirituality," in S.H. Nasr (ed.) *Islamic Spirituality: Manifestations*, New York: 1991, 393–446.

Needleman (ed.), *The Sword of Gnosis*, Baltimore: Penguin Books, 1973.

Netton, I.R., *Allah Transcendent: Studies in the Structure and Semiotics of Islamic Philosophy, Theology and Cosmology*, London: Routledge, 1989.

Pines, S., *Studies in Arabic Versions of Greek Texts and in Mediaeval Science*, Jerusalem: Magnes Press; Leiden: E.J. Brill, 1986.

______ "What was original in Arabic Science?," *Scientific Change*, ed. A.C. Crombie, New York: Heinemann Educational Books, 1963, 181–205.

al-Qazwīnī. *Die Wunder des Himmels und der Erde*. trans. A. Giesse, Stuttgart: Thienemann, 1986.

Rahman, F., "Ibn Sīnā's theory of the God-world relationship," in D.B. Burrell and B. McGinn (eds.), *God and Creation: An Ecumenical Symposiun*, Notre Dame: University of Notre Dame Press, 1990, 38–55.

Rescher, N., *Studies in Arabic Philosophy*, Pittsburgh: Pittsburgh University Press, 1966.

Roszak, T. *Where the Wasteland Ends*, New York: Anchor Books, Doubleday and Company, Inc., 1973.

Sabra, A.I., "The Exact Sciences," *The Genius of Arab Civilization*, 149–163.

Saeed Shaikh, M., *Studies in Muslim Philosophy*, Lahore: Pakistan Philosophical Congress, 1962.

Schuon, F., *Understanding Islam*, trans. D.M. Matheson, London: Unwin Paperbacks, 1981.

______ *Dimensions of Islam*, trans. P.N. Townsend, London: George Allen and Unwin, 1970, paperback, 1976.

______ *Formes et substance dans les religions*, Paris: Dervy-Livres, 1975.

______ *Islam and the Perennial Philosophy*, trans. J.P. Hobson, London: World of Islam Festival Publishing Company and Thorsons Publishers Ltd., 1976.

______ *Logic and Transcendence*, trans., P.N. Townsend, New York: Harper Torchbooks, 1975.

Sezgin, F., *Geschichte des arabischen Schrifttums*, vols. 3–5, Leiden: E.J. Brill, 1970–1974.

Smith, H., *Forgotten Truth, The Primordial Tradition*, New York: Harper and Row, 1976.

Suyūṭī, Jalāl al-Dīn and Heinen, A.M. *Islamic Cosmology: A Study of as-Suyūṭī's al-hay'a as-sanīya fi'l-hay'a as-sunnīya*. Wiesbaden: Steiner, 1982.

Theories and Philosophies of Medicine, Delhi: Institute of History of Medicine and Medical Research, 1962.

Tomlin, E.W.F., *Philosophers of East and West: The Quest for the Meaning of Existence in Eastern and Western Thought*, London: Oak-Tree, 1986.

Ullmann, M., *Islamic Medicine*, Edinburgh: Edinburgh University Press, 1978.

______ *Die Natur-und Geheimwissenschaften im Islam*. Leiden: E.J. Brill, 1972.

Vernet, J. *La cultura hisranoárabe en Oriente y Occidente*. Barcelona: Editorial Ariel, 1978.

______ (ed.) *Estudios sobre historia de la ciencia árabe*. Barcelona: Instituto de Filologia, 1980.

Walzer, R., *Greek into Arabic*, Oxford: Oxford University Press, 1962.

Wiedemann, E., *Aufsätze zur arabischen Wissenschaftgeschichte*. 2 vols., ed. W. Fischer, New York: George Olm Verlag, 1970.

______ *Gesammelte Schriften zur arabischislamischen Wissenschaftsegeschichte*, ed. D. Girke, Frankfurt a.m.: Institut für Geschichte der Arabisch-Islamischen Wissenschaften an der J.W. Goethe-Universität, 1984.

Wolfson, H. A., *The Philosophy of the Kalam*, Cambridge: Harvard University Press, 1976.

Yoshida, S., *The Ontological Weltanschauung of Islam: A Comparative Study of the Concept of Time*, Niigata: Institute of Middle Eastern Studies, 1986.

Zolla, E., *Le meraviglie della natura. Introduzione all'alchimia*. Milan: Bompiani, 1975.

Ikhwān al-Ṣafā'

Bausani, A., *L'enciclopedia dei Fratelli della purità*, Naples: Istituto Universitari Orientale, 1978.

______ "Le dimensioni dell'Universo nel Kitâb Iḫwân aṣ-Ṣafâ'," *Actes 8 Congrès Union europ. arabisants et islamisants*, 1976, 23–28 bis.

______ "Scientific elements in Ismā'īlī thought: the epistles of the Brethren of Purity (Ikhwān al-Ṣafā')", in S.H. Nasr (ed.), *Ismā'īlī Contributions to Islamic Culture*, Tehran: Imperial Iranian Academy of Philosophy, 1977, 23–49.

Bauwens, J., "Les épîtres des Frères Sincères: une imago mundi," *Acta Orientalia Belgica*, 10:7–18 (1966).

______ "Zeventiende Zendbrief van de 'Rasā'il Ikwān aṣ-Ṣafā'.' Over de fysische lichamen," *Orientalia Gandensia*, 1:171–185 (1964).

Blumenthal, D.R., "A comparative table of the Bombay, Cairo and Beirut editions of the *Rasā'il Iḫwān al-Ṣafā'*," *Arabica*, 21:186–203 (1974).

Diwald, S., *Arabische Philosophie und Wissenschaft in der Enzyklopädie Kitāb Ikhwān aṣ-Ṣafā' III. Die Lehre von Seele und Intellekt*. Wiesbaden: Otto Harrassowitz, 1975.

Goodman, L.E., *The Case of the Animals versus Man before the King of the Jinn: a Tenth-Century Ecological Fable of the Pure Brethren of Basra*. Boston: Twayne, 1978.

Halm, H., *Kosmologie und Heilslehre der frühen Ismā'īliya.Eine Studie zur islamischen Gnosis*. Wiesbaden: Franz Steiner, 1978.

Hamdani, A., "The arrangement of the *Rasā'il Ikhwān al-Ṣafā'* and the problem of interpolations," *Journal of Semitic Studies*, 29: 97–110 (1984).

Ikhwān al-Ṣafā', *La disputa de los animales contra el hombre*, trans. E. Tornero Poveda, Madrid: Edition de la Universidad Complutense, 1984.

Marquet, Y., "Coran et création," *Arabica*, 11 (3): 279–285 (1964).

______ "Imāmat, résurrection et hiérarchie chez les Ikhwān al-Ṣafā'," *La Revue des Etudes Islamiques*, 30:490142 (1962).

______ *La philosophie des Ikhwān al-Ṣafā'. De Dieu à l'homme*, Lille: Université de Lille, 1973.

______ "Quelles furent les relations entre 'Jâbir ibn Ḥayyân' et les Iḫwân as-Ṣafā'?", *Studia Islamica*, 64:39–51 (1986).

______ "Sabéens et Iḫwān al-Ṣafā'," *Studia Islamica*, 24:35–80 (1966); and 25:77–109 (1966).

Nasr, S.H., (ed.). *Ismā'īlī Contributions to Islamic Culture*. Tehran: Imperial Iranian Academy of Philosophy, 1977.

Netton, I.R. *Muslim Neoplatonists: An Introduction to the Thought of the Brethren of Purity (Ikhwān al-Ṣafā')*. London: Allen & Unwin, 1982.

Plessner, M., "Beiträge zur islamischen Literaturgeschichte IV: Samuel Miklos Stern, die Ikhwān aṣ-Ṣafā' und die Encyclopedia of Islam," *Israel Oriental Studies*, 2:353–361 (1972).

Shiloah, A., "L'Épître sur la musique des Ikhwān al-Ṣafā'," *La Revue des Etudes Islamiques*, 32:125–162 (1964).

Widengren, G., "The pure brethren and the philosophical structure of their system," *Islam: Past Influence and Present Challenge (in Honor of W.M. Watt)*, Edinburgh: Edinburgh University Press, 1979, 57–69.

AL-BĪRŪNĪ

Ahmad, N., "Some glimpses of al-Bīrūnī as a geographer," *Al-Biruni Commemoration Volume*, Karachi, 1979, 141–148.

Anas, M., "Al-Beruni's mathematics and astronomy," *Afghanistan*, 26i:76–85 (1973).

Arnaldez, R., *Conception et pratique de la science chez Avicenne et Biruni*, Karachi: al-Biruni International Congress (Pakistan), 1973.

______ "La science arabe à travers l'oeuvre de Bīrūnī," *Lumières arabes sur l'occident médiéval*, Paris, 1978, 41–54.

Azkaï, P., *Karname-e-Biruni (Essai Bibliographique) d'après Biruni et Boilot*, Tehran: Ministère de la Culture et des Arts, 1973.

Bausani, A., "Al-Bîrûnî, un genio del x secolo," *Islam: Storia e Civiltà*, 4:5–15 (1985).

______ "Some considerations on three problems of the anti-Aristotelian controversy between al-Bīrūnī and Ibn Sīnā," *Akten VII. Kong. Arabistik (Göttingen 1974)*, 1976, 74–85.

al-Bīrūnī, *Al-Biruni's Book on Pharmacy and Materia Medica*, Hakim Mohammed Said (ed.), Karachi: Hamdard National Foundation, 1973.

______ *The Determination of the Coordinates of Cities (Taḥdīd al-Amākin)*, trans. J. Ali, Beirut: American University of Beirut, 1967.

______ *The Determination of the Coordinates of Positions for the Correction of Distances between Cities*, Beirut: American University of Beirut, 1966.

______ *Fihrist-i kitābhā-yi Rāzī*, ed. and trans. M. Mohaghegh, Tehran: Tehran University Press, 1352 (1973).

______ *Izbrannye Proizvedeniya* (Russian translation of his works), 6 vols., Tashkent: Akademiya Nank Uzbekskoi SSR, 1964 on.

______ *Kitāb al-Jamāhir Fī Ma'rifat al-Jawāhir*, (trans. from Arabic) (*Book of Precious Stones*), Islamabad: Pakistan Hijrah Council, 1989.

______ *Kitāb al-tafhīm li awā'il ṣinā'at al-tanjīm*, new edition by Jalāl al-Dīn Homā'ī, Tehran: Anjuman-i āthār-i millī, 1352 (1973).

______ *Kitāb taḥdīd nihāyāt al-amākin li taṣḥīḥ masāfāt al-masākin*, trans. A. Ārām, Tehran: Tehran University Press, 1352 (1973).

______ *Kitāb taḥdīd nihāyāt al-amākin li taṣḥīḥ masāfāt al-masākin*, ed. P.G. Bulgakov, *Majallat ma'had al-makhṭūṭāt al-'arabiyyah*, Cairo: 1962.

______ *Ṣaydanah*, ed. M. Sotudeh and I. Afshar, Tehran: High Council of Culture and Arts, 1973.

al-Bīrūnī and Ibn Sīnā, *al-As'ilah wa'l-ajwibah* (*Questions and Answers*), *Including the Further Answers of al-Bīrūnī and al-Ma'ṣūmī's Defense of Ibn Sīnā*, S.H. Nasr and M. Mohaghegh (eds.), Tehran: High Council of Culture and Art, 1973. 74–85.

Chelkowski, P.J. (ed.), *The Scholar and the Saint. Studies in Commemoration of Abu'l-Rayhān al-Bīrūnī and Jalāl al-Dīn al-Rūmī*, New York: New York University Press, 1975.

Essays on al-Bīrūnī, Tehran: High Council of Culture and Arts, 1973.

Fakhry, M., "Al-Bīrūnī and Greek philosophy—an essay in philosophical erudition," *Al-Biruni Commemoration Volume*, Karachi, 1979, 344–349.

Habib, K.M., "The 'Kitāb al-Ṣaydanah': structure and approach," *Al-Biruni Commemoration Volume*, 458–473.

Hamarneh, S.K., *Al-Bīrūnī's Book on Pharmacy and Materia Medica*, Karachi: Al-Biruni International Congress (Pakistan), 1973.

______ *Introduction to al-Biruni's Book on Precious Stones and Minerals*, Karachi: Hamdard Foundation, 1988.

Hartner, W., and M. Schramm, "Al-Bīrūnī and the theory of the solar apogee: an example of originality in Arabic Science," *Scientific Change*, ed. A.C. Crombie, New York: Heinemann Educational Books, 1963, 206–218.

Harvey, J.H., "Al-Bīrūnī on plants," *Islamic Quarterly*, 20,21,22: 30–35 (1978).

Haschmi, M.Y., "Die griechischen Quellen des Steinbuches von al-Beruni, *Extrait des annales archéologiques de Syrie*, 15 (2):21–56 (1965).

Heinen, A., "Al-Bīrūnī and Al-Haytham: a comparative study of scientific method," *Al-Biruni Commemoration Volume*, 501–513.

Hermelink, H., "Bestimmung der Himmelsrichtungen aus einer einzigen Schattenbeobachtung nach al-Bīrūnī," *Archiv für Geschichte der Medizin*, 44:329–332 (1960).

Kennedy, E.S., "Al-Bīrūnī's Maqālīd 'ilm al-hay'a," *The Journal of Near Eastern Studies*, 30:308–314 (1971).

______ "Al-Bīrūnī's Masudic Canon," *Al-Abhath*, 24:59–81 (1971).

______ *A Commentary upon Bīrūnī's Kitāb Taḥdīd al-Amākin*, Beirut: American University of Beirut, 1973.

Mahdihassan, S. "Interpreting al-Bīrūnī's observations on Indian alchemy," *Al-Biruni Commemoration Volume*, 524–529.

Maqbul Ahmad, S., "Al-Beruni and the decline of science and technology in medieval Islam, and his contributions to geography with special reference to India," *Afghanistan*, 26ii:91–96 (1973).

Nasr, S.H., *Al-Bīrūnī: An Annotated Bibliography*, Tehran: High Council of Culture and Art, 1973.

______ "Al-Bīrūnī as philosopher," *Al-Biruni Commemoration Volume*, 400–406.

______ *Abū Rayḥān Bīrūnī, Scientist and Scholar Extraordinary*, Tehran: Ministry of Culture and Arts, 1973.

Nowshervi, A.R., "Al-Bīrūnī's contribution to natural sciences," *Al-Biruni Commemoration Volume*, 582–586.

Qadri, M.A.N., "Kitāb al-Jamāhir fī Ma'rifah al-Jawāhir: Al-Bīrūnī's contribution to biological studies and concepts," *Al-Biruni Commemoration Volume*, 587–593.

Qudsi, O., "Al-Bīrūnī's methodology and its resources," *Al-Biruni Commemoration Volume*, 594–604.

Qurbani, A., *Bīrūnī-nāmah*, Tehran: Anjuman-i āthār-i millī, 1353 (1974).

Rosenthal, F., "Al-Biruni between Greece and India," in E. Yarshater (ed.), *Biruni Symposium*, New York: Iran Center, Colunbia University, 1976, 1–12.

Safa, Z., *Al-Biruni, ses oeuvres et ses pensées* (in French), Tehran: Ministère de la Culture et des Arts, 1973.

______ *Al-Biruni, ses oeuvres et ses pensées* (in Persian), Tehran: Ministère de la Culture et des Arts, 1973.

Said, Hakim Mohammad (ed.). *Al-Biruni Commemoration Volume*. Karachi: Hamdard Academy, 1979.

Said, Hakim Mohammad, *Al-Bīrūnī's Book on Pharmacy and Materia Medica*, Karachi: Al-Biruni International Congress (Pakistan), 1973.

Said Khan, A., *The Bibliography of al-Biruni*, trans. A. Habibi, Tehran: High Council of Culture and Art, 1973.

______ *A Bibliography of the Works of al-Beruni*, Kabul: Ministry of Education of Republic of Afghanistan, 1973.

Sayili, A., "Al-Bīrūnī and the history of science," *Al-Biruni Commemoration Volume*, 706–712.

al-Shābī, 'A., *Biographie de Biruni*, trans. P. Azkaï, Tehran: Ministère de la Culture et des Arts, 1973.

al-Shaḥāt, 'A.A., *Abu'l-Rayḥān al-Bīrūnī*, Cairo: Dār al-Ma'ārif, 1968.

Timsfeev, I., *Biruni*, Moscow: Molodaya Gvardiya, 1986.

Youssefi, G.H., "Abu-Reyhan Biruni, a lover of truth," in *Biruni Symposium*, 13–26.

Yusuf, S.M., "Al-Biruni as a mathematician," *Al-Biruni Commemoration Volume*, 713–715.

IBN SĪNĀ

Adivar Adrian, A., "Ibn Sina et alchimie," *Professor Muhammad Shafi' Presentation Volume*, S.M. Abdullah (ed.), Lahore: University of the Punjab, 1955, 1–3.

Anawati, G.C., "Les divisions des sciences intellectuelles d'Avicenne," *Institut Dominicain d'Etudes Orientales du Caire*, (*MIDEO*), 13:323–335 (1977).

Arnaldez, R., "The theory and practice of science according to Ibn Sīnā and al-Bīrūnī," *Al-Biruni Commemoration Volume*, 428–436.

Baratov, R.B., "Ideas of Ibn Sīnā in natural sciences," *Acta Antiqua Academiae Scientiarum Hungaricae*, 29:49–55 (1981).

Bell, J.N. "Avicenna's *Treatise on Love* and the non-philosophical Muslim tradition," *Der Islam*, 63:73–89 (1986).

Brentjes, B. *Ibn Sina (Avicenna): der furstliche Meister aus Buchara*, Leibzig: Teubner, 1979.

______ (ed.), *Avicenna. Ibn-Sina. 980–1036 (Materialen einer wissenschaftlichen Arbeitstagung am 25 und 26.2.-1980)*, 2 vols., Halle/Saale: Martin-Luther Universität, 1980.

Burrell, D.B., "Essence and existence: Avicenna and Greek philosophy," *Institut Dominicain d'Etudes Orientales du Caire* (MIDEO), 17:53–66 (1986).

Campanini, M. "Essenza ed esistenza di Dio in Ibn Sînâ," *Islàm: Storia e Civiltà*, 3:173–179 (1984).

Davidson, H.A., "Alfarabi and Avicenna on the Active Intellect," *Viator*, 3:109–178 (1972).

Dinoshoev, M., M.S. Asimov (ed.), *Naturfilosofiya Ibn Siny*, Dushanbe: Donish, 1985.

Durray, K.S., "Ibn Sīnā's concept of man," *Studies in History of Medicine*, 6:161–194 (1982).

Finianos, Gh., *Les Grandes divisions de l'être "mawjūd" selon Ibn Sīnā*, Fribourg: Editions universitaires, 1976.

Galindo, E., "Anthropologie et cosmogonie chez Avicenne," *Institut des Belles Lettres Arabes*, 22:287–323 (1959).

Gilson, E., *Etudes médiévales*, Paris: J. Vrin, 1986.

Girs, G.F., "Main results of research in the scientific heritage of Abū 'Alī Ibn Sīnā (Avicenna) in the Soviet Union," *Acta Antiqua Academicae Scientiarum Hungaricae*, 29:43–48 (1981).

Gohlman, W.E., *The Life of Ibn Sīnā. A Critical Edition and Annotated Translation*, Albany: State University of New York Press, 1974.

Gutas, D., *Avicenna and the Aristotelian Tradition, Introduction to Reading Avicenna's Philosophical Works*, Leiden: E.J. Brill, 1988.

Hamarneh, S. "Abu 'Ali al-Ḥusayn bin 'Abdallah bin Sina (Avicenna) (980–1037)," in J.R. Hayes (ed.), *The Genius of Arab Civilization: Source of Renaissance*, London: Eurabia, 1983, 196–197.

Haschmi, M.Y., "Die geologischen und mineralogischen Kenntnisse bei Ibn Sīnā," *Zeitschrift der Deutschen morgenländischen Gesellschaft*, 116:44–59 (1966).

Hourani, G., "Ibn Sina: treatise on the secret of destiny," *Muslim World*, 53:138–140 (1963).

Ibn Sīnā (Avicenna), *Avicenna Latinus: Liber de Philosophia Prima sive Scientia Divina I-X*, S. Van Riet (ed.), Louvain: Peeters, 1983.

______ *Avicenna Latinus. Liber tertius naturalium de generatione et corruptione*, G. Verbeke (intro.), ed. S. Van Riet (ed.), Louvain: Peeters, 1988.

______ *Avicenna's Poem on Medicine*, H.C. Krueger (trans. and ed.), Springfield, Ill.: Thomas, 1963.

______ *Das Buch der Genesung der Seele eine philosophische Enzyklopädie Avicennas. II. Serie die Philosophie III. Gruppe und XIII. Teil die Metaphysik, Theologie, Kosmologie und Ethik*, Frankfurt am Main: Minerva B.m.b.H., 1960.

______ Liber de anima, seu sextus de naturalibus, S. Van Riet (ed.), with an introduction on Avicenna's psychological doctrines by G. Verbeke, Leiden: E.J. Brill, 1968.

______ *Le Livre de science*. 2 vols., trans. M. Achena, Paris: Les Belles Lettres/ UNESCO, 1986.

______ *The Metaphysics of Avicenna (ibn Sīnā)*, trans, P. Morewedge, New York: Columbia University Press, 1973.

______ *La Métaphysique du Shifā'*. trans. G.C. Anawati, 2 vols., Paris: J. Vrin, 1978 and 1985.

______ *Qāmūs al-qānūn fi 'l-ṭibb*, New Delhi, Idārah ta'rīkh al-ṭibb wa'l-taḥqīq al-ṭibbī, 1967.

______ *Remarks and Admonitions. Part One: Logic*, Trans. Sh. C. Inati, Toronto: Pontifical Institute of Mediaeval Studies, 1984.

______ *Al-Shifā'*, under the general direction of I. Madkour, Cairo: Wizārat al-ma'ārif al-'umūmīyah, al-idārat al-thiqāfah, 1371 (1951) on.

______ *al-Ta'līqāt*, ed. 'A. Badawī, Cairo: al-Hay'at al-miṣriyat al-'āmmah li'l-kitāb, 1973.

Janssens, J. "Le Dânesh-nâmeh d'Ibn Sînâ: un texte à revoir?", *Bulletin de Philosophie Médiévale*, 28:163–177 (1986).

Kaur, M., "Avicenna: his life, works and impact," *Studies in History of Medicine*, 7:216–235 (1983).

Khan, M.S., "Ibn Sīnā: Philosopher, physician and scientist," *Islamic Culture*, 56:249-264 (1982).

Lambrechts, M-C. "Les 'Lexiques' de la 'Métaphysique d'Avicenne'," *Revue Philosophique du Louvain*, 81:634–637 (1983).

Ley, H., "Ibn Sina (980-1037): Gründe für 1000 Jahre Rückerinnerung," *Deutsche Zeirschrift für Philosophie*, 28:1309–1323 (1980).

Lewis, G.L., "Two alchemical treatises attributed to Avicenna," *Ambix*, 10:41–82 (1962).

Listfeldt, H.G., "Some concepts of matter of Avicenna, Averroes, St. Thomas and Heisenberg," *Aquinas*, 17:310–321 (1974).

Madkour, I., "Avicenne en Orient et en Occident," *Institut Dominicain d'Etudes Orientales du Caire (MIDEO)*, 15:223–230 (1982).

______ "Ibn Sīnā Savant," in G.F. Hourani (ed.), *Essays on Islamic Philosophy and Science*, Albany: State University Press of New York, 1975, 76–82.

______ "Introduction à la Metaphysique du Shifa'," *Mélanges de l'Institut Dominicain d'Etudes Orientales au Caire (MIDEO)* 6:281–308 (1959–1961).

Marmura, M.E., "Avicenna on the division of the sciences in the *Isagoge* of his *Shifā'*," *Journal of the History of Arabic Science*, 4:239–251 (1980).

______ "The metaphysics of efficient causality in Avicenna (Ibn Sina)," in M.E. Marmura (ed.), *Islamic Theology and Philosophy: Studies in Honor of G.F. Hourani*, Albany, State University of New York Press, 1984, 172–187 and 304–305.

Michot, J.R., *La Destinée de l'homme selon Avicenne: le retour à Dieu (ma'ād)*, Louvain: Peeters, 1986.

______ "Les sciences physiques et métaphysiques selon la Risālah fī aqsām al-'ulūm d'Avicenne; essai de traduction critique," *Bulletin de Philosophie Médiévale*, 22:62–73 (1980).

Monteil, V., "Ibn Sina and Avicennism," *Cultures*, 7 iv:186–199 (1980).

Nabi, M.N., "The theory of emanation in the philosophical system of Plotinus and Ibn Sīnā," *Islamic Culture*, 56:233–240 (1982).

Nasr, S.H., "Ibn Sīnā's prophetic philosophy," *Cultures*, 7 iv:165–180 (1980).

Ormos, I., "The theory of humours in Islam (Avicenna"), *Quaderni di Studi Arabi*, 5–6:601–607 (1987-1988).

Sabri, T., "Avicenne philosophe et mystique dans le miroir de trois récit: Ḥayy ibn Yaqẓān, l'Oiseau, Salāmān et Absāl," *Arabica*, 27:257–274 (1980).

Shah, M.H., *The General Principles of Avicenna's Canon of Medicine*, Karachi: Naveed Clinic, 1966.

Stapleton, H.E., R.F. Azo, Hidayat Husain and G.L. Lewis, "Two alchemical treatises attributed to Avicenna," *Ambix*, 10–41–82 (1962).

Tirmizi, S.M.A., "Ibn Sīnā as a scientist," *Studies in History of Medicine*, 5:233–238 (1981).

Ushida, N., *Etude comparative de la psychologie d'Aristote, d'Avicenne et de St. Thomas d'Aquin*, Tokyo: The Keio Institute of Cultural and Linguistic Studies, 1968.

Van Riet, S., "Données biographiques pour l'histoire du shifā' d'Avicenne," *Académie Royale de Belgique: Bulletin de la Classe des Lettres et des Sciences Morales et Politiques*, 66:314–329 (1980).

Yassin, J. al-, "Avicenna's concept of physics," *Bulletin of the College of Arts*, 7:55–62 (1964).

Index

Ibn Buṭlān, 189; *al-Maqālat al-miṣrīyah*, 190
Ibn Ḥajjāj al-Shā'ir, 26
Ibn Khaldūn, 36, n53
Ibn Khallikān, 177, n1
Ibn Masarrah, 83, 278
Ibn Muqaffa', 39
Ibn Nadīm al-Warrāq: *Fihrist*, 13
Ibn Rushd. *See* Averroes
Ibn Shāhūyah, 26
Ibn Sīnā. *See* Avicenna
Ibn Taimīyah, 26, 36, n53
Ibn Ṭufail, 185–186, n22
Ibn Turkah. *See* 'Alī ibn Turkah Iṣpahānī
Ibn Yūnus, 13
Ibn Zar'ah, 26
Ibrāhīm ibn Sīnān, 12
'īd al-aḍḥā, Islamic feast, 35
'īd al-fiṭr, Islamic feast, 35
'īd al-ghadīr, Islamic feast, 35
Idrīs, 13, n28, 15, n33, 34, 35, 75, 132, 239; *see also* Hermes
Ifrād al-maqāl fī amr al-ḍalāl (of al-Bīrūnī), 112
iḥsān, 34
Ikhwān al-Ṣafā' (Brethren of Purity), 12, 13, 21, 25–104, 122, 127, 138, 141, 142, 147, 207, n32, 210, n37, 220, 275, 277–280 passim
ilāhīyāt (metaphysics), 187–188, n26
'illat al-'ilal ("Cause of Causes"), 203
Illuminationist. *See Ishrāqī*
'ilm al-'adad (science of number), 46–51
'ilm al-khawāṣṣ ("science of the elite"), 267
īmān, 34
'Imrān al-Ṣābī, 14
India, 38, 38–39, n62, 66, 80; al-Bīrūnī on, 142–143
India (of al-Bīrūnī), 108, 109, 112, 114, 174
Indus Valley, 125
al-insān al-kāmil (Universal Man), 66, 163
al-Insān al-kāmil (of al-Jīlī), 83, 158
Intellect, 40, 102, 150, 159, 160, 162, 173; Avicenna's concept of, 200–205, 210, 211, 218, 257, 259, 269; First Intellect, 203, 204; Second Intellect, 203; Third Intellect, 203; *see also* Active Intellect; Divine Intellect; Tenth Intellect; Universal Intellect
intellectus materialis, 269
Intelligences, 181, 199, 206, 209, 220, 229, 236, 237, 238, 240, 243, 258, 259, 262, 268, 280; *see also* Tenth Intellect
Isagoge, 42
al-Ishārāt wa'l-tanbīhāt (*The Book of Directives and Remarks*), 180, 181, 194, 263, 264, 266
'ishq (love), 53, 189, 206, 237, 261
Ishrāqī, 2, 10, 19, 21, 38, n60, 89, 115, 185, 190, 195, n53, 196, 243, 263, 276, 278, 279
islām, 34
Ismā'īl al-Zāhid, 178
Ismā'īlī, 17, 19, 20, 21, 27, 29, 30, 36, 83, 115, 182, 209, 275, 278
Ispahān, 179, 180
Israelites, 38–39, n62
Ivanov, V.A., 29

Jābir ibn Ḥayyān, 9, n17, 14, 36, 49, 51, n26, 111, 148, 206, n31, 211, 246, 278
Jābirian alchemy, 90, 149, 247
Jābirian balance, 49
Jābirian corpus, 14, n31, 37, 38
Ja'far al-Ṣādiq (*Imām*), 14, 26
jafr, science of, 210
al-Jāḥiẓ, 39, 111
Jāma-yi Bahādur Khānī, 108, n6
Jāmī, 'Abd al-Raḥmān, 266, n10
Jāmi'at al-jāmi'ah (of the Ikhwān al-Ṣafā'), 37
Jerusalem, 89
Jesus Christ, 31, 32, 83
Jews, 38–39, n62, 117
al-Jīlī, 'Abd al-Karīm, 13, n29, 195, 196; *al-Insān al-kāmil*, 83, 158
jinns, 100, 270
jism (Body), 52, 200
al-jism al-muṭlaq (Absolute Body), 58
Joseph, 32
Judaism, 70
Jundishāpūr, 11, 188
al-Jurjānī, Sayyid Sharīf, 21; *Maṭāli' al-anwār*, 21
al-Juzjānī, Abū 'Ubaid, 177, n1, 178, 179, 180

Ka'bah, pilgrimage to, 103
Kabbalists, 51, 188
kalām (of Ibn Sīnā), 184
kamāl (perfection), 53
Kant, 222
al-Kāshānī, 'Abd al-Razzāq, 195, n53
al-Kāshānī, Ghiyāth al-Dīn Jamshīd, 279
Kashf al-maḥjūb (*The Unveiling of the Hidden*), 209, n36
Kashf al-ẓunūn (of Ḥājjī Khalīfah), 107, n3, 110
Kashkūl (of Bahā' al-Dīn al-'Āmilī), 194
Kennedy, E. S., 111, n17
keshvars, 144